Mainstreaming Handicapped Students:

A Guide for the Classroom Teacher

Ann P. Turnbull
University of North Carolina at Chapel Hill

Jane B. Schulz
Jackson County Public Schools, North Carolina

Allyn and Bacon, Inc.
Boston   London   Sydney

Library of Congress Cataloging in Publication Data

Turnbull, Ann P   1947–
        Mainstreaming handicapped students.

        Includes bibliographies and index.
            1. Handicapped children—Education—United States.
2. Mainstreaming in education.   3. Individualized
instruction.   I. Schulz, Jane B., 1924–   joint
author. II.   Title.
LC4031.T86   371.1'02   78-23724
ISBN 0-205-06107-9

Printed in the United States of America.
Second printing . . . August, 1979

*To our families, comprised of individuals—
each our teacher, each our student*

Contents

Contents

Preface

Mainstreaming is a reality. The basic principle underlying mainstreaming is that handicapped students can benefit educationally and socially from being in programs with nonhandicapped students. Mainstreaming is based on the assumption that handicapped students have more similarities than differences in comparison to their nonhandicapped peers, and that "separate" education can result in "unequal" education. The impetus for mainstreaming has come from many sources, including educational research, litigation, legislation, and civil rights. Mainstreaming is being implemented on a large scale in school systems across the country.

Few educators argue with the principle of mainstreaming as it relates to basic notions of equality and justice. Belief in the principle has led some educators and school systems to expect miracles for handicapped students in regular classes. Mainstreaming has been thought to be the panacea for the educational problems of handicapped students by some professionals in the field, as handicapped students have sometimes been haphazardly returned from special classes to regular classes. In the process, many classroom teachers have been put at a disadvantage by being expected to adapt their curriculum easily to meet the needs of the mentally retarded speech impaired, learning disabled, physically handicapped, visually impaired, hearing impaired, and emotionally and/or behaviorally disturbed student. Special educators in the past have typically specialized in one area of exceptionality; classroom teachers have been expected to be competent almost overnight in teaching students who might represent the full range of handicapping conditions. Further, special educators have usually worked with handicapped students in special classes with a limited enrollment (usually fewer than fifteen students) or in a resource room in a one-to-one or small group situation. Classroom teachers may have 30 or more students at a given time which substantially decreases the same opportunities that the special educator may have for individualized instruction.

The idea for this book evolved partially from an experience one of us had in delivering a workshop on individualized instructions to a large group of elementary and junior high classroom teachers. Many of the instructional strategies used in the resource room with handicapped students were shown and described. The individual programs for each student were impressive. About midway through the session a teacher raised her hand and commented in a skeptical fashion, "This all is very nice. But could you tell me, please, what I should do with the other twenty-nine students in my class while I do what you are suggesting with the handicapped student?"

This book is directed at providing a response to that question. *Mainstreaming Handicapped Students* has a strong curriculum focus and reflects the day-to-day life of regular classrooms. It provides a bridge between the principle of mainstreaming and its educational implementation by highlighting instructional strategies and curriculum adaptations that are possible even with twenty-nine other students in the class. Additionally, this book provides an analysis of the characteristics of handicapped students and the educational implications associated with those characteristics. Public Law 94–142, the Education for All Children Act, is explained, with emphasis given to what this legislation means for classroom teachers. An important feature is that the book helps to answer the immediate questions of what to do on "Monday morning."

We are advocates of classroom teachers. We believe that teachers basically respect the individuality of children. We believe that teaching is one of the most demanding professions that exists. We believe that teachers want to put forth their best effort. We reject the opinions of some professionals that teachers have negative attitudes toward mainstreaming owing to a lack of humanism. If a lack exists, it is in the area of training. Many teachers have been expected to implement mainstreaming in spite of being provided with little or no preservice and/or inservice training. If handicapped students have a right to an education in a regular program, teachers have both a right and a responsibility to be prepared for the task. It is hoped that this book will enhance the training opportunities for classroom teachers and increase their competencies in mainstreaming.

We wish to acknowledge deep appreciation. to the classroom teachers, special educators, handicapped children and adults, and parents of handicapped persons who have shared their thoughts and experiences with us. We are specifically grateful to Tom Schulz and Mary Schulz for their illustrations in Chapters 4 and 5; to Kathy Burroughs for her assistance with the manuscript preparation; to Bonnie Strickland for her support and ideas; to Richard Clontz, Dorris Beck, and John Rosenthal for the photography; and to the Jackson County and Chapel Hill-Carrboro school systems for their cooperation in making their facilities and personnel available to us.

Mainstreaming Handicapped Students

■ Chapter One

Educational Characteristics of Handicapped Students

Diversity characterizes regular classrooms—children are different. They possess unique characteristics along the dimensions of achievement levels, language acquisition, social interaction, physical size, motor development, general health, vision, hearing acuity, and other personal attributes. The students in each regular classroom have a unique mixture of abilities/disabilities, strengths/weaknesses, likes/dislikes, and successes/failures. A sixth-grade class might give the impression of homogeneity to a casual observer. Upon close inspection of the twenty-five children in this sixth-grade class, no two are exactly comparable in their development and achievement. Some are extremely bright, learn new material quickly, and never seem to have their intellectual curiosity satiated. Others are slow to grasp new concepts, giving up quickly and losing attention easily. The academic achievement levels in a sixth-grade class often range roughly from second- to ninth-grade levels. In social areas, the class leader may be chosen as "most popular" by almost every member of the class. Other children are isolates and are always picked last when the class is choosing teams. There are those who love school and those who are bothered by having to attend; those with perfect attendance and those continually absent. Differences of educational significance also occur in the profiles of each individual student. The child who excels on the playground in gross motor activities may have extreme difficulty in fine motor areas such as handwriting. The eager scientist in the class may dread mathematics. Every person represents a unique combination of strengths and weaknesses. Along every possible dimension of human behavior, children exhibit differences that create diversity in educational settings.

Individual differences of children in regular classrooms fall along a continuum. The differences of the great majority of children in the class are not extreme and can be accommodated within the usual routine of the regular class program. Other children deviate significantly from the expected norm at a given grade level along varying dimensions. This deviation may single them out as being handicapped in learning capability, communication, motor development, sensation, and/or emotional adjustment. What does it mean to be handicapped? Webster's *New Collegiate Dictionary* defines *handicap* as "a disadvantage that makes achievement unusually difficult." The disadvantage experienced by handicapped children in regular classes can be minimized as teachers recognize the students' mixture of assets and liabilities and tailor the curriculum to their special needs. Before teachers can make necessary curriculum adaptations, they must become familiar with the population of students who are operating at a disadvantage in terms of school success—the 10 to 12 percent of school-age persons who are considered handicapped.

This chapter will focus on the various types of disadvantages that create educational handicaps for students. Disadvantages in the following areas will be examined: (1) cognitive; (2) physical; (3) communicative; (4) sensory; and (5) emotional/behavioral. Attention will be directed to general characteristics and the educational implications of these characteristics in each area. The information in this chapter should help teachers identify the types of educational disadvantages that occur in regular classes. Awareness of these factors is the first step in planning successful instructional strategies. This chapter also serves as an overview to the rest of the book. The reader will be directed to particular chapters for "how-to" suggestions related to specific student characteristics and educational implications.

Cognitive Disadvantages

Cognitive disadvantages are related to delayed intellectual development in areas considered important for school success. Students who are handicapped in the cognitive area in most cases achieve below grade level in academic subjects and usually experience difficulty throughout their total school career. *Cognitive disadvantage* is used synonymously in this text with the term *mental retardation*. Cognitive impairment or mental retardation does fall along a continuum, as some students have mild disadvantages and others severe ones. Students with the potential for placement in a regular class are ones whose handicaps can be classified on the continuum from mild to moderate. Specialized services for the student with severe cognitive impairment will always be needed.

The concept of individual differences applies to students with cognitive disadvantages, as well as to all other students. No two children who experience school difficulty have identical problems. Identifying the individual mixture of strengths and weaknesses is a key to successful instruction. Certain characteristics of this student group do exist. They do not apply to every student in equal proportions; however, teachers of regular classes should be aware of the types of disadvantages that are often associated with cognitive impairment. Some of these disadvantages are discussed below with particular focus on resulting classroom implications

Educational Implications

Intellectual Functioning.   The aspects of intellectual functioning related to mental retardation considered in this section include attention span, memory, generalization, and conceptualization. With respect to *attention span,* students may be able to work for relatively short periods before they need a change of pace. Every teacher is familiar with the student who almost never stays on task for more than five minutes. A student with this type of problem is not only at a personal disadvantage, but also often disrupts the concentration of others. A typical response to this type of cognitive handicap has been to consider the student a "troublemaker" and to continually punish him for the inappropriate behavior. This approach has usually met with minimal success. As teachers recognize that in many

3

cases attention problems are cognitively based rather than deviously contrived by the student, teachers can learn systematic management procedures, as discussed in chapter 9, to teach the student to increase his attention span, thus minimizing this disadvantage.

Another deficit associated with students with cognitive handicaps is *memory*. Teachers may find that they can repeat directions over and over and still the student forgets. These situations can be frustrating for everyone, and an automatic response is often to assume the student was not listening. Research has clearly indicated that many of these students are at a distinct disadvantage in recalling information immediately after they have received it (Ellis 1970; Belmont and Butterfield 1969). They do not automatically use active strategies to remember, as most students do who are not cognitively impaired; therefore, these students forget much important classroom information. The most encouraging aspect of memory research with mentally retarded students is that they can successfully be taught memory skills, significantly improving their performance in this area (Butterfield, Wambold, and Belmont 1973; Turnbull 1974).

Other cognitive disadvantages may be in the areas of *generalization* and *conceptualization*. In respect to generalization, a third-grade student may learn the essential elements for living things in science, yet not realize that his shaded backyard garden is dying for lack of sunlight. Teachers who help students form linkages between academic content and application to everyday living assist those with cognitive impairments in learning to make generalizations. Students who have difficulty conceptualizing may be referred to as "concrete thinkers." Students who have difficulty with the abstract principles of a mathematical problem, inferring the meaning of a poem, or formulating the hypothesis of a scientific experiment are placed at a cognitive disadvantage.

Learning Rate. Considering the characteristics of intellectual functioning associated with students who are mentally retarded, it automatically follows that their learning rate in most instances is slower than their classmates'.

There are several significant curriculum implications of a decelerated learning rate. First, many students enter kindergarten and first grade who lack academic readiness. When their peers are ready, for example, to move ahead in academic areas such as reading, students at a cognitive disadvantage might need more priority placed on important readiness areas such as language development, visual and auditory skills, and increasing attention span. These students from the first day of school are at a cognitive disadvantage, as compared to their peers. Many compensatory educa-

4

tion programs have been quite successful in giving students inclined to start school at a disadvantage a "head start" for school success. Regardless of the quality of many of these programs, learning rate will continue to impede many students upon their initial entry into school.

A second curriculum implication is that new concepts and/or skills presented will require more practice for the child to reach mastery. For example, the concept of regrouping in subtraction will require far more practice for these students; therefore, when other classmates are ready to move on to higher-order mathematical skills, the students with cognitive handicaps will probably not be ready to move with them. If they are required to leave the concept of regrouping before they have mastered it, they will be penalized for their lack of understanding from that point on, and failure on subtraction problems will be inevitable. Systematic instruction and student success depend upon a solid foundation of step-by-step mastered skills and concepts. The additional time required to build this solid foundation has a snowballing effect on learning rate. In a standard curriculum devised for students with no cognitive disadvantage, students with this type of handicap sometimes fall farther and farther behind their classmates in academic achievement.

As for the curriculum for students whose learning rate places them at a disadvantage, it is necessary for teachers to make adjustments in goals and objectives. Mentally retarded students will probably learn less than other students. Quantity adjustments have to be carefully focused on the most relevant and functional information, by omitting content less applicable to everyday living. For example, it is far more important for a student to learn about his city and county rather than customs associated with foreign countries in an adjusted social studies curriculum. To minimize cognitive disadvantages, the teacher must continually ask, "What essential information must this student know to get along in everyday living?"

Environmental Factors. It has been estimated that approximately 80 to 90 percent of the students identified as mentally retarded have no evidence of organic brain damage (Hewett and Forness 1974). Their disadvantages are attributed to lack of early educational stimulation, malnutrition, poor health, parental deprivation, and other related factors. They may be recognized by the teacher as those who come to school hungry or sleep through a large portion of the school day because they were up so late the night before. They may have chronic respiratory problems attributable to lack of medication, inadequate clothing, or a host of other reasons. Students coping with a variety of environmental problems simply cannot concentrate fully on academic subjects. Teachers can help minimize the cognitive disadvantages imposed on these students by being sensitive to their environmental needs. Taking the time to get a carton of milk and crackers from the school cafeteria for a hungry student will greatly increase the likelihood that the student will concentrate on his reading lesson.

A barrier for many students from minority backgrounds in school is language. Consider the student whose major language is Spanish and who attends school where he hears only English. The student is automatically at a significant disadvantage. Often teachers are understandably at a loss in . knowing how to handle this problem. Do they learn Spanish to communicate with the student in his language or do they teach him English in order to facilitate his communication with the great majority of the persons in the school who speak English? Value questions such as these have proponents on both sides and deserve much greater analysis in formulating strategies to effectively bring together people from different backgrounds. One strategy many school systems have used with success is hiring teachers' aides who are bilingual.

Students whose environmental backgrounds have contributed to their mental retardation have, in the past, been prime targets for placement in special classes. Based on a below-average performance on verbal and nonverbal intelligence tests, a significant number of students from minority backgrounds have been classified as educable mentally retarded (EMR) when their IQ score falls roughly between 50 and 70. The abuses of the IQ test will be discussed in greater detail in the next chapter. Let it suffice here to say that various combinations of factors such as impoverished backgrounds, language barriers, different sociocultural mores, impaired intellectual functioning, and a general lowered learning rate have resulted in categorizing a group of students as mentally retarded. The term *mental retardation* is used basically to refer to students who score below 70 on an IQ test and who have an associated impairment in adaptive behavior which, during school years, generally refers to an impairment in school success (Grossman 1973). The whole movement in special education is away from classifying students according to diagnostic labels, which often has resulted in lowered expectations, thus overlooking the student's abilities (Hobbs 1975). For example, there was a psychological report that stated, "This student has an IQ of 58 and, with this retarded capability, will never be able to do so much as write her own name or cross the street by herself." What an educational life sentence! Luckily, the child's parents and teachers disregarded this gloomy prospect and made a commitment to teach her systematically at her level of understanding. She made consistent progress and was reading on a third-grade level when she was eleven years of age. Many students' life sentences have not been reversed; they have been the casualties of our educational system because diagnostic labels have resulted in disastrous wasted potential. Teachers are alerted to this problem because they will probably read cumulative folders of students in their classes with scores that can haunt the students, unless teachers are clearly aware of the educational significance. The label *mentally retarded* does not mean that the student cannot make academic progress; it does not mean that the student is socially deviant; it does not mean that the student belongs in a special class; it does not mean that the child is a failure in all he attempts. It basically means that he scored below 70 on an IQ test. It also most likely means that the student is at a disadvantage in terms of school achievement. But remember—every student is a mixture of assets and liabilities, strengths and weaknesses. The opportunity exists for the teacher to minimize the disadvantages by insuring step-by-step achievement. The purpose of this book is to join with teachers in successfully taking advantage of this opportunity.

■ **Case Study**
Cognitive Disadvantages

Larry is in my sixth-grade class and teaching him is not always easy. His cumulative records state that he has been classified as EMR, which stands for educable mentally retarded. Do not misunderstand or underestimate him. Although he does have learning and behavior problems, Larry is capable of far more than most people realize. His life history is a story of moving from one place to another. He has been in four different schools in six years and has moved away from his parents to live with his aunt.

From the time Larry entered first grade, he has been behind academically. He must have lacked the readiness that the teacher expected from the day he first set his foot in the school door. Because his learning rate is slower, he has increasingly fallen behind over the years. Now in the sixth grade he reads on a fourth-grade level and is learning to multiply in math. He has real problems with spelling but has nice handwriting and excels in physical education. Sometimes I am unsure if I am doing the right thing with him, but I have had some success hitting on some strategies that seem to work. First, he works with the resource teacher for one hour per day in reading. With this kind of intensive help, he seems to be making progress. I plan special work for him to do in math, since his achievement is below all the other students'. Recently he has been working with cuisenaire rods which seem to help him understand abstract concepts. In social studies, we are studying Europe. I found a fourth-grade textbook also on Europe which Larry uses in place of the regular sixth-grade text. He really likes having a book he can read. Film-strips and visual aids are his favorites. He seems to learn more effectively when we use them.

The biggest concern I have about Larry is his short attention span and low frustration level. On most days he will work for a short while and then just give up. I try to accommodate this by giving him short tasks that can be completed before he runs out of steam. After he works, he sometimes will play a game like *Easy* or *Monopoly;* or read library books about sports. I let him do this, because I think he is learning from these games and books.

Another problem is that he has a temper. Yesterday during art Larry got angry and threw a sponge down into a box of metal pans. It caused a loud noise, and he refused to pick it up. I try to get him to take responsibility for his own behavior. When the rules of the classroom are clear and he knows what to anticipate, he often will follow through on expectations. He loves to help out in the classroom on tasks like giving out books or setting the room up for a special activity. Larry would work all day long to help me. He loves to do things and move about. When he has control of his temper, he is thoughful.

Larry's behavior is as much a problem as his academic work. There is no doubt about the fact that he does have some strengths. I think he benefits from being around the classroom peers. I know he is making some progress, but sometimes I wonder if he is working up to his potential.

Ms. Tyson
Glenwood Elementary School

Physical Disadvantages

Physical disadvantages may stem from disorders of the nervous system; handicaps associated with muscles, bones, or joints; and/or chronic health problems. They may be congenital—present from birth—or acquired during childhood or adult years, sometimes resulting from accidents. Similarly to all other handicapping conditions, physical disadvantages vary greatly depending upon the age of onset, the level of severity, the extent of involvement, and the treatment provided by special therapists, the family, and teachers. Sometimes students with physical handicaps also have secondary problems, possibly in speech, vision, or cognitive impairment. In other cases, students may have the singular disadvantage of a physical handicap, such as dwarfism, but have gifted intelligence and accelerated academic achievement. Some physical disadvantages occur only periodically, such as epileptic seizures, and others are constantly present and apparent, as in the case of students who must constantly interact in their environment from a wheelchair. It is also important to realize that physical handicaps that are educationally and socially debilitating to one student may not be to another. Different persons have differing coping abilities in minimizing handicaps. Consider the student with paralyzed legs who has satisfactory or above-average academic achievement. He adapts games such as basketball, tennis, and softball to be played from his wheelchair and participates in peer and family activities. Another student with an identical physical impairment may be both academically deficient and socially excluded. What is the difference? It is the individual flair which characterizes all students coupled with the support the student has received from his parents, teachers, other helping professionals, and peers. Physical disadvantages may only be evaluated in regard to the relevant behavior of each person affected. This chapter, rather than focusing on etiology of physical handicaps from a medical perspective, highlights educationally relevant behaviors that are often associated with physically handicapping conditions.

Educational Implications

Mobility. Mobility basically refers to one's capacity to move about, stand, or to use the hands in manipulating environmental objects. Students with limited mobility may need to develop compensatory ways of moving around the classroom, entering and leaving the school building, going to the school cafeteria, participating in playground activities, or learning to write. In educational implications, mobility must be considered in light of three factors: the locus of involvement, the nature of the handicap, and the rate and stability of motion.

Locus of Involvement. Restrictions in mobility may occur in various parts of the body and in various combinations of body parts. For example, a student in a regular class may have mobility problems in any of the following aspects: one limb, all four limbs, only the legs, only the arms and hands, the right side of the body, the left side of the body, and speech mechanisms (larynx, oral cavity, diaphragm, lungs). The educational implications and the resulting adaptations planned by the teacher are dependent upon the student's particular locus of involvement.

Nature of the Handicap. Disadvantages of mobility differ, depending upon the nature of a student's handicap. One way to think about the nature of these disadvantages is from the perspective of paralysis, problems with coordination, and loss of limbs. Paralysis results in the limitation of moving parts of the body, ranging from mild limitations to total incapacity. Students whose legs are paralyzed gain mobility through the use of a wheelchair, braces, and crutches. The elimination of architectural barriers in schools is necessary for these students to gain access to educational services and opportunities. Minimizing the disadvantages of these students means creating accessibility through ramps, aisles and doorways, desks adjusted to the comfort of the students, and accommodations in toilet facilities and water fountains. Plans for fire drills and other emergency procedures sometimes have to be adapted according to the particular needs of the physically handicapped student and the physical plant of the school. Paralysis can also affect bowel and bladder functions of students with physical handicaps. Rehabilitative techniques are used quite successfully in managing these problems. An excellent description of these techniques is provided by Bigge (1976) for readers interested in more detailed information. Teachers should talk with the student's parents, doctor, and special therapists in devising a workable toileting procedure during school hours.

Students with handicaps related to coordination may have too much movement as opposed to the limited movement resulting from paralysis. Coordination problems might also be characterized by tenseness, jerkiness, or difficulty in directing one's movements in desired patterns. Helping the student to position himself while sitting, standing, or moving about can significantly contribute to the student's adaptability to coordination handicaps. Correct positioning is an individual matter based on the particular needs of each physically handicapped student. Teachers should discuss positioning with the student's parents and physical therapist for specific classroom guidelines. Academically, impairment in coordination is usually reflected in a student's writing. Remedial techniques and compensating strategies discussed in chapter 5 can help the teacher minimize this type of handicap.

Finally, some students have lost limbs either through congenital malformations, accidents, or diseases. In almost every case, students are fitted with a prosthesis—an artificial arm or leg. Prosthetic devices, in most cases, drastically minimize the educational disadvantages of these students.

Rate and Stability of Motion. Mobility rate is an important factor in classroom success. Some students with no major, overt physical impairment may generally have slow mobility. They may be those who are chosen last on the playfield, because they can never make it to first base before the ball gets there. They may be those who rarely have time to complete classwork or tests because of the snail's pace at which they write. These students are at a definite disadvantage in attaining school success, even though there may be no medical diagnosis of their physical disability. Other students do have chronic medical problems, such as diabetes, allergies, asthma, heart condition, nephritis, or others. In some cases, these problems can interfere with the rate of motion. The characteristics of mobility problems discussed in the previous two sections also frequently result in lowered rates of motion.

Curriculum accommodations to such problems can be fairly simple. If a student requires significantly more time to complete a written assignment, the teacher might reduce the length of the assignment so that it is not physically overwhelming. All classroom tasks can be reduced in length if necessary. This often allows the student with a low mobility rate to complete assignments and to achieve success. With students capable of increasing mobility rates, the behavior management principles discussed in chapter 9 can be very helpful.

As to the stability of motion, some students with physical handicaps and health problems fatigue more quickly than others. Teachers should be alert to this factor and minimize it by making provisions for such students to rest at necessary intervals throughout the school day. Some teachers have successfully used a cot or lounge chair in the corner of the classroom for this purpose. Another important factor related to stability is the progressive nature of some physical conditions. For example, the voluntary muscles of children with muscular dystrophy slowly degenerate until they are totally physically incapacitated. The teachers of these students often are able to detect deterioration of mobility from month to month throughout the school year. In addition to making adjustments in academic and physical activities tailored to the child's capacity, the teacher also has a role in helping the child with decelerated mobility and his peers with the social and psychological implications. Suggestions on how to handle these affective concerns are included in chapter 10.

Seizures. *Seizures* most often are associated with epilepsy, although they can occur in other convulsive conditions. Many teachers are fearful of teaching children with seizures, since they are afraid they will not know how to handle a child in seizure in the classroom. This is an understandable concern which can be alleviated by adequate information.

When nerve cells in the brain are charged with excessive electricity, the brain may temporarily lose control of functions, such as attention, sensation, perception, and muscle control. This phenomenon is referred to as a seizure. The two most common seizures teachers might encounter in the regular class are petit mal and grand mal.

When petit mal seizures occur, a child is likely to appear to be daydreaming in the classroom. The student might stare straight ahead, blink his eyes, drop books or pencils, or nod his head for a few seconds. The student does not comprehend classroom information for the brief period of

11

the seizure. The teacher must first be alert to the fact that the child is not just failing to pay attention. A teacher who suspects the possibility of seizures should discuss this concern with the school nurse, child's family, or medical doctor. The second responsibility of teachers is to make sure the student has an opportunity to get the information missed in class. Both the teacher and the student's classmates can help him fill the gaps of classroom activities and instruction missed during the occurrence of the seizure.

A grand mal seizure is a more severe manifestation. It is usually preceded by an aura, a strange sensation which can alert the person that a seizure is about to occur. The student probably will first stiffen the muscles of the body and then proceed into a stage of jerking movements. During this period, he will lose consciousness, might emit sounds and/or saliva, and possibly lose bladder and bowel control which can result in extreme embarrassment to the student. The actual seizure only lasts several minutes and is followed by the need for rest or sleep. Teachers can help to manage seizures that occur at school by following some guidelines.

1.   Collect information and plan ahead about what you will do in your classroom so that you can remain calm when the seizure occurs. Talk with the student, his parents, and doctor to make sure your questions about the student's particular seizure pattern are answered. Write the Epilepsy Foundation of America (see appendix A for address) which has pamphlets for classroom teachers on school management of seizures.

2.   Try to help the student respond to the aura or warning signal by getting to an open space away from desks and tables. He should lie on the floor and be free to move around. The teacher should not attempt to restrict movement or place anything in the student's mouth other than possibly a soft handkerchief between the teeth. It is important for the teacher to remember that the seizure is painless to the student.

3.   After the seizure occurs, the teacher should let the child sleep (he does not necessarily need to be sent home) and report the seizure to the student's parents and doctor.

Most seizures are controlled very effectively by medication and rarely occur in classrooms. Unfortunately, there is often stigmatization of students with histories of seizures. Teachers have a major responsibility in helping classmates understand the nature of seizures, as well as the strengths and talents of students who are inclined to seizures.

School Absenteeism.   Various types of physical handicaps often require special medical care or the services of rehabilitation centers. The educational implication is that some physically handicapped children are excessively absent from school and thus are at a disadvantage in keeping up with academic work. Teachers can minimize the disadvantages associated with frequent absences from school by working with special services personnel in the school system to arrange for the students to have hospital/homebound tutoring. The majority of school systems have employed special teachers or have contracted with other educational agencies to provide this type of instruction. Whatever the particular arrangement, school systems are responsible for providing educational services when students must be out of school on a long-term basis because of physical handicaps or chronic health conditions. Teachers may also be able to locate volunteers to work with the student, in addition to the hospital/homebound teacher. In these situations, it is necessary that the classroom teacher coordinate the instructional program with all persons working with the student, including the hospital/homebound teacher, volunteers, and the student's parents. Instructional objectives will be met far more quickly when everyone is working toward the same goal. Weekly or biweekly meetings might be set up to handle this coordination.

To keep up with classroom discussions, a student in the class who excels in organizing major concepts during classroom discussions could be asked to make a duplicate copy of the notes for the student who is absent, by using carbon paper. Classroom discussions and various activities might also be taped so that the student who is in the hospital or at home can still share in what goes on at school by listening to the tape.

When the student is back at school, the teacher might be called on to supervise medication schedules, arrange for rest periods, or to be aware of special nutritional or diet requirements. All these responsibilities can be handled in the regular class with minimal disruption. The important point is that they should be carefully discussed with the student, his parents, and his physician.

■ **Case Study**
Physical Disadvantages

When we were told that Jason would be in our class we were apprehensive. We had observed him when he was in kindergarten and our impression was that his every motion was painful and lengthy. Frankly, we felt it was an imposition to ask us to have a physically handicapped child in a class with fifty-one first- and second-graders. We thought it would be a burden; we didn't know how to cope.

Actually, we have been pleasantly surprised this year. Jason is such a delightful, happy child that we feel fortunate to have him in our class. Our chief problem has been that he must be taken to the bathroom by one of us; this requires ten to fifteen minutes away from the class and may mean that we have to leave in the middle of a lesson. His coordination is poor; writing takes him longer. However, he takes his unfinished work home

Photograph by Dorris D. Beck

and his mother helps him, so it's no problem. When he is absent (which is often) his mother helps him keep up. His home situation has been a definite asset.

We have received more help than we expected. Recently we acquired the services of a part-time aide; this helps with the bathroom problem. The special education teacher in our school, who had known Jason previously, reassured us from the beginning and informed us of resources where we could find manipulative materials for children who need special help. We have a high school student who works with Jason in physical education.

Jason is well liked by his peers. They look after him without being protective. For example, during the last fire drill one child reminded us, "Don't forget Jason!" The other children try out Jason's crutches and are very accepting of his problems. They like and respect him.

Jason wants to be treated like everyone else. At cleanup time, he picks up paper and crawls to the wastebasket with it. He is on grade level and is helping his cousin with his reading.

We think it would be a shame to have Jason in a special class; We think it would be harmful to him. We hope to have him in our class next year!

Ms. Allman
Ms. McMahan
Team teachers
Fairview Elementary School

Communicative Disadvantages

The communicative disadvantages of children in regular classes can be classified in various ways, since almost all handicapping conditions create

14

communication concerns. In this section, however, these disadvantages will be divided into two groups, learning disabilities and oral communication.

Learning Disabilities

Many regular teachers have had the experience of working either directly or indirectly with children who have significant gaps between their educational achievement and their expected intellectual potential. These students may experience severe academic difficulty in one or two, but not all, subject areas. They may have difficulty attending to their assigned task, sitting still for seemingly brief intervals, decoding or comprehending in reading, using expressive and receptive language, writing legibly, solving arithmetic problems, or generally following instructions. They can be characterized by a large combination of these factors or by only one or two. Frequently, students who fit this description are described as "underachievers," "poorly motivated," and "reluctant learners." An adult with some of these educational disadvantages recalled her school career as a period of being labeled "everything from lazy to crazy," when, in fact, she was part of the population of students who might be referred to as learning disabled.

The definition probably most widely used in schools was offered by the National Advisory Committee on Handicapped Children (1968) and is as follows:

Children with specific learning disabilities exhibit a disorder in one or more of the basic psychological processes involved in understanding or in using spoken or written language. These may be manifested in disorders of listening, thinking, talking, reading, writing, spelling, or arithmetic. They include conditions which have been referred to as perceptual handicaps, brain injury, minimal brain dysfunction, dyslexia, developmental aphasia, etc. They do not include learning problems which are due primarily to visual, hearing or motor handicaps, to mental retardation, emotional disturbance, or to environmental disadvantage (p. 4).

To gain a clearer understanding of learning disabilities, a closer examination of four of the component parts of this definition is warranted (Myers and Hammill 1976).

1. "...a disorder in one or more of the basic psychological processes involved in understanding or in using spoken or written language."

Since the term *psychological processes* is not operationally defined, it is open to different interpretations. Perhaps the most frequent referents are learning modalities, such as visual, auditory, tactile, and motor, in addition to learning processes such as memory, comprehension, and generalization. For these processes, the disorder may result from a developmental lag or impaired functioning. A developmental lag occurs when the learning process becomes refined at a slower rate than that of other children. For example, some students may not have the necessary fine motor skills for successfully learning to write in manuscript in the first grade, but the refinement of these readiness skills may be present one to two years later. Impaired functioning of modalities or processes refers to a basic distortion in interpretation, organization, and/or expression. As for language, an example of impaired functioning would be a student who routinely is unable to find the words he wants to say to respond to an oral or written question. This word-finding difficulty represents impaired functioning of learning processes. It is often difficult for teachers to distinguish accurately between the disorders representing a developmental lag in which remediation might reasonably be expected to occur in the future and impaired functioning in which the possibility exists that the student will always experience difficulty.

2. "These may be manifested in disorders of listening, talking, reading, writing, spelling, or arithmetic."

It is these subjects that form the core of academic success and in which the learning disability may be manifested. The majority of questions from classroom teachers revolve around questions concerning methods and materials for teaching these subjects to students with learning problems. Chapters 3 through 9 respond directly to these concerns.

3. ". . . conditions which have been referred to as perceptual handicaps, brain injury, minimal brain dysfunction, dyslexia, developmental aphasia, etc."

These terms do not have operational meanings, and even experts in the field of learning disabilities do not agree on their definitions. Teachers are wise to develop the habit of discussing characteristics of students in educational terms, such as the specific strengths and weaknesses in subject areas. It is *that* information which is educationally relevant to classroom teachers. Jargon is superficial and often adds more confusion than clarity to the development of a student's individual educational program.

4. "They do not include learning problems which are due primarily to visual, hearing or motor handicaps, to mental retardation, emotional disturbance, or to environmental disadvantage."

Learning disabilities are often diagnosed through the process of elimination. When the child's primary handicap is not attributable to other conditions, yet a gap exists between achievement and potential, the student often is considered to have a learning disability. The key word in this portion of the definition is *primarily*. The student with learning disabilities may have secondary problems related to other handicapping conditions. Furthermore, students with other handicapping conditions (emotional problems, sensory deficits) may have secondary educational concerns which fit the description of a learning disability. The decision between primary and secondary handicapping conditions is not always clear-cut. Again, the important consideration for teachers is pinpointing the student's individual strengths and weaknesses and developing a systematic instructional program geared to the student's needs. Losing valuable teacher time on lengthy discussions revolving around which handicapping condition is primary and secondary is often just spinning educational wheels. Getting on with the task of academic instruction is a priority item.

Educational Implications

Academic Difficulty. Students with learning disabilities experience substantial difficulty in school subjects. Frequently they have a peak profile across all school subjects with very distinct abilities and disabilities. Sometimes the student is deficient in only one subject and at other times in a combination of subjects. A student in the sixth grade, for example, might be working on basic addition in arithmetic which would be significantly below grade level expectations, yet be entirely commensurate with his peers in reading achievement. Individual strengths and weaknesses are particularly striking with these students.

When students are impaired in language areas (reading, spelling, and writing), other subject areas are also affected. Special considerations must be made when students are unable to read science, social studies, and health books. Chapter 8 includes suggestions on adaptations teachers can make in regular classes to accommodate these types of educational consideration.

Academic difficulty associated with learning disabilities is an outgrowth of the disorders related to developmental lags or impaired functioning in learning modalities and processes. Teachers should be aware that students can have deficits in one or more learning modalities that can make it very difficult for them to process information. Some learning disabled students will respond to a phonics approach to reading instruction and others will experience tremendous difficulty and frustration in discriminating the differences between isolated sounds. Just because several instructional methods have failed is not an indication that the student cannot learn. Rather, it is a message to the teacher to keep looking for the instructional technique that provides the best match with the student's learning characteristics.

Other factors that frequently contribute to the academic difficulty associated with learning disabilities are problems in the area of memory and generalization. Both these learning processes are critically important to the development of academic competence in every subject.

Attention. The nature of learning disabilities often results in an impairment in the student's ability to pay attention selectively to the relevant stimuli. Students may be unable to screen out interfering noises like the ticking of a clock, the squeak of desks, and the buzzing of neon lights in the classroom. Sometimes these noises, unnoticed by most teachers and students, significantly impede the student with learning disabilities from paying attention to the task at hand. Open classrooms with a large number of children and movement within the room can be a serious educational disaster to students who are already at a distinct disadvantage in ability to maintain attention. If teachers suspect that students are having difficulty screening out background noise, they might arrange seating close to the point where the teacher most frequently stands in giving instructions, have a classroom peer repeat instructions to the students, and/or create a quiet work center for the student away from more distracting parts of the classroom. These suggestions are discussed in more detail in chapter 4.

Other problems with attention relate to the amount of time a student can work on a given task before becoming restless or getting involved in something else. Short work periods followed by a break are often helpful to these students.

Motor Activity. Frequently a portion of the student's learning disability is actually a motor disability, which can be categorized in many ways. For our purposes, we will discuss them as follows: activity levels, fine motor skills, and gross motor skills.

The activity level of students refers to the frequency and intensity of movement in which they engage. Some students handicapped by learning disabilities are described as hyperactive and others as hypoactive. Hyperactivity refers to an activity level significantly above norm expectations. Students who are prone to hyperactivity could be described as unable to sit still, distractible, restless, and fidgety. They might be the ones scooting around the classroom while the teacher is trying to lead a class discussion. Keogh (1971) has provided a review of hyperactivity for those who would like more in-depth information. It is sometimes easy to consider the student a behavior problem and troublemaker and overlook the fact that he may not be able to control some of the disruptions strictly on his own. The behavior modification techniques discussed in chapter 9 should be helpful to classroom teachers in controlling hyperactivity. Drug therapy is an alternative for children with severely excessive activity levels. Teachers might discuss this possibility carefully with the school nurse who might observe the child in the classroom. On the basis of behavioral observations, the nurse might talk with the students' parents who then should work closely with the family doctor. It is encouraging for teachers to remember that excessive activity levels generally decrease with age. Hypoactivity is the reverse of hyperactivity; its characteristics include lethargic, passive, and quiet behaviors. Students affected in this manner are usually very slow and have low energy levels. They often do not complete their work and sometimes go unnoticed in the classroom. Either extreme places the student at a disadvantage in successfully functioning in a regular class.

Fine motor handicaps are related to difficulty in writing, using scissors, or manipulating small objects. The student might use tense, labored movements or be generally awkward in motoric skills. Severe deficiencies in handwriting can interfere with performance in all academic subjects.

The final area of disturbance in motor activity is gross motor skills. Students with difficulty in this area might be characterized as clumsy, uncoordinated, or awkward in tasks such as playground activities, walking, or general movement within the classroom. The students may experience special problems in finding noncompetitive physical activities they can participate in and enjoy. It is important for students with motor problems to strengthen their motor skills but, at the same time, they should be recognized for their abilities in other areas.

■ **Case Study**
Learning Disabilities

Photograph by John Rosenthal

Having Tom in my eighth-grade language arts class means that there is never a dull moment. At the beginning of the year, his capabilities and performance were not easy to figure out. With some students, all the pieces of information fall into place immediately. Tom puzzled me. I knew he had high ability, yet he demonstrated real problems in getting his work done. His math teacher told me that he was having major problems in her class, since his achievement was significantly below the other students'. After observing his behavior closely and talking with the resource teacher in the school, I now seem to have a handle on some of his learning strengths and weaknesses.

In the language arts areas, Tom is able to read just slightly below grade level. Although he does not have the reading proficiency of most of his classmates, he is able to read his textbooks, rarely needing help with a word. In written assignments, his handwriting can be neat; however, he usually approaches a written task in a harum-scarum fashion, writing quicky to get through as soon as possible. More often than not, his papers are messy and difficult to read. When he gets down to work, he is able to make a passing grade on his spelling test. That is the heart of the problem—"when he gets down to work."

It is basically organization that poses extreme difficulty for Tom. He seems almost constantly distracted, having a difficult time sitting down and getting settled. On some days I think he spends more time wandering around the classroom than sitting in his seat. When he goes to sharpen his pencil, he will look out the window and become captivated watching a bird or he will pass the magazine rack and flip through several magazines before returning to his seat. He's fidgety, constantly turning in his seat and moving around. As to his work, he often does not complete it. Since it takes him longer because of his attention span, he sometimes will hand in work several days late. With that much delay and his general difficulty with organization, it is not unusual for him to lose assignments that he has started but not completed. I have to watch Tom about taking short-cuts with his work. If he has ten questions to answer, he sometimes will answer the first, a couple in the middle, and the last, and state that he has finished the assignment. Sometimes I purposefully shorten his assignments so that the length is adjusted to his learning pattern. In this way, he can achieve success and demonstrate a mastery of the content without being penalized for his distractibility. Another approach which seems to help him is for me to write instructions for the class period on the board and sometimes even an outline of class discussions. Since Tom does not always generate his own structure, he seems to benefit from as much as I can impose. I have been pleased with the encouragement and direction he gets from the other students in the class. They tell him things like: "Turn around and do your work." "Come on, Tom, I don't have time to talk to you."

I tried separating him into a part of the room without other desks and students. For Tom, this did not seem to help. He still turned around and talked across the room. Tom does seem to respond to reasoning. He usually knows when he is off track and wants to do better. He often says, "I know, Ms. Allison; I am going to do my work."

His mother and I were talking last week about his overall recent improvement in settling down and following class instructions. She had an insight that made sense to me. During the last month Tom has joined the YMCA swimming program, and he swims almost every afternoon. She thinks that the swimming is a good outlet for a lot of his excess energy. That could possibly be contributing to the fact that some of his classroom restlessness seems to be decreasing.

Tom has his good and bad days, just like all of us. He's got the ability, and it's a continual challenge for me to capitalize on his strengths.

Ms. Allison
Culbreth Junior High School

Oral Communication Handicaps

Oral communication refers basically to speech and language. Speech includes various processes related to producing sounds, combining sounds into words, and further combining words into phrases and sentences. Language is the total system of symbols used in both the expression and comprehension of ideas. Speech and language processes involve receiving, associating, comprehending, analyzing, synthesizing, and evaluating concepts and then transferring these concepts into the production of speech that can be comprehended by others. Since this process can be a very complicated one for some children to master, deviations with oral communication commonly occur with students in regular classes. Sometimes it is difficult to determine when a difference in speech patterns falls outside the range of normality and is considered to be a handicap. The criterion generally accepted for speech handicaps was specified by Van Riper (1972): "Speech is defective when it deviates so far from the speech of other people that it calls attention to itself, interferes with communication, or causes the possessor to be maladjusted" (p. 29). This definition focuses mainly on the effects of speech. Sometimes speech handicaps are in the eye of the beholder but, for the most part, it is the actual production by the speaker that is deficient. The criterion set by Van Riper for speech handicaps may also be applied to language disorders.

Oral communication handicaps are related to other disabilities. Students with lowered cognitive ability frequently have delayed language development. Conditions related to physical handicaps, such as paralysis, can seriously impede the production of speech. Since hearing-impaired children are at a distinct disadvantage in developing oral communication, these special concerns will be discussed separately. The significant contribution of language impairment to learning disabilities has been highlighted. Almost across the board, speech and language factors are major considerations in every handicapping condition. Aside from the implications of speech and language deficits that are discussed elsewhere in this chapter, the major types of disorders with educational implications that receive focus in this section include articulation, voice, delayed language, and stuttering.

Educational Implications

Articulation. Articulation problems generally refer to consistent mispronunciation of syllables or of the entire word. These mispronunciations occur very commonly among children in the primary grades and frequently disappear as children mature. Other articulation disorders create significant communication problems. Articulation problems can be categorized as follows:

Substitutions. Examples of this error are wove for love, tite for kite, yeth for yes. Some children consistently substitute at various word positions (initial, medial, and final).

Omissions occur when sounds are dropped from words, such as when *h* is dropped from *house*. When this problem is severe, language is extremely difficult to understand.

Distortions of sounds can be considered one kind of substitution; however, their distinctiveness comes from being unidentifiable as any other consonant or vowel.

In classroom situations articulation errors might interfere with the student's performance in the following ways: expressive language might be difficult to understand, phonics training which could effect spelling and reading skills could be held back, and the student's social interactions could be influenced. The teacher needs to be alert to these possibilities and work cooperatively with the student and the school's speech therapist to eliminate these problems to the greatest extent possible.

Lubker's example (1972) demonstrates the difficulty of changing the articulation skills of children. Stop reading at this point and produce an /s/ sound. Do it again and note whether you have the top of your tongue up, down, or in the middle. After you have identified the placement of your tongue, change the position and make another /s/ sound. It feels a bit awkward, doesn't it? Next time you talk to someone, try to make all your /s/ sounds with your tongue in the new position. Often we expect children with articulation errors to concentrate on hearing the difference in speech sounds and to change the production of the sound to the correct form immediately. Changing articulation habits can be a difficult task.

Voice. Teachers will encounter voice problems of children which typically fall into four categories—pitch, intensity, quality, and flexibility. Again, voice characteristics are noted as problems when they call attention to themselves, interfere with communication, or cause the student to be maladjusted. An overview of these categories should help the teacher be aware of possible areas of concern (Kirk 1972; Hull and Hull 1973).

    Pitch. Pitch, of course, refers to the highness or lowness of the voice. The most frequent problems associated with pitch are high falsetto voices in adolescent males. Speech therapy can help students raise or lower the pitch of their voice. Appropriate pitch should be considered in light of the student's age.

    Intensity. Loudness or softness of voice relates to intensity or volume. Children who routinely speak too loudly create difficulty for their listeners and can also disrupt the concentration of their peers during class periods. On the other hand, students who speak too softly often are not heard or ignored. This significantly interferes with their oral communication.

    Quality. Characteristics of voice quality include hoarseness, huskiness, breathiness, and nasality. The first three of these characteristics can result in undue strain on the vocal cords which can cause more permanent disorders. Teachers should be alert to quality disorders and immediately seek the services of a speech therapist. Disorders of quality are the most frequent types of voice problems among children.

    Flexibility. All teachers are familiar with monotone speakers who rarely vary the pitch and loudness of their voices. Flexibility creates interest for the listener, adds expression, indicates emotion, and gives emphasis to major points the speaker wants to communicate. Often flexibility problems are considered part of the normal language characteristics of a given child and are accepted as unalterable. Automatic acceptance is not the solution. Teachers working closely with speech therapists can help the student increase his flexibility of pitch and loudness.

Delayed Speech and Language. Some students are significantly behind chronological age expectations in production of speech and/or comprehension of ideas. Sometimes the cause can be pinpointed as cognitive impairments, hearing loss, severe emotional problems, or bilingual considerations. In other cases, children can have speech and language delays, and it is impossible to identify the origin of the problem. Regardless of the particular cause, handicaps of this nature can put the student at a distinct disadvantage in achieving classroom success. These handicaps might be characterized by an insufficient vocabulary, difficulty expressing or comprehending complex sentence structures, problems with sequencing ideas or organizing information, or difficulty with inferring the meaning of words or sentences. Speech and language are developmental processes, and some children proceed through the levels of higher-order functioning at slower rates than others.

Specific educational implications could be delays in reading, writing, and spelling since these subjects are dependent on understanding the language process; difficulty in understanding classroom discussions or mastering concepts in content subjects such as science and social studies; and difficulty in following directions. Helping students overcome speech and language delays and avoid these educational handicaps is the responsibility of teachers and speech therapists. Chapter 5 offers suggestions on educational approaches for the remediation of these problems.

Stuttering. Stuttering is manifested in disruptions in the normal flow of speech (Hull and Hull 1973). These disruptions may be prolongations or repetitions of sounds and words. Stuttering can vary tremendously as to circumstances, particular sounds or words, location of syllables in words or words in sentences, fatigue, and emotional comfort. Although a significant amount of research has been conducted on stuttering, resulting in numerous theories of causation, experts still debate and disagree over the definitive causes (Van Riper 1972; Ainsworth 1970; Brutten and Shoemaker 1967). Some people believe it is learned, others that it represents a developmental lag, and still others that it is emotionally and environmentally based. These debates are likely to continue; however, the important consideration for teachers is learning to minimize the educational implications of stuttering in the classroom.

It is important for teachers to remember that normal disfluencies occur in everyone's speech at various times. Also, prolongations and repetitions normally are more frequent in the speech of young children, generally up to the age of eight. Therefore, caution should be taken in interpreting normal disfluencies as actual stuttering. Going back to Van Riper's definition, stuttering becomes a problem when ". . . it calls attention to itself, interferes with communication, or causes the possessor to be maladjusted." In these situations, teachers should refer the child to the speech therapist for evaluation and therapy. The therapist should give the teacher and parents particular suggestions of ways to follow through with therapy in the classroom and at home. General suggestions that the teacher can follow include the following:

Avoid calling attention to the stuttering. Let the child finish what he is trying to say and maintain good listening habits, such as eye contact and positive facial expressions.

Make a special note of the classroom circumstances (discussions, oral presentation, free play) and the times of day when a child's stuttering seems to be the most severe. On the basis of each student's particular pattern, minimize the difficult situations and maximize the situations characterized by more fluency as much as possible.

Talk with the student and his parents and cooperatively discuss ways of helping other students in the class react positively to stuttering episodes. Classroom peers may resort to teasing and mimicking if they do not know other ways to react positively.

Reduce anxiety over speaking situations as much as possible. If the student who stutters is particularly fearful of being called on to answer a question orally in class, the teacher could let him know that he would not be called on unless he raised his hand. Often this strategy can prevent students with stuttering problems from sweating out every discussion period.

■ **Case Study**
Oral Communication Handicaps

Photograph by John Rosenthal

Jane is the brightest student in my third-grade class. In every subject area, her achievement is outstanding to the point that every assignment is practically perfect. In contrast to all these strengths, she has a significant stuttering problem. At the beginning of school, it was immediately apparent. I was concerned because I have never before encountered this type of handicap. I was relieved when Jane's mother asked to meet with me during the second week of school. She openly discussed Jane's problem, which helped me understand it. It seems that Jane started talking very early and was using complete sentences long before her second birthday. Around the age of three she started stuttering and went through periods of mild to more obvious disfluencies. She has been receiving therapy since she was five. Her mother told me the name of her current therapist and the types of work he is doing with her. Since I was unsure how to handle the stuttering in the classroom, she suggested that I listen carefully to Jane, let her finish what she is trying to say, and try to be relaxed about it. I really appreciate the open channels of information with Jane's mother.

As the school year has progressed, the stuttering has become worse. I have noticed that it seems to be very bad during spontaneous conversation in the classroom and during oral reading. Sometimes she jerks her neck and twists her mouth as she is struggling to say something. She seems to stutter less in free-play situations on the playground and with her peers. Lately her stuttering has been so severe that I have difficulty understanding her. I realize that I am having a problem handling the stuttering, because I feel uncomfortable when I see her struggling so much. Sometimes I almost want to skip over her in the reading group. I realize that this is a problem I must deal with.

The other children in the class are very sensitive. They have great respect for Jane's intelligence and would never tease or mock her. She is popular with her peers and very friendly. It concerns me that she rarely discusses her feelings. She's very closed about her personal reactions. Sometimes she looks sad and alone, but during these times she never will open up with me. She seems to be very conscious of the stuttering, yet she never mentions it. Her therapist has suggested that I not call attention to her problem, but I would like to talk with her about it. I operate better when I can be open with the students. I want to talk with him again about the possibility of talking openly with Jane. Since her speech therapist is handling her program, it is important to coordinate things with him. At the same time, it is important for him to be aware of techniques and approaches that fit comfortably into the atmosphere and routine of the classroom.

I will have to admit that I am concerned about Jane. Stuttering is a difficult handicap. I just hope that her problem can be decreased.

Ms. Tully
Ephesus Road School

Sensory Disadvantages

Children's sensory disadvantages can be manifested in a number of different ways. Those that place children at the greatest disadvantage in achieving success in regular classes are impairments related to vision and to hearing.

Visual Impairment

Billy's medical records state that he is legally blind. He attends the sixth grade with his sighted neighborhood friends. He can read large print, write legibly in cursive, find his way around the community without special help, and play softball with his friends. Other than obtaining large-print books and seating him close to the board, Billy's teacher needs to make few classroom adaptations for him.

Polly also has been evaluated as legally blind. She is unable to see anything. In her sixth-grade classroom, she uses taped textbooks in order to get the same information as her peers in content subjects. The special education resource teacher is working with her classroom teacher in developing a program to teach her to type. She also is learning braille reading. After Polly became familiar with the arrangement of furniture and learning centers in the classroom, she was able to move freely about the room with the use of a cane. She still has some difficulty getting around crowded hallways and finding her way on field trips taken by the class. Other students often walk with Polly telling her about the obstacles in the surrounding area.

Although Billy and Polly are both considered legally blind, their visual functioning differs. It is for this reason that the educational definition of blindness or visual impairment usually differs from the medical or legal definition. Basically, the traditional definition of blindness has been visual acuity less than 20/200 after correction, while partial sightedness is considered visual acuity of 20/70 after correction. There are several educational problems with this definition. In the criterion for blindness, 20/200 means that a person can read the 200-foot letter on the Snellen Chart at a distance of 20 feet. This type of visual examination takes into account only distance vision. Education experiences primarily involve close-distance vision, such as reading. Other factors such as color, light, and object perception are not included in the traditional definition. Finally, a major drawback to the traditional definition is that measurement of acuity does not correspond to a person's actual utilization of vision

(Gearheart and Weishahn 1976). The cases of Billy and Polly offer a clear example of this point. Billy had more residual or useful vision remaining than Polly. If he were treated as a blind person, his visual abilities would be grossly underestimated. Teachers and parents of blind children frequently comment on the fact that the child's ability to use his residual vision effectively may vary from day to day. Adaptations in the classroom vary with the child. For educational purposes we shall consider a blind child to be visually impaired to the extent that he needs to read braille, whereas a partially sighted child is one who is able to read large print. A basic definitional principle is that whether the student is blind or partially sighted, educational adaptations are required to accommodate for the visual limitations.

Since children with visual problems traditionally have received their education in residential schools, many teachers have had limited exposure to these students. Teachers are often understandably uncomfortable about situations for which they have little information. Also, since almost everyone has banged his head or stubbed his toes trying to get around his bedroom in the middle of the night when the lights were out, it is sometimes difficult for sighted people to imagine how a blind person is able to get around and participate in his environment. As with all other handicapping areas, the capabilities of blind persons are frequently underestimated. Again, the same condition has a different effect on different people. Some blind people withdraw from involvement and participation, while others make their way around busy city streets, engage in advanced academic study, make significant contributions in their career, participate in sports of all kinds, and have a meaningful and enjoyable family life as a husband or wife, mother or father. Readers who would like greater insight into the world of the blind are referred to *If You Could See What I Hear* (Sullivan and Gill 1975). Mr. Sullivan shares his lifetime experiences as a blind person. This book expands one's awareness of human adaptability and causes one to question his perceptions of a handicap.

In the majority of cases, severe visual problems are identified early in the first years of life; however, teachers should be alert to warning signals of visual problems which have previously gone undetected. Warning signals (Kirk 1972; Gearheart and Weishahn 1976) could include chronic eye irritations such as encrusted lids, recurring sties, wateriness, or reddened eyelids; excessive blinking, squinting, or facial contortions when reading or doing close work; arranging reading material or classroom charts unusually close or far away; overconcern for establishing awareness of body in relationship to other children or classroom fixtures, or bumping into peers and fixtures; difficulty in copying from the chalkboard and paper or writing in general with respect to quality of letter formation, spacing, and staying on the line; tilting the head or shutting one eye while reading; and complaining of headaches, burning eyes, or dizziness.

When teachers suspect visual problems based on these symptoms, they should discuss their concern with the student's parents and the school nurse. The disadvantages associated with visual problems can be drastically minimized through the use of corrective aids (e.g., glasses) and sound educational programming.

Educational Implications

Cognitive Functioning. Visually impaired children have been found to have a normal curve of intellectual development (Bateman 1963). There are no particular language deficits characteristic of children with visual problems (Telford and Sawrey 1972); however, these students have been found by some researchers to have mild to moderate lags in academic achievement (Hayes 1941; Bateman 1963). Their underachievement could be attributable to a number of reasons, including slower concept development associated with impaired vision, slower reading rates, and inappropriate instructional procedures. Instructional procedures for teaching blind students will be included in chapters 3 through 10. Problems in achievement resulting from difficulty in concept development will be discussed here.

Concept development basically refers to the process of attaching meaning to ideas and clustering them into units of information to form a conceptual framework. A concept can be thought of as the "hook" on which children can attach ideas when they are first perceived. This type of concept formation adds clarity, meaning, and organization to the thousands of inputs students receive each day. Vision contributes significantly to the quality of concept development. It is considered the "unifier" of experience. We can hear an airplane, ride on an airplane, smell an airplane, and listen to a story about an airplane; but the sensory experience that can pull all those bits of information together is actually seeing an airplane. When vision is impaired to the extent that visual sensory input is impossible, teachers must capitalize on the use of other sensory channels such as listening, feeling, tasting, and smelling. It is also important to use the remaining, useful vision. In many cases, the more the vision is used, the more efficient it will become. Another significant aid to concept development is concrete experiences. One aspect of concreteness involves touching and manipulating in order to understand concepts of size, texture, and shape. If algae are being discussed in the science class, do not rely just on verbally describing this concept to a blind student. Have him feel the side of an aquarium as a more concrete encounter. Real objects and their models can be valuable learning aids. Learning from concrete experiences could involve field trips. These types of experiences are good for all students, not just the blind and partially sighted.

Some blind students may be able to memorize definitions of words without having any clear understanding of how to relate that information to anything meaningful. A program which starts at a concrete level using practical experiences and a multisensory approach can help students with visual problems move from concrete to abstract levels of understanding.

Orientation and Mobility. Orientation and mobility have similar, yet different, meanings. They are often confused as they relate to blind and partially sighted people. Orientation is the person's awareness of his position in space as related to other objects and people in his environment. Mobility refers to the person's movement within the environment as he goes from one place to another (Gearheart and Weishahn 1976).

Students with severe visual impairment probably will have started mobility training prior to entering school. Many students will have an orientation and mobility instructor to work with them, their family, and teachers in helping prepare them for getting around the classroom and school independently. Teachers should follow through carefully on the suggestions of the instructor to insure that consistent expectations and guidelines are set for the child. Some general tips for teachers in this area include:

Have the student spend time in the classroom for a couple of days prior to the beginning of the school year. Guide him around the room explaining the layout, learning centers, arrangement of desks, location of special equipment, and other important information. Let him ask questions and generally spend the necessary time to feel comfortable in moving about. Practice walking to the bathroom, playground, cafeteria, library, and other special areas. Again, explain the layout of each and practice moving about in them. Practice the procedure of exiting the building for fire drills.

When the arrangement of the classroom or parts of the school change, tell the student in advance and provide for practice in learning orientation and mobility again, if necessary.

Instruct the blind or partially sighted student to ask for help when he needs it. Classmates should be prepared for acting as guides. Have blindfolded classmates role-play being guided by holding on to a peer's arm. This will help them establish proper guidelines for serving as guides.

Call the blind or partially sighted student by name (he will not know when you are looking at him) and give explicit directions. For example, if he is being asked to get a particular library book, describe the location precisely.

Blind students who have attended public schools report on the horror of walking down the steps when a mass of students is thundering down past them. Encourage sighted classmates to take precautions against possible collisions or schedule the blind student's transition time a few minutes earlier or later than other students'.

Adaptations in Classroom Procedures and Equipment. Relatively few adaptations in general classroom procedures are necessary for students with visual impairment. Some helpful considerations, depending upon the individual student, might include seating close to the teacher and chalkboard; avoiding glare created by having the student work facing a window; keeping doors either opened or closed, since ajar doors can be a potential safety hazard in mobility; providing adequate space for the storage of special equipment, such as braille books and typewriters, and adequate desk space for using it; providing a verbal explanation of board work, filmstrips, or other visual presentations; and alternating periods of using residual vision with other educational experiences to reduce fatigue and strain.

A substantial amount of adapted instructional equipment has been developed for partially sighted and blind students. As each curriculum area is discussed in this book, this special equipment will be identified and explained. Catalogs of materials and the necessary equipment, braille books, and other materials are available free of charge from the Commission for the Blind in each state.

■ **Case Study**
Visual Impairment

When I learned that I would have a blind student in my home room and social studies class, my first thought was "What can I do for him?" I had misgivings about things I would say, such as "Look at the board, we're going to see a film." After talking with a friend, I decided that the first day I would tell David that I would treat him just like the other students. This worked out well; his attitude made it easy for me and we both relaxed.

David wants to learn more than any kid in my class. He wants to learn because he's behind. He will have to work hard just to finish high school.

Before David came into the class and the home room, I talked with the other students. At first he was a curiosity to them but soon it was evident

31

Photograph by Richard Clontz

that the others liked him and wanted to help in any way they could. David talks about his handicap and thus there is no pressure on the other kids; they don't view him as very different.

Actually, David has been an asset to the class. I put him at a table of boys who like him; they are conscious that they must verbalize so David can take part in whatever is going on. As they read or look for answers for questions, they talk about it for David's benefit and they all profit. He has helped the whole class verbalize their feelings and their findings.

I have had to take a good look at my instructional techniques and I am not altogether happy with what I am doing. For one thing, I like showing "war movies"; the kids like them and are motivated by them. But I feel David is cheated when we have movies and that this emphasizes his disability.

Lectures are totally unsuccessful with David. We've tried taping lectures for him to replay, but I find that he learns best through discussion. He enters into activities with other students and derives a lot from them, but not from my talking.

Sometimes I feel that I neglect David, and that I need to let him know I'm there. The lack of eye contact makes me feel he may think I have forgotten him.

I have not been easy on David; I feel it would be demeaning to expect less of him than I do of the other students. I have given him tests equal to the ones the rest of the class took. We started with verbal tests, then I asked him to type the answers. He didn't like this, but I required him to do it. I don't feel I've measured his understanding of concepts, such as on the subject of communism.

Next year I will be better prepared for David. I want to involve him in the whole curriculum, rather than in social studies and science only. I need to develop some way to teach him map skills, among other things.

The best thing David and I have going is that we like each other. He's helped me more than I've helped him.

Mr. Rayburn
Fairview Elementary School

Hearing Impairment

Imagine not being able to hear favorite sounds often taken for granted, such as a symphony, rain on the roof, a crackling fire, the song of a bird, children's laughter, or the voices of loved ones. Also devastating to consider is not being able to hear the sounds signifying safety warnings, such as the honking of a horn on a city street, ambulance sirens, fire alarms, weather alerts, and the ring of a telephone. Hearing impairment must also be considered in classroom settings. Some students have difficulty hearing or are unable to hear the teacher's instructions, conversations of their peers, educational TV, classroom discussions, the comradely comments on the playground, or even the noise in the cafeteria. Undoubtedly, these students are at a distinct disadvantage in achieving school success. However, hearing-impaired students and their teachers can minimize hearing handicaps to the point that these students frequently can function effectively in regular class settings.

Hearing impairment is an extremely complex phenomenon. To explain its influence on a person's development, Birch (1975) identified five factors for consideration.

The *nature* of the hearing impairment refers to a person's hearing pattern as it relates to frequency and intensity. Frequency can be thought of as pitch, while intensity refers to loudness. Frequency must be considered in terms of the pitch range needed for communication purposes in order to understand the nature of a hearing loss. Some students may be able to hear the majority of sounds, missing those at one extreme of pitch or the other. Students with the greatest educational handicap are those who are unable to hear the pitch range of normal conversation. As for intensity, students vary in their ability to hear different levels of amplification. Some students, unable to hear faint or even conversation intensity, can hear when these sounds are amplified. The nature of hearing impairment varies in many ways. In addition to frequency and intensity, the nature of hearing impairment is also determined according to whether the acuity of one or both ears is damaged and the type of hearing loss. The two major types of losses are conductive and sensorineural. Conductive losses result from middle ear deficiencies while sensorineural losses result from inner ear deficiencies.

The *degree* of hearing impairment is the second important factor. Some students with residual (remaining) hearing benefit from the use of a hearing aid to the extent that total regular class assimilation is effectively accomplished without major adaptations. Other impairments range along every point of the continuum to the point of total deafness. Students who are totally deaf do not benefit from the amplification of hearing aids. Classification systems have been developed which describe the degree of hearing impairment at the levels of mild, moderate, moderately severe, severe, and profound. Educationally, those systems often lose their meaning, since no two hearing-impaired students are affected in exactly the same way or to the same extent. An elementary teacher who had been notified at the beginning of the school year that he would have responsibility for teaching a student with a "severe" hearing loss was extremely concerned over his self-assumed lack of competence to teach the student. He imagined that his instruction would need to be in sign language and did not know whether he should learn to sign himself or hurriedly try to find an interpreter, which he knew would be virtually impossible. He was shocked on the first day of school when the student with the severe loss was engaged in spontaneous oral conversation with other students and was able to read only slightly below grade level. Although the student's voice quality was raspy and some articulation errors were present, the student was able to talk and to hear the speech of others with the use of a hearing aid and lipreading. What a relief to this teacher to realize that "severe" does not always mean lack of communication. On the other hand, sometimes the educational handicaps of a severe loss are significantly greater than in this case. Teachers who observe the behavior of a hearing-impaired student and carefully talk with his parents, physician, and speech teacher about his specific abilities and disabilities are able to determine the degree of educational impairment. Teachers should beware of labels. They are sometimes functionally on target, but many other times misconvey information related to classroom performance.

The *age of onset* is the third factor for consideration. A hearing impairment creates far more significant educational handicaps when it is congenital (present from birth) or its occurrence is in the first or second year of development. The reason early onset is more significant is that language has not yet been learned; therefore, the child has no frame of reference for understanding language. When the onset occurs later, for example, at the age of ten, the child has the vocabulary and syntax of language and reading achievement developed to the point that continued, steady growth could be strongly anticipated.

A fourth factor for consideration is *level of intelligence*. Hearing-impaired students who are intellectually capable are often able to compensate more for their handicap in learning strategies to work around it. Language development is a difficult process under normal conditions. Requirements for abstractness and generalization are increased drastically in the language development process of hearing-impaired students.

The final factor affecting the influence of a hearing impairment is the *quality of stimulation*. When hearing-impaired children are identified early and receive intensive language stimulation during preschool years, the prognosis of their success in the regular class is usually better than if the stimulation had not occurred. It is not only preschool intervention that is necessary. Daily language stimulation throughout a student's school career by parents and teachers has minimized the educational disadvantages of many hearing-impaired children.

All these factors interact to determine the specific educational handicap of a given student. It is impossible to consider them in isolation as a basis for educational planning. The teacher should take a dynamic view and consider the totality of the student's strengths and weaknesses. It is impossible for teachers to be experts in understanding and interpreting the intricate details of specific hearing problems. Again, each student's condition will vary according to the five factors. Teachers are advised to talk carefully with the student's parents, doctor, speech teacher, and audiologist to gain information on the educationally relevant influences of the hearing impairment.

The educational classification used by many states distinguishes between deaf and hard of hearing. Students whose hearing loss has precluded normal acquisition of language are considered deaf; those whose hearing loss has not precluded normal language acquisition are referred to as hard of hearing. Sometimes these students are not identified prior to entering school. In other situations, hearing problems can follow immediately after diseases or accidents. Upper respiratory diseases and infected tonsils and adenoids can create temporary or sometimes permanent hearing loss. The teacher should observe carefully any behaviors indicative of hearing problems. Some of these behaviors (McConnell 1973; Gearheart and Weishahn 1976) include turning one side of the head toward the speaker or touching the ears when trying to listen; delayed language; standing very close to someone when he is talking; frequently asking for comments or instructions to be repeated; lack of attention; inappropriate responses to questions signaling lack of understanding; and complaints of earaches, runny discharges from ears, sore throat, and constant colds. The teacher who observes some of these symptoms should contact the student's parents and the school nurse. Initial screening of problems might indicate the need for a medical, audiological, and educational evaluation.

Educational Implications

Communication. The greatest single educational handicap of deaf and hard-of-hearing students revolves around the development of communication skills. There are two basic approaches, referred to as oral and total communication (Birch 1975; Kirk 1972). The oral method requires the student with a hearing impairment to use a combination of residual hearing, a hearing aid, and speech reading (the ability to understand another person while watching his lips and face) in comprehending what he hears. In expressing himself, the student using the oral approach verbalizes. The total communication approach also involves the use of residual hearing, a hearing aid, speech reading, and oral speech. Additionally, this approach includes the use of sign language and the manual alphabet. In sign language, concepts are represented by movement of the hands and arms, each sign representing a concept. As opposed to concept representation, the manual alphabet has a movement for each letter of the alphabet and is often referred to as finger spelling. Words can be spelled by use of a particular movement for different letters. The manual alphabet has been likened to writing in the air.

The form of communication a student uses has tremendous implications for the classroom. Although there is some debate over the most advantageous approach, many specialists seem to follow the pattern of intensively stimulating oral communication with hearing-impaired students during preschool and early elementary years (Nix 1976). If the child has not developed adequate language by the age of nine or ten, consideration is given to teaching the two forms of manual communication at that time. The oral approach to language facilitates mainstreaming in that the student with a hearing handicap can understand and be understood by his classroom peers. When signing is necessary, however, hearing children often enjoy the intrigue of learning signing as a way of communicating with their friend. In some mainstream situations, teachers also have learned signs for basic classroom terminology. Certainly the educational goal for students with hearing handicaps is to prepare themselves to live in a hearing world. Many students with hearing handicaps have been limited by teachers and parents excusing them from the rigorous requirements of language training on the basis that it was too difficult for them. The capabilities of these students in obtaining language proficiency often exceed our expectations. Specific instructional strategies for developing communication skills will be discussed in chapter 5.

Special Equipment in the Classroom.   Hearing-impaired students frequently wear hearing aids. Teachers, therefore, must have a basic understanding of how hearing aids work and of basic maintenance operations. The hearing aid itself is composed of three parts: a receiver for picking up the sound, an amplifier for making it louder, and a speaker for transmitting the sound to the hearing-impaired person. The aid runs on batteries. Any specific questions as to its operation or maintenance and all major repairs should be directed to the hearing aid dealer who sold it. General guidelines (Gearheart and Weishahn 1976; Birch 1975) important for the classroom follow:

Hearing aids cannot be assumed to result in normal hearing. Aids do make sounds, including background noises, louder. Preferential seating should be provided to a student wearing an aid to accommodate his need to hear classroom discussions and instructions, as well as his need not to have sounds drowned out by loud background noises. Sometimes it is difficult to know the best seating location automatically. Perhaps the special education teacher in the school could offer some suggestions. A good strategy is to start with the "best educated" guess and try the student in a particular seating arrangement. Seek feedback from him as to his ability to hear and also observe his behavior to see if he seems to be straining or missing important language information. Make modifications in the seating pattern until the optimal location is identified.

If a hearing aid has been prescribed for a child, he should wear it at all times unless otherwise directed by his doctor. When children repeatedly try to remove their aids at school, it is often an indication that the aid is not doing the proper job by making sounds too loud or not loud enough. The teacher can put the aid to his ear to get an idea of possible disturbances. Aids should be checked intermittently.

Students who wear a hearing aid should learn early to care for it. When they first detect a change in its functioning, they should report it to their parents and teacher. Teachers should keep an extra battery and cord on hand at school. As children advance in elementary years, they usually are able to change batteries or insert cords themselves. The teacher should be knowledgeable in these procedures and carry them out for young children. Hearing aid dealers are usually the best people to give teachers and parents detailed information on this type of maintenance. Another maintenance problem is eliminating the occasional squeal of the aid. Shrill squealing can disrupt the attention of everyone in the classroom. The squeal is often caused by a slippage of the speaker or earmold and can be eliminated by properly fitting the earmold in the ear and sometimes turning down the volume.

Hearing students are naturally curious about the operation of a hearing aid. The teacher, working with the hearing-impaired student and his parents, can help classroom peers understand the hearing aid by presenting a lesson on how it works. The hearing students might be given an opportunity to listen to the aid's amplification of sound. This type of openness and understanding is the foundation for facilitating the social adjustment of everyone in the class.

In addition to hearing aids, some schools purchase auditory training units which generally have stronger amplification and a wider frequency range than hearing aids. The student wears the trainer, which has the same three parts as the hearing aid—receiver, amplifier, and speaker. Additionally, the teacher wears a portable microphone around his neck which sends his voice directly to the student wearing the auditory trainer. A distinct advantage of the trainers is that they can be adjusted to close off all sound except for the teacher's voice. By having background distractions cut down, the student is able to focus completely on what the teacher is saying. Typically, trainers are used for speech and language development. Hearing aid dealers can give teachers more specific information on the use of auditory trainers.

Adaptations in Classroom Procedures. In considering necessary adaptations in classroom procedures, the teacher must realize that the needs of hearing-impaired students vary according to the details of their particular handicap. General suggestions will be given for classroom adaptations that might be considered and modified for the particular student in a regular classroom.

If the student needs specialized services to keep up with achievement in the classroom or to develop communication skills, help should be obtained from the special education resource teacher or speech therapist. The student may receive individual tutoring outside the classroom or the resource teacher and/or speech therapist might work with the child within the regular class. The total coordination of the program will be a key to success.

The teacher (classroom or resource, or both) may have to introduce the vocabulary of lessons to hearing-impaired students ahead of time or seek the help of the student's parents in this preliminary preparation for the lesson. This language orientation can facilitate speech reading and understanding. Another helpful hint is to write key words and phrases on the chalkboard for the student as an outline during a class discussion.

The teacher should try to remain stationary when talking and not stand near a window that creates a glare for the student. Teachers positioned with light on their face are most helpful to students with hearing impairments. Of course, it is important to face students when talking. Using an overhead projector rather than the chalkboard can increase the amount of time a teacher faces a class.

Fancy hairstyles, mustaches, beards, and excessive jewelry worn by teachers often create distractions and interfere with the hearing-impaired student's ability to read lips. Other obstructions to be avoided around the face include pencils, books, cigarettes, and pipes.

Teachers should not exaggerate lip movements, rate, or volume of their voices. Complete sentences should be used so that individual words can be interpreted in the context of their meaning.

Visual aids can be extremely helpful. Consider using captioned films, pictures, and the chalkboard.

Written assignments and announcements can be advantageous to increasing the successful integration of hearing-impaired students. A classroom discussion could be taped and then typed by a volunteer, so that the student is able to read what he was not able to hear.

Students who work very hard to hear in the classroom often tire more quickly than other students. Academic subjects may be interwoven with physical activity and short intervals of free time to minimize fatigue and frustration.

A hearing-impaired student in the class can benefit significantly from having a "hearing buddy" make an outline or carbon copy of notes, repeat directions, clarify concepts, or help him stay on the right page of his book. Buddies could be rotated on a weekly or biweekly basis. The teacher has to instruct classroom peers carefully on how much help is needed or when help is not needed. Striking the proper balance is an important educational decision.

Sometimes hearing-impaired students make unintentional noises, interrupt conversations, and speak too loudly or not loudly enough when they are unaware of it. They need guidance in appropriate verbal interactions. Overlooking or excusing these types of behaviors with students who are perfectly capable of appropriate communications skills is denying them an opportunity to learn otherwise.

■ Case Study
Hearing Impairment

My experiences in mainstreaming hearing-impaired children had a terrible beginning and a very happy ending. It all started last year when Dave, a severely hearing-impaired student was placed in my class. Prior to the first day of school with Dave, I had received no training in teaching children with hearing handicaps. I had seen Dave around the school the year before and had always felt sorry for him, because he seemed to be unhappy. The truth was that he was unhappy because his second-grade teacher never seemed to include him in instructional activities. She was not ignoring him on purpose; she simply did not know what to do.

When Dave started in my third-grade class, I thought I could adapt my program to meet his needs. Although I was promised consultation and help from a special education teacher, I received none. Dave's language and reading skills were very low and his handwriting was all done in tall manuscript letters. I shudder now to think of all the mistakes I made with him. For example, we always give standardized achievement tests to students in the third grade. Not knowing any better, I gave him a group test on the third-grade level. Dave scored very low, and I recommended him for possible placement in a special class with cognitively handicapped children. His mother got very upset and contacted the state department of education. Someone from the hearing-impaired program in the state department called and fussed at me for using a test that required third-grade reading and language skills with Dave. I could then understand that the test was inappropriate for him and that his hearing handicap had penalized his performance. I did not mean to treat him unfairly, but I simply did not know what was best for him. I developed a very negative attitude about teaching Dave.

Just when I was relieved that the school year was over and I had made it through the year, the principal asked me to move up to the fourth grade and teach the same class the following year. This meant another year of having Dave in class. The only hope I had was that a new special education teacher had been hired to work with me and with other classroom teachers. I was very skeptical, but I agreed to give it a try. Ms. Goulding, the new teacher, held a short workship before school started and gave me lots of suggestions on good instructional tips to use with Dave. I don't want to sound like I am overstating it, but she was truly like a ray of sunshine. All of a sudden I knew help was close by and that she had much to offer. She started working with Dave every day in reading and math. He seemed to do well in programmed series like the Sullivan. Instead of always taking Dave out of the room, she frequently popped into my class and worked with him there. She then could remind me of important considerations like facing the children when I talk, avoiding standing in front of the window, and writing assignments on the board. Even though she had told me these things before, sometimes I would forget and not even realize it. Another thing that I really appreciate is that she always gives me suggestions in such a nice way. There's nothing threatening or negative about it.

I am responsible for the social studies and science portion of Dave's program. I use the overhead projector frequently to introduce vocabulary, and I always try to put new words into context for him. He enjoys captioned films and supplementary library books. Dave always wears an auditory trainer at school. I wear the microphone so that my voice is amplified for him and background noises are screened out. At first he tended to wear his coat over the trainer to hide it, but now it is a normal thing in our classroom. I have never heard any teasing by the other students. One thing that has helped tremendously is that hearing-impaired children have been attending our school for the last ten years. It is nothing new for the other children.

As I look back on this year, I realize that I have made great strides as a teacher. I can honestly say that the key has been Ms. Goulding. The great thing about it is that the techniques I have learned for Dave have benefited all the students. I am excited over what has happened this year. It seems that all of us have made gains in different ways.

Ms. Fracker
Cary Elementary School

Emotional/Behavioral Disadvantages

Like other handicaps that place children at a disadvantage in terms of school success, emotional/behavioral problems vary along a continuum in terms of their specific type, severity, duration, and classroom manifestation. The literature related to emotional/behavioral handicaps sometimes has added confusion rather than clarity to the teacher's need to learn how to help the child with problems in the regular class, since there are many different opinions on what exactly constitutes an emotional/behavioral problem. A definition adopted in this text is: An emotional/behavioral handicap is a marked deviation from age-appropriate behavior expectations which interferes with positive personal and interpersonal development. It is important to realize that people's emotional/behavioral development must be considered in light of chronological age. Young children, for example, typically are expected to have difficulty delaying gratification. Waiting for special treats or the celebration of holidays can be frustrating to a preschooler. When a twelve-year-old child experiences similar difficulty in delaying gratification, it usually is considered, according to an age perspective, as cause for concern. The latter part of the definition focuses on both personal and interpersonal areas. Teachers should remember that healthy emotional/behavioral development takes into account how a person feels about himself, as well as how he relates to others. In the area of personal development, the way a student views himself, or his self-concept, is learned. Experiences at school help students shape their own identity: successful or failing; willing or hesitant; lively or withdrawn; leader or follower; confident or unsure. These aspects of self-concept form the foundation of personal or emotional/behavioral development. A student's self-concept influences all areas of school performance. Students who expect success are often more willing to risk a challenging task. Those who continually fail may get the message to "give up." Since self-concepts are learned, they can be positively influenced. Students who are handicapped because of their view of themselves do not always have to remain that way. Teachers who recognize that personal development has just as much, or sometimes more, educational relevance as basic academic subjects can help students feel more successful, capable, happy, and confident through their careful attention to emotional/behavioral needs. Personal development is closely tied to interpersonal development. Bower (1969b) has provided an excellent description of interpersonal development:

It isn't just getting along with others that is important here. Satisfactory interpersonal relations refers to the ability to demonstrate sympathy and warmth toward others, the ability to stand alone when necessary, the ability to have close friends, the ability to be aggressively constructive, and the ability to enjoy working and playing with others as well as enjoying working and playing by oneself (pp. 22–23).

Sometimes in the rush of classroom activities the relationship of one student to another may become more observable to the teacher than how a troubled student is viewing himself. It is important to establish the interdependence of both elements—personal and interpersonal—in understanding the individual nature of emotional/behavioral handicaps.

Since teachers are generally familiar with the range of behavioral differences found among children at a given age level, their identification of children who have emotional/behavioral problems is particularly relevant. In a major research effort conducted by Morse, Cutler, and Fink (1964), sixty teachers rated the problem behavior characteristics of 441 children. The ratings of these teachers were found to cluster into three groups:

1. Conduct disorder—Children described as defiant, disobedient, uncooperative, attention seeking, restless, and negative.

2. Personality problem—Children described as lacking self-confidence, fearful, depressed, and anxious.

3. Inadequacy/immaturity—Children described as sluggish, lazy, daydreaming, and passive.

Some behaviors indicative of emotional problems may be situational (e.g., related to a family crisis) and others occur over a long period of time. Students who may be considered emotionally/behaviorally handicapped by one teacher in a given classroom may not be so considered by another teacher in a different classroom. Students perform differently in various situations according to expectations, guidelines, responses, and personality traits of teachers. Tolerance is a reciprocal factor between student and teacher. Some teachers are more tolerant of particular student behavior and vice versa. An important educational principle is matching student and teacher characteristics/styles to the greatest degree possible in order to maximize the potential of a "comfortable fit."

Educational Implications

Learning Problems. Students with higher vulnerability to emotional/behavioral pressures who are coping with a host of factors that are distracting to goal-directed activity often encounter academic difficulty. Bower (1969a) reported that emotionally handicapped students scored lower on reading and arithmetic achievement tests than their nonhandicapped counterparts. Sometimes the problem becomes one of the chicken and the egg. Which came first—the emotional/behavioral or the learning problem? Consider the fourth-grade child who reads on a second-grade level. Such a child is recalled who was expected to function academically with textbooks all on the fourth-grade level. Since he could not read them, he received an *F* in every subject for the entire school year. He was characterized by his teacher with almost the exact description of the behaviors listed previously in the personality problem dimension of the Morse, Cutler, and Fink (1946) classification—"Lacking in self-confidence, fearful, depressed, and anxious." As his emotional/behavioral problems became more pronounced, his achievement came to a halt as he refused to attempt assignments. This example illustrates the interaction between learning problems and emotional/behavioral problems, as well as the interaction between student and teacher behavior. Just as "success begets success," often "failure begets failure." Students who experience difficulty in personal and interpersonal development also often have learning problems. When a student gets on this type of failure treadmill, he needs help in breaking out of it.

How can the teacher help? There are many ways. Motivation and interest have to be established—useful techniques are discussed in chapters 3 and 9. Using these techniques requires a teacher's willingness to try a number of novel approaches until a successful one for the particular student's difficulty can be identified. Sometimes the initial investment of more individualized teacher time can ultimately be extremely efficient in preventing future classroom disruptions and more exaggerated emotional handicaps on the student's part. When motivation and interest have been established, the teacher might begin instruction in a structured, systematic format which stresses the step-by-step development of skills. This instruction should be based on thorough academic assessment. When students know they are making progress and are receiving positive recognition for their gains, they are much more likely to be emotionally/behaviorally healthy. The major purpose of this book is to bring together strategies and resources to make individualization possible in order to ameliorate many of the learning and emotional/behavioral problems experienced by students. It is conjectured that teachers will see a substantial reduction in the number of children with emotional/behavioral handicaps as students are able to state with confidence, "I can learn. I am competent. Good things happen to me. I make positive accomplishments."

Inappropriate Behavior Leading to Classroom Disruptions

When teachers are responsible for approximately twenty to thirty students in a given class period, they must consider the impact the student with emotional/behavioral handicaps makes on the entire class.

When John gets angry, he loudly curses the teacher, gets into fights with his peers, and destroys classroom materials.

Jane develops physical symptoms every time she is given a test. Most often she becomes nauseated. In particularly stressful situations, she is unable to control her bladder.

These two situations require excessive demands upon classroom time and interfere with ongoing activities. Teachers often need help in managing these types of problem situations. In the next chapter, the team approach will be emphasized. Changing the inappropriate behavior of students requires shared responsibility by many educators in the school.

Some students with emotional/behavioral problems engage in otherwise appropriate behavior at inappropriate times. For example, rowdy behavior associated with the playground or clowning appropriate in some social interactions might be carried out by some students in the midst of a reading group or math lesson. As a rule, students with emotional/behavioral handicaps function better when teachers provide structure and clearly set limits to classroom behavior and assignments. Some students who do not personally generate their own stability and orderliness can benefit substantially from teachers who help provide this structure. Additionally, when the classroom disruptions of students with emotional/behavioral handicaps are reduced, all students benefit.

Getting Lost in the Shuffle

In spite of teachers' best intentions, it often happens that students who tend to be overly passive, shy, and withdrawn get overlooked in the teacher's effort to respond to the seemingly most demanding aspects of the school day. Acting-out, aggressive behavior almost always requires an immediate response in the best interest of the student relative to safety and personal/interpersonal disruption. When students say nothing, cower from attention, and generally do what is asked of them, they frequently are overlooked in classroom situations.

Severe withdrawn and passive behavior is a clear signal of an emotional/behavioral handicap. Active intervention in building trust and understanding is required to insure both personal and interpersonal development. Many of the suggestions included in chapter 10 regarding the development of relationships are particularly applicable to these students.

Peer Relationships

Students with emotional/behavioral handicaps often suffer in silence as they eat lunch alone in a crowded cafeteria, get into arguments in the restroom, or feel excluded immediately before or after school when informal groups occupy the schoolyard. Sometimes the quality of peer relationships is more telling outside the formal classroom situation than within. Loneliness and isolation can exaggerate emotional/behavioral handicaps. Again, we have the treadmill situation:

A person engages in annoying or bothersome behavior associated with an emotional/behavioral problem.

Peers become irritated with the behavior and reject the individual.

The individual is hurt by the rejection and loneliness.

The harder the individual tries to be accepted, the more annoying he becomes.

Greater annoyance leads to further rejection.

Peer relationships are significant aspects of the educational experiences of students. When students within a class are factionalized, effective instructional strategies involving the range of group activities become

45

greatly reduced. The breakdown of peer relationships is a major implication of emotional/behavioral handicaps and creates significant educational disadvantages.

■ Case Study
Emotional/Behavioral Disadvantages

Maria came to my third-grade class after attending school for the first two years in the Dominican Republic. Moving from one country to another represented a tremendous change for Maria. Also involved in this process was a transition for Maria from Spanish to English as a primary language. In a conference with Maria's father, he shared another factor which I found had to be considered in understanding Maria's needs. He and Maria's mother had recently divorced. Her mother and two siblings stayed in the Dominican Republic, and Maria and her father were starting a new life in North Carolina.

This background information helped me interpret some of the first warning signals from Maria with respect to her self-concept and her interaction with her classmates. Some of these warning signals included general fussiness and grouchiness. For instance, when someone would inadvertently bump into her, Maria would scream out, "He hit me!" She often "tattled" on her peers, which caused some of them to exclude her. At the beginning of the year, she tended to sulk and seemed to have quite a stubborn streak. Sometimes I would call on her when I was confident she knew the answer, and she would refuse to say anything. Another observation was that Maria was extremely lonely. Since my class is made up almost entirely of boys, there were few girls with whom to develop close friendships. Maria often seemed to feel isolated at school and after school she had neither friends nor siblings with whom to interact. As for academics, her achievement is below that of most of her classmates. I was initially unsure if her general unhappiness was affecting her academic progress. On the one hand, the concerns related to Maria's emotional status; on the other hand, it was important not to overlook her learning needs.

In trying to help Maria, I have tried to help her gain recognition from her peers. One nice thing occurred when the advanced reading group in the class had to read a story about a Spanish family. The story included various Spanish phrases. Maria, who is in a lower reading group, was able to pronounce the Spanish words for her peers. She seemed to enjoy being in the special position of knowing something no one else knew. It was beneficial for her peers to recognize her bilingual ability. Maria's reading achievement seems to have improved significantly since we discovered that she needed glasses. The way she held her head back and squinted her eyes alerted us to this problem. As Maria has received classroom recognition and improved in her schoolwork, she seems to have a more positive attitude in interaction with her peers. Another positive factor that seems to have contributed to her overall happiness is her father's remarriage, as she enjoys having a new mother.

On a particularly bad day Maria asked if she could talk with the counselor about her feelings. I was pleased that she sought this help when she needed it. She is beginning to establish a close friendship with one peer, which is a positive sign. Overall, Maria's emotional problems seem to be improving for a number of reasons.

Ms. Koon
Glenwood Elementary School

Summary

After various areas of handicapping conditions are highlighted, common threads can be identified. The most obvious one, language, cuts across every handicap in some aspect. Other common threads are attention span, generalization, mobility, lowered academic achievement, and emotional/ behavioral considerations. These characteristics should be approached in light of the particular student with whom the teacher is working. It is impossible to define a set of successful instructional strategies for all learning disabled or all hearing-impaired students. There is no assurance that what is successful for one student will automatically work with another. In each curriculum area, basic principles will be discussed with many different possibilities for application in classroom settings. Methods and materials will be suggested for student characteristics or those particular strengths and weaknesses that have educational relevance. Although these characteristics often cluster according to the different handicapping condition, every child is unique and must be approached on that basis. The *characteristics* pointed out in each handicapping area in this chapter should help readers direct their attention to correlating remediation strategies discussed in the following chapters.

In summarizing the introduction to disadvantaged or handicapped students in school situations, we emphasize several points.

All students have various combinations of strengths and weaknesses. It is important for the teacher to be aware of both. Accentuating or building on strengths, while working to remediate weaknesses, is a key to successful instruction.

The seemingly most obvious handicap does not necessarily impede the student's progress. Students may possess tremendous ability to overcome obstacles and compensate for deficits. Recently an eighth-grade blind student making all *A*s in a regular public school was asked to consider being transferred to the state school for the blind. The reason given by the administrator at his school was that he would be able to be around "more people of his kind." Why should he transfer? He had successfully performed in all subjects and had minimized the disadvantage of blindness. A difference is only a difference when it makes a difference. Handicapped children have far more similarities than differences with the nonhandicapped.

Often the most critical educational disadvantage for handicapped students is that instructional strategies in education classes are often not tailored to their needs. Classroom teachers have both a challenge and an opportunity in developing competency to teach these students. The methods and materials discussed in this book are not only useful with handicapped students; they can also enhance the teacher's effectiveness with all children. There is no substitute for sound educational principles and systematic instruction.

References and Selected Readings

Ainsworth, S. 1970. Report and commentary. In *Conditioning in stuttering therapy: Application and limitations.* Pub. no. 7. Memphis, Tenn.: Speech Foundation of America.

Bateman, B. 1963. Reading and psycholinguistic processes of partially seeing children. *CEC Research Monograph,* Series A, no. 5. Arlington, Va.: Council for Exceptional Children, pp. 1–46.

Belmont, J. M., and Butterfield, E. C. 1969. The relations of short-term memory to development and intelligence. In L. C. Lipsitt and H. W. Reese, eds., *Advances in child development and behavior,* vol. 4. New York: Academic Press.

Bigge, J. L. 1976. *Teaching individuals with physical and multiple disabilities.* Columbus, Ohio: Merrill.

Birch, J. W. 1975. *Hearing impaired children in the mainstream.* Minneapolis: Leadership Training Institute/Special Education, University of Minnesota.

Bower, E. M. 1969a. A process for identifying disturbed children. In Henry Dupout, ed., *Educating emotionally disturbed children.* New York: Holt, Rinehart and Winston.

Bower, E. M. 1969b. *Early identification of emotionally handicapped children in schools.* Springfield, Ill.: Thomas.

Brutten, G. J., and Shoemaker, D. J. 1967. *The modification of stuttering.* Englewood Cliffs, N.J.: Prentice-Hall.

Butterfield, E. C., Wambold, C., and Belmont, J. M. 1973. On the theory and practice of improving short-term memory. *American Journal of Mental Deficiency* 77:654–669.

Clarizio, H. F., and McCoy, G. F. 1976. *Behavior disorders in children.* New York: Crowell.

Dunn, L. M., ed. 1973. *Exceptional children in the schools.* New York: Holt, Rinehart and Winston.

Ellis, N. R. 1970. Memory processes in retardates and normals. In N. R. Ellis, ed., *International review of research in mental retardation,* vol. 4. New York: Academic Press.

Gearheart, B. R., and Weishahn, M. W. 1976. *The handicapped child in the regular class.* St. Louis, Mo.: Mosby.

Grossman, H. J., ed. 1973. *Manual on terminology and classification in mental retardation.* American Association on Mental Deficiency Special Publication, Series no. 2.

Hayes, S. P. 1941. *Contributions to a psychology of blindness.* New York: American Foundation for the Blind.

Hewett, F. M., and Forness, S. R. 1974. *Education of exceptional learners.* Boston: Allyn and Bacon.

Hobbs, N. 1975. *The futures of children.* San Francisco, Calif.: Jossey-Bass.

Hull, F. M., and Hull, M. E. 1973. Children with oral communication disabilities. In Lloyd M. Dunn, ed., *Exceptional children in the schools.* New York: Holt, Rinehart and Winston.

Keogh, B. 1971. Hyperactivity and learning disorders: Review and speculation. *Exceptional Children* 38:101–110.

Kirk, S. A. 1972. *Educating exceptional children.* Boston: Houghton Mifflin.

L'Abate, L., and Curtis, L. T. 1975. *Teaching the exceptional child.* Philadelphia: Saunders.

Lubker, B. B. 1972. An introduction to the study of exceptional children. University of North Carolina Television in conjunction with Division of Special Education and Extension Division.

McConnell, F. 1973. Children with hearing disabilities. In L. M. Dunn, ed., *Exceptional children in the schools.* New York: Holt, Rinehart and Winston.

Morse, W. C., Cutler, R., and Fink, A. 1964. *Public school classes for the emotionally handicapped: A research analysis.* Arlington, Va.: Council for Exceptional Children.

Myers, P. I., and Hammill, D. D. 1976. *Methods for learning disorders.* New York: Wiley.

National Advisory Committee on Handicapped Children. 1968. First Annual Report, Special Education for Handicapped Children. Washington, D.C.: U.S.O.E., Department of Health, Education, and Welfare.

Nix, G. W. 1976. *Mainstream education for hearing impaired children and youth.* New York: Grune and Stratton.

Smith, R. M., and Neisworth, J. T. 1975. *The exceptional child.* New York: McGraw-Hill.

Sullivan, T., and Gill, D. 1975. *If you could see what I hear.* New York: Harper and Row.

Telford, C. W., and Sawrey, J. M. 1972. *The exceptional individual,* 2nd ed. Englewood Cliffs, N.J.: Prentice-Hall.

Turnbull, A. P. 1974. Teaching retarded persons to rehearse through cumulative overt labeling. *American Journal of Mental Deficiency* 79:331–337.

Van Riper, C. 1963. *Speech correction: Principles and methods,* 5th ed. Englewood Cliffs, N.J.: Prentice-Hall.

Chapter Two

Principles of Mainstreaming

Photograph by Richard Clontz

At a recent statewide conference, experts were flown in from around the country to discuss the educational significance of mainstreaming with practicing school administrators, teachers, and support personnel. These experts gave dozens of definitions of mainstreaming which were loaded with multisyllabic words, reported an array of figures concerning current trends, and postulated on the philosophical and ethical implications of this educational movement. Many of the participants became perplexed with the overwhelming amount of information being disseminated and questioned the real meaning of the jargon with respect to the pupil responsibilities they would resume on Monday morning. One superintendent of a school system was overheard asking someone why all the presenters were making such a "big deal" over mainstreaming. He went on to say that mainstreaming is certainly nothing new; in his school system handicapped students had been educated with nonhandicapped students for the last twenty-five years. He commented that he did not see any need to call that kind of arrangement "mainstreaming." Rather, he called it "helping kids." Perhaps this superintendent interpreted with far greater insight and precision the educational significance of mainstreaming than did any of the experts at the conference.

Purposes of Mainstreaming

Mainstreaming is the educational arrangement of placing handicapped students in regular classes with their nonhandicapped peers to the maximum extent appropriate. In the words of the superintendent, the underlying purpose of mainstreaming is "helping kids." Both in the literature and in practice, mainstreaming is open to countless, ambiguous interpretations. For this reason, the very word *mainstreaming* is a red flag to many persons, indicating classroom chaos and futility. It is important for educators to consider carefully what mainstreaming is and what it is not. In order to allay "red flags" immediately, let us first consider what mainstreaming is not.

What Mainstreaming Is Not

Mainstreaming is not the wholesale elimination of special education self-contained classes. It does not mean that all handicapped students will be placed in regular classes. Further, it does not automatically imply that those handicapped students who are placed in regular classes will be in that setting for the entire school day.

Total mainstreaming is not an arrangement that can be accomplished overnight in a school system. Instant change often leads to threatening and unstable classroom environments.

Mainstreaming is not just the physical presence of a handicapped student in the regular class.

Mainstreaming does not mean that the placement of handicapped students in regular classes creates jeopardy for the academic progress of nonhandicapped students.

Mainstreaming does not mean that the total responsibility for the education of handicapped students placed in regular classes will fall to the regular class teacher.

Mainstreaming does not mean putting educators "out on a limb" and expecting them to accomplish tasks for which they are not prepared.

What Mainstreaming Is

Mainstreaming is the creation of new and different educational alternatives for handicapped students rather than the elimination of alternatives. Deno (1970) has proposed a cascade of educational services to illustrate the continuum of programming from special to regular education. This cascade, illustrated in figure 2-1, emphasizes individuality by including various options for the student, depending upon particular needs. The tapered design is indicative of the differences in the numbers of students requiring the various levels of service. The largest number of handicapped students can be accommodated in the regular class with or without supplementary services, whereas the fewest number of handicapped students would require hospital/homebound instruction. It is important to note that the cascade model does not do away with special classes or special schools. These settings may be the most educationally appropriate for some students. Consider the moderately to severely cognitively impaired student who at the age of eight has less than twenty-five words in his oral vocabulary, has an attention span of thirty to forty-five seconds, and is not toilet trained. Placing this student in a regular first- or second-grade class would further handicap him by making it almost impossible for him, his teacher, and peers to turn the classroom into a constructive facilitating situation.

When handicapped students are placed in regular classes, they often need various types of support services. They might be in a regular class for a portion of the school day and a resource room or special class for the remainder of the day. A resource room is an educational setting that provides assessment services and remedial instruction to handicapped students on a regularly scheduled basis for a portion of the school day (Wiederholt 1974). The special education teacher who assumes responsibility for instruction in the resource room is referred to as the resource teacher. The special education self-contained class in most schools provides a more permanent educational arrangement. Rather than moving back and forth for specified periods between the regular and special class, students in the special class usually receive the majority of their instruction in that setting. In many school systems, mainstreaming has resulted in the transition of many former special classes to resource room programs. Rather than eliminating special education, the resource arrangement has the distinct advantage of being more accessible to regular teachers and their classrooms. Many educators erroneously believe that the state and federal

Figure 2–1
Cascade Model of Special Education Service

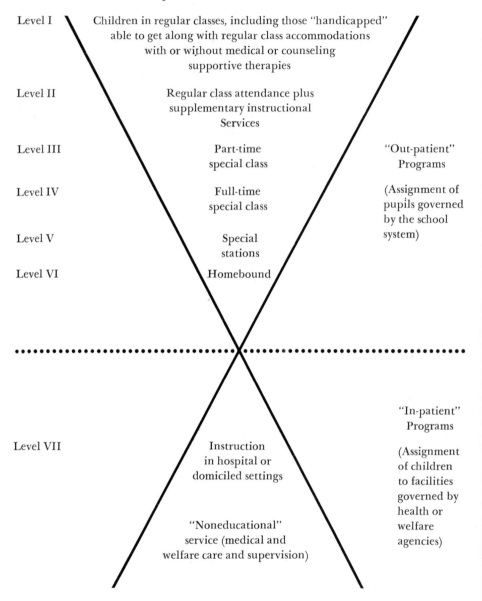

Level I — Children in regular classes, including those "handicapped" able to get along with regular class accommodations with or without medical or counseling supportive therapies

Level II — Regular class attendance plus supplementary instructional Services

Level III — Part-time special class — "Out-patient" Programs

Level IV — Full-time special class — (Assignment of pupils governed by the school system)

Level V — Special stations

Level VI — Homebound

"In-patient" Programs

Level VII — Instruction in hospital or domiciled settings — (Assignment of children to facilities governed by health or welfare agencies)

"Noneducational" service (medical and welfare care and supervision)

From Evelyn Deno, Special education as developmental capital, *Exceptional Children* 37:229–237, 1970. Reprinted by permission.

law pertaining to handicapped students requires that *all* handicapped students be placed in regular classes. Rather than a legal requirement, there is a legal preference for mainstreaming when it is appropriate to the needs of a handicapped student. The legal interpretation of mainstreaming will be highlighted later in the chapter.

To be successful, mainstreaming must be an ordered, systematic, and step-by-step process of moving older handicapped students, formerly segregated in special classes, and younger handicapped students, initially entering kindergarten and first grade, into regular programs. In many school systems mainstreaming has been expected to be accomplished overnight. A desire for rapid accomplishment and instant action in mainstreaming has resulted in some very unfortunate situations when handicapped students have been blindly included in regular programs. One such example involved Bill, a seventh-grader. After spending the first six years of his school career in a special class, Bill was immediately "mainstreamed" into a regular seventh-grade class. His teacher felt insecure over her capability to teach him and was not given the inservice training or back-up support to approach the situation with confidence. Bill's peers were unprepared for some of his learning and behavior problems, and they resorted to teasing and excluding him. Although Bill was initially excited about being in a "real class," as he described it, he was quickly squelched by his failure, frustration, and exclusion. He began running around the classroom, screaming out in class, and throwing textbooks, to the point that he had to be removed from the class. This particular school system had approached mainstreaming in a totally pell-mell fashion by dissolving all special classes. Since there was no program that met Bill's need, the administrator suggested suspending him from school. Rather than the regular class placement resulting in a least restrictive placement, Bill was on the verge of being excluded from school, which would have been the most restrictive alternative. Bill ended up as the catalyst for major change in this school system. The educators backed up and started creating the range of alternatives previously discussed, developed comprehensive inservice training programs for teachers, and began to plan systematically for individual students.

Bill reentered the regular class for one hour per day as a student in a new resource program. As he was able to attain success for the one-hour period, his time in the regular class gradually increased until he was able to spend the majority of time in the regular class. His teacher became more effective in planning instruction for him as he received training and help from the resource teacher. This one situation highlighted the requirement of step-by-step, careful planning to the educators working with Bill.

Many systems have been involved in similar incidences. Educators should take heed and realize the importance of mainstreaming the "system" before mainstreaming students. The effective implementation of mainstreaming involves accomplishing many tasks prior to the actual placement of handicapped students in regular classes, such as a needs assessment, development of a systematic plan, inservice training, acquisition of resources, coordination of services and support personnel, and the development of evaluation procedures (Paul, Turnbull, and Cruikshank 1977). Teachers should be consulted continuously in this total process and be actively involved in decision making. Insuring success at each step and avoiding the inevitable backlash that comes from abrupt change are guidelines that are essential to constructive mainstreaming practices.

Mainstreaming is the social and instructional integration of handicapped students in regular classes. It is not just their physical presence. Social integration involves peer relationships, an opportunity to gain status and acceptance, and feeling comfortable and secure as a full member of the classroom group with the corresponding rights and responsibilities of membership. At the basis of social integration is a respect for the strengths and weaknesses of all students. This concept will be developed in much greater detail in chapter 10. Instructional integration refers to the handicapped student being involved in the curriculum of the classroom. It means that appropriate instructional strategies are used to teach the student through individual, small group, and large group activities. Some people might interpret instructional integration as the handicapped student working on the same skills and concepts as all other students, but this is not the case. All students need some personalized instruction. The essential criterion of instructional integration is whether the handicapped student is making educational progress commensurate with his abilities.

The best environment for mainstreaming is a classroom that is appropriate to the needs of the handicapped student. If the classroom is appropriate and the teacher is knowledgeable in a variety of techniques to individualize instruction, there is no basis for concern that the presence of a handicapped student will interfere with the progress of nonhandicapped students. If teachers feel that there is interference, they should examine the specific mainstreaming problems and devise a plan to eliminate them. Concerns often center around the amount of individual time required, behavior problems, or lack of appropriate instructional materials. These concerns typically are related to the teacher's information and skill requirements, rather than serving as a basis for excluding the handicapped student because of interference with other students. This book will include many strategies for handling these problems. Teachers may want to follow up on some of the suggested readings or to ask for help from resource people within their communities and school system. Before a handicapped student is allowed to become the culprit for the lack of progress of nonhandicapped peers, the teacher has a responsibility to try a variety of techniques and approaches. The creative and persistent teacher is usually successful in eliminating the possibility of peer interference. When a variety of approaches has been tried and the handicapped student still is unable to be socially and instructionally integrated into a classroom without disrupting the atmosphere and requiring an inordinate amount of time, the appropriateness of the placement should be carefully examined by the school faculty.

Nonhandicapped students stand to learn a great deal from handicapped classmates. Children never learn to respect differences until they are exposed to them and have an opportunity to gain information. A third-grade teacher of a visually impaired child developed an excellent unit on the sense of vision to prepare the nonhandicapped students for feeling comfortable around and being helpful to the visually impaired child. The students had a variety of experiences including being blindfolded for portions of the day as lessons were presented, studying the various parts of the eye, learning about braille, listening to lessons on tape and learning to make tapes for blind students, visiting a special school for blind students, and studying the contributions of famous blind adults. The teacher reported on the students' overwhelming interest, attributable primarily to their classmate and friend who made it a realistic concern. In many different ways, the interrelationships of handicapped and nonhandicapped students in mainstreaming programs can be of a two-way nature—reciprocal teaching and learning.

Mainstreaming requires shared responsibility among all educators in a school. For example, Larry, a hearing-impaired student in the second grade, typically spends 75 to 80 percent of the school day in the regular class, with his teacher assuming primary responsibility. In addition, he works with the resource teacher on basic academics thirty minutes per day and with the speech therapist on language development for forty-five minutes three days a week. The music teacher at his elementary school has responsibility for the class for thirty minutes every Friday. Occasionally a volunteer from the PTA helps out in the classroom and is particularly interested in spending time with Larry. Larry's parents are eager to be involved in his educational program and to follow up on his language development at home. Involvement with Larry is definitely a shared responsibility: the regular teacher, resource teacher, speech therapist, music teacher, PTA volunteer, and his parents all have a direct role to play and responsibilities to assume to insure the success of his mainstreaming. A word of caution: uncoordinated shared responsibility is self-defeating. If all these persons have different goals with no knowledge of what others are doing, progress will be minimal and Larry will be very confused trying to make sense out of all that is happening to him. Chapter 4 offers particular suggestions on ways to coordinate the instructional programs of students. Perhaps having all these different resource persons available to work with a student is possible in some systems and totally unrealistic in others. Later in this chapter we will return to the concept of shared responsibility and suggest a host of resource persons, agencies, and organizations that might have either direct or indirect roles to play in the implementation of mainstreaming.

Mainstreaming does require skills and knowledge different from those many teachers have previously acquired in either preservice or inservice training. Many special education teachers primarily emphasize one type of handicapping condition in their training program. They might be extremely competent in the area of learning disabilities and totally at a loss in assessing and planning an instructional program for a blind student. Additionally, many special education teachers work with approximately fifteen students in a self-contained class (sometimes with the help of a teacher aide) or possibly twenty to thirty students throughout the school week in a resource program. This type of student-teacher ratio is an advantage in individualizing instruction. Many special education teachers have not had the opportunity to face the complex task, for example, of many junior high teachers who teach 120 to 150 students per day for five or six periods of roughly fifty minutes per period. In a given period of a seventh-grade science class, a teacher may have twenty-five students, including two students totally unable to read the textbook, one student with visual problems, and one student with aggressive behavior. Special education teachers are called upon to develop new skills to help the regular teacher plan instruction effectively under these circumstances. Just as special education teachers recognize the need to expand their skills, regular teachers find themselves in a similar situation. In pinpointing the particular concerns of regular teachers in inservice training sessions, we have consistently found that regular teachers generally ask for more information on assessing a student's level of achievement, strategies for individualizing instruction, appropriate instructional materials for various student characteristics, and ways to manage behavior problems. College and universities are challenged to prepare *all* education majors for successful mainstreaming practices. A corollary to the college and university responsibility is the need for school systems to develop inservice training programs for all school personnel. It is not just the teachers who need this information; it is also the principal, school psychologist, counselor, special therapists, school-based consultants, and central administrators. All educators are in this together and have a responsibility in preparing themselves to be competent. Mainstreaming is a fact and a reality in the great majority of schools across the country. Our tasks are to become knowledgeable about the principle of mainstreaming and skillful in its implementation.

Background of Mainstreaming

Reynolds (1973) discusses the history of the education of handicapped students that has preceded their placement in regular classes as characterized by "progressive inclusion," which is illustrated by the following rough historical breakdown modified from his study.

General Time Frame	*Predominant Education Service*
1. Ancient times	No education. Handicapped individuals were generally neglected and abused.
2. 1850–1900	Development of residential schools for the purpose of providing education and training.
3. 1900–1950	Special schools and special classes became more prevalent; residential schools continued to grow and expand.
4. 1950–1970	Special classes became the preferred type of educational service for students with mild cognitive impairments. Residential institutions and special schools flourished for blind, deaf, and physically handicapped students.
5. 1970–	Movement toward placement in regular classes of handicapped students who are able to be socially and instructionally integrated (mainstreaming). Development of special classes for some handicapped students formerly placed in residential institutions and special schools.

A clear trend of movement from more to less restrictive settings is evidenced on the chart. The general reasons for the total trend of progressive inclusion is that the most conducive and humanizing educational environment has typically been found to be in community and school environments. Again, handicapped students have more in common with nonhandicapped students than uncommon. These students can benefit significantly from being a part of the schools neighborhood peers attend rather than apart from these schools. The Supreme Court decision in Brown v. Board of Education (1954) can be applied to separate schooling for the handicapped population as well as to different racial groups. The finding was "separate is inherently unequal." Broadly speaking, this philosophical and sociological perspective has largely accounted for the progressive inclusion of handicapped students. In considering the more specific trend of mainstreaming in the seventies, there were some very specific reasons for questioning the value of special class placement for the majority of handicapped students. These reasons are briefly outlined below.

Efficacy of Special Classes

A significant amount of research has been directed toward assessing the academic progress and/or social adjustment of handicapped students placed in special classes as opposed to handicapped students who remained in regular classes (Goldstein, Moss, and Jordan 1965; Smith and Kennedy 1967; Bradfield 1973; Vacc 1972; Cegelka and Tyler 1970). Although there have been methodological problems with some of the research projects, findings offer negligible support to the placement of mildly handicapped students in full-time, self-contained, special classes. The data generally indicate stronger academic gains for handicapped students in regular classes than in special classes. As for social adjustment, studies are divided in terms of support for more positive adjustment in the regular, as opposed to the special, class. It is on the basis of the heightened academic gains that educators began to question the efficacy of special classes. One of the first cautions came from Johnson (1962) during the period when the development of special classes was flourishing. He commented:

It is indeed paradoxical that mentally handicapped children having teachers especially trained, having more money (per capita) spent on their education, and being designed to provide for their unique needs, should be accomplishing the objectives of their education at the same or at a lower level than similar mentally handicapped children who have not had these advantages and have been forced to remain in the regular grades (p. 66).

Labeling

Labeling basically refers to assigning the name of a categorical condition to a student and then referring to the student on the basis of the categorical condition. An example is a teacher who refers to the student in her class who stutters as a stutterer. The so-called stutterer might be a child who talks fluently 60 to 70 percent of the time, has achievement in some subjects above grade level, and has distinct talents in artistic areas. Nonetheless, the way the student is perceived and identified is as the stutterer. In some cases, the label becomes the child and immediately creates a stigma under which the child must perform in school. The greatest furor over labeling has been with students described in the first chapter as having cognitive disadvantages. These students traditionally have been classified as mentally retarded. Some states classify students with mild mental retardation as educable mentally retarded or EMR. Many educators have, in the past, referred to particular students in the school as the EMRs or the retardates. One teacher was overheard threatening her fifth-grade class with the statement, "If you cannot make a passing grade on this easy math assignment, you belong with the EMRs in the special class." These labels can have disastrous academic and social implications. The President's Committee on Mental Retardation (1970) discussed the result of many of the labeling practices as the creation of the "six-hour retarded child." These children are labeled as retarded in school based on having low IQ scores; however, they are capable of functioning normally in their neighborhoods and community when out of school. The unfortunate result of labeling is that the six-hour label can be sufficient to cloud the teacher's perception of the student's strengths, cause a student to have a lowered self-concept, make friendships more difficult to establish, and interfere with the student's postschool adjustment (Jones 1972). Partly as a result of the questionable past research findings on labeling (Macmillan, Jones, and Aloia 1974), a major national project on classification of exceptional children was undertaken to review current issues on classification and labeling, assess their implications, and make policy recommendations to improve professional practices (Hobbs 1975). A portion of the recommendations of this project call for classification made on the basis of educationally relevant behavior including specification of the student's strengths as well as weaknesses. The implications of this recommendation are very significant. Rather than simply classifying a student as mentally retarded or learning disabled, describing educationally relevant behavior means documenting level of performance, learning styles, types of appropriate reinforcement, and other such factors. This classification should lead directly into instructional intervention. The project also resulted in a recommendation that educational services for handicapped students be provided in settings determined to be as "normal" as possible.

Racial Imbalance

One of the first major criticisms of special classes regarding racial imbalance was made by Dunn (1968) who pointed out that 60 to 80 percent of the students in special classes are from "low status backgrounds" including Mexican American, Puerto Rican American, black, and poverty homes. Racial imbalance has largely been attributed to the use of standardized intelligence tests which have resulted in a disproportionately large number of students from minority backgrounds being labeled as intellectually subnormal and a strikingly small number of these students considered to be gifted (Mercer 1973). Since most intelligence tests generally reflect the culture and language patterns of Anglo-Americans and are mostly standardized on this population, persons from other backgrounds are automatically put at a disadvantage for performing successfully on this test. Low socioeconomic status students are put at a similar disadvantage to minority students on these tests. Racial desegregation contributed to focusing attention on special classes predominantly composed of students from minority backgrounds. In carrying out the decision of the Supreme Court in Brown v. Board of Education (1954), the Office of Civil Rights in HEW has required some school systems to eliminate special classes which were interpreted to be a vehicle for de facto segregation.

Parental and Court Action

On the basis of a combination of the foregoing reasons questioning the value and effects of special class placements, many parents of handicapped students began to seek help through the judicial system for what they considered to be educational inequities. They were joined by groups of parents whose handicapped children had been completely denied any type of free public appropriate education. These parents had essentially been told that the schools offered no programs for their children. Parent groups were, therefore, the first to bring legal suits against schools for failing to provide appropriate educational services for handicapped students. These suits, which have been heard in many states throughout the country, have resulted in rulings that all handicapped children have a right to an education (Mills v. Board of Education 1972; Pennsylvania Association for Retarded Children v. Commonwealth of Pennsylvania 1972), that students may not be inappropriately evaluated with tests reflecting culture bias and subsequently placed in special classes based on the results (Hobson v. Hansen 1967; Diana v. State Board of Education 1972), and that tracking is discriminatory (Hobson v. Hansen 1967). This type of wide-scale litigation resulted in almost every state adopting special legislation regarding the education of handicapped students. Readers are encouraged to get a copy of their state legislation on the education of the handicapped from their State Department of Public Instruction, the attorney general's office, or the legislative library. A further result of parental and court action was the passage of federal legislation in November 1975, referred to as Public Law 94–142, the Education for All Handicapped Children Act. This legislation sets forth regulations and requires actions by teachers and school systems. These actions can be interpreted as legislative remedies to some of the past failures of schools in providing appropriate education to handicapped students. P.L. 94–142 has a striking correspondence to the legislation of most states regarding the education of the handicapped in terms of legal and educational principles. This law became enforceable in October 1977, requiring program and fiscal accountability. A summary of the major principles and requirements is included below to acquaint readers with the law (*Federal Register* 1977).

Federal Legislation Requirements

Free Appropriate Public Education

Free appropriate public education must be available to all handicapped students between the ages of three and eighteen no later than September 1, 1978, and for handicapped students between the ages of three and twenty-one no later than September 1, 1980. There is an exception for providing services to the preschool, handicapped age group (ages three to five) or to high school students (ages eighteen to twenty-one) if this is inconsistent with state law or practice regarding public education to these age groups. The educational implication of this legal requirement is that school systems may no longer refuse to admit handicapped students into educational programs.

Protection in Evaluation Procedures

Procedures must be established and practiced in each school system to assure that testing procedures used for the purpose of evaluation and educational placement of handicapped students are selected and administered to assure racial and cultural fairness. Further, evaluation must be conducted prior to placing or denying placement of a handicapped student in a special education program or transferring or denying transfer to a student in a special education class to a regular class setting. Evaluation requirements include: testing the child in his native language or mode of communication; using tests that are appropriately validated; having licensed personnel to administer the test; testing specific areas of educational need rather than focusing only on general intelligence; insuring that sensory and/or physical handicaps of students do not jeopardize their capability to demonstrate their aptitude and achievement level on the test; making the decision for educational placement on the basis of giving a minimum of two tests or types of tests; considering information concerning physical development, sociocultural background, and adaptive behavior in conjunction with test scores; setting up a *team* of persons in the school who possess knowledge about the child, the placement alternatives, and available resource personnel to interpret evaluation data in order to provide an appropriate education; and placing the student in a regular class if, according to the evaluation results, he does not require a special setting for his education.

In most school systems, responsibility for developing procedures adhering to these legislative requirements regarding evaluation is assigned to one of the central administrators in charge of special education, special services, school psychology, or another related area. Classroom teachers are encouraged to ask for a copy of the system's written policies in this area, if this information is not routinely provided. In situations when classroom teachers refer students for evaluation, the teacher automatically is placed in a responsible position for seeing to it that these legal requirements are followed.

Individualized Education Programs

Each school system must establish a procedure for developing and implementing an individualized education program for each handicapped student in accordance with the specification of P.L. 94–142. Because the requirements for individualized education programs have such tremendous implications for all teachers, chapter 3 is devoted to outlining the requirements and suggesting strategies to implement them.

Least Restrictive Environment

The law requires that state and local education agencies set up policies to assure that handicapped students are educated to the maximum extent appropriate in programs with nonhandicapped students and that they be placed in special classes or special schools only when the handicap is so severe that education cannot be satisfactorily accomplished in the regular education program with the use of supplementary aids and services. School systems are required to include a continuum of educational alternatives, as depicted in figure 2–1 earlier in this chapter. In regard to implementing the least restrictive requirement, schools should review the placement of handicapped students on at least an annual basis. The placement decision should be based on the student's individual education plan; and unless the plan requires some other arrangement, the handicapped child should be educated in the same school that he would attend if he were not handicapped. Although the legal preference is unquestionably in favor of the least restrictive appropriate placement, P.L. 94–142 does provide a safeguard that steps must be taken to insure that the least restrictive placement does not result in a harmful effect on the student or reduce the quality of his educational program.

Procedural Safeguards

Parents of handicapped students are entitled by law to the opportunity to examine all their child's educational records for identification, evaluation, and placement information. They also have the right to obtain an independent evaluation of their child by a professional examiner outside of the school system and to have this evaluation considered when decisions are made by the school about educational placement.

Procedural safeguards also apply to providing prior notice to parents of handicapped students whenever a change is proposed or refused regarding the identification, evaluation, or placement of the handicapped child. Additionally, prior parental consent is necessary when a student is initially evaluated for special education placement with psychological or educational tests which are over and above those routinely given to non-handicapped students. The parental notice should meet the following specifications: a complete explanation of all procedural safeguards afforded to parents; a description of the proposed or refused action with respect to placement or obtaining special services for the student, the rationale for the action, and a description of other options considered with a justification of why the options were not chosen; a description of the evaluation procedures, reports, and records upon which the proposed action is based; a statement documenting the right to challenge the proposed action; and the language of the notice must be understandable to the parent.

Again, one of the central administrators of the school system will most likely be charged with the responsibility of preparing the format of letters to be sent to parents. A manual entitled *Functions of the Placement Committee in Special Education* published by the National Association of State Directors of Special Education (1976) provides excellent examples of letters that could serve as a model for implementing these procedural safeguards.

Parents must be afforded the opportunity to present complaints to the school system with reference to any issue related to identification, evaluation, or educational placement. When the school does receive a parental complaint, the parents have a legal right to an impartial due process hearing, which must be conducted by the local educational agency according to state policies and regulations. Parents shall have the opportunity to be represented by counsel or by persons having expertise in the area of handicapping conditions, present evidence and cross-examine the school witnesses, and have a written record of the hearing. Either the parents or the school system may appeal the hearing decision from the local education agency to the state education agency and, in turn from that point, to the appropriate state or federal court. While the proceedings of the hearing are pending, the handicapped student should remain in his current educational placement.

The law has tremendous implications for all teachers. It can basically be viewed in two ways: as a mandate to be bucked or as a catalyst to improve the quality of education. It is hoped that teachers will take the latter view. Knowledge of its requirements can help teachers provide appropriate educational services and insure their own professional behavior in teaching handicapped students. Readers who would like more detailed information on legislative issues are referred to the texts, *Free Appropriate Public Education: Law and Implementation* (Turnbull and Turnbull 1978) and *Public Policy and the Education of Exceptional Children* (Weintraub et al. 1976).

Shared Responsibility

The implementation of mainstreaming is a complex educational task which requires a team approach. Many school systems have expected classroom teachers magically to have all the skills and time to accomplish the successful mainstreaming of students representing the full range of educational handicaps—in most cases an impossible expectation for teachers. A sound approach to mainstreaming requires shared responsibility on the part of all educators in the school.

Regular Teachers

Classroom teachers of the regular grades will undoubtedly be called upon to assume major responsibility in the mainstreaming process. As they teach handicapped students for a portion of the school day or in some cases for the entire day, they will coordinate the student's instructional and social integration which is the essence of mainstreaming. Often it is the classroom teacher who is the focal point for marshaling the resources to implement the individual education plan effectively. Since such a large portion of mainstreaming requirements occurs in the regular classroom, it is very important for these teachers to know from whom help can be expected. The following sections briefly outline responsibilities that might generally be expected to be shared with other mainstreaming team members. These suggestions are offered as a general guide and must be adapted to the particular staffing pattern of each school.

Special Educators

Resource Teachers. Many handicapped students in regular classes receive individual or small group instruction from a special education resource teacher. Handicapped students may leave the regular class to receive instruction in the resource room for a specified period of time each day or each week, or the resource teacher may come into the regular class and instruct the handicapped student in his everyday setting. To insure maximum educational progress, resource and regular teachers need to coordinate their programs carefully and maintain close communication relative to the student's performance. The individual education plan is the curriculum and instructional guide; however, as the plan is implemented, information between or among teachers needs to be shared. Regular teachers can expect the resource teacher to give them suggestions on instructional techniques and curriculum adaptations that are appropriate for the student when he is in the regular class. Some resource teachers are assigned to work with students having only one type of educational handicap, such as learning disabilities. Many school systems are moving toward the plan of having "noncategorical" resource teachers—teachers who are not restricted to working with only a particular diagnostic group of students. The function of a resource teacher is to do just what the job title implies: to serve as a resource to the handicapped students and classroom teacher. Regular teachers are encouraged to take advantage of this assistance. Asking for help is no sign of weakness; rather, it is indicative of concern and conscientiousness.

Itinerant Teachers. Itinerant teachers usually function in a manner similar to resource teachers. They are considered to be itinerant as they travel from one school to another and usually work with individual students on a regularly scheduled basis. This model is usually followed in sparsely populated areas or in schools that have too few handicapped students to justify a full-time resource teacher.

Self-contained Class Teachers.   Special classes are one alternative in the full continuum of educational services for handicapped students. These classes typically serve students with substantial handicaps who may not be appropriately served in regular classes. The teacher of this class has the job responsibility of working with handicapped students in the self-contained class setting and also integrating these students into school activities and curriculum blocks as appropriate. Although self-contained class teachers usually do not have the consultative duties of the resource or itinerant teacher, they do readily share instructional suggestions and materials with regular teachers in many situations.

Special Education Consultants.   Larger school systems often employ a special education consultant whose job might be to provide inservice training to classroom teachers and to offer backup support to classroom, as well as resource, teachers. The consultant usually has advanced training and is knowledgeable about a variety of instructional strategies. Systems which do not directly employ a consultant are likely to have consultative services available from the Division of Exceptional Children in the State Department of Public Instruction (the agency titles vary from state to state) or from a regional educational service agency. It is disconcerting that often teachers believe no help is available when it really is. At the beginning of the school year, teachers are advised to check with their principal and central administrators in finding out how to obtain the services of the special education consultant.

Director of Special Education.   Most school systems have either a part-time or full-time director or coordinator of special education. This person is responsible for knowing about legal requirements and for administering, and often supervising, special education services. Classroom teachers who have specific questions about obtaining needed services, resources, or evaluation of a handicapped student should consider working through their principal to contact the director of special education.

Principals

Principals have been identified as one of the keys to mainstreaming success (Payne and Murray 1974). Teachers should consider them as partners in carrying out mainstreaming responsibilities. They might be called on to arrange inservice training, consider hiring additional personnel, instigate a volunteer program to help with individualization, locate appropriate instructional resources, and/or work toward the reduction of the student-teacher ratio. Teachers should share their concerns about mainstreaming constructively with principals in order for principals to respond most effectively to teachers' needs.

Counselors

Counselors have various roles to play in the implementation of mainstreaming. They often serve as chairperson of the evaluation team which is responsible for pinpointing educational problems and devising the individual education plan. They might help teachers with problems of social adjustment or coordinate parent involvement. Specific responsibilities vary from school to school, but the important thing for teachers to remember is that counselors share in the responsibility for mainstreaming.

School Psychologists

Many schools employ a part-time or full-time psychologist. Frequently psychologists are similar to itinerant teachers in that they are responsible for serving more than one school. Psychologists typically assume major responsibility in evaluation and placement decisions, in addition to participating in the development of the individual education plan. Other mainstreaming involvement could be in working with teachers on behavior management and on ways to individualize instruction effectively.

Librarians

Librarians can be of great assistance in curriculum adaptation, particularly in helping to identify textbooks and a large variety of supplementary materials appropriate to the student's achievement level and interests. Many handicapped students who read significantly below grade level need books of a high interest/low vocabulary nature. Librarians are uniquely qualified to identify such materials and to make them available to students and teachers. They can also be called upon to assist the teacher in gathering resource materials for units of instruction and concept development for students requiring more repetition and practice than the majority of the class to acquire mastery.

Therapists

Mainstreaming requires the expertise of many specialists, such as those in speech, physical development, occupational development, dramatics, art, and music. All schools do not employ therapists in these areas on a full-time basis; however, their services may often be available through mental health clinics, hospitals, special schools, colleges and universities, and state department consultants. When the teacher finds that the needs of individual handicapped students require the expertise of a therapist, the teacher, along with other team members, should seek the special help that is needed. Many handicapped students in regular classes have previous histories of working with therapists, particularly those in speech and physical development. Parents can provide this background information to teachers and might assist in arranging the continuation of services, as the need is documented in the individual education plan. Therapists can also train teachers in special techniques which the teacher can provide routinely in the regular class.

Paraprofessionals

Paraprofessionals or teacher aides can contribute significantly to the quality and quantity of individualized instruction. Even if their help is available for only a portion of the school day or week, every bit of "extra-hands" time can be helpful. When working with handicapped students, paraprofessionals should be thoroughly aware of the individual education plan and the total educational program in which the student is included (resource program). Teachers are wise to provide careful guidance to the paraprofessional to capitalize on generalization from one portion of the curriculum to the other.

Students

Students, both handicapped and nonhandicapped, have a significant role to play in successful mainstreaming. Handicapped students should be involved in the development of their individual education plan, when this is appropriate to their age and maturity. They should be encouraged to share their perspectives on their social acceptance in the regular class. Problems can often be pinpointed and eliminated when students bring them to the attention of teachers in early stages before they reach a crisis point. Handicapped students often know how to adapt the curriculum or school environment to their needs most effectively. Sometimes teachers waste time by trying to second-guess, for example, the needs of a blind student. Asking the student directly about when help is needed and when it is not needed can assist teachers in getting on with the task of appropriate instruction. Mainstreaming should be viewed not as an arrangement to be imposed on handicapped students, but rather as a process involving reciprocal information sharing and responsibility.

Nonhandicapped students often are helpful as "peer tutors" providing instruction to their handicapped friends. This arrangement will be explained more fully in chapter 4. Nonhandicapped students also can be helpful in making instructional materials, such as taping the textbook or making charts explaining concepts. The buddy system, which pairs nonhandicapped and handicapped students, to be discussed in chapter 4, has the potential for significant contribution to the successful integration of handicapped persons in regular classes.

Parents

Parents can be tremendous partners to teachers in mainstreaming programs. There are many ways in which parents can enhance the success of handicapped students at school. First, they have a significant responsibility as members of the team developing the individual education plan. As they participate in specifying priority instructional goals, they help shape the curriculum through which their children will progress. Educational decision making and accountability, therefore, becomes a shared responsibility with parents. Other participatory involvement of parents might be in serving in the role of a teacher aide in their child's class or in another class in the school; sharing information on helpful hints regarding possible classroom/environmental adaptions or motivational suggestions; making instructional materials to be used at school; reviewing and reinforcing concepts taught at school in the evenings; and helping to foster their child's social adjustment.

Community Volunteers

Volunteers from the community have made beneficial contributions to mainstreaming in some school systems by serving, in a way similar to that described for parents, in the role of teacher aide. They might work individually or in small groups with handicapped students needing extra help or might be involved in projects or assignments with other class members in order to free teachers to spend more time with students having special problems. Some communities have organized volunteer effort for the purpose of making instructional materials needed by handicapped students or raising money to purchase expensive equipment, such as auditory trainers for hearing-impaired students, wheelchairs, large-print typewriters, or braille readers. Civic groups and service clubs in many communities have a particular interest in the needs of handicapped persons. One of the best examples of this interest on a national basis is the Lions Club, an organization that has made a tremendous contribution to services for the blind. Generally speaking, communities are rich in possibilities for volunteer help. Often the failure to capitalize on volunteer contributions may be traced to the fact that there is no single person in the school system charged with the responsibility of recruiting, training, and matching the needs of teachers/students with the willingness and capability of volunteers to be involved in educational programs. Teachers are encouraged to consider the possibility of seeking help for mainstreaming from interested community citizens.

Professional and Consumer Organizations

Educators involved in mainstreaming should call on the resources of professional and consumer organizations. These organizations are high in number and most have, as one of their major goals, information dissemination. A list of some of these organizations is included in appendix A. Readers with particular interest in a certain type of educational handicap or a focused area of mainstreaming are encouraged to write the organizations which would represent corresponding target groups and concerns. A wealth of information is available from these sources. Additionally, many of these organizations have local and state chapters which increase the possibility of "on-site" contributions to the implementation of mainstreaming, such as providing consultants to conduct inservice training, offering specific instructional suggestions for particular handicapped students, or sharing information on appropriate instructional materials.

Team Approach

Mainstreaming requires shared responsibility involving many team members working cooperatively with classroom teachers to provide quality educational programs to handicapped students. Mainstreaming does not mean that classroom teachers must assume all the responsibility; rather, special educators, principals, counselors, school psychologists, librarians, therapists, paraprofessionals, students, parents, community volunteers, and professional/consumer organizations all have responsibilities and opportunities in planning and implementing mainstreaming for handicapped students. Paul, Turnbull, and Cruikshank (1977) provide a more detailed examination of roles and responsibilities of various team members for readers interested in further information. Emphasis again is directed to the need to coordinate carefully all involvement to maximize the ultimate benefit to students. Since "we are all in this together," coordination, communication, and cooperation are keys to shared responsibility and successful programming.

References and Selected Readings

Bradfield, R. H., Brown, J., Kaplan, P., Rickert, E., and Stannard, R. 1973. The special child in the regular classroom. *Exceptional Children* 35:384–390.

Brown v. Board of Education, 347 U.S. 483 (1954).

Cegelka, W. J., and Tyler, J. L. 1970. The efficacy of special class placement for the mentally retarded in proper perspective. *Training School Bulletin* 67:33–68.

Deno, E. 1970. Special education as developmental capital. *Exceptional Children* 37:229–237.

Diana v. State Board of Education, No. C-70 37 RFP, District Court for Northern California (Feb. 1970).

Dunn, L. M. 1968. Special education for the mildly retarded: Is much of it justifiable? *Exceptional Children* 35:5–22.

Federal Register. 1977. Washington, D.C.: U.S. Government Printing Office.

Functions of the placement committee in special education: A resource manual. 1976. National Association of State Directors of Special Education.

Goldstein, H., Moss, J., and Jordan, L. J. 1965. *The efficacy of special class training on the development of mentally retarded children.* Urbana: University of Illinois.

Hobbs, N. 1975. *The futures of children.* San Francisco, Calif.: Jossey-Bass.

Hobson v. Hansen, 269 F. Supp. 401 (1967).

Johnson, G. O. 1962. Special education for the mentally retarded—A paradox. *Exceptional Children* 29:62–69. Copyright 1962 by The Council for Exceptional Children. Reproduced by permission.

Jones, R. L. 1972. Labels and stigma in special education. *Exceptional Children* 38:553–564.

MacMillan, D. L., Jones, R. L., and Aloia, G. F. 1974. The mentally retarded label: A theoretical analysis and review of research. *American Journal of Mental Deficiency* 79:241–261.

Mercer, J. R. 1973. *Labeling the mentally retarded: Clinical and social system perspectives on mental retardation.* Berkeley: University of California Press.

Mills v. Board of Education of the District of Columbia, No. 1939–71 (D.D.C. 1971).

Paul, J., Turnbull, A. P., and Cruikshank, W. 1977. *Mainstreaming: A practical guide.* Syracuse, N.Y.: Syracuse University Press.

Payne, R., and Murray, C. 1974. Principals' attitudes toward integration of the handicapped. *Exceptional Children* 41:132–135.

Pennsylvania Association for Retarded Children v. Commonwealth of Pennsylvania, 334 F. Supp. 1257 (E.D. Pa. 1971).

President's Committee on Mental Retardation. 1970. *The six-hour retarded child*. Washington, D.C.: U.S. Government Printing Office.

Reynolds, M. C. 1973. Changing Roles of Special Education Personnel. Paper presented to UCEA.

Smith, H. W., and Kennedy, W. A. 1967. Effects of three educational programs on mentally retarded children. *Perceptual and Motor Skills* 24:174.

Turnbull, H. R., and Turnbull, A. P. 1978. *Free appropriate public education: Law and implementation*. Denver, Colo.: Love.

Vacc, N. A. 1972. Long term effects of special class intervention for emotionally disturbed children. *Exceptional Children* 39:15–22.

Weintraub, F. J., Abeson, A., Ballard, J., and Lavor, M. L. 1976. *Public policy and the education of exceptional children*. Reston, Va.: CEC.

Wiederholt, J. L. 1974. Planning resource rooms for the mildly handicapped. *Focus on Exceptional Children*, January.

Chapter Three

*Developing Individualized
Education Programs*

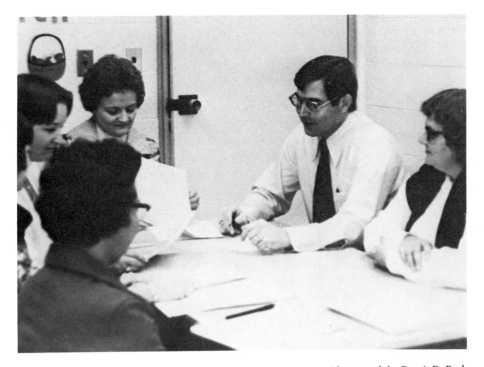

Photograph by Dorris D. Beck

Complete individualization is a goal for educators much as democracy is a goal for Americans or Christianity is a goal for Christians. Everyone in education should strive to reach the goal, knowing that complete individualization is rare, if not impossible. Anytime, however, that the school situation is focusing on the individual student in the teaching-learning process, another step is being made toward the ultimate goal (Musgrave 1975, p. x).

Individualized education has been the goal for educators for a number of years. Programs designed to provide instruction meeting individual needs have been adopted and implemented in many schools. The philosophy of special education has been based on individual needs of handicapped children. This philosophy is reflected in Public Law 94–142, the Education for All Handicapped Children Act, where special education is defined as: "specially designed instruction, at no cost to parents or guardians, to meet the unique needs of a handicapped child, including classroom instruction, instruction in physical education, home instruction, and instruction in hospitals and institutions."

Abeson and Weintraub (1977) interpret this definition to imply that special education proceeds from the basic goals and expected outcomes of general education and that special programming does not occur because a child is handicapped but because he has a unique educational need that requires specially designed instruction. Public Law 94–142 has four overriding purposes:

1. To guarantee the availability of special education programing to handicapped children and youth who require it.
2. To assure fairness and appropriateness in decision making about the provision of special education to handicapped children and youth.
3. To establish clear management and auditing requirements and procedures regarding special education at all levels of government.
4. To financially assist the efforts of state and local government through the use of federal funds (Abeson and Weintraub 1977, p. 4).

This law requires the formation of a placement committee or team which will have the responsibility for making specific decisions concerning each handicapped child and the development, by the committee, of an individual education program.

The Placement Committee

The placement committee functions as an interdisciplinary team to insure that all needed information is available. The National Association of State Directors of Special Education (1976) outline the functions of the committee:

1. Preplanning functions.
   a. specifying committee composition and procedures,
   b. gathering information needed to make decisions.
2. Planning functions
   a. developing an individual educational plan,

      b.   determining eligibility for special education placement.
3.   Implementation functions
      a.   providing for individual program implementation,
      b.   providing for individual program monitoring and evaluation (p. 9).

Composition of the Committee

The law stipulates who will be involved in developing the Individual Education Program: (1) A representative of the local education agency or intermediate educational unit who is qualified to provide or supervise the provision of special education; (2) The teacher or teachers of the child; (3) The parents or guardian; (4) Whenever appropriate, the child.

Inclusion of the teacher in program development insures that considerations related to the learning environment of the class as well as the skills of the teacher are reflected. Teacher involvement also helps to establish a common basis for understanding with the child's parents. It is more effective for the teacher to communicate with the parents than for psychologists or administrators to be the exclusive communicators (Abeson and Weintraub 1977).

Parents have the right to participate in planning and monitoring services provided for their children. Their knowledge of the medical and behavioral history of their children, their experience in dealing with the children, and their observations of the needs and skills of their children are of great value in helping to decide what will comprise a relevant and appropriate educational program. Winslow (1977) suggests information which might help parents organize a working notebook to assist professionals in planning: observations of behavior at home; any medical, educational, or psychological test results as well as questions about these reports; significant differences between test reports and a parent's observations; and any attempts that have been made to change or intervene in a child's handicap.

Parents will be informed by the school as to a proposed date and time of the meeting. If it is impossible for parents to attend, telephone calls can be used to assure their participation. The planning conference can be held without parent participation if school personnel have sufficient documentation that attempts were made through telephone calls, letters, and home visits to secure parent participation and such attempts were rejected.

Parent involvement is a highly desirable part of the process. Using parents as volunteers in the instructional program may be a preamble or an outgrowth of the Placement Committee meeting. Cory (1974) says: "When parents can be transformed from angry and hostile critics into friendly and helpful critics, all involved—kids, teachers, administrators and the parents themselves—benefit" (p. 76).

Parents of handicapped children may, themselves, have problems. They may be on the defensive regarding the inference that their child is "different"; they may have struggled themselves to accept this difference. Such parents may appear disinterested or hostile but may, in time, respond to the idea that their opinion is valued and needed.

On the other hand, some parents may *be* disinterested. If repeated efforts are not acknowledged, the school may be forced to accept the fact that this is part of the child's problem and, if this is the case, the efforts of Social Services or Mental Health may be needed. Parents are important; the results are usually worth the effort.

Mattson (1977) observes that the team approach has been legally broadened to include a significant component, the parents. "Basic to the expediting of parent involvement on the 'team' is the need for professionals to examine their attitudes toward these nonprofessional teammates whose roles in child-rearing are central and whose nonsymbolic involvement is crucial" (p. 358).

The Individualized Education Program

Abeson and Weintraub (1977) specify the concepts implied by the term *individualized education program:*

Individualized means that the program must be addressed to the educational needs of a single child rather than a class or group of children. *Education* means that the program is limited to those elements of the child's education that are specifically special education and related services as defined by the Act. *Program* means that the individualized education program is a statement of what will actually be provided to the child, as distinct from a plan that provides guidelines from which a program must subsequently be developed (p. 5).

The individual education program must include:

1. a statement of the student's present level of educational achievement in areas such as academic achievement, social adaptation, prevocational and vocational skills, psychomotor skills, and selfhelp skills.
2. a statement of annual goals that describes the educational performance to be achieved by the end of the school year under the child's individualized education program.
3. a statement of short-term instructional objectives, which must be

measurable intermediate steps between the present level of educational performance and the annual goals.

4. a statement of specific educational services needed by the child, including a description of all special education and related services that are needed to meet the unique needs of the child, also including the type of physical education program in which the child will participate.

5. the date when those services will be initiated and terminated.

6. a description of the extent to which the child will participate in regular education programs.

7. objective criteria, evaluation procedures, and schedules for determining, on at least an annual basis, whether the short term instructional objectives are being achieved (Torres 1977, pp. 52–53).

In order to prepare or revise individual programs for each handicapped student on an annual basis, a planning conference must be held at the beginning of the school year. For students already receiving special education services, the planning may be done at the end of the school year in preparation for the following school year. The purpose is to develop a comprehensive and coordinated instructional program. There is no intent to hold teachers accountable for teaching all specified objectives if it becomes obvious throughout the school year that the student is not making progress commensurate with expectations at the beginning of the year. The school is responsible for providing the services specified in the plan. However, ongoing adjustments of anticipated progress may be needed.

The individual education program requires teacher involvement and involves significant amounts of teachers' time. However, if done constructively, the individual program can facilitate sound educational planning, student progress, and professional accountability. It can be the vehicle for communication between special education teachers and classroom teachers, between teachers and administrators, and between school personnel and parents.

While forms for consolidating the information required are suggested by the National Association of State Directors of Special Education (see appendix B), local districts may design forms more appropriate for their own use. Suggestions for developing components of the individual education program are discussed in the following sections and a completed individual program is presented in table 3–1.

Level of Educational Performance:
Assessment

While the essential ingredient of individualized instruction is *continuous* assessment or evaluation, there are a number of preliminary steps that pro-

79

vide the framework for making decisions about each child's current level of educational performance. For the handicapped child, a multidisciplinary evaluation team is responsible for administering the necessary and appropriate psychological, social, and educational evaluations according to specific regulations of Public Law 94–142 about the elimination of cultural and racial bias. According to federal requirements, a teacher must be included as a member of the multidisciplinary evaluation team. The types of evaluation required by a particular handicapped child will differ with the needs of the child and will be determined in many cases by the placement committee. Procedures that have proved to be valuable to multidisciplinary evaluation teams in defining levels of functioning are standardized tests, criterion-referenced tests, and observation. Level of performance should be stated on the individualized educational program in terms of the student's precise skill development.

Standardized Tests.   Standardized, or norm-referenced, tests describe how a person performs in comparison with others. Used primarily to measure intelligence and achievement, the scores arrived at are viewed in relation to the child's agemates or some standard norm. The basis for such comparisons is usually established through research and repeated testing of persons at various age or grade levels.

Educators and psychologists have expressed a concern about the discriminatory aspects of standardized *intelligence testing*. As mentioned in chapter 2, one of the most serious issues has been raised by minority segments of the population. Test items, devised by people from the cultural majority, are more representative of that group than others.

Psychologists must exercise caution in evaluating children whose experiences have not been in the social mainstream: children who may be threatened or unmotivated by the test situation and items. Children who have impairments of speech, neurological, sensory, or motor functions require special consideration and interpretation to insure that handicaps irrelevant to intelligence are not allowed to interfere with performance.

Efforts have been made to develop "culture fair" tests of intelligence; the results have been disappointing. However, it has been demonstrated repeatedly that standardized intelligence tests do predict success in school. The question remains: is this the fault of the tests or the fault of society? Robinson and Robinson (1976) resolve the question in the following way:

To expect tests not in any way to favor one cultural group or another is . . . to deny both the complexity and the importance of environmental determination of intellectual development and the unavoidable truth that intelligent

Identification Information

Name: John Doe
School: Beecher Sixth Grade Center
Birthdate: 5-15-65   Grade 6
Parents:
Name: Mr. and Mrs. John Doe
Address: 1300 Johnson Street Raleigh, N.C.
Phone: Home none   Office 932-8161

Testing Information

Test Name	Date Admin.	Interpretation
		spell—1.7, math—5.7, read recog—1, read comp—N.A., gen. info—6.3
PIAT	9-10-77	
test of initial consonants (CRT)	9-11-77	knows eight out of twenty-one initial consonant sounds total 2.0
CRT Reading Checklist 9-12-77		oral comprehension—6th grade reading skills—primary level
Carolina Arith. Inventory (Time)	9-2-77	Level IV
Carolina Arith. Inventory (Number concepts)	9-2-77	Level IV

Health Information

Vision: good
Hearing: excellent
Physical: good
Other:

Yearly Class Schedule

	Time	Subject	Teacher
1st semester	8:30–9:20	math	Franks
	9:30–10:20	language arts	Bambara (Resource)
	10:30–11:20	social studies	Bambara
	11:30–12:20	science	Franks
		lunch	
	1:10–2:00	art	Shaw
	2:10–3:00	P.E.	King
2nd semester	8:30–9:20	math	Franks
	9:30–10:20	language arts	Bambara (Resource)
	10:30–11:20	social studies	Bambara
	11:30–12:20	science	Franks
		lunch	
	1:10–2:00	art	Shaw
	2:10–3:00	P.E.	King

Continuum of Services

	Hours per week
Regular class	20 hours
Resource teacher in regular classroom	
Resource room	6 hours
Reading specialist	4 hours
Speech/language therapist	
Counselor	
Special class	
Transition class	
Others:	

Checklist

9-1-77   Referral by Louise Borden
9-3-77   Parents informed of rights; permission obtained for evaluation
9-15-77 Evaluation compiled
9-16-77 Parents contacted
9-18-77 Total committee meets and subcommittee assigned
9-28-77 IEP developed by subcommittee
9-30-77 IEP approved by subcommittee

Committee Members

Mrs. Louise Borden
Teacher
Mrs. John Thomas (Sp. Ed. Coordinator)
Other LEA representative
Mrs. John Doe,
Parents
Mrs. Mary Franks
Mrs. Joan Bambara
Mrs. Alice King
Date IEP initially approved 9-30-77

Table 3–1
Individual Education Plan (IEP)

Student's Name ___John Doe___ Subject Area ___Reading___

Level of Performance ___primary reading recognition, 6th grade comprehension of oral material.___ Teacher ___Mrs. Bambara—resource teacher___

ANNUAL GOALS: 1) John will successfully complete the primer level of the Bank Street Reading Series.

2) John will recognize and correctly say 90 new sight words.

3) John will master 14 initial consonants.

	SEPTEMBER	OCTOBER	NOVEMBER	DECEMBER	JANUARY
OBJECTIVES	Referred	1. Recognize and correctly state the sounds of the initial consonants *b* and *f* 100% of the time. 2. Recognize and correctly say ten new sight words 100% of the time. 3. Complete the first three stories of the primer, reading the material with 50% accuracy.	1. Recognize and correctly state the sounds of the initial consonants *s* and *m* 100% of the time. 2. Recognize and correctly say ten new sight words 100% of the time. 3. Complete the next three stories in the primer, reading the material with 50% accuracy.	1. Correctly recognize and state the sound of the initial consonant *g* 100% of the time. 2. Recognize and correctly say five new sight words 100% of the time. 3. Complete the next story in the primer, reading the material with 50% accuracy.	1. Review and correctly state the sounds of the initial consonants *b, f, m, s,* and *g* 100% of the time. 2. Recognize and correctly state the sound of the initial consonant *h* 100% of the time. 3. Review and correctly say 25 previously learned sight words 100% of the time. 4. Recognize and correctly say five new sight words 100% of the time. 5. Review the previously read stories in the primer, reading the material with 60% accuracy.

Table 3–1 Continued
Individual Education Plan (IEP)

Table 3–1 Continued
Individual Education Plan (IEP)

	SEPTEMBER	OCTOBER	NOVEMBER	DECEMBER	JANUARY
MATERIALS		Bank Street Basal Reading Series, Hoffman Phonetic Reading Program, teacher-made materials	Bank Street Basal Reading Series, Hoffman Phonetic Reading Program, teacher-made materials	Bank Street Basal Reading Series, Hoffman Phonetic Reading Program, teacher-made materials	Bank Street Basal Reading Series, Hoffman Phonetic Reading Program, teacher-made materials
AGENT		regular teacher resource teacher	regular teacher resource teacher	regular teacher resource teacher	regular teacher resource teacher
EVALU-ATION		1. informal assessment 2. Criterion Referenced Test (CRT)	1. informal assessment 2. CRT	1. informal assessment 2. CRT	1. informal assessment 2. CRT

Turnbull, A. P.; Strickland, Bonnie; and Brantley, John C. *Developing and Implementing Individualized Education Programs*. Columbus: Charles E. Merrill Publishing Co., 1978.

Student's Name John Doe Subject Area Reading

Level of Performance reading recognition (1.2 PIAT), 6th grade comprehension of oral material (CRT). Teacher Mrs. Bambara—resource teacher

ANNUAL GOALS:
1) John will successfully complete the primer level of the Bank Street Basal Reading Series.
2) John will recognize and correctly say 90 new sight words.
3) John will master 14 initial consonants.

	FEBRUARY	MARCH	APRIL	MAY	JUNE
OBJECTIVES	1. Recognize and correctly state the sounds of the initial consonants *l* and *d* 100% of the time. 2. Recognize and correctly say 15 new sight words 100% of the time. 3. Complete the next three stories in the primer, reading the material with 60% accuracy and mastering the skills that accompany the stories.	1. Recognize and correctly state the sounds of the initial consonants *r* and *w* 100% of the time. 2. Recognize and correctly say 15 new sight words 100% of the time. 3. Complete the next three stories in the primer, reading the material with 60% accuracy and mastering the skills that accompany the stories.	1. Recognize and correctly state the sounds of the initial consonants *c* and *t* 100% of the time. 2. Recognize and correctly say 15 new sight words 100% of the time. 3. Complete the next three stories in the primer, reading the material with 95% accuracy and mastering the skills that accompany the stories.	1. Recognize and correctly state the sounds of the initial consonants *n* and *y* 100% of the time. 2. Recognize and correctly say 15 new sight words 100% of the time. 3. Complete the next three stories in the primer, reading the material with 95% accuracy and mastering the skills that accompany the stories.	Evaluation
MATERIALS	Bank Street Basal Reading Series, Hoffman Phonetic Reading Program, teacher-made materials	Bank Street Basal Reading Series, Hoffman Phonetic Reading Program, teacher-made materials	Bank Street Basal Reading Series, Hoffman Phonetic Reading Program, teacher-made materials	Bank Street Basal Reading Series, Hoffman Phonetic Reading Program, teacher-made materials	
AGENT	regular teacher resource teacher	regular teacher resource teacher	regular teacher resource teacher	regular teacher resource teacher	
EVALUATION	1. informal assessment 2. Criterion Referenced Test (CRT)	1. informal assessment 2. CRT	1. informal assessment 2. CRT	1. informal assessment 2. CRT	

Table 3–1 Continued
Individual Education Plan (IEP)

84

behavior will always tend to be defined and evaluated in relation to what the culture and, of course, the test maker, choose to foster and to prize (p. 330).

Psychometric and psychological tests may include the Wechsler Preschool and Primary Scale of Intelligence (Wechsler 1967), the Wechsler Intelligence Scale for Children—revised (Wechsler 1974), and the Stanford-Binet Intelligence Scale (Terman and Merrill 1960). Tests such as the Slosson Intelligence Test (Slosson 1963) and the Columbia Mental Maturity Scale (Burgemeister, Blum, and Lorge 1972) may be given by the teacher as screening tests or to provide additional verification.

Many handicapped children will have been referred for special education evaluation by the classroom teacher on the basis of poor academic achievement as indicated by standardized *achievement test* scores. However, it is usually wise to complete some individual testing both to verify the referral information and to observe specific types of problems as the child approaches the various subject areas. While assessment tools will be discussed in chapters relating to subject areas, the following are general achievement tests which may be useful to the teacher.

The Wide Range Achievement Test (WRAT) (Jastak, Jastak, and Bijou 1965) assesses a child's performance in three areas: reading, spelling, and arithmetic. While the test does not provide much detail in terms of specific skill areas, it is useful as a screening device. The Peabody Individual Achievement Test (PIAT) (Dunn and Markwardt, 1970) includes subtests in math, reading recognition, reading comprehension, spelling, and general information. The resulting profile permits the observer to note the child's strengths and weaknesses and to use the information for individual planning.

Once the area for remediation is determined, in-depth assessment of one content area may be helpful. For example, if the child's profile indicates a weakness in mathematics, the Key Math Diagnostic Arithmetic Test (Connelly, Nachtman, and Pritchett 1971) assesses the areas of content, operations, and applications. Scores, recorded on a profile, describe strengths and weaknesses that may be used for instructional programming (see chapter 7 for a more detailed discussion).

While information from standardized tests has been helpful in screening for placement in special education, it has not been useful in planning and teaching. Some norm-referenced tests, properly administered and interpreted, do provide guidance for instruction. Frequently, however, a single score has been used for decisions on placement in special education, with little information provided about the child's specific strengths and weaknesses.

Criterion-Referenced Tests. Unlike the norm-referenced test, the criterion-referenced test does not measure one child's performance against another's, but determines whether or not the child in question has actually reached specified levels of competence. It attempts to assess very specific skill areas individually rather than yielding a score based on a composite testing of several skills. The more specific an assessment is, the more potential there is for drawing implications for instruction.

Following the sequential arrangement of tasks, a person's performance is viewed in terms of absolute level of performance or the actual number of operations completed. If a child, being tested on counting skills, can count by twos but not by threes, his performance is viewed as follows: the child can count by twos with 100 percent accuracy but cannot count by threes. The teacher asks, "Is this level of proficiency adequate for this child at this time?" The level of proficiency necessary for the child is the criterion. If he needs the skill of counting by threes, instruction is pinpointed. As the child progresses, the criterion will change (Chinn, Drew, and Logan 1975).

Criterion-referenced assessment not only describes a person's level of performance but also indicates how far a pupil must progress to reach some specified level of achievement. The teacher knows where the child is starting and where he is going (Haring and Gentry 1976). In short, criterion-referenced tests formulate specific goals and assess a child's progress toward them.

Criterion assessment requires stating behavioral, or instructional, objectives, which aids greatly in educational planning. Behavioral objectives will be discussed later in this chapter.

Frequently in check-list format, criterion-referenced tests become records of achievement and may be used as progress evaluation devices. They are tools to assist the teacher in establishing specific educational objectives for individual students. Table 3–2 is an example of a criterion-referenced test in reading. Many commercial materials, based on behavioral objectives, have built-in assessment.

Table 3–2

Criterion-Referenced Test

Language Arts—Level B (Those children building sight vocabulary)
_____ 1. Dictates experience stories to build sight vocabulary
_____ 2. Can copy and reproduce words from the dictated stories
_____ 3. Recognizes main idea of selection
_____ 4. Recalls story sequence
_____ 5. Finds details in story

Table 3–2 Continued

_____ 6. Can draw inferences

_____ 7. Understands pronoun references

_____ 8. Predicts events in a story

_____ 9. Recognizes rhyming words

_____ 10. Identifies characters

_____ 11. Reads orally to answer specific questions

_____ 12. Recognizes letters and sounds of these beginning consonants

    _____ (a) *M T B H P N*

    _____ (b) *D W G C J*

    _____ (c) *F L R S*

    _____ (d) *K Q V X Z Y*

    _____ (e) Recognizes vowels

_____ 13. Identifies capital and small letters

_____ 14. Reads to express feelings to characters

_____ 15. Uses picture and context clues to get meaning

_____ 16. Illustrates stories

_____ 17. Predicts outcomes on basis of previous experience

_____ 18. Uses table of contents

_____ 19. Uses punctuation marks at ends of sentences

_____ 20. Recognizes opposites

_____ 21. Recognizes singular words and plural words ending in *s*

_____ 22. Participates in informal conversations

_____ 23. Interprets material through dramatic play

_____ 24. Recognizes and uses variant endings—*s, ed, ing*

_____ 25. Shows improvement in manuscript writing

_____ 26. Knows how to attack a new word by:

    _____ (a) Using picture clues

    _____ (b) Reading to the end of a sentence and making a guess

    _____ (c) Checking that guess by use of phonetic clues—beginning and ending

    _____ (d) Using structural clues

    _____ (e) Checking himself by asking the teacher

Lee L. Smith, *Teaching in a nongraded school* (West Nyack, N.Y.: Parker Publishing, 1970), p. 85.

With the utilization of standard procedures, cooperation with other teachers, parents, specialists, and researchers, criteria can be determined by the classroom teacher. Instead of merely discriminating between children, as norm-referenced tests are designed to do, criterion-referenced tests help the student achieve successful learning experiences (Haring and Gentry 1976).

Observation.   In addition to gathering information, techniques of observation include investigation of medical, educational, and psychological records that are available. If the child being considered has a particular health problem, the teacher needs to be aware of the implications for his educational planning. Will he need medication or require a limited schedule of activities? If the child is cognitively disadvantaged, does the psychological report indicate abilities or limitations that would serve as a starting point? Have his visual and auditory acuity and his general health been recorded? If pertinent information is not available, appropriate referrals should be made immediately.

Smith and Neisworth (1975) emphasize the importance of evaluating a child's appearance. Handicapped children may be physically unattractive, have offensive odors, or wear unkempt clothing. These factors may affect other people's reactions and need to be considered and dealt with.

If the child has a prosthesis, such as a hearing aid, crutches, or a cane, the observer will note the ease or difficulty with which he handles his particular device. Other children's reactions are important, too.

Jimmy, who has cerebral palsy, recently entered a kindergarten class. His teachers, when informed that he would be coming, were apprehensive about other children's acceptance. They were particularly concerned about Jimmy's crutches. Wisely, they decided to observe before they planned any strategy. The other children asked Jimmy about the crutches and wanted to inspect them. The openness with which Jimmy and the children discussed the crutches revealed that this would not be a problem.

With a background of knowledge gained from existing information and reports, the teacher is ready to learn from personal experiences with the child. The teacher's observations may be focused on a certain behavior that warrants attention (such as social interaction) or concern with the child's overall behavior pattern and personality.

Observation may be defined as "getting to know the child." One teacher describes her method:

I interview each child, asking him to tell me about his home, hobbies, vacations, friends, clubs, travel, sports, animals, and so forth. I try to evaluate his needs and his level of confidence as he speaks. Some other ways in which I begin to diagnose the children are as follows: I listen to them speak and read, ask them to write and compute, watch them socialize, and look for evidence of empathy with others, of original thinking, of common sense, of sense of worth, and of ability to take responsibility (Huffman 1974, pp. 15–16).

Learning Style.   An area of assessment that is receiving a great deal of attention is that of learning style. Interest in children with learning disabilities has added impetus to investigation of modalities, or channels of learning. It has been demonstrated, for instance, that some children learn better by visual than by auditory methods, and that some children can attend successfully to only one modality at a time, negating the value of the multisensory approach (Clinger and Van Osdol 1974).

In spite of the interest in learning styles, this area of assessment has been neglected, even for children with obvious sensory handicaps. Chase (1971) points out that understanding of the learning modalities of the majority of visually handicapped children is limited. She claims that educational practices continue by tradition in settings for blind students, rather than by analysis and specific prescriptions.

In planning for remediation of a particular problem, it is necessary to know which modality can be used to acquire information and which modality needs to be strengthened. Unless such information is known, frustration for the child and for the teacher is likely to develop.

Melvin was making no progress in his fourth-grade reading program. The teacher had "tried everything" without success. Melvin was given a standardized test to determine his method of learning sight words. It was found that the only way he learned was visual. The reading program he was working in was a phonics program. His skills and self-concept began to improve with the use of an auditory training program to remediate his weakness and the use of a visually oriented program to help him acquire reading skills.

There are several instruments designed to furnish information about a child's learning style. The *Learning Methods Test* (Mills 1964) purports to aid the reading teacher in determining the student's ability to learn and retain new words under different teaching procedures. Dunn and Dunn (1974) suggest that students should be grouped for instruction by matching how they learn with how the program will require them to learn. By charting the students' behavior, it is possible to determine how they are affected by the physical environment, the emotional framework in which they are functioning, the sociological setting, and their own physical being and needs.

Self-examination and classmate surveys are suggested by Atwood (1975) as a means to help students recognize their own learning styles. The surveys include some of the following items:

a. I am most alert for learning new things in the: (1) early morning, (2) midday, (3) late afternoon or (4) evening.

b. The easiest way(s) for me to learn something is to: (1) read it, (2) hear it, (3) see it in pictures, (4) try it, (5) write it in my own words, (6) explain it to someone else or (7) draw a diagram or picture of it.

c. The kinds of learning situations that bother me most are: (1) large group sessions, (2) small group sessions, (3) using learning games such as spelling bees, (4) working with a partner who chose me, (5) working with a partner the teacher chose for me, (6) working with a partner I don't know, (7) working by myself, (8) working on team projects, (9) working in a very quiet place, (10) working in a very noisy place, (11) being interrupted while I'm working, (12) having to break in the middle of my work, (13) having to stop when I'm not finished or (14) having nothing to do while I wait for others to finish (pp. 73, 75).

A learning style questionnaire can be filled out by a student, or read to him and recorded by the teacher. A sample of such a questionnaire is in appendix C.

Skillful, continuous teacher observation is necessary in arriving at a child's learning style. With the help of a paraprofessional, a volunteer, or a college student, the teacher can compile a checklist similar to the one presented in table 3–3. Analysis of the findings can assist in providing the appropriate environment, materials, and programs to suit each child's learning style.

Long-Term Goals

The first requirement for individualizing instruction is the establishment of long-term goals. The National Association of State Directors of Special Education (1976) suggests critical areas to consider in deciding where to start:

What are the priority parental concerns?
What are the priority teacher concerns?

Table 3–3
Inventory of Learning Styles

Elements	Choice
Time	_____morning _____afternoon _____evening _____night _____other:
Place	_____learning centers _____library _____media corner _____home _____other:
Structure	_____strict _____flexible _____jointly determined _____self-determined _____other:
Affiliation	_____alone _____small groups _____large groups _____with partner _____other:
Movement	_____active _____still _____sporadic _____other:
Modality	_____visual _____auditory _____kinesthetic _____combination _____other:
Environment	_____floor _____desk _____sitting _____reclining _____other:
Sound	_____quiet _____music _____conversation _____working groups _____other:
Motivation	_____self _____teacher expectations _____deadlines _____extrinsic rewards _____other:

Adapted from R. Dunn and K. Dunn, *Practical approaches to individualizing instruction: Contracts and other effective teaching strategies* (West Nyack, N.Y.: Parker Publishing, 1972).

What are the appropriate developmental sequences of tasks or behaviors that the child would be expected to move through?

What behaviors appear to be the most modifiable, as determined from baseline assessment data including the child's strengths, weaknesses, and learning style?

Are there any other crucial considerations one needs to make in selecting areas of educational need, such as any problem areas that are truly dangerous for the child, injurious to his or her health, or others? (p. 30).

Hayes (1977) suggests the use of curricular areas when setting annual goals. This will enable the program developers to focus on specific goals and insure that nothing relevant is omitted. She suggests the following partial topical list of content areas that might appear on a district program planning form:

Reading Skills
  readiness
  comprehension
  vocabulary
  word attack

Prevocational-Vocational Skills
  job readiness
  work experience

Language Arts Skills
  writing
  spelling
  grammar
  speech

Arithmetic Skills
  numeration
  computation
  application
  measurement
  time

Perceptual Motor Skills
  auditory and visual
    sequencing
    memory
    acuity
    discrimination
    association
  eye-hand coordination
  fine motor development

Gross Motor Skills
  large motor activity
  general physical health
  body localization
  directionality
  laterality (pp. 15–16).

Goals may also be expressed in terms of social behavior, such as ability to attend to a task, interaction with other children, or curtailment of aggressive behavior. Since goals may be numerous, it is important to utilize the foregoing procedures to establish priorities. It is also important to include the child in planning. There may be particular areas about which he is concerned. One rather large fifth-grader, for example, said that he did not know how to tie his shoelaces! Since it was important to him that he not be subjected to ridicule, teaching him this skill became a top priority.

In planning with students, it must be remembered that some children like to set a course for the entire year while some may function better by setting smaller goals. The individualized educational program must specify annual goals; however, these goals can be broken down into smaller units. Atterbury (1974) gives examples of the diversity of goals:

Within four weeks, the student will be able to multiply two-digit numbers by two-digit numbers with 90 percent accuracy.

By the end of the year, the student will be able to construct a small computer and describe how it functions.

By the end of the quarter, the student will have written at least forty different selections and have collected them in a scrapbook.

Before next week, the student will be able to pass the one-digit addition test.

By the end of the year, the student will be able to select books which he can read with good comprehension and will select at least one book to read per week.

During the year, the student will show the ability to avoid physical confrontation when an adverse situation arises.

By the end of the week, the student will be able to write a paragraph containing one main idea.

By the end of the year, the student will be using cursive writing more often than printing (pp. 36–37).

Short-Term Objectives

Within the determined goals, teachers usually have some freedom in specifying instructional objectives. Curriculum areas are usually defined by the school and the school district; completion of textbooks within grade levels is often expected. Where individual differences exist in pupils, teachers are expected to deal with the differences. In practice, teachers have considerable freedom to specify and formulate objectives (Haring and Gentry 1976).

An objective, which may be derived from a general goal, is a specific statement. It is necessary to develop precise instructional objectives for the learner and the curriculum used for instruction. Only when teachers know what children are to learn will they be able to create the appropriate learning environment.

What must we teach? How will we know when we have taught it? What materials and procedures will work best to teach what we wish to teach? Mager (1962) suggests that effective instruction must respond to these questions. In discussing the preparation of objectives, he defines the following terms to be used:

Behavior—any visible activity displayed by a learner.

Terminal behavior—the behavior you would like your learner to be able to demonstrate at the time your influence over him ends.

Criterion—a standard or test by which terminal behavior is evaluated (p. 2).

A meaningfully stated objective is one that succeeds in communicating to the reader the writer's instructional intent. Ambiguous terminology such as *to know, to understand, to appreciate* should be avoided. Objectives are stated in terms that will answer the question: What will the learner be *doing?*

Butler (1970) makes a comparison of two objectives.

A. The student will have a good understanding of the letters of the alphabet, *A* through *Z.*

B. The student will be able to pronounce the names of the letters of the alphabet, *A* through *Z* (p. 45).

Statement B tells what the student will be able to do. However, statement B does not describe the conditions under which the performance is to take place: letters could be pronounced from memory or on sight. By adding such a condition, the statement could read: Given a box of cards containing the letters from *T* to *Z* in a predetermined order selected by the teacher, the student will be able to pronounce the letters of the alphabet from *A* through *Z* (Butler 1970, p. 45).

While this statement is more definitive, there is no minimum standard of performance level expressed. The following statement includes a definitive performance level: Given a box of cards containing the letters from *A* to *Z* in a predetermined order selected by the teacher, the student will be able to pronounce twenty of the twenty-six letters of the alphabet from *A* through *Z.*

As outlined by Butler, a well-written objective should say at least three things: what the student who has mastered the objective will be able to *do,* under what *conditions* the student will be expected to do this and, if appropriate to the situation, to what *extent* a certain kind of student performance can be expected to take place.

The preparation of behavioral objectives to cover *all* instructional intents would be an impossible task. Many instructional materials will list behavioral objectives; curriculum guides and books may list objectives that would fit into long-range goals projected by the teacher. Another shortcut is suggested by Charles (1976). After a teacher acquires the ability to write good behavioral objectives, a brief form may be adopted which includes only an action verb and its object. Examples would be:

Add	decimal fractions
Jump	rope
Associate	words with pictures

An important rationale for behavioral objectives is communication to the learner. Rosenbaum (1973) expresses the problem:

One of the most common origins of student nonperformance on tasks that they apparently should be capable of learning from is the failure of the immediate environment to communicate effectively to the learner what he is supposed to do, how he is supposed to do it, and then to check, through careful observation of what he in fact does, to make sure that he has understood all of this (p. 153).

A behavioral objective is a statement that tells the student what to do, suggests how to do it, tells him what he should do it with, and, at times, suggests why he should do it. Behavioral objectives make teaching and learning more precise and efficient.

Task Analysis. Although some behavioral objectives may be reached in a single step, many others may be more effectively reached through a series of small steps. In the example used in the foregoing section, the objective "the student will be able to pronounce the names of the letters of the alphabet, *A* through *Z*" might be more appropriately reached by teaching three letters at a time instead of starting with all twenty-six. Each group of letters would then be a step.

Task analysis makes mastery of a subject possible by identifying small learner steps, each of which can be mastered with adequate learner practice. In this process, each learning task (objective) is broken into component tasks, each of which must be mastered as a prerequisite to mastery of the total task.

To analyze a learning task, first state the terminal objective, which tells what the learner will be able to do after instruction. To analyze the overall task, ask questions like: What must the learner be able to do to achieve the objective? What kinds of learning are involved? What prior skills are necessary? What specific knowledge is required? What concepts or meanings must be understood? What is prerequisite to ultimate success? (Johnson and Johnson 1970).

Instruction time is frequently wasted because the teacher has no knowledge of prerequisite skills essential to learning a task. A student teacher was observed attempting to teach a child to tell time. Her materials were carefully prepared, the child was well-motivated, and still the child would sometimes respond to 12:15 as fifteen minutes before twelve and sometimes as fifteen minutes after twelve. An experienced observer immediately identified the problem: the child did not have the concepts of "before" and "after," prerequisite skills to telling time. A similar problem was encountered when an experienced teacher attempted to offer typing instruction to a visually impaired child. In dictating simple sentences, she learned that the student had limited phonics and spelling skills. It was necessary, therefore, that he be instructed in basic word attack skills before advanced typing could be offered.

The determination of how many steps are necessary is based on the complexity of the objective and the learner's current abilities. The method recommended by McCormack (1976) for a group of learners working toward the same objective but functioning at different levels is to construct the instructional sequence for those learners demonstrating the least competence. The task is analyzed into the simplest steps; the more capable learners may simply skip tests.

Frank (1973) presents an example of a task analysis which leads to an informal test constructed from the steps. The objective is stated as follows: The child is able to count correctly a specified number of coins handed to him by the teacher. A partial task analysis includes:

1. Child can verbally identify a penny and nickel.
2. Child states that a nickel is equivalent to five pennies.
3. Child can correctly count a row of pennies placed in a straight line.
4. Child can correctly count pennies placed in scattered fashion.
5. Child can count one nickel and several pennies which are placed in a straight line where the nickel is first.

The following items comprise a corresponding test:

Test Item Number	Test Item	Directions Given by Teacher
1	Coins or pictures of coins	Teacher asks child to name each coin as he points to it
2	Same	Teacher asks child how many pennies he can get for one nickel
3	Same	Teacher asks child to count the money
4	Same	Teacher asks child to count the money
5	Same	Teacher asks child to count the money

After administering the test to each child who will be learning about money, the teacher is able to determine what steps each needs to reach the stated objective.

For some tasks it is possible to determine the steps by observing and recording the sequential activities of a person performing the task. In most cases, the teacher decides what activities presented in what order will most assist the learner in acquiring the skill (McCormack 1976).

Task analysis is a major element in the individualization of instruction. An ability to analyze tasks allows the teacher to determine pupil readiness, to teach groups of children with varying skills, and to produce alternatives to instructional failure. It identifies the demands that a task will make on a child and allows the teacher to prepare the child to meet each demand (Junkala 1973). Task analysis is a tool that helps to carry out the goals and objectives specified in the Individualized Education Program.

Specifying Educational Services

The Individual Education Program must include statements that specify services necessary to accomplish the goals and objectives identified. Documentation of the services a child needs is required without regard to the availability of those services. Greer and Torres (1977) suggest that developing this statement will be difficult for the parents and the school personnel, since the services needed may not exist within the local education agency. Services include speech therapy, physical therapy, transportation, counseling, and other related school functions.

Specifying Percentage of Time

The extent to which the handicapped child will participate in the regular classroom must be defined. The nature and severity of the problem determine whether a child will receive direct services from a special educator or indirect services through consultation with the classroom teacher. For example, social behavior and minor academic problems can be handled through structured consultation while severe academic problems usually require direct service (Jenkins and Mayhall 1976).

The child who has severe academic or social problems may require some special education services outside the regular classroom while the child with minimal difficulties may be accommodated in the regular classroom on a full-time basis, with adaptations made by the regular teacher or with indirect services provided by the special educator.

Setting Timelines

It is necessary to establish a time when services for the child will start and when they are expected to end. As soon as the child has been determined eligible for special services, the placement committee and the classroom teacher should devise and begin implementation of the individual plan.

The committee will also set dates on which it will review the child's progress toward the annual goals and the short-term objectives. Review of programs at regular intervals will help the teacher determine whether or not changes in the plan are indicated.

Evaluating the Program

The effectiveness of the program for each child is determined by the accomplishment of the goals and objectives outlined for him. If they have been stated in measurable terms, the criteria have been set. The evaluation procedures should determine "(a) if satisfactory progress toward the annual goals is being achieved, (b) if the annual goals or short-term instructional objectives need revision, (c) if services need to be altered, and (d) if the student can benefit from a less restrictive environment" (National Association of State Directors of Special Education 1976 p. 32).

Evaluating the Child

It is the same as placing a chicken and a fox in the same cage and asking them to live together. Individualized instruction and comparative grading cannot exist in harmony with each other (Musgrave 1975, p. 129).

Noar (1972) refers to a nationwide study concerning the use of reporting procedures. It is noted that the report card is gradually being supplanted by the progress report and that schools are revising instruments to provide parents with more detailed information in terms of the development of pupil skills. She observes that many pupil progress reports "still place their emphasis almost entirely on the subjects in the curriculum rather than on the learner while many teachers and administrators reveal a greater concern about *how* to report than *what* to report" (p. 88).

If reporting procedures are prescribed by the school district, they can be modified to accommodate individual differences. One school uses the following notation on the report card:

LEVEL CODE
A—above grade level
B—on grade level
C—below grade level

On the card, there is a space for level and a space for evaluation. Thus, a student may receive *C/A,* indicating that he is doing excellent work at a level below his peers. While this permits some individualization, teachers still find themselves averaging grades on group-oriented tasks, with the handicapped child in many cases receiving a failing grade.

An individualized reporting form has strengths and advantages over traditional reporting forms:

Both students and teachers are held accountable for learning.

The teacher reports achievement in concrete terms rather than making value judgments based on subjective data.

Teachers evaluate students in terms of their own abilities and are not forced to compare students with others.

Individualized evaluation may be defined as evaluation of an individual student's attainment and progress in relation to his own starting point. Musgrave (1975) finds that persuading people that individualized evaluation is this simple is a formidable task, because they cannot separate student evaluation practices from reporting methods.

One teacher describes her method of reporting to parents:

I encourage any parent to visit without appointment and take an interest in the education of his child. I use the parent-teacher conference as our first report session and use a checklist-type report card as our second, third, and final report. I do not give letter grades. In assessing the child, I try to see the whole child in relation to his health, his environment, his learning needs, his social development (Huffman 1974, p. 18).

The use of the individual education program simplifies the process of evaluation. It also simplifies the reporting procedure, since teachers, administrators, parents, and the child can examine the program in terms of the child's progress and know where he started, where he went, and how he got there.

Perhaps the mandate requiring the development of an individualized program for all handicapped children can be a catalyst for positive change in the learning environments of all children. With the acquisition of knowledge in assessing the needs of handicapped and nonhandicapped children and with the development of skills and techniques in meeting those needs, each teacher is taking a step toward the ultimate goal of complete individualization.

References and Selected Readings

Abeson, A., and Weintraub, F. 1977. Understanding the individualized education program. In S. Torres, ed., *A primer on individualized education programs for handicapped children*. Reston, Va.: Foundation for Exceptional Children.

Atteberry, D. 1974. Personalized learning. In D. A. Shiman, C. M. Culver, and A. Lieberman, eds. *Teachers on individualization: The way we do it*. New York: McGraw-Hill.

Atwood, B. S. 1975. Helping students recognize their own learning styles. *Learning* 3:8, 72–78.

Burgemeister, B. B., Blum, L. H., and Lorge, I. 1972. *Columbia mental maturity scale, third edition*. New York: Harcourt Brace Jovanovich.

Butler, L. 1970. Performance objectives for individualized instruction. *Audiovisual Instruction* (May):45–46.

Charles, C. M. 1976. *Individualizing instruction*. St. Louis: Mosby.

Chase, J. B. 1971. Evaluation of Severely Visually Impaired Children. Address, American Foundation for the Blind, New York.

Chinn, P. C., Drew, C. J., and Logan, D. R. 1975. *Mental retardation*. St. Louis: Mosby.

Clinger, P. A., and Van Osdol, B. M. 1974. Remediation of learning disabilities —methods and techniques. *Teaching Exceptional Children* 6:192–202.

Connelly, A. J., Machtman, W., and Pritchett, E. M. 1971. *Key math*. Circle Pines, Minn: American Guidance Service.

Cory, C. T. 1974. Two generations of volunteers: Parents. *Learning* (October): 76–83.

Dunn, L. M., and Markwardt, F. C. 1970. *Peabody individual achievement test manual*. Circle Pines, Minn: American Guidance Service.

Dunn, R., and Dunn, K. 1974. Learning style as a criterion for placement in alternative programs. *Phi Delta Kappan* (December):275–278.

Frank, A. R. 1973. Breaking down learning tasks: a sequence approach. *Teaching Exceptional Children* (Fall):16–19.

Garcia, V. C., and Pinkelton, M. 1977. The teacher's role in development. In S. Torres, ed., *A primer on individualized education programs for handicapped children*. Reston, Va: Foundation for Exceptional Children.

Greer, J., and Torres, S. 1977. Arranging specific educational services to be provided. In S. Torres, ed., *A primer on individualized education programs for handicapped children*. Reston, Va: Foundation for Exceptional Children.

Haring, N. G., and Gentry, N. 1976. Direct and individualized instructional procedures. In N. G. Haring and R. L. Schiefelbusch, eds., *Teaching special children*. New York: McGraw-Hill.

Hayes, J. 1977. Annual goals and short term objectives. In S. Torres, ed., *A primer on individualized education programs for handicapped children.* Reston, Va: Foundation for Exceptional Children.

Huffman, S. 1974. Notes to a new teacher. In D. A. Shiman, C. M. Culver, and A. Lieberman, eds., *Teachers on individualization: The way we do it.* New York: McGraw-Hill.

Jastak, J. F., Jastak, S. R., and Bijou S. W. 1965. *Wide range achievement test, revised edition.* Wilmington: Guidance Associates of Delaware.

Jenkins, J. R., and Mayhall, W. F. 1976. Development and evaluation of a resource teacher program. *Exceptional Children* 43:21–29.

Johnson, S. R., and Johnson, R. B. 1970. *Developing individualized instructional material.* Palo Alto, Calif.: Westinghouse Learning Press.

Junkala, J. B. 1973. Task analysis: The processing dimension. *Academic Therapy* 8:401–409.

Knight, N. 1976. Working relationships that work. *Teaching Exceptional Children* 8:113–115.

McCormack, J. E. 1976. Using a task analysis format to develop instructional sequences. *Education and Training of the Mentally Retarded* 11:318–323.

Mager, R. F. 1962. *Preparing instructional objectives.* Palo Alto, Calif.: Fearon.

Mattson, B. D. 1977. Involving parents in special education: Did you really reach them? *Education and Training of the Mentally Retarded* (December):358–362.

Mills, R. E. 1964. *The teaching of word recognition.* Ft. Lauderdale, Fla.: Mills Center.

Musgrave, G. R. 1975. *Individualized instruction.* Boston: Allyn and Bacon.

National Association of State Directors of Special Education. 1976. *Functions of the placement committee in special education.* Washington, D.C.: National Association of State Directors of Special Education.

Noar, G. 1972. *Individualized instruction: Every child a winner.* New York: Wiley.

Robinson, N. M., and Robinson, H. B. 1976. *The mentally retarded child.* New York: McGraw-Hill.

Rosenbaum, P. S. 1973. *Peer-mediated instruction.* New York: Teachers College Press.

Slosson, R. L. 1963. *Slosson intelligence test (SIT) for children and adults.* New York: Slosson Educational Publications.

Smith, R. M., and Neisworth, J. T. 1975. *The exceptional child: A functional approach.* New York: McGraw-Hill.

Terman, L. M., and Merrill, M. A. 1960. *Stanford-Binet intelligence scale: Manual for the third revision, form L-M.* Boston: Houghton Mifflin.

Torres, S., ed. 1977. *A primer on individualized education programs for handicapped children.* Reston, Va: Foundation for Exceptional Children.

Turnbull, A. P., Strickland, B., and Brantley, J. C. 1978. *Implementing Individualized Education Programs.* Columbus: Merrill Publishing Co., 1978.

Wechsler, D. 1967. *Manual for the Wechsler preschool and primary scale of intelligence.* New York: Psychological Corp.

Wechsler, D. 1974. *Manual for the Wechsler intelligence scale for children—revised.* New York: Psychological Corp.

Winslow, L. 1977. Parent participation. In S. Torres, ed., *A primer on individualized education programs for handicapped children.* Reston, Va: Foundation for Exceptional Children.

Chapter Four

Implementing Individualized
Education Programs

Photograph by Richard Clontz

Teachers who know how to individualize instruction will have no difficulty in integrating handicapped children into their classrooms. They are aware of individual differences and are skillful in meeting the needs of each child they teach. They know that good teaching and good learning take place when the educational processes are varied according to the interests, abilities, achievements, learning styles, and preferences of the students. They realize that the need to label and categorize students in order to attend to their differences is lessened when each class member is individually attended to. They would agree that "individualized learning is the process of developing and retaining *individuality* by a classroom organization that provides for the effective and efficient learning experiences of each class member" (Kaplan et al. 1973, p. xiii).

However, just as children cannot be expected to learn a difficult task in one step, teachers cannot be expected to plan and implement individualized programs in one operation. If teachers are to succeed in the integration of handicapped students in the regular classroom, administrators must recognize the additional time, training, and assistance that is required.

Individualizing instruction in a classroom containing thirty children who exhibit wide ranges of differences is a complex task. Many teachers are overwhelmed with the prospects confronting them. However, with proper planning and assistance, individually tailored programs are possible, practical, and desirable. Successful implementation requires changes in teacher expectations and responsibilities, in the learning environment, and in instructional techniques.

Teacher Role

Once the Individualized Education Program is developed, implementation of the goals and objectives is begun. The teacher is responsible for planning the activities to help the child meet the specified goals. Since the program is specific, formulating daily lesson plans (see table 4–1) is simplified and reporting progress to the planning committee is facilitated. The teacher is then able to concentrate on strategies for accommodating the individual needs of his students.

Teachers and administrators are quick to admit that children learn by talking and doing as well as by listening. Yet most classes operate with the teacher as the active person, while the children are expected to listen, pay attention, and play a fairly passive role in the learning process. Dunn and Dunn (1972) claim that "Youngsters often merely serve as an audience for teachers when they sit politely and listen to diatribes that essentially serve to reinforce the teacher's knowledge—not necessarily adding to the children's understandings, skills or abilities" (p. 22).

A well-organized, individualized program appears to run itself. One such program, a prevocational program for students identified as "potentail dropouts," consisted entirely of learning stations on cosmotology, typewriting, horticulture, leathercraft, and photography. The children, who were familiar with the system, proceeded to a chosen learning station, took

Table 4–1
Daily Lesson Plan

Child's Name: George Allen

Date of Program Entry: 9/10/76

Projected Ending Date: 10/15/77

Goal Statement: Improve mathematical skills

Short-term Instructional Objectives:
Develop concept and skills in multiplication

Behavioral Objectives	Task Analysis	Strategies and/or Techniques	Materials and/or Resources	Date Started	Date Ended	Comments Evaluation
George will demonstrate concept of multiplication by grouping objects and writing equations: $1 \times 6 =$ $2 \times 3 =$ $3 \times 2 =$ $6 \times 1 =$ $4 \times 2 =$ $2 \times 4 =$ $8 \times 1 =$ $1 \times 8 =$ $5 \times 3 =$ $3 \times 5 =$ Equations will be solved with 80% accuracy	1. Arrange objects in sets 2. Verbalize problems from objects; e.g., "two eights" 3. Read problem as written 4. Verbalize answer 5. Write answer	1. Use arrays 2. Group objects 3. Verbalize process to develop concept of sets as multiplication facts ------- e.g., * * * * * * * * $(4 \times 2 = 8)$ $(2 \times 4 = 8)$	Drinking straws Rubber bands Poker chips File folder with discs and problems	9/11/76		

the pretest, gathered the appropriate task cards, and went to work. The teacher was free to circulate, lending help where needed and providing continuous feedback to the students. The teacher was relaxed; the children were excited about the things they were learning.

In this role, the teacher is a manager: of the objectives, the environment, and the instructional activities. The teacher must know when to intervene, when to allow exploration to continue, and when to offer help. Lectures, explanations, and demonstrations are still necessary. Concepts need to be presented to groups of children; the individualized activities take place as each child approaches learning at his rate and in his fashion. It is the teacher's task (and opportunity) to provide the situation in which this can occur.

When one talks with people about mainstreaming handicapped children, one misconception becomes apparent. Classroom teachers seem to feel they will have to "go it alone." Actually, the mainstreaming process requires more ancillary help than self-contained special classes have ever had. Depending on the model adopted by a particular school system, the special education support may be provided by a resource teacher, an itinerant teacher, or a supervisor. Other support and advice will come from psychologists, social workers, parents, volunteers, college personnel and students, paraprofessionals, and peer teachers as suggested in chapter 2.

Scheduling

When direct services are provided by a resource teacher, scheduling students' time away from the regular classroom may become difficult. Although proper scheduling is time-consuming, it is extremely important for smooth operation and good working relationships. The classroom teacher may consider several time blocks during which it would be appropriate for the handicapped child to be away from the classroom without jeopardizing his instructional program. Generally, it is wise to schedule the student during the period of the subject being remediated. For instance, if the child is provided with special services in reading, he should be taken from the class during his regular reading period. Thus he will be absent from his class during a time when he does not usually experience success.

The child should not be scheduled for direct services during his physical education, music, art, or speech classes. Children enjoy and need all special services; the resource room should not be punitive.

It is extremely important for all teachers to adhere to the schedule once it is determined. From the resource teacher's point of view, every minute counts, since children are usually scheduled in short, consecutive blocks. From the classroom teacher's point of view, lack of adherence to a schedule can mean interruptions of group activities.

Coordinating Services

Each of the service areas listed by the committee on the Individual Education Program is responsible for developing an implementation plan. The primary implementation plan will be the responsibility of the receiving teacher or other implementer. This person or persons will take the committee's plan and break it into finer steps.

Frequently the resource teacher (special educator) and the classroom teacher will be designated to implement the program. To facilitate the development and the implementation of the program, a close working relationship must be established. Knight (1976) suggests questions a classroom teacher might pose:

Just what does a resource teacher do?
Will the resource teacher listen to me?
Does the resource teacher know what it's like to have 28 children all in one room? (p. 113).

It is the task of the special educator and the administrator to clarify the role of the special educator or resource teacher and to answer any questions the classroom teacher may have in relation to both roles.

For students whose primary education will be in regular programs, it is necessary to identify and strengthen the link between the regular and special education programs (Garcia and Pinkelton 1977). Although the committee defines the essential mainstream skills, the classroom teacher observes the child performing tasks, establishes criteria for acceptable performance, and judges performance against these criteria (Jenkins and Mayhall 1976). When direct services are provided, constant feedback to the classroom teacher is essential to successful implementation of a program.

Indirect services can add greatly to successful programming. Based on objectives stated by the committee, materials to be used in the classroom can be provided for a particular child. Self-instructional packets (to be described later in this chapter) can be placed in the classroom for handicapped or all children to use. In one school, the resource teachers developed a library of materials for classroom teachers to use. Placed in the media center, it is available for anyone's use and contains activities, at many levels of difficulty, in all subject areas. Not only is this useful to the classroom teachers, but it is evidence that the special educator wants to help.

Communication

One of the most difficult tasks is finding time to plan. Teachers are physically and mentally exhausted at the end of the day; planning and talking should take place *during* the school day. Many resource programs have failed because the special educator and the classroom teacher did not have time to communicate and to coordinate services. The result is that frequently the instruction provided in the resource room has no relation to that provided in the regular classroom. In fact, sometimes the child is penalized for missing regular instruction. It is hoped that the cooperative efforts initiated in developing the Individual Education Program will prevent such a problem. In any event, it is essential that the classroom teacher and the special educator have established times, convenient for both, to talk, to plan, and to explore.

Communication can be facilitated if the principal is aware of the need for planning time. The principal can also assist in planning for in-service training for classroom teachers and for making clear the purposes of the particular program in practice. If specific roles are determined, responsibilities delegated, and planning time provided, adequate communication is likely to take place.

Environment

While individualized instruction is usually associated with "open" education, it can take place in any structure. The learning environment is more closely associated with the teacher's philosophy than with the physical setting of the classroom. One of the teacher's most important jobs is to create an environment conducive to emotional and intellectual growth for each child in the classroom.

Environmental factors that affect a student's achievement rate at a given time include the elements of sound, light, temperature, and design (Dunn and Dunn 1974). These factors become particularly important for children who have learning and/or emotional problems. Children who are distractible may have difficulty sorting out or attending to visual or auditory stimuli; other children may be distracted by movement. It is important to determine what source and degree of stimuli distract the student, so that a proper learning environment can be established and training procedures started to help him cope with these distractions (Clinger and Van Osdol 1974).

There are environmental considerations relevant to many specific handicaps. Prosthetic adjustments may have to be made for children who are physically disabled. Smith and Neisworth (1976) state the problem:

"Prostheses are applied to the person, to his environment, or to both to maximize interaction between person and environment and, thus, to facilitate behavioral development" (p. 234). The example refers to a child whose hands are missing. The doors in a school could be designed so the child could bump them with his elbow; the child could be fitted with artificial hands that would allow him to open a standard door; or the child could be trained to grasp a doorknob with both elbows and open doors without an individual or an environmental prosthesis. The type of adaptation that is necessary is an individual matter.

Considerations of space for handicapped children are important and require special consideration. A blind student, for example, needs a listening center in the classroom; he needs a space for his braille books and his braille writer. A child who is hearing-impaired needs placement near the teacher or may require environmental adaptations to permit him to maximize his residual hearing. Distractible children may not function well in an open situation. Carrels, cubicles, or partitions may be necessary to modify an overly stimulating environment.

Settings can be provided for small group or individual tasks with the use of large cardboard cartons to be used as "offices," movable screens (which also serve as display space), bookcases, and planters. Tables which comfortably seat five to six children suggest small group activities; shelves to accommodate storage bins enable children to keep their personal belongings organized.

Creative teachers view their classrooms as a challenge. They get ideas from reading, from other teachers, and, most of all, from the children who share the room.

Instructional Techniques

Perusal of the literature on individualized instruction will reveal techniques to facilitate individualization. Among ideas presented are programmed instruction, learning stations, interest centers, media corners, contracts, and games. All are strategies worth investigation. Many ideas can be gained from visiting schools and classes where individualized instruction is a policy. Several techniques that have proved to be effective with handicapped children are peer teaching, learning centers, contracts, and learning activity packets.

Peer Teaching. Children learn from each other. It is a common misconception that individualized programs do not allow for group work. Children need individual activities, small group, and large group experiences.

109

Learning to interact, cooperate, and work as a group member is part of a child's development. Flexible groups which pull students together for a specific purpose aid the teacher in individualizing learning.

Students find satisfaction in working together. They find that knowledge and skills can be shared in a profitable way. They also find that they can teach each other and that the teacher also is a learner! Integrating handicapped children into regular classrooms can be facilitated immeasurably by students teaching students. This can be observed in any classroom; there is always a student asking for help and there is usually one giving it. If this inclination can be used systematically, it is a powerful instructional technique.

Debbie, who receives help with math in the resource room, was reviewing multiplication tables. Kevin, who has severe emotional problems, was asked to help her. He used drill cards and became the "teacher." His self-image and Debbie's multiplication skills both improved.

Frequently a nonhandicapped child will help a handicapped child. It is interesting to observe the process in reverse.

David, who is blind, has mastered the use of the Numberaid, a pocket-sized abacus. He was asked to demonstrate its use to a group of fourth-graders who were having difficulty with the concepts of place value and regrouping.

Peer teaching may occur in an informal way or in a more structured fashion. Jenkins and Mayhall (1976) describe a program in which peer teachers were trained and supervised by a resource teacher. Results of the one-to-one tutoring indicated an overwhelming superiority over small group teacher instruction.

There are a number of techniques that can be used to initiate peer teaching. Potential teachers may be identified with the use of a classroom resource bank. In the posted directory may be listed each class member with information and resources about him. To develop the directory, students may be paired to interview each other to discover "who's good at what." The teacher encourages and supports active use of the directory at any time and makes frequent referrals to it when a student needs help.

Training for students who want to be peer teachers can be made available. One type of training helps students to learn to relate well with younger children or to handicapped children, with instruction on helping them achieve success and feel important. Another type of training emphasizes the development of teaching strategies in specific content areas.

110

Training sessions can be held by teachers, administrators, school counselors, or experienced peer teachers.

The book of Ecclesiastes states the principle of peer teaching: "Two are better than one . . . For if they fall, the one will lift up his fellow; but woe to him that is alone when he falleth; for he hath not another to help him up" (4:9–10).

Learning Centers

A good beginning toward individualization is through learning centers or learning stations. The learning center is an area in the classroom where students can go to work on facts, concepts, or skills. In the specified area, materials and resources related to a given curriculum are collected and presented in an attractive and well-organized manner.

Developed by the teacher with student help, learning centers have specific objectives to fulfill. They have multilevel activities and materials requiring various modes of learning to meet individual needs and styles. Choices and alternatives are offered with clear and simple instructions which a child can follow without constant teacher guidance.

Piechowiak and Cook (1976) describe four types of learning centers:

1. Basic Learning Skills. A skills center may utilize close-ended activity cards such as math drill cards, phonics, or sentence scrambles, or open-ended task cards such as: make a list of all the ways that you can use the number *4*. Activity task cards state the main goal, specific objectives, preassessment, and evaluation.

2. Listening Center. This is the ideal choice for a teacher who is just beginning to use learning centers. The use of a listening post with eight headsets enables the teacher to add variety and offer some independence to the class, yet offers little threat to classroom control.

3. Discovery Center. This is the place for exploration and discovery. An example would be a science center where the child may float a variety of objects in a large container of water, leading to the discovery that heavy objects sink and light objects float.

4. Creative Center. The creative center includes language arts, art, music, and crafts activities.

The following is a description of a Math Skills Learning Center; it is illustrated in figure 4–1.

NUMBER FACTS

Objective:
Students will discover and write addition facts of numerals from 2 to 10.

Task Card:

Number	Date	Facts
2		$1 + 1 = 2$
3		$2 + 1 = 3$ $1 + 1 + \_\_\_ = 3$
4		
5		
6		
7		
8		
9		
10		

Name _____

Activities:
Poker chips for manipulation
Concept cards for each numeral indicating various
   addition facts, color coded
Drill cards for practice with a friend

Extended Activity:
Make colored dot pictures to show:
   11, 12, 13

Reinforcing Activity:
Card game (Make 10)

1. Deal 1 card to each player.
2. Player asks Banker for 1 card to make 10.
3. Player lays down 2 cards that make 10.
4. Player writes number facts.

Learning centers may be added to the classroom as slowly or completely as the teacher wishes. They may be added to emphasize materials that support basic skill programs or relate to a unit of study or as an enriching element to the classroom. On the other hand, the teacher may elect to alter the course and convert the self-contained classroom to a total learning center scheme. Since learning centers are designed for individuality, a center in the second grade ought to be useful to any other child if it fits his maturity, interests, and learning style, without regard to grade level (Voight 1971).

Learning centers may be used to provide activities for independent study, follow-up for teacher-taught concepts, activities in place of regular assignment or an enrichment activity. An additional use as a reinforcer is described in chapter 9.

Figure 4–1
Learning Center

1. Identifying poster
2. Materials container
3. Concept cards
4. Manipulative materials
5. Drill cards
6. Task card
7. Extended activities
8. Reinforcing activity

Kaplan et al. (1973) suggest steps necessary in creating a learning center:

1. Select a subject area.
2. Determine the skill or concept to be taught, reinforced, or enriched.
3. Develop the skill or concept into a learning activity which should include manipulating (such as cutting, pasting, or matching); experimenting (observing, charting, keeping a log); and listening or viewing.
4. Prepare the skill or concept into an applying activity, such as filling in; arranging in order; putting together; taking apart; listing; classifying; matching; tracing; writing; locating or labeling.
5. Incorporate the skill or concept into an extending activity, such as comparing; developing your own; researching; reconstructing; finding what other or deciding what if.
6. Place all the games, worksheets, charts, etc., together in one area of the room for children to use in a self-selected manner (pp. 21–22).

Piechowiak and Cook (1976) claim that the learning center approach is humane to children with learning difficulties since they are not pressured to perform at a level exceeding their skill nor chastised because they cannot do the work. "When students perform self-selected and self-scheduled tasks, the opportunities for comparison are less frequent. Who can tell if the immature child is *still* working on math, or if he has just started it later in the day?" (p. 68).

Because learning centers contain a variety of activities ranging from simple to difficult and from concrete to abstract, they enable the handicapped student to participate in interests shared by his classmates. The wide use of media permits the auditorily impaired child, the poor reader, and the mentally retarded child to take part in activities appropriate for their abilities. Instructions should be simple and clear; they may be on tape or pictured rather than written. Learning centers provide alternatives related to the ability and the learning style of each person.

Contracts

A contract is an agreement written for, by, or with the student. It provides opportunities for a child to learn independently and usually includes a variety of learning resources, such as tapes, records, books, films, pictures, loops, slides, and games (Dunn and Dunn, 1972).

Blackburn and Powell (1976) define the following types of contracts:

Structured contracts, in which all component parts are predetermined by the teacher. The student and the teacher negotiate a contract from these components.

Partly structured contracts, in which some components are predetermined by the teacher and others are designed and developed by the teacher and the student.

Mutually structured contracts, in which no components are predetermined; the teacher and the student cooperatively develop and negotiate the contract.

Unstructured contracts, in which no components are predetermined; the student initiates and develops the parts and negotiates with the teacher.

Contracts include behavioral objectives, a listing of many kinds of learning resources, and a series of activity alternatives that provide the student a choice in applying and reporting the information he has gathered.

Contracts are useful for the teacher who has handicapped children in his room, because they help remove the time variable from learning and permit the student to work at his own pace. With the choices provided, they are a means to achieving independence and assuming responsibility for learning.

Contracts allow the teacher to prescribe activities on individual bases for a great many students. As students are engaged in activities, the teacher has time to spend with those encountering difficulties or needing assistance. The following is an example of a contract:

PLANT IDENTIFICATION

A.   Identify 15 plants in the chart below. You may use plants, labels, seed catalogs, and library reference books.

1.   Fill in the plant name.
2.   Draw a leaf.
3.   Draw the flower if there is one.
4.   Identify the plant type (annual, biennial, perennial).
5.   Give the use of the plant (potting plant, bedding plant, shrub, tree, etc.)
6.   Tell or show how the plant may be propagated (seed, leaf cutting, stem cutting, etc.).

The student agrees to fulfill this contract by performing the above duties.

Date: _____   _____
                                                      Student

                                             _____
                                                      Teacher
                                                   (Schulz 1972)

115

Learning Activity Packets

A learning activity packet is a self-instructional unit designed to aid students in learning one basic concept or idea in which the idea to be learned is broken into its several components. A learning activity packet is designed for a specific ability level and provides flexibility in activities students may choose for reaching stated goals. The student proceeds at his own pace. The format of the learning activity packet is structured in a way that insures its success. The following components are essential:

1. A specific objective or set of objectives.
2. A pretest designed to assess the student's level of achievement relevant to the objective or objectives prior to the instructional experience.
3. A series of instructional activities designed to help the student meet the objective or objectives.
4. A posttest designed to assess the student's level of mastery relevant to the objective or objectives.
5. Remediation procedures for those students who do not demonstrate mastery on the posttest.

The objective is based on teacher observation, formal and informal testing, and student interest. As in all behavioral objectives, it should be stated in terms that will answer the question: What will the learner be *doing?*

The pretest may be used to determine whether the objective is appropriate or at what level the student may enter the activities. The pretest will also indicate that some activities may be bypassed.

Instructional activities may be as limited or numerous as is deemed necessary, depending on the sophistication of the topic and the abilities and needs of the student. Regardless of the simplicity or complexity, the activities should be varied and highly motivational.

The posttest may be the same as, or a different form of, the pretest. If the student does not pass the posttest, it may indicate that: the objective was not appropriate; the activities were not relevant to the objective; or more activities are required for the student to meet the performance criteria.

In the latter case, remediation activities (sometimes called branching activities) may be used to approach the task through a different sense modality or a related topic. After completing these activities, the student may again take the posttest and, it is to be hoped, be ready for a new packet.

The learning activity packet is a valuable tool in integrating the handicapped child into the regular classroom. It enables the child to work at his own speed; it provides additional material to insure learning; it offers alternatives to learning styles; and it allows the child to work alone or with a group.

Learning activity packets may be prepared by the teacher or by volunteers or paraprofessionals. Once prepared, they can be used individually by a student or with the help of a volunteer or peer teacher. Although the packets are planned for individual needs, many children have similar needs. Therefore, a library of various kinds of learning activity packets would assist tremendously in the individualization process.

The following learning activity packet is illustrated in figure 4–2.

TIE A BOW

Objective:
Student will tie his shoestrings every time they need it, at school and at home.

Pretest:
Student is instructed to tie his shoestring.

Activities:
Follow illustrated task analysis of tying a bow
1. Tie strings on tennis shoe (colored shoestrings correspond with pictorial directions)
2. Practice with lacing board
3. Tie own shoestring.

Branching activity:
Forty knots—a visual aid for knot tying
Packet is contained in box which ties to close. Packet may be used at home or at school.

The learning activity packet as a means to individualized instruction has advantages for the learner and for the teacher:

1. The student learns at his own rate.
2. The student is successful.
3. The student is motivated to learn and to acquire independence.
4. The teacher's time and energy are extended.
5. Students who perform at different levels may work in the same classroom.

Although it is highly structured, the learning activity packet consists of a variety of methods and materials from which the student may

Figure 4–2
Learning Activity Packet

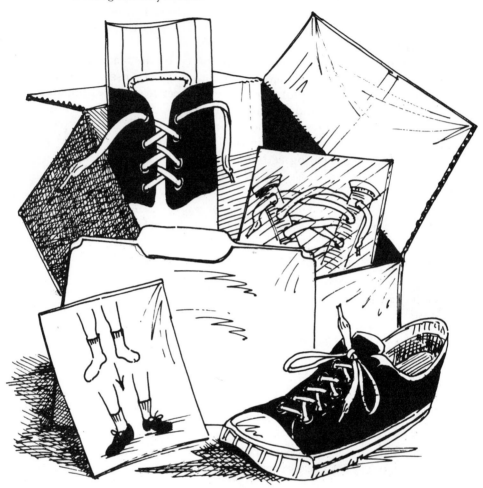

1. Container
2. Behavioral objective
3. Pretest, posttest
4. Pictorial instructions, activity A
5. Instructional activity B
6. Branching activity

choose. Structure is more evident in the instructional objectives, with emphasis on "what you must arrive at" rather than a forced "how you must get there."

Curriculum Adaptation

Although the general curriculum of a school may be prescribed, there is generally some leeway in the choice of curriculum materials. Perhaps more emphasis needs to be placed on this aspect of curriculum planning if individualization is to be practical.

Several criteria presented by Keller and Ribes-Inesta (1974) are relevant to these needs:

1. Does the curriculum describe the terminal behavior?
2. Does the curriculum measure the students' entry level?
3. Does the curriculum require frequent student response?
4. Does the curriculum contain clear criteria for correct response?
5. Does the curriculum contain check points and prescriptions?
6. Does the curriculum accommodate individual differences? (p. 132).

If available materials can fill these needs, they can be used to meet each child's curriculum demands. If the materials available to the teacher are more rigid, a number of adaptations will have to be made for the handicapped learner. Such adaptations will be discussed in chapters relating to specific subject areas; several general suggestions will be made in this chapter.

Many of the problems encountered in presenting the regular curriculum to the handicapped child are related to reading disability. The tape recorder is a tremendous aid in circumventing this problem. Recently a student teacher recorded a social studies lesson for a mildly handicapped student in a fifth grade. The teacher reported that a group of students listened to the tape with him, enjoying the change in presentation. Responses can be recorded by the student if he is a poor writer or speller, giving the teacher valuable feedback without penalizing the student. If the student's vocabulary is poorly developed, chapters in textbooks may be rewritten by the teacher or volunteer on a lower cognitive level, in simpler terminology, without destroying the concepts dealt with in the lesson. Filmstrips, records, and tapes may be used to strengthen the concepts.

Johnson and Johnson (1970) suggest an audio-tutorial lesson to permit the student to learn at his convenience and pace. Such a lesson is composed of an audio tape with either a workbook, a filmstrip, a slide, or an 8 mm film loop. The audio tape controls the entire lesson, and the student is in complete control over all medium sources.

A compact, simple way to provide manipulative materials is illustrated in figure 4–3. Pockets attached to file folders add concrete learning

Figure 4–3
File Folders

materials to help in the development of concepts. Such folders can be prepared as supplements to regular textbook or group assignments and are useful to children with learning disabilities, cognitive disabilities, perceptual problems, or visual impairments.

It is quite possible for the handicapped student to deal initially with a concept in some concrete way, on a different cognitive level, and still participate in class discussions and group projects. Open-ended questions, the availability of audiovisual material, and alternatives in assignments permit the handicapped student to operate within a structured curriculum.

Teachers who are willing to learn to individualize instruction will be better teachers of *all* children. Educators are finding that existing predetermined curricula do not provide for the unique characteristics of all learners; that children learn different amounts of content at different rates at different times; that children learn by talking, doing, and teaching as well as by listening. They are also learning that teachers are different; they have individual strengths and preferences which they bring to the teaching/ learning task. Individualization of instruction requires that each teacher bring unique characteristics, skills, and knowledge to the challenge of meeting the unique characteristics and needs of each student.

References and Selected Readings

Blackburn, J. E., and Powell, W. C. 1976. *One at a time all at once: The creative teacher's guide to individualized instruction without anarchy.* Pacific Palisades, Calif.: Goodyear.

Clinger, P. A., and Van Osdol, B. M. 1974. Remediation of learning disabilities —methods and techniques. *Teaching Exceptional Children* 6:192–202.

Cruickshank, W. M., and Hallahan, D. P. 1975. *Perceptual and learning disabilities in children,* vol. 1. Syracuse, N.Y.: Syracuse University Press.

Dunn, R., and Dunn, K. 1972. *Practical approaches to individualizing instruction: Contracts and other effective teaching strategies.* West Nyack, N.Y.: Parker.

Dunn, R. and Dunn, K. 1974. Learning style as a criterion for placement in alternative programs. *Phi Delta Kappan* (December):275–278.

Garcia, V. C., and Pinkelton, M. 1977. The teacher's role in development. In S. Torres, ed. *A primer on individualized education programs for handicapped children.* Reston, Va.: Foundation for Exceptional Children.

Gearheart, B. R. 1976. *Teaching the learning disabled.* St. Louis: Mosby.

Gold, M. W. 1976. Task analysis of a complex assembly task by the retarded blind. *Exceptional Children* 43:78–84.

Hammill, D. D., Crandell, J. M., Jr., and Colarusso, R. 1970. The Slossom intelligence test adapted for visually limited children. *Exceptional Children* 36:535–536.

Jenkins, J. R., and Mayhall, W. F. 1976. Development and evaluation of a resource teacher program. *Exceptional Children* 43:21–29.

Johnson, S., and Johnson, R. B. 1970. *Developing individualized instructional material.* Palo Alto, Calif.: Westinghouse Learning Press.

Junkala, J. B. 1972. Task analysis and instructional alternatives. *Academic Therapy* 8:33–40.

Junkala, J. 1970. Teacher evaluation of instructional materials. *Teaching Exceptional Children* 2:73–76.

Kaplan, S. N., Kaplan, J. A. B., Madsen, S. K., and Taylor, B. K. 1973. *Change for children*. Pacific Palisades, Calif.: Goodyear.

Keller, F. S., and Ribes-Inesta, E. 1974. *Behavior modification: Application to education*. New York: Academic Press.

Knight, N. 1976. Working relationships that work. *Teaching Exceptional Children* 8:113–115.

Leles, S., and Bernabei, R. 1969. *Writing and using behavioral objectives*. Tuscaloosa, Ala.: Drake.

McCormack, J. E., Jr. 1976. The assessment tool that meets your needs: The one you construct. *Teaching Exceptional Children* 8:106–109.

Neujahr, J. L. 1976. *The individualized instruction game*. New York: Teachers College Press.

Piechowiak, A. B., and Cook, M. B. 1976. *Complete guide to the elementary learning center*. West Nyack, N.Y.: Parker.

Popham, W. J. 1967. *Educational objectives*. UCLA; VIMCET Tape and Filmstrip #1. Los Angeles, Calif.: Vimcet Associates.

Pronovost, W., Bates, J., Clasby, E., Miller, N. E., Miller, N. J., and Thompson, R. 1976. Hearing impaired children with associated disabilities: A team evaluation. *Exceptional Children* 42:439–443.

Rudman, M. K. 1976. Standardized test taking. *Learning* 4:76–82.

Sattler, J. M. 1974. *Assessment of children's intelligence*. Philadelphia: Saunders.

Schulz, J. P. 1972. "Simulated Work Laboratory." Unpublished program of instruction, Columbus, Ga.

Smith, R. M., and Neisworth, J. T. 1945. *The exceptional child: A functional approach*. New York: McGraw-Hill.

Voight, R. C. 1971. *Invitation to learning*. Washington, D.C.: Acropolis.

Volkmor, C. B., Langstaff, A. L., and Higgins, M. 1974. *Structuring the classroom for success*. Columbus, Ohio: Merrill.

Weiner, B. B. 1967. Assessment: Beyond psychometry. *Exceptional Children* 33:367–370.

Chapter Five

Teaching Language Arts:
Listening, Speaking, Writing

Photograph by Dorris D. Beck

The language arts, or communication skills, comprise a larger part of the school curriculum than any other subject area. While other subjects may be taught in isolation, the language arts are part of all areas and are used throughout the day. The receiving skills are listening and reading; the sharing skills are speech and writing.

For most human beings, the acquisition of language arts follows a hierarchy of development: listening, speaking, reading, and writing. Spelling and handwriting may be considered part of writing (Lerner 1971).

Each of these skills is related to the others, since the mental processes involved are similar and each has a definite function in communication. Speech has no purpose unless associated with listening; the mental processes used to understand and evaluate the ideas on a printed page are almost identical to those employed in listening to a teacher present the same ideas orally (Anderson 1964).

The tools of communication are essential to social and academic development. Not only is communication related to every area of school, it is related to every area of life. The person who is deficient in communication skills is unable to follow directions in school (or on the job); he is unable to gain information from textbooks (or from news media); he is limited in his interaction with other children (or adults).

As indicated in chapter 1, communication problems are common in most handicapping conditions. The physical and mental abnormalities causing children to be handicapped are most evident in the processes of communication. Teaching language arts, therefore, is of prime importance in program planning for handicapped children. Programs should be based on the following objectives.

Children will develop language skills permitted by their abilities.

Children will develop abilities to employ listening, speaking, reading, and writing in the solution of problems confronting them as individuals and as members of groups.

Children will improve abilities to secure personal satisfaction through competent use of language in getting and sharing ideas.

Children will develop sufficient skill in language usage to make their meaning clear to those with whom they wish to communicate.

The communication skills of listening, speaking, reading, and writing are closely interrelated. While they are used and taught simultaneously, discussion requires their separation. Listening, speaking, and writing will be presented in this chapter and reading in the following chapter.

Listening

Fritz, a curly-haired, snaggle-tooth "outdoor" boy, had trouble controlling his "indoor" behavior. After a particularly rough day, Fritz's kindergarten teacher was talking to him about her expectations of him in the classroom. After the serious talk, the teacher asked, "Now, Fritz, do you have any questions?" "Yes, teacher. Why do you wear green on your eyes?"

Not listening may be a natural defense against the reception of undesirable or useless information that constantly assaults the ear. Or not listening may be the result of limited auditory perception or training.

Lerner (1971) comments that while special concern for instruction of speaking and reading is common, children are expected to acquire the ability to listen without special instruction. She declares that "listening is the foundation of all language growth, and the child with a deficit in listening skills has a handicap in all the communication skills" (p. 160).

Investigations of listening in the elementary classroom led to the discovery that 57.5 percent of class time was spent in listening (Taylor 1973). Much of this listening is without purpose and, therefore, without efficiency. Lack of ability and inattention in children may be failure on the part of the child and the teacher to identify the purpose of the listening. The process should not be a one-way affair; children should do more talking and listening to each other instead of to the teacher (Barbe and Myers 1971).

Taylor (1973) describes the process involved in translating sound into meaning:

1. *Hearing* designates the process by which speech sounds in the form of sound waves are received and modified by the ear.

2. *Listening* refers to the process of becoming aware of sound sequences. In listening to speech, the person first identifies the component sounds and then recognizes sound sequences as known words through the avenues of auditory analysis, mental reorganization, and/or association of meaning.

3. *Auding* refers to the process by which the continuous flow of words is translated into meaning. Auding involves one or more avenues of thought—indexing, making comparisons, noting sequence, forming sensory impressions, and appreciating.

Factors involved in the total process are hearing, attention, auditory discrimination, mental reorganization, association of meaning, sensory impressions, and thinking skills. It is obvious that many handicapped children would have deficits in some or all of these areas.

Lerner (1971) identifies the listening skills which contribute to the process:

1. Auditory perception of nonlanguage sounds.
2. Auditory perception and discrimination of isolated single language sounds.
3. Understanding of words and concepts, and building of a listening vocabulary.
4. Understanding sentences and other linguistic elements of language.
5. Auditory memory.
6. Auding or listening comprehension:

a. Following directions.
b. Understanding a sequence of events through listening.
c. Recalling details.
d. Getting the main idea.
e. Making inferences and drawing conclusions.
f. Critical listening (p. 162).

She claims that listening is a basic skill that can be improved through training and suggests teaching strategies for each of the levels of listening.

Listening as a skill is particularly valuable for handicapped children. As suggested in several chapters of this book, use of audiovisual materials is frequently necessary for poor readers. And yet, Bliesmer (1966) claims that "bright children are superior to dull children of comparable mental ages with respect to listening comprehension" (p. 134).

Obviously, the deaf or hard-of-hearing child cannot develop speech and language through avenues of casual hearing or listening. Specific auditory training is necessary to help him develop his limited hearing into listening skills.

The visually impaired child is dependent upon listening to a greater extent than any other child. Not only is his education dependent upon it; his safety and existence depend on his ability to listen to the sounds in his environment.

Early (1971) suggests the following reasons for teaching listening:

1. The large proportion of time pupils spend in listening in school and outside.
2. The increasing influence of oral communication in adult life.
3. The need for training the ear as well as the eye, since listening and reading require different, as well as similar, skills.
4. The importance of listening as a substitute for reading, especially when the latter ability is impaired (pp. 36–37).

Assessment of Listening Skills

Listening vocabulary is much larger than reading vocabulary at all lower grade levels; only at grade eight does reading vocabulary equal listening vocabulary (Durrell 1971). Comparisons between listening comprehension and reading comprehension may be useful in program planning. *The Durrell Reading-Listening Series* (Harcourt, Brace & World) permits a comparison of these two language skills.

Brassard (1971) describes two tests of listening comprehension:

The Brown-Carlsen Listening Comprehension Test. Harcourt, Brace & World. Grades 9–13. A receptive language test designed for group use to determine ability to understand spoken English.

Sequential Tests of Educational Progress. Educational Testing Service. Grades 4–12. Tests designed to measure a student's skill in understanding, interpreting, applying, and evaluating what he listens to.

Kelly (1966) claims that "listening ability tests are not different enough from measures of general mental ability to be considered as reliable measures of 'listening' " (p. 140).

In the absence of formal instruments to test listening skills, criterion-referenced tests or checklists may be used by the teacher. The following items are examples:

_____ 1. Uses records, earphones, tape recordings, radio, and television to develop listening skills.
_____ 2. Participates in audience situations (programs, etc.)
_____ 3. Listens to poetry and stories read by teacher (Smith 1970, p. 84).

Observation and informal questioning may be the best indication of the child's listening skills. Having the child retell a story to another child will indicate to the teacher how much detail and meaning he derived from listening.

Improving Listening Skills

As there is growing awareness of the importance of listening, there is also awareness that listening skills can be taught and that listening instruction produces improvement in reading and language usage (Taylor 1973). Because learning is dependent on listening and because most students are not accomplished listeners, a developmental listening improvement program is recommended by many educators.

Chaney and Kephart (1968) feel that listening is a learned process and is learned in conjunction with experiences. Unless a child learns to listen and attend to the activities in his environment, he cannot learn maximally from that environment. The following are some of the activities suggested to help the child to listen, to retain, and to recall auditory information.

Learning to Listen
1. Several times a day, play a game of being quiet and relaxed with eyes

shut. The voice and the whole body should be quiet so that not a sound is made.

2. Once he can maintain reasonable quiet for thirty seconds or more, whisper a child's name and have him rise quietly and come to you. As the child's listening ability improves, give simple directions in the same whispered voice and move to different areas of the room.

3. To encourage the child to listen and to prevent him from shouting, make a habit of using a low, quiet tone of voice when presenting tasks or play items that the children really enjoy.

Actions Performed from Auditory Clues

1. Give simple one sentence, one action commands.
2. Increase the number of words and commands.
3. Use clues other than words for starting and stopping an activity. The activity may be a simple motor movement, a game, or a task. The task may be as simple as sitting still until a buzzer sounds.

Developing Auditory Memory

1. Have the child repeat unrelated words.
2. Have the child repeat digits and/or letters after you.
3. Increase the length of time between naming of the digits, words, or sounds as the child demonstrates his competency.
4. Read or tell a short, simple story containing two or more elements in a sequence.
   a. Ask the child to retell the story.
   b. Ask the child "What did I say first . . . last?"

As educators have become more aware of the importance of auditory training for many children, commercial programs have become available. The following programs are designed to improve auditory perception.

Developmental Learning Materials. Auditory Perception Training. Tapes and spirit masters are designed to provide sequential training for auditory memory, auditory motor, auditory figure-ground, auditory discrimination, and auditory imagery.

Mafex Associates Inc. Learn to Listen. Cassette tapes and duplicator activity sheets are designed to help children discriminate and classify sounds and their possible causes.

Auditory Training for Hard-of-Hearing Children

The hard-of-hearing child who is trained to use his residual hearing to the fullest extent develops better understanding of relationships between sounds and objects, sounds and actions, and sounds and people. Techniques in auditory training are designed not only to stimulate responses to sound but to improve the child's whole response to his environment. The training is more effective when combined with lipreading, speech preparation, and other activities. The following are the four major steps of auditory training:

1. Development of awareness of sound.
2. Development of gross discrimination.
3. Development of broad discrimination among simple speech patterns.
4. Development of finer discrimination of speech (Adler 1964).

If a child has a hearing loss, steps can be taken to improve hearing conditions in the classroom. Since noise should be kept at the lowest level possible, classrooms in noisy locations may need acoustical treatment.

The use of individual learning stations or study carrels reduces noise and may be used for students with auditory problems. Carrels may be useful for other students in reducing visual distractions and providing better illumination.

Creating a Good Listening Climate

Many improvements can be made in listening skills of all children by careful inspection of the quality of the listening climate. Taylor (1973) suggests that a reevaluation of teaching methods may lead to greater variety of listening situations, including independent activities, pupil-team learning, and greater use of audiovisual approaches.

The teacher provides a model for listening. When he listens to the children with interest, he is helping to establish an environment in which listening is valued.

Listening skills are important for all children. While many children acquire the skills incidentally, the teacher of handicapped children cannot assume that such acquisition is taking place. Development of listening skills is a prerequisite to speaking and should be programmed accordingly.

Speaking

We walked down the path to the well-house, attracted by the fragrance of the honeysuckle with which it was covered. Some one was drawing water and my teacher placed my hand under the spout. As the cool stream gushed over one hand she spelled into the other the word water, first slowly, then rapidly. I stood still, my whole attention fixed upon the motions of her fingers. Suddenly I felt a misty consciousness as of something forgotten—a thrill of returning thought; and somehow the mystery of language was revealed to me. I knew then that "w-a-t-e-r" meant the wonderful cool something that was flowing over my hand. That living word awakened my soul, gave it light, hope, joy, set it free! (Keller 1954, p. 36).

Just as the impact of language on thought is revealed by the description of a handicapped individual, much of present knowledge of language development comes through the observation of handicapped children and their language deviations (Lerner 1971).

Language acquisition is a special problem for many children. Most of the children referred to in chapter 1 have some language deficit. Therefore language must be a critical part of any educational plan for them. Each child's success in his social and academic environment depends largely on how he uses language. His ability to express language (speech) and to utilize language interpersonally (communication) must be increased through activities built into his educational program (Schiefelbusch, Ruder, and Bricker 1976).

Miller and Yoder (1972), in discussing the language behavior of mentally retarded persons, conclude that the retarded child develops language in the same order as children without intellectual deficits, but at a slower rate. Gearheart and Litton (1976) feel that this idea is a common misconception; that because of the variety of physical problems present in many retarded children, they follow different developmental patterns. Regardless of the pattern, the fact remains that there are no developmental sequences established for retarded and other handicapped persons; the content for language training must be taken from the data available on language development in normal children.

There appear to be three major components necessary for language to develop in the child: cognitive-perceptual development, linguistic experience, and nonlinguistic experience. In order to acquire the language system, the child must be capable of perceiving objects, events, and relationships in his environment; he must be exposed to the linguistic system that can be used to express those objects, events, and relationships he recognizes; he must have direct experience with those objects, events, and relationships in his environment (Bloom 1970). It is obvious that children who have cognitive, perceptual, physical, and emotional deficits cannot be expected to achieve normal language development.

Children with language problems do not display consistency in the severity of their various deficiencies. A child with a mild problem may have good comprehension of language yet produce relatively unintelligible speech. Another child may possess all the tools for becoming a competent speaker and listener but may lack the communicative skills to comprehend or to use language appropriately in a learning environment (Schiefelbusch, Ruder, and Bricker 1976). For good program planning to evolve, therefore, individual assessment is necessary. Since language assessment is based on comparisons with normal children, some idea of normal language development is desirable.

Normal Language Development

Communication, an exchange of ideas and information, can be nonverbal, through the use of facial expression or gestures, or verbal, through spoken language. *Speech* is uniquely human and is a part of a larger system of symbols that carry meaning. The system of making sounds into words which carry meaning is called *language.* The way words are said is *speech;* the way words are used is *language* (Molloy and Witt 1971).

Phonemes, the basic vowel and consonant sounds, are the raw materials of the spoken language. During the babbling period, infants produce all sounds that form the basis of language and typically speak their first word at about the end of the first year. At this time the use of single words standing for whole sentences begins; at about eighteen months of age the child's earliest "sentences" begin. These sentences are abbreviated adult sentences, consisting largely of essential nouns and verbs. The adult sentence "I see a dog" would be said as "See dog." These first sentences occur in all cultures and express a broad range of meanings. Slobin (1973) finds that everywhere language consists of utterances performing a universal set of communicative functions, expressing a universal set of underlying semantic relations, and using a universal set of formal means.

As the child's sentences become longer and more complex, he adds prepositions and articles, plurals, and possessives. Children make enormous progress in the comprehension and production of language during the preschool years and continue to make important advances throughout childhood (Mussen, Conger, and Kagan 1974). By the time he is six years old, the average child can tell what several words mean, can answer questions, responds to pictures, and has an average sentence length of six to seven words. Detailed information on acquisition of receptive and expressive language may be found by using the Developmental Scale for Language Levels (appendix D).

Because language is so distinctively human, because it is so important in social interactions, and because it plays such a prominent part in cognitive functioning, many attempts have been made to explain its acquisition.

131

Although there is lack of agreement on how language is acquired, it is generally recognized that while there are many individual differences, children follow established patterns in speech and language development.

Assessment of Language Development

Ruder and Smith (1974) establish three levels of assessment: informal assessment, formal assessment, and ongoing assessment.

Informal Assessment. Informal assessment in its simplest form is the parent's or teacher's report of the child's language capacity or their impressions of the language problem (Ruder and Smith 1974). A somewhat more structured assessment by the teacher may include the following features:

Receptive Language

1. Awareness or attention: include items that require observable responses to sound or speech (e.g., eye contact).
2. Discrimination: ability to respond differently to sound or speech sounds.
3. Understanding: speech accompanied by
   a. gestures
   b. situational clues (e.g., "Turn on water" while in bathroom)
   c. speech alone

Expressive Language

1. Imitating
2. Initiating
3. Responding

Samples may be taken of the child's interaction with persons and reactions to elicited speech, such as "Tell me about the picture." Such language samples may be useful in planning developmental programs.

Formal Assessment. The most common formal language tests assess comprehension of vocabulary. Procedures for these tests present the child with a verbal stimulus; the child is asked to point to the appropriate initial stimulus, the picture that best depicts the stimulus word (Ruder and Smith 1974). The Peabody Picture Vocabulary Test is an example of this type of assessment.

Another instrument viewed as assessing the language area is the Illinois Test of Psycholinguistic Abilities. The initial usage of the ITPA was primarily with children designated as learning disabled. As concepts of prescriptive education have grown in popularity it has been applied more broadly (Chinn, Drew, and Logan 1975). Hammill and Bartel (1975) point out a major shortcoming in the omission of subtests for linguistic abilities (syntax, phonology, or transformations). They consider the ITPA valuable when the examiner is concerned with such variables as memory or closure, or with receptive, associative, or expressive performance.

A limitation of formal assessment is that it frequently indicates whether or not the child possesses a certain structure but gives little indication of where to begin training. The assessment instrument, to be maximally beneficial, should show some relevance to the training program being used. A list of instruments may be found in Table 5–1.

Table 5–1
Instruments for Assessment of Speech and Language Skills

Test for Auditory Comprehension of Language. Elizabeth Carrow. Learning Concepts, 1973.
Designed to measure auditory comprehension of language structure and to permit assignment of the child to a developmental level of comprehension. Performance on specific items and groups of items allows the examiner to determine the areas of linguistic difficulty.

Communication Evaluation Chart from Infancy to Five Years. Ruth M. Anderson, Madeline Miles, and Patricia A. Matheny. Educators Publishing Service, Inc., 1963.
The information provided can give the examiner significant data on the child's abilities and disabilities in language performance. The chart is useful as a screening tool by suggesting language and performance areas requiring further evaluation. The chart is also useful in the early detection of childhood communication disabilities.

Goldman-Fristoe Test of Articulation. Ronald Goldman and Macalyne Fristoe. American Guidance Service, Inc., 1969.
Measures a person's articulation performance; major emphasis is placed on production of consonant sounds. The tool describes sound production in a wide variety of contexts and is easily administered.

Illinois Test of Psycholinguistic Abilities, Revised Edition. Samuel A. Kirk, James J. McCarthy, and Winifred D. Kirk. University of Illinois Press, 1972.
The ITPA is used to specify areas of difficulty in communication; it delineates specific abilities and disabilities in children so that remediation may be instituted. The psycholinguistic processes analyzed are receptive, expressive, and organizing.

Peabody Picture Vocabulary Test. Lloyd M. Dunn. American Guidance Service, Inc., 1965.

§

Table 5–1 Continued

An individual test, the PPVT consists of 150 test plates with four pictures on each plate and requires no reading. The score that is derived can be converted to mental age, percentile rank, or deviation IQ. It is easy to administer and score and requires minimal preparation by the examiner.

Utah Test of Language Development. Merlin J. Mecham, J. Lorin Jex, and J. Dean Jones. Communication Research Associates, Inc., 1967.

This test was designed as a direct-test version of the informant-interview *Verbal Language Development Scale* (Mecham 1963). The items were selected to assess the child's receptive and expressive language skills in listening, reading, speaking, and writing.

Ongoing assessment. Assessment procedures built into language development programs will probably be most useful to the teacher. Such procedures provide for placing a child in a particular phase of a training program and provide feedback concerning the relevance of a particular training sequence and the prerequisite behaviors required to enter particular stages of a program (Ruder and Smith 1974).

Once the behavioral objectives for the language development program are stated, the teacher may create his criterion-referenced test. Familiarization with developmental scales will help with the task analysis and provide an ongoing assessment instrument. An optimal assessment procedure should provide the teacher with data concerning the most effective training sequence for achieving a particular terminal goal.

Speech and Language Problems

The purpose of assessment and identification of language and speech disorders is the facilitation of program planning. In determining which children should be considered as having a communication disorder, McLean (1974) compares the child's language with the standard language form of the culture and with the language of other children at the same age level. He categorizes the most common disorders as nonverbal children, language-disordered children, and speech-impaired children. He states:

Because language is learned behavior, it can be affected by the factors which affect any learning. Factors like intellectual ability, motivation and/or good models of the behaviors to be learned can all affect language acquisition. Because language models are received in the auditory mode, the auditory sensory channel is critical to natural language learning. Because the natural language production mode is a motor behavior, disrupted or diminished motor systems can affect language acquisition. Because language is connected with the child's world and learned within relationships in that world, a child's emotional status can be a factor. Language carries the marks of whatever problems have affected the child (p. 474).

The factors that appear to be most critical in poor speech and language development are related to physical, sensory, intellectual, and environmental differences in the child.

Physical Disabilities. Children with physical disabilities, particularly those with cerebral palsy, frequently have speech and language problems (see chapter 1). Molloy and Witt (1971) state that a child's speaking mechanism is usable for speech if he is able to swallow, suck, maneuver his tongue by controlling its action and employing some speed in tongue action. Exercises for developing and strengthening the muscles involved can be prescribed and demonstrated by the speech clinician.

Sensory Deficits. *Hearing* provides contact with the environment and with other people. It is designed to permit the learning of the spoken language system and plays a major role in the development of abstract concepts and temporal sequence. The child who is hard of hearing misses much of this association of sound with experience (Lowell and Pollack 1974).

Hearing children learn the sound, shape, and sense of their language through their auditory modality; the hearing-impaired child depends on vision to learn about his language. Comparisons of the written language of the deaf and the hearing suggest that the deaf are significantly inferior in all aspects of language development and facility (Moores 1972). Adler (1974) suggests that when hearing is faulty, the development of speech is likely to be retarded or imperfect. The child learns faulty interpretations of sound or he learns to substitute other senses for the ear. Gestures tend to replace speech as a method of communication.

Because of his limited interaction with his environment, the hearing-impaired child has difficulty in the acquisition of concepts. A speech therapist described a sequence of steps necessary for a hearing-impaired child to develop the understanding of the word *mammals:*

The student was asked to use a dictionary to find meanings of words she did not know and to write a sentence with the words to demonstrate her understanding of their meaning. She found that the dictionary defined mammal as any class of animals that nourishes its young with milk. Her first sentence read "I don't want to go to mammal today." The therapist asked the student what the meaning of mammal was. The student replied that it was a class and that the sentence meant that the student didn't want to go to class today.

135

After discussing the entire meaning of the word with the student, the therapist asked her to write another sentence. The second sentence read "The puppy is mammals its mother." The definition of the word was discussed again and again and examples were given. When the student presented her third sentence, it read, "My kitten is a mammal."

The hearing-impaired child has a low vocabulary and experiences difficulty with words that have more than one meaning. Prefixes and suffixes added to words may confuse him. Word order is often improper, prepositions and articles may be omitted from sentences, and syntax is generally poor.

The *visually* impaired child experiences much of the same experiential deprivation as the hearing-impaired child and has similar problems with concepts.

A blind child was in a language arts group playing the game Password. The word to be discovered was room. *In giving a clue, the boy who was blind gave the word* box. *While he may have used models to help develop spacial concepts, he had a poor understanding of* room.

Suggestions made for the classroom teacher of the hearing-impaired child could be used as well for the visually impaired child:

The child should be given preferential seating in class, sitting close to the teacher at all times.

A classmate "buddy" should be assigned to him. The buddy should be a responsible youngster who would assure that he understands the ongoing activity at any given time, has his correct place in reading, or knows and understands an assignment.

The teacher can give assignments verbally and also write them on the board. After the assignment is given, it should be reviewed and understanding determined.

If a film is shown in class, it should be remembered that the child who wears a hearing aid will experience some distortion in picking up sound from another mechanical device (the speaker from the projector). The topic of the film should be reviewed with the hearing-impaired or the visually impaired child so he will be "set" for its content. After the film, another review and simple questioning will help insure understanding.

To help in concept development, many visual aids for the hearing-impaired child and many auditory aids for the visually impaired child should be used. Tactile experiences should be provided whenever possible.

Questions or messages should be rephrased if the child does not appear to understand them in their original form.

The child and, if necessary, his parents, should be given a preview of topics to be discussed the next day or week so he may prepare at home for coming topics. The resource teacher can assist in the coordination of this procedure.

Intellectual Deficits.   Bloom (1970) states that "the acquisition of language is a complex process that is crucially related to the child's cognitive-perceptual growth and his interaction in an environment of objects, events, and relations" (p. 1). The cognitive prerequisites for the development of grammar relate to the meanings and the forms of language; the first linguistic forms to appear in a child's speech will be those that express meanings consistent with the child's level of cognitive development (Slobin 1973). In discussing cognitive development, Miller and Yoder (1972) conclude that "children do not talk in the absense of something to talk about" (p. 9).

The mentally retarded child frequently exhibits delayed language. Data available on language development in normal children may be used to plan language training.

The child first learns aspects of language within the scope of his current cognitive development; as he develops cognitively he will gradually learn to use more complex linguistic formulations (Clark 1974). Miller and Yoder (1972) suggest that each child's target language behavior should have some functional relevance to his environment and to his personal and physical needs. They present the following procedures and constructs essential in coordinating implementation of content with teaching strategies in developing programs for language training:

Before the child becomes a language user, he has to have something to say (concepts) and a way to say it (linguistic structure).

Throughout the entire program the teacher works from comprehension to production.

New words and syntactical relationships are best established by supplying the underlying concepts through environmental manipulation and experience.

For the child who is mentally retarded, as for other children, language is acquired through interaction with the environment. Language is a part of the child's mental development and should not be isolated.

Environmental Differences.   Molloy and Witt (1971) feel that the child's environment is favorable to the development of good social language if "he has a need to talk (the parents do not anticipate his every need), if there is some stimulation in the home, and if he is neither ignored nor abused" (p. 451). The child may also have such poor models that his language may

137

be inadequate in its relationship to more standard language forms. Homes in which no one listens to another can also frustrate language learning (McLean 1974). Other factors limiting verbal communication may be lack of communication with adults in large families, the frequent absence of fathers, the necessity for mothers to work away from home, and crowded conditions which force children out of doors (McConnell, Love, and Clark 1974).

In describing the inner-city child, Lerner (1971) says, "It is estimated that a good beginning reader at age 6 has a speaking vocabulary of 2,500 to 8,000 words; whereas the inner-city child at age 6 has been judged to have a speaking vocabulary of less than 500 words, which is equivalent to that of an average 3-year-old in a more favored environment" (p. 145). She offers two solutions: help them secure a broad oral language base before introducing them to more complex language skills such as reading; and change learning media and materials—teach them to read by using the child's own language as the basis for initial readers.

This point of view has been expressed in relation to dialects (Goodman 1969), in stating that the problems stem from differences rather than from deficiencies. Persons concerned with cultural differences caution teachers to be careful what they do to the language a child brings to school, not just because of his self-image, but because his language makes it possible for him to communicate with the world. If teachers attack the child's language, they cut him off from the world. Houston (1973), for instance, finds that black children anxiously cover their flair for language to please teachers who feel that black English is inferior.

Activities for Language Development

There are strong bases for language development programs for handicapped children: The child may have no language through which a teacher can provide basic instruction; many of the activities performed in classroom groups require the communication of messages which exclude the language-deficient child; and language is a basic part of cognitive behavior and must be included in the curriculum (Schiefelbusch, Ruder, and Bricker 1976).

Language develops as the child becomes aware of his surroundings. Awareness of the environment may be developed through experiences that stimulate the senses:

Smell. Associate smells with experience: the smell of pepper, "AhChoo!," cinnamon, "Mmmm," vinegar, "Ugh!" Call the child's attention to smells in the environment, such as flowers and food.

138

Touch. Make a touch box. Children will enjoy some "feels" and not others. Include yarn, velvet, silk, flannel, rocks, sandpaper, rope, cotton, emery board, wool, wood, string.

Enjoy the sand box; mix sand with water to build objects from moistened sand. Mud is fun for most children. Clay can be formed, flattened, and pounded.

Finger paint provides exciting language and artistic experiences. Other media which can be used in the same way are shaving cream, whipped cream, and whipped soap flakes.

Sound. Play with noise makers: bells, sticks, whistles, drums, rattles, horns. Fill boxes with various objects; listen to the objects as they are shaken. Listen to familiar recorded sounds: telephone, typewriter, sneeze. Imitate animal noises. Listen to noises and select a picture appropriate to the noise. Listen to sounds outside: wind, cars, train, for example.

Vision. When giving a child an object, place it in front of him and say its name before handing it to him. Meaningful objects should be identified with an action word: "I lift the chair," "I tie the bow." Name the objects in simple pictures as the group looks at them; if possible show the children the real object as well as a picture. Provide some toys with brightly colored moving parts; provide experiences with colors using colored blocks, beads, paper, and so on.

Language is stimulated in a classroom where experiences are encouraged and promoted. Pasamanick (1976) states that this means organizing and equipping the room with materials that act as stimulants to language, drama, and thought. She suggests materials for a Language Center which will enrich the possibilities for dialogue.

A round table and perhaps one or two others to house language games. Storage shelves and a comfortable chair, rug, or mats.

A good supply of blank pages bound into books for children's original stories. Some of these might be precut into different animal and geometric shapes.

A good stock of colorful magazines—*Woman's Day, Family Circle, Ebony, Sports Illustrated.*

A picture file of interesting "trigger" pictures on various subjects chosen for the stimulation they offer to concept development and problem solving. Pictures evocative of emotional reaction are very valuable, too. Be sure to include pictures of many different peoples: black, Indian, Chinese, old, young, urban, and rural. All pictures could be trimmed, mounted on stiff bright paper, and covered with transparent Con-Tact to insure their longevity.

139

Language games such as lottos, alphabet letters of various kinds (sand-paper, felt, wood), small and large flannelboards and felt pieces. Your ditto sheets and task cards (simple ones with more drawing than words) belong here, too. So do sequence cards and other homemade language materials.

Crayons, felt markers, fat pencils, and scissors stored in attractively covered or painted cans should be placed beside stacks of paper for writing and drawing.

Small "treasures" of doll figures (such as are often found in penny-candy machines); figures of animals, people, vehicles, and furniture are often stimulants to story making. Store them in transparent containers along-side trays for manipulation.

And finally, there's the primer typewriter This is a distinct asset to letter recognition and word building. If you possibly can, get one and keep it, along with an abundant supply of paper (pp. 20–21).

Pets in the classroom offer opportunities for observation and description. Gerbils, hamsters, rabbits, guinea pigs, snakes, lizards, and fish are attractive and provocative choices.

Language may be stimulated through play activities in which children enact pretended or real-life situations. Doll houses, puppets, household centers, and "dress-up" clothing facilitate such experiences.

Many of the materials suggested can be made from inexpensive products. Puppets can be made from wooden spoons, paper plates, popsicle sticks, and paper bags (Deen and Deen 1977). In addition, there are numerous commercial products available. The following list suggests appropriate materials.

Developmental Learning Materials, 7440 Natchez Avenue, Niles, IL 60648. *Language Big Box*. Designed to promote the acquisition of basic language skills, the materials reinforce auditory and conceptual skills by building upon the student's existing language strengths. The Big Box includes 170 activity cards for lesson planning and twenty-four products to be used for language development.

Educational Design Associates, P.O. Box 915, East Lansing, MI 48823. *Caption Cards*. Designed for creative writing and language development, the cards are cartoons without captions which form the basis for learning activities. All cards have a situation and a verbal action. The idea is to design verbal interaction displayed in the picture.

Learning Concepts, 2501 N. Lamar, Austin, TX 78705. *Developmental Syntax Program*. A programmed approach to the development of syntax, this program is designed to teach the child the grammatic and morphologic structure of his language. The most common syntactic structure errors have been selected and sequenced to reflect a developmental sequence.

Love Publishing Company, 6635 East Villanova Place, Denver, CO 80222. *Language Development Pak.* Develops language skills including word formation, contractions, phonics, classification, dictionary skills, and others. Includes open-ended, multilevel spirit masters and perforated worksheets.

American Guidance Service, Publishers Building, Circle Pines, MN 55014. *Peabody Language Development Kit.* Designed to stimulate oral language development, activities are highly motivating. The kits include lesson plans, stimulus cards, hand puppets, taped stories, transistorized battery-operated intercommunication set and cards to stimulate imagination and continuity in story telling. The kits require no special training, can be used effectively in large or small groups, and are effective in promoting oral language expression.

Word Making Productions, Inc., 60 West 400 South, Salt Lake City, UT 84101. *Language Making Action Cards and Stickers.* Sets of pictures designed to make the teaching of communication skills easier and more effective, the cards in the set are action verb pictures, designs for teaching color, number, and plural concepts. Also included are pictures helpful in teaching prepositions, personal expression modifiers, polars, comparatives, and multiple attributes. Other cards are comprised of sequence pictures for verb tense and story telling.

Finally, the emotional climate of the classroom must be conducive to expression. Frostig and Maslow (1973) emphasize the value of this condition: "The most important factor in encouraging a child to talk is the provision of an environment in which each child feels comfortable. A child who is insecure and fearful will not talk" (p. 229).

For most children, language evolves naturally as they interact with their environment, family, and friends. For children who do not acquire language naturally, this interaction may have to be provided by the classroom teacher. The experiences provided will be most effective if they are related to each child's life—to his home background, to his experiences in and out of school, and to his past and future learning.

Writing

There are three expressive communication areas of written language: handwriting, spelling, and written expression. Handwriting and spelling are tools of written expression and are, therefore, prerequisites to it.

Handwriting

Handwriting is the most concrete of the language arts; it can be observed, evaluated, and used to provide a permanent record of the child's productive efforts. Although largely a motor skill, handwriting also requires visual ability.

Handwriting is not as important in the elementary school curriculum as it once was. Beautiful handwriting used to be the mark of a scholar; it is now rare. The thought communicated is considered to be far more important than the means of transmitting it. Kean and Personke (1976) declare that the only purpose in teaching handwriting is the production of letters and that "Instruction in handwriting beyond this point seems an inefficient use of valuable classroom time" (p. 239). Although handwriting is viewed as a means of expression rather than an end in itself, this does not mean that instruction in the mechanics of writing should be neglected.

Objectives.   The handicapped child, like the normal child, is expected to identify forms and to make movements producing forms. The forms include those for manuscript and cursive letters, punctuation marks, Arabic numerals, conventions for arrangement and spacing, and conventions for margins and headings (Blake 1974). The objective for handwriting is legibility. In addition to the primary purpose, Strauss and Lehtinen (1947) give two additional goals: (1) Writing is a valuable and effective means of developing visual-motor perception; (2) writing is an important tool in learning to read, partly through its stimulating and organizing effect upon the visual perception of words and partly through the additional kinesthetic factors involved.

There is an additional advantage to handwriting instruction for children who are mentally retarded. Since it is motor rather than cognitive based, it provides an area in which children with good motor skills can excel.

Assessment.   Screening criteria are not so clear in handwriting as in other areas. Classroom teachers may not agree upon the criteria because of differing emphases on the importance of speed, legibility, and form. While individual differences in handwriting style are generally accepted, the primary criterion is response to the question: Can it be read with ease?

Criteria for legibility can be established by each teacher as a base for assessment in manuscript and in cursive writing. The following checklist is an example of a form used in analyzing and evaluating handwriting:

_____ Appearance of writing
_____ Margins
_____ Slant of writing
_____ Quality of pen or pencil line
_____ Letter forms
_____ Size of writing
_____ Alignment of letters
_____ Figures
_____ Proportion

Areas needing improvement can be indicated and instructional procedures initiated. An ongoing assessment can be maintained through samples of the child's handwriting. He may be asked to write such sentences as "This is a sample of my handwriting on October 1." The difficult part of assessment is in deciding upon the minimum standard of acceptance.

Otto, McMenemy, and Smith (1973) describe handwriting scales developed by Freeman (1959), West (1957), and Ayres (1912). While the scales are used for purposes of rating the quality of writing produced by school children, fine distinctions that would be useful for instructional purposes are not provided.

Beginning Instruction. Anderson (1964) specifies three kinds of experiences that lead to writing readiness. The first group, manipulative experiences, is designed to strengthen muscles needed for writing and to gain control over tools used in writing. The second group of experiences is designed to increase the child's use of language. Children have to be able to express their ideas orally before learning to write. The third group of experiences is designed to give practice to the basic movements of writing itself.

Children with learning problems may be unable to control movements well enough to hold a pencil. Exercises may be needed for developing coordination and strengthening the muscles involved in grasping. Spring clothespins can be used for this purpose—the child squeezes the pins to open them and places them on the edge of a box. Strong tactile feedback may be needed to monitor movements. Such experience can be provided through tracing with finger paint, letters made from sandpaper, felt, velvet, or clay. Frostig and Maslow (1973) suggest that kinesthetic feedback provided from tracing soft, warm materials may be more effective for many children than tracing sandpaper letters.

Anderson (1964) suggests development of the small muscles of the hands through playing with toys, dialing the telephone, setting the table, putting puzzles together, cutting with scissors, and clay modeling. The first writing exercise should be with chalk on the board or with crayons on large pieces of paper.

Manipulative experiences are combined with experiences to increase use of language by Pasamanick (1976). In her early childhood language development resource book, she presents the idea that every activity and experience has a language component.

Practice in the basic movements of writing is begun with variations of the circle, the curved line, and vertical, horizontal, and oblique lines. Ebersole, Kephart, and Ebersole (1968) describe three generalizations that apply to the teaching of these markings: (1) Move from freedom to confinement. The child is gradually required to start and stop within boundaries; templates should be used for children having difficulty; (2) Progress from working at large areas, such as the chalkboard, to smaller areas, such as a piece of paper; (3) Make the majority of markings from left to right. This also complements prereading readiness.

Handicapped children may benefit from tracing exercises. Tracing paper or a plastic cover can be placed over the forms to be traced. While there are commercial vinyl overlays for this purpose, inexpensive page covers or even the plastic inserts found in bacon packages work just as well.

The initial pattern may consist of lines and simple geometric forms oriented in different positions in space and drawn in a constantly varying assortment of colors. The exercise is planned for the primary purpose of supplying practice in visual motor perception. The next step is to copy the pattern on a paper without the aid of tracing.

A useful variation is the use of modeling clay. Strips of clay may be used to form the patterns or letters of the alphabet. A very distractible child will often benefit from copying the forms with a stylus in modeling clay rolled out on the bottom of a shallow pan or meat tray. The modeling clay affords resistance which helps to strengthen the kinesthetic perception (Strauss and Lehtinen 1947).

The position in writing is important. The child should be seated in a comfortable chair, the table should be at a proper height, and the paper should be properly placed. For manuscript writing, the paper is not slanted; for cursive writing it should be tilted approximately 60° from the vertical to the left for right-handed children and to the right for left-handed children. A strip of tape can be placed at the top of the desk to indicate position; some children may need the paper attached to the desk with tape.

As soon as possible, writing should say something. Children should be encouraged to label pictures they have drawn. The child should know the names of the letters before writing them and realize that he has made a word when he finishes (Anderson 1964).

Manuscript Writing. Children are usually taught to print in kindergarten or first grade, with the transition to cursive writing occurring during the second or third grade. Recently educators have suggested that cursive writing not be introduced in the handwriting program. Kean and Personke (1976) state the rationale to this position: some research indicates that manuscript print can be produced as rapidly as cursive writing once the individual has practiced it; manuscript printing may be more legible than cursive writing; manuscript print has received acceptance in business and commercial contexts; and a printed signature has the same legality as one written in cursive.

While the acceptance of individuality in writing may permit the continuance of manuscript writing, many children feel the importance of learning "real writing," and many parents and teachers see it as an indication of progress. The transition should be demonstrated (see figure 5–1) and practice sessions scheduled if cursive writing is to be taught. A child should be permitted to choose his mode of writing for spelling, tests, and expressive writing.

Cursive Writing. Although children are taught to print before they learn cursive writing because the letters are easier to form and more closely resemble book print, printing is not the easiest form for some children to write. Cursive writing may be easier because of its connective lines which indicate the order, position, and grouping of letters (Bigge 1976).

The flow of cursive writing may help children to establish a smooth left-right progression and avoid reversals; it helps them to experience words as wholes. It is usually quicker, less laborious, and helps to establish spelling patterns (Frostig and Maslow 1973).

Figure 5–1
Transition from Manuscript to Cursive Writing

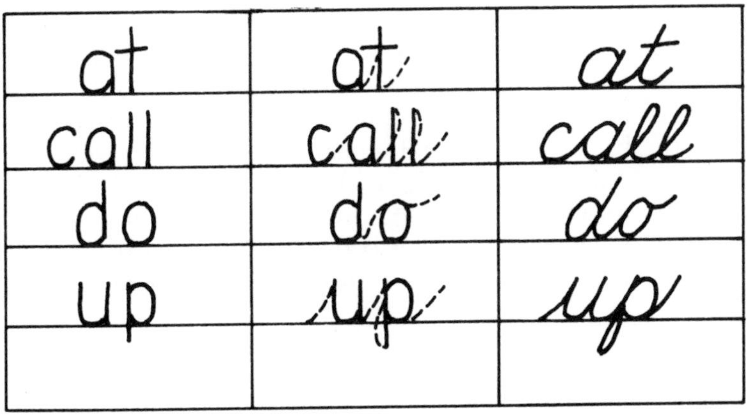

Strauss and Lehtinen (1947) advocate an early start in teaching cursive writing to children with perceptual or neurological problems. They feel that the learning of two alphabets (one for writing, one for reading) is an advantage. The knowledge that a word can be written in different letter forms may assist in making the generalization that it is the order and sound of letters which is significant; this avoids the inflexibility resulting from extended use of only one type of alphabet.

Children who are experiencing difficulty with forming the letters in cursive writing may profit from the Alpha-Line (Lectro-Stik Corporation) shaping cord and writing card. The cards are printed with cursive letters numbered to insure proper form sequence; the cord will adhere to the letters when the child follows the sequence. This inexpensive device provides individual practice and can be used without a great deal of teacher direction.

If the child is unable to indicate the line on which letters should rest, he will be helped with cues, such as outlining the major writing space with colored or heavy black crayon. The use of felt tip pens also adds color and contributes to the ease of writing.

Handwriting Problems. Handicapped children may be unable to perform the motor movements required for writing or to copy; they may be unable to transfer the input of visual information to the output of motor; and activities requiring motor and spatial judgments may be difficult for them. The shortcomings that contribute to such problems are poor motor skills, unstable and erratic temperament, faulty visual perception of letters, and difficulty in retaining visual impressions (Lerner 1971).

The child with poor motor skills may experience difficulty in holding a pencil, pen, chalk, or crayon. A commercial pencil grip or a ball of clay or sponge molded around the pencil (see figure 5–2) will prevent his fingers from slipping; if the problem is severe, pencil holders or mechanical devices may be needed. Care must be taken to equip persons with the adaptations to fit specific functional problems (Bigge 1976).

Since handwriting is a visual as well as a motor task, visually impaired children need special accommodations. Even if braille is used, the child will need some method of communicating with sighted persons in writing. With the aid of an APH signature guide (American Printing House for the Blind), he can write letters, spelling words, and his signature. The guide provides tactile lines which fit over a paper on a clip board; the guide may be made of metal or cord. A small signature guide which can be carried in the wallet is easily made from tagboard or plastic (see figure 5–3).

Figure 5–2
Pencil Grips

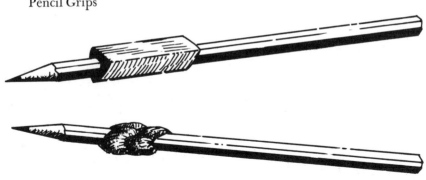

Figure 5–2
Pencil Grips

The visually impaired child will need dark lined paper and may need to continue to write with large pencils past the primary grades. He will profit from writing in sand and in clay.

For visually impaired children and for children who write slowly, typewriting may be a useful skill. An electric typewriter for the child with severe motor difficulties would facilitate written expression.

An additional problem in handwriting may be poor instruction. Hofmeister (1973) cites five common instructional errors in teaching writing: massed practice without supervision; no immediate feedback given; emphasis on rote practice rather than discrimination (perhaps the most important skill the child should acquire is the ability to compare

Figure 5–3
Signature Guide

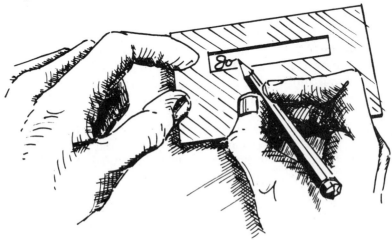

his effort with a model and determine for himself the changes necessary); failure to provide good models; no differentiation between good and poor work. Many times the consequences of trying to improve are the same as not trying.

Hofmeister (1973) presents a progressive approximation approach in which worksheets with a model at the top and space for practice lines below are used. In the steps outlined, the child completes the first line and informs the teacher; the teacher corrects by overmarking with a "high-lighter" only those letters needing improvement; the child erases incorrect portions of the letters and traces over the teacher's marking; and the student moves to the next line, repeating only the letters that were incorrect on the preceding line.

With knowledge of the developmental aspects of handwriting, regard for individual needs and differences, and skill in instructional procedures, the classroom teacher can provide activities to initiate and improve handwriting for handicapped and nonhandicapped children.

Spelling

There appears to be a conflict in discussions of the importance of spelling in the elementary school curriculum. Proponents of the linguistic approach to the language arts view spelling as relatively unimportant. "It seems clear that writing, or composition, is the linguistic process actively concerned with communication; spelling is little more than a copy-editing operation within this larger process" (Lefevre 1970, p. 83).

The evidence, however, indicates that poor spellers are on the increase at elementary, secondary, and college levels. There are, in fact, programs at the college level which start out with the same words introduced at the elementary level (Rivers 1974).

Another conflict occurs in approaches to diagnosing spelling problems. Otto, McMenemy, and Smith (1973) declare that "Severe, deep-seated problems that result in poor spelling will almost always result in generally poor performance in the related skills of reading, listening, handwriting, and oral and written expression" (p. 267). Burling (1976), on the other hand, denies the association of spelling and reading:

I suspect that the missunderstandings that good spellers so ofen have about their less fortunate brethrin stem from a failure to grasp the profound difference between converting letters to sounds on the one hand, and converting sounds to letters on the other. To a hoapless speller like me, the difference betwene these tasks can never, for a moment, be in dout. It is a difference that was allreddy completely clear to me in the first graid, because reading—going from letters to sounds—never caused me special difficulty, while righting—gowing from sounds to letters—caused me endless agoney (pp. 76–77).

Spelling is necessary for daily written communication. Although there is a paucity of recent research dealing with methods for teaching it, spelling does occupy a large portion of school instructional time. The inability to spell carries with it a social stigma and complicates efforts at written communication.

Lerner (1971) demonstrates the many subskills and abilities demanded in the spelling process. The child must be able to read the word; he must be knowledgeable and skillful in certain relationships of phonics and structural analysis; he must be able to apply the appropriate phonic generalizations; he must be able to visualize the appearance of the word and have the motor facility to write it.

Since handicapped children may have problems in visual and auditory discrimination, in making generalizations and with motor skills, spelling success may be difficult to acquire. And yet, there are many instances in which handicapped children have succeeded in this area.

Larry, Libby, James, and David comprise a spelling group that comes to the resource room daily from the sixth grade. The resource teacher and the classroom teacher have worked out a weekly list of ten words, taken from the sixth-grade spelling book, for this group to learn. After several months, this group became the best spellers in their class, sometimes even scoring well on the twenty words given to the whole class. Larry and Libby are mentally retarded, James is learning disabled, and David is blind.

The resource teacher used a combination of discovery and drill. One of the most effective drill methods was to have one of the students dictate the words to David, who brailled them on cards. He could then drill the others orally, since they could not read his cards.

Objectives.   While many spelling programs focus on graded lists of words to be mastered, one series presents as its primary purpose the development of *spelling power* (Kottmeyer and Claus 1972). This concept refers to the ability to spell unfamiliar words by applying previously learned generalizations.

Another objective of spelling programs is to spell commonly used words. Spelling lists compiled by various researchers indicate that approximately three thousand words account for about 98 percent of the words people use in normal writing (Kean and Personke 1976).

A third objective in spelling is the ability to spell words related to one's environment or occupation. This approach has been used frequently

149

with mentally retarded children, who have been taught service words dealing with safety, social necessities (such as "men" and "women" on rest room doors), and occupational requirements.

Spelling, like other areas of learning, is individual. Therefore, the objectives for programming must be based on each child's abilities and needs. Each child should be aware of the relationship of the spelling program to other areas of the curriculum. Clanfield and Hannan (1961) suggest development of the following concepts:

The purpose for learning to spell correctly is to be able to say something in writing in a way that other people can read.

Pronouncing words correctly in speaking and oral reading contributes to correct spelling.

Carefully observing words in reading enables pupils to spell many words without further study.

Phonics learned during the reading period will be helpful in spelling many words.

Learning about roots, suffixes, prefixes, homonyms, antonyms, contractions, syllabication, and so on, in reading and language classes are aids to spelling.

One of the important reasons for learning to use the dictionary is to be able to increase one's spelling power.

There is a group of important words that is used over and over in writing and should be mastered as quickly as possible.

Handwriting plays an important part in spelling because letters must be formed correctly for readers to be able to interpret the writing.

Assessment. Standardized survey tests assist the teacher in screening his classes for children who need help with spelling. Such tests as the *Iowa Tests of Basic Skills* (Houghton Mifflin Co., 1 Beacon Street, Boston, MA 02107), the *Metropolitan Achievement Tests* (Harcourt Brace Jovanovich, 757 Third Avenue, New York, NY 10017), and the *Stanford Achievement Tests* (Harcourt Brace Jovanovich) have age and grade norms and are based on word counts and lists of general utility. Informal testing can be done by administering reading vocabularies from basal readers to the entire class; the words missed can form the basis for the beginning spelling program.

Observation of students' written work offers the best assessment tool for the teacher, for being able to spell in context is the utlimate goal of the spelling program. Since the purpose of assessment is remediation, the spelling teacher should note the nature of the child's spelling errors, attempt to perceive the pattern presented, and plan a program to help him overcome the errors. Otto, McMenemy, and Smith (1973) have developed a schemata to demonstrate the process (see table 5–2).

Table 5–2
Selecting Remedial Procedures

Spelling Errors	Probable Cause	Remedial Procedure
"bad" for "bat" "cown" for "clown"	poor auditory discrimination	Give practice in hearing likenesses and differences in words that are similar. Have the student look at a word as it is pronounced to hear all the sounds and see the letters that represent them. Play rhyming games.
"enuff" for "enough" "clim" for "climb" "krak" for "crack"	poor visual imagery	Expose words that are not entirely phonetic for short periods of time and have the child reproduce them in writing from memory. Have child trace words with his finger and write them from memory.
"comeing" for "coming" "happyly" for "happily" "flys" for "flies" "payed" for "paid"	pupil has not learned rules for formation of derivatives	Stress visual imagery. Teach generalizations of forming tenses and adding suffixes.
"form" for "from" "abel" for "able" "aminal" for "animal" "mazagine" for "magazine"	poor attention to letter sequence in certain words	Have pupil pronounce words carefully. Stress sequence of sounds and letters.
"there" for "their" "peception" for "perception" "sasifactry" for "satisfactory"	carelessness	Discuss the importance of good spelling for social and vocational purposes. Encourage careful proofreading of all writing.
"hires" for "horses" "bothry" for "brother" "meciline" for "medicine"	lack of phonics ability	Use a multisensory approach whereby the student sees the word, says the word, spells the word orally, and copies the word.

Reprinted from W. Otto, R. A. McMenemy, and R. J. Smith, *Corrective and remedial teaching*, pp. 273–274. Copyright © 1973 by Houghton Mifflin Company. Used by permission.

Study Plans. Boyd and Talbert (1971) suggest the *test-study-test* plan as an effective method for teaching spelling. In this plan, the child is tested on the words assigned and studies the words he misspells. It consists of the following features: a preliminary test to determine the general level of spelling achievement; a test on each week's assignment before instruction is begun on that assignment; words that each pupil misspells become his study list; each child uses a series of steps in learning to spell each word; one or more tests are given to determine the degree of mastery of the words. Spelling exercises and activities are used throughout the week. Each child keeps a progress chart and words missed on the final test of the week are added to the following week's list.

The *study-test* plan is organized in much the same way, except that the pretest is omitted and all the words in the lesson become the study list for each pupil. Various activities such as defining the words, writing sentences with the words, working crossword puzzles, and playing spelling games are usually assigned to the students.

Kean and Personke (1976) advocate the use of the *corrected test,* a procedure in which each child corrects his own test. With this approach, children are tested on the words of a lesson either before the words have been introduced or any time thereafter. The child corrects his own test, either independently or in a group. The child receives immediate, positive feedback and corrects his errors immediately.

A *discovery* approach to spelling allows children to discover and apply spelling generalizations rather than memorizing individual words. Usually the teacher decides upon a generalization to be taught and guides the children to discover the generalizations for themselves (Kean and Personke 1976). On an independent level, the lesson might be presented to a student in the following way:

future	manage	captain
mixture	average	fountain
adventure	message	curtain

How is each group of words alike?
Form a rule about the spelling of each group.

The *cover and write* method has been advocated for slow learners and mentally retarded children because of the overlearning feature. The following steps are included

1. Look at the word; say it.
2. Write the word two times while looking at it.
3. Cover the word and write it one time.
4. Check your spelling by looking at the word.
5. Write the word two times while looking at it.

6. Cover the word and write it one time.
7. Check the word.
8. Write the word three times while looking at it.
9. Cover the word and write it one time.
10. Check the spelling.

This approach is useful in making an initial breakthrough with poor spellers, which is motivating in itself. However, it becomes dull if used too often.

A procedure that supports the importance of active teacher involvement during spelling instruction is presented by Stowitschek and Jobes (1977). Instruction is provided through a process of imitation training in which teachers model spelling words, orally and in writing, for students to imitate. This direct, tutorial approach has been successful where previous spelling instruction has failed and would be useful if volunteer help or paraprofessionals were available.

Other programs are outlined in teachers' editions of spelling series and in other sources. The plans described are adaptable to the classroom that includes handicapped children. The words can be chosen to fit each person's needs and the plan carried out with the help of a resource teacher or with peers. Learning Activity Packets (see chapter 4) are useful in providing practice and motivating activities, which can be done on an individual basis.

Activities. For children who need a multisensory approach to spelling, the *Language Master* is an effective tool. An audiovisual instructional system (Bell and Howell, 7100 McCormick Road, Westchester, IL 60645), the Language Master provides visual, auditory, and some kinesthetic experiences for the child. There are programmed cards available as well as blank cards which can be programmed by the teacher. The blank cards may be reused if the top portion is laminated so the spelling words may be erased and changed. The blank cards also permit the teacher to add clues such as pictures or tactile stimulation (e.g., letters in yarn or sandpaper).

The *typewriter* can offer many advantages in the language arts program. The following benefits have been found:

1. Primary children quickly learn the uppercase and lowercase forms of the alphabet letters.
2. Punctuation marks are easily mastered.
3. The left to right and top to bottom movements of the typewriter carriage help in reading readiness activities.

153

4. Students have greater success with spelling, perhaps because of the clear image presented by the typed word and the combined use of sight, sound and touch.

5. Handwriting and neatness problems are minimized.

6. The performance of children with perceptual problems improves, perhaps because the visual and tactile senses work together.

7. Self-confidence increases.

8. Concentration improves.

9. Students' thinking and creative abilities seem to improve (Ray 1977, p. 45).

Exploring words and patterns improves spelling and is highly motivating. Anagrams are puzzles in which one letter is changed at a time until the top word is changed into the bottom word.

N O N E	Not one
— — — —	Dial __ __ __ __
— — — —	Weights of 2,000 pounds
— — — —	Sits in the sun
T A P S	Hits gently

(News for You, 1975)

Concrete poetry is another example of the exploration of words and patterns. Either with a typewriter or a pen or pencil, students arrange the word in as many different patterns as they can.

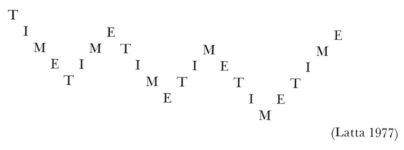

(Latta 1977)

Additional activities for promoting spelling can be found in teachers' magazines, in children's weekly newspapers, and in children's magazines. While there are a number of commercial games available for this purpose, some of the most successful ones have been created by children and teachers (see appendix E).

It must be remembered that spelling is a tool for communication.

It should be integrated with writing instruction and activities at all levels of instruction. The best motivating activity in spelling is for the child to need to use particular words.

Written Expression

Expressive writing may be viewed as either functional or creative. Functional writing refers to letters, reports, and other means of relaying information in a structured form. Creative writing permits the author to express, through poetry or prose, his thoughts, experiences, and observations in his own unique fashion.

Many people feel that writing has been neglected in today's schools. Albert (1977) attributes much of the problem to teachers who place "an uncontrollable, abnormal dependence on blank-filling and labeling exercises which eat away at vital time for learning to write" (p. 43).

This criticism may be particularly applicable to teachers who have worked with handicapped children. In the effort to provide control, models, and structure for children with learning problems, teachers may not have emphasized creative endeavors. Thus many children have not acquired skills which permit them to communicate, to express themselves, and to learn to think.

Functional Writing. Letter writing is a valued social, as well as business, skill. As with handwriting, this is an area in which many children (including those who have not been successful academically) can excel.

Robert, who is mentally retarded, has been writing thank-you notes since he was quite young. At first, he told his mother what he wanted to say; she wrote it and Robert copied it. As he acquired a small sight vocabulary, his mother put the words he used most frequently on small cards. With her help, he could form sentences from the cards and copy them into letter form. Last year, following his high school graduation, Robert wrote all his notes to thank friends and relatives for graduation gifts.

Classroom teachers can encourage letter writing in many ways. Noar (1972) suggests the use of individual mailboxes. These can be made from milk cartons, with the top cut off and a sign with the owner's name on it. The teacher can put into the mailboxes welcome back notes for absentees and notes to go home. Children can put in birthday cards, friendly notes to classmates, and notes to the teacher and to parents.

If the teacher wishes to plan a program in letter writing, a visit to the post office could be a starting point. The post office has a writing kit which may be requested for classroom use. One teacher (Brokamp 1976) has a post office in her classroom. She writes to two or three students each evening and places the letters in the class post office. The students answer the letter with one of their own and drop it in the box the next day.

The forms of writing should be introduced as vehicles for conveying information rather than rigid models or patterns to be imitated. Since writing is, for everyone, a very personal and individual production, the handicapped child is not at a disadvantage. Leeson (1977) describes a project in which eighth-grade students assisted third-grade students in the revision, composition, and evaluation of their writing projects. Both groups improved their use of grammar and spelling, learned to proofread and read aloud clearly, and developed admiration for each other's accomplishments. A similar plan could improve the writing skills of handicapped children and their nonhandicapped peers.

Creative Writing. Writing is a threat to many people. For children who view reading, spelling, and school as areas in which they have failed, writing may appear to be impossible. Yet it may be the vehicle for expression and growth vital to their intellectual and emotional development.

A program in creative writing for children with learning disabilities (Cady 1975) demonstrated the value of writing and contributed some excellent techniques in teaching it to children whose reading skills were below the level at which written expression is usually introduced. The topic was introduced to the class by the teacher's reading aloud each day. In addition to such classics as *Charlotte's Web* and *Helen Keller,* she read stories and poems which had been written by children of all ages. The children were instructed to write as if they were talking and were provided with copies of *The Spelling Reference Book* (Developmental Learning Materials, 3505 North Ashland Avenue, Chicago, IL 60657). Topics were chosen with or without students' help, and they were free to write at any suitable time, provided a story was completed or a reasonable beginning was made on a particular day. Upon completion, the children shared their stories. Their pleasure in hearing each other's stories suggested that "real communication occurred and that some of the isolation of struggling with a learning disability was diminished" (p. 29).

In the early stages of writing, it is important that children not be restricted by emphasis on the mechanics of writing. While editing is important, concern with punctuation may be inhibiting. The classroom climate should permit children to feel free to dare and to explore.

Children who have never written may feel less inhibited if they are granted privacy in their early endeavors. Kohl (1967) used this technique effectively in introducing writing to children of the ghetto. The children were encouraged to write about their lives and were assured that the teacher would see their products only if they wished. The results were moving experiences which helped the teacher understand the children and their problems.

For children who will not write, who do not have the skills to write, and who still need to express themselves, the tape recorder provides an excellent medium. The teacher may provide a list of topics or pictures from which to choose; the child may have his own topic. When left alone, many children will use the tape recorder with a great deal of creativity. One teacher placed the tape recorder on a table with a folder beside it and the following instructions written and recorded: The pictures in this folder are illustrations for stories. Select one you like and write a story to go with it. You may use the tape recorder if you wish to tell your story. I will write it down later.

A number of pictures cut from magazines were placed in the folder. As stories were written by the teacher and read to the class, the children began to read their own as well as others' stories. One student, who had never written a story, chose a picture showing an old house on a hill. This is his story:

Three ole men were standing in the street. This old preacher guy walked by and they were talking about this old haunted house up on the hill. This old man and woman lived up there years ago and was dead and nobody ever knowed what happened to them. The old preacher was talking and wanted to know who would go up there and stay all night. That old preacher was talking that he'd go up there and stay all night. He went home and got his Bible and a little lamp. And that night, after he went up there, he was sitting there, reading his Bible and he heard something upstairs rattling a chain; he said "Whoooo's up there?" It hushed and after a while he heard something rattling and he said "Whooooo's up there?" After a while he heard something coming down the stairs and he looked up and saw a ghost up there with his eyes hooked back in his head and he said, "That preacher left a new door in the side of that house!" He went down through there and he sat down on a log and that thing sat down beside him and he said, "Tight race, huh?" He said "It's gonna be a dang sight tighter the way he went!"

He tore down the door and went home and his wife told him, "I thought you were going to stay all night." He said, "NO MORE!"

By Larry

The Language Experience Approach. The communication skills of listening, speaking, reading, and writing are closely interrelated. In the language experience approach, children develop certain fundamental concepts about themselves and communication so that they will have a framework on which to hang the skills they find functional and meaningful.

1. What a child thinks about he can talk about.
2. What he can talk about can be expressed in painting, writing, or some other form.
3. Anything he writes can be read.
4. He can read what he writes and what other people write.
5. As he represents his speech sounds with symbols, he uses the same symbols (letters) over and over.
6. Each letter in the alphabet stands for one or more sounds that he makes when he talks.
7. Every word begins with a sound that he can write down.
8. Most words have an ending sound.
9. Many words have something in between.
10. Some words are used over and over in our language and some words are not used very often.
11. What he has to say and write is as important to him as what other people have written for him to read.
12. Most of the words he uses are the same ones which are used by other people who write for him to read (Lee and Allen 1963, pp. 5–8).

A university teacher was visiting in a kindergarten class. She had just observed a little boy as he completed a building with blocks. She commented on the beauty of the production and was directed by the child, "Write it!" Since the teacher obviously did not understand, the boy took her by the hand and led her to a large tablet on an easel. Under his direction, the teacher wrote about the block building which had been constructed.

At a very early age, children are aware of the importance of the written word. It is exciting to them to see their own experiences and their own words written down. The language experience approach has no age limits; it is as valuable to the high school student as it is to the young child. It may be especially effective for the student who has not learned to read and to write by other methods.

Mike, a fifteen-year-old, was embarrassed because he could not read. Discovering Mike's interest in camping, his teacher brought in several camping magazines. She pasted several pictures on paper and asked Mike to tell a story about them. She wrote the stories beneath the pictures and

Mike could *read them: they contained words in his own vocabulary and were based on his interest.*

Language experience stories may be written by the whole class or by one person. A class experience may be interpreted in many different ways by participants in it. The important factor is the experience. While many children have a background of experiences to draw from, some will have to be provided with experiences in school.

Me and my daddy are going coon hunting tonight. When I started to go my dog had pups.
Tommy

We went on the nature trail. We heard crows. We seen dogs. I found a acorn. I found some tree limbs. Jake climbed a tree. We saw trees turning colors. Marty and Lewis and Tommy saw doves. We heard a jeep.
Edward

We saw gerbils having babies. The babies didn't have no hair yet. We seen that other gerbil running around that wheel. The father was happy. The gerbils was pretty. I seen the daddy gerbil washing his face. The gerbils had brown fur and black eyes.
Lewis

We drawed a big funny nose. We drawed the eyes. We drawed the mouth. The teacher cut the pumpkin. We ate some pumpkin. We pulled out guts. We put the candle in it. We lit it up. We sat down and watched it burn. We saved the seeds. We might plant them. We might eat them.
Sue

More than a method of learning to read, the language experience approach illustrates the interrelatedness of all the language arts. Based on the prerequisite skill of oral language expression, it adds skills of spelling, writing, and reading to create a total communication process. As a method of teaching reading, it is only a beginning, since a child's own experiences limit his vocabulary acquisition and his ability to decipher new words. As a bridge from speaking to reading, it is an excellent tool.

References and Selected Readings

Adler, S. 1964. *The non-verbal child.* Springfield, Ill.: Thomas.
Albert, B. 1977. Are you giving writing its due? *Instructor* (October):41–48.
Anderson, P. S. 1964. *Language skills in elementary education.* New York: Macmillan.

Ayres, L. P. 1912. *A scale for measuring the quality of handwriting in school children.* New York: Russell Sage Foundation.

Barbe, W. B., and Myers, R. M. 1971. Developing listening ability in children. In Sam Duker, ed., *Teaching listening in the elementary school: Readings.* Metuchen, N.J.: Scarecrow Press.

Bigge, J. L. 1976. *Teaching individuals with physical and multiple disabilities.* Columbus, Ohio: Merrill.

Blake, K. A. 1974. *Teaching the retarded.* Englewood Cliffs, N.J.: Prentice-Hall.

Bliesmer, E. P. 1966. Mental age and listening. In Sam Duker, ed., *Listening: Readings.* New York: Scarecrow Press.

Bloom, L. 1970. Language development: Form and function in emerging grammars. *Research Monograph No. 59.* Cambridge, Mass.: M.I.T. Press.

Boyd, G. A., and Talbert, E. G. 1971. *Spelling in the elementary school.* Columbus, Ohio: Merrill.

Brassard, M. B. 1971. Present tests of listening comprehension. In Sam Duker, ed., *Teaching listening in the elementary school: Readings.* Metuchen, N.J.: Scarecrow Press.

Brokamp, M. 1976. Good morning, Mr. Mailman. *The Elementary Teacher's Ideas and Materials Workshop* (November):8.

Burling, R. 1976. Poor spellers of the world, unite! *Learning* (March):76–78.

Cady, J. L. 1976. Pretend you are . . . an author. *Teaching Exceptional Children* (Fall):26–31.

Chaney, C. M. and Kephart, N. C. 1968. *Motoric aids to perceptual training.* Columbus, Ohio: Merrill.

Chinn, P. C., Drew, C. J., and Logan, D. R. 1975. *Mental retardation.* St. Louis: Mosby.

Clanfield, M., and Hannan, C. 1961. *Teach spelling by all means.* Palo Alto, Calif.: Fearon.

Clark, E. V. 1974. Some aspects of the conceptual basis for first language acquisition. In R. L. Schiefelbusch and L. L. Lloyd, eds., *Language perspectives—Acquisition, retardation, and intervention.* Balitmore: University Park Press.

Deen, B., and Deen, F. 1977. Oral language development. *The Elementary Teacher's Ideas and Materials Workshop* (March).

Durrell, D. D. 1971. Listening comprehension versus reading comprehension. In Sam Duker, ed., *Teaching listening in the elementary school: Readings.* Metuchen, N.J: Scarecrow Press.

Early, M. J. 1971. Developing effective listening skills. In S. Duker, ed., *Teaching listening in the elementary school: Readings.* Metuchen, N.J.: The Scarecrow Press.

Ebersole, M., Kephart, N. C., and Ebersole, J. B. 1968. *Steps to achievement for the slow learner.* Columbus, Ohio: Merrill.

160

Freeman, F. N. 1959. A new handwriting scale. *Elementary School Journal* 59:218–221.

Frostig, M., and Maslow, P. 1973. *Learning problems in the classroom.* New York: Grune & Stratton.

Gearheart, B. R., and Litton, F. W. 1975. *The trainable retarded.* St. Louis: Mosby.

Goodman, K. J. 1969. Let's dump the uptight model in English. *Elementary School Journal* (October):1–13.

Hammill, D. D., and Bartel, N. R. 1975. *Teaching children with learning and behavior problems.* Boston: Allyn and Bacon.

Hofmeister, A. M. 1973. Let's get it write. *Teaching Exceptional Children* (Fall): 30–33.

Houston, S. H. Black English. 1973. *Psychology Today* (March):45–48.

Kean, J. M., and Personke, C. 1976. *The language arts.* New York: St. Martin's Press.

Keller, H. 1954. *The story of my life.* Garden City, N.Y.: Doubleday.

Kelly, C. M. 1966. Listening test results and actual day-to-day listening performance. In Sam Duker, ed., *Listening: Readings.* New York: Scarecrow Press.

Kohl, H. 1967. *36 children.* New York: New American Library.

Kottmeyer, W., and Claus, A. 1972. *Basic goals in spelling.* New York: McGraw-Hill, Webster.

Latta, R. 1977. Creative spelling activities. *The Elementary Teacher's Ideas and Materials Workshop* (May):3.

Lee, D. M., and Allen, R. V. 1963. *Learning to read through experience.* New York: Appleton-Century-Crofts.

Leeson, J. 1977. Story partners. *Teacher* (May/June):68–69.

Lefevre, C. A. 1970. *Linguistics, English, and the language arts.* Boston: Allyn and Bacon.

Lerner, J. W. 1971. *Children with learning disabilities.* Boston: Houghton Mifflin.

Lowell, E. L., and Pollack, D. B. 1974. Remedial practices with the hearing impaired. In Stanley Dickson, ed., *Communication disorders.* Glenview, Ill.: Scott, Foresman.

McConnell, F., Love, R. J., and Clark, B. S. 1974. Language remediation in children. In Stanley Dickson, ed., *Communication disorders.* Glenview, Ill.: Scott, Foresman.

McLean, J. 1974. Language development and communication disorders. In N. G. Haring, ed., *Behavior of exceptional children.* Columbus, Ohio: Merrill.

Miller, J. F., and Yoder, D. E. 1972. On developing the content for a language teaching program. *Mental Retardation* 10 (2):9–11.

161

Molloy, J. S., and Witt, B. T. 1971. Development of communication skills in re-tarded children. In J. H. Rothstein, ed., *Mental retardation*. New York: Holt, Rinehart & Winston.

Moores, D. 1972. Language disabilities of hearing-impaired children. In J. V. Irwin and Michael Marge, eds., *Principles of childhood language disabilities*. Englewood Cliffs, N.J: Prentice-Hall.

Mussen, P. H., Conger, J. J., and Kagan, J. 1974. *Child development and personality*, 4th ed. New York: Harper & Row.

Nation, J. E., and Aram, D. M. 1977. *Diagnosis of speech and language disorders*. St. Louis: Mosby.

News for you. *New Readers Press*, August 13, 1975.

Noar, G. 1972. *Individualized instruction: Every child a winner*. New York: Wiley.

Otto, W., McMenemy, R. A., and Smith, R. J. 1973. *Corrective and remedial teaching*. Boston: Houghton Mifflin.

Pasamanick, J. 1976. *Talkabout*. Little Neck, N.Y.: Center for Media Development.

Ray, M. L. 1977. Type and learn. *Teacher* (March):45–47.

Rivers, C. 1974. Spelling: Its tyme to du somthing. *Learning* (November): 72–78.

Ruder, K. F., and Smith, M. D. 1974. Issues in language training. In R. L. Schiefelbusch and L. L. Lloyd, eds., *Language perspectives—Acquisition, retardation, and intervention*. Baltimore: University Park Press.

Schiefelbusch, R. L., Ruder, K. F., and Bricker, W. A. 1976. Training strategies for language-deficient children: An overview. In N. G. Haring and R. L. Schiefelbusch, eds., *Teaching special children*. New York: McGraw-Hill.

Slobin, D. I. 1973. Cognitive prerequisites for the development of grammar. In C. A. Ferguson and D. I. Slobin, eds., *Studies of child language development*. New York: Holt, Rinehart & Winston.

Stowitschek, C. E., and Jobes, N. K. 1977. Getting the bugs out of spelling. *Teaching Exceptional Children* (Spring):74–76.

Strauss, A. A., and Lehtinen, L. E. 1947. *Psychopathology and education of the brain-injured child*. New York: Grune & Stratton.

Taylor, S. E. 1973. *Listening*. Washington, D.C.: National Education Association of the United States.

Thursby, D. D. 1977. Everyone's a star. *Teaching Exceptional Children* (Spring):77–78.

West, P. V. 1957. *Manual for the American handwriting scale*. New York: A. N. Palmer.

Chapter Six

*Teaching Language Arts:
Reading*

Photograph by Dorris D. Beck

While learning difficulties in one skill area are usually associated with and interrelated to those in other areas, reading problems are frequently the first indication that a potential disability exists. Reading is considered the most basic of the basic skills; teachers, parents, and students are more concerned with failure in reading than in any other area. Going to school is equated with learning to read. Such emphasis is justified when it is understood that success in all academic areas is dependent upon success in reading.

163

Assessment

There is national interest in and emphasis on accountability and assessment at all levels of instruction. The thrust is particularly strong in the area of reading, since attention has been called to the number of nonreaders" in the schools and even graduating from the high schools. Reading programs funded by the Office of Education require evaluation of such programs in terms of students' achievement.

The accountability emphasis in most school districts includes three basic requisites in order of priority: first, a statement of objective outcomes for reading instruction; second, specification of learning conditions leading to the outcomes; and third, selection of measurement instruments to evaluate the degree to which the objectives have been achieved (Ruddell 1974). Because of the pressure resulting from accountability requirements, this priority may be altered, with the objectives of measurement instruments determining the objectives of instruction.

Venezky (1974) stresses the idea that "assessment, whether done by formal testing or informal observation, is an integral component of any instructional program and is legitimatized by the need to make decisions at various points during the program's use" (p. 24). The decisions to be made are based on evaluation of programs, materials, and children.

Much recent development of the evaluation concept has resulted from decision-making requirements of the Elementary and Secondary Education Act (ESEA). The initial development focused on evaluation as a tool for administrators. While such evaluation is necessary and appropriate, it should be remembered that evaluation within the classroom permits the most important decisions concerning instruction for individual children (Farr and Brown 1971). In planning reading instruction for handicapped children, group testing has little value.

Standardized Reading Tests

During a schoolwide testing program, Tommy was observed by a monitor, who noticed that his test booklet was closed. The monitor pointed out to him that his booklet should be in use. Tommy replied, "Oh, I don't need it; I was the first one through." Tommy, who does not read, scored a reading grade level of 3.5.

Myers (1976) claims that an alliance of the U.S. Office of Education and the publishers of standardized tests dominates reading programs in most American schools. Standardized reading survey tests, most of which have been produced as part of achievement batteries (such as Stanford, Metropolitan, and California), were not constructed as instruments intended to indicate with maximum accuracy the reading level achieved by particular students (Durost 1971).

While standardized group reading tests may be ineffective, the teacher may use various sections of standardized individual diagnostic reading tests for prescriptive purposes. Such tests as *Diagnostic Reading Scale* (California Testing Bureau, McGraw-Hill Division, 100 Colony Square, Suite 1801, Atlanta, GA 30361), *Durrell Analysis of Reading Difficulty* (Harcourt Brace Jovanovich, 757 Third Avenue, New York, NY 10017), and *Gates-McKillop Reading Diagnostic Tests* (Teacher's College Press, 1234 Amsterdam Avenue, New York, NY 10027) offer more information than group standardized reading tests. However, several limitations are of particular importance; they give grade levels that are of little diagnostic value to the teacher because of the lack of correlation of levels between tests and reading materials; they are time-consuming; they require considerable practice and study by the teacher; and they do not provide diagnostic information that is necessary in developing a program for the child (Gillespie and Johnson 1974).

Individual diagnostic reading tests may yield valuable information when used to measure word recognition, sentence reading, and comprehension. Test makers themselves disclaim much precision when their instruments are applied to one specific youngster. Certainly children should not be assigned to books according to standardized test results, since the achievement test score typically represents the child's frustration level (Hardin and Carroll 1976).

Criterion-Referenced Tests

Standardized tests do not reveal what a child can do relative to a predetermined criterion or mastery level; yet it is this concern which is the basis of most instructional decisions that teachers make. Writers of test items for criterion-referenced tests begin with a definition of desired behaviors, from which test items are derived. Because they are based on well-defined instructional goals, they are more compatible with instructional alternatives than norm-referenced tests (Venezky 1974).

The proponents of criterion-referenced testing in reading consider it useful in evaluating the effectiveness of a teacher's instruction and in making decisions concerning appropriate instructional programs for students. Prescott (1971) states the assumptions underlying the criterion-referenced approach: (1) Mastery is a reasonable criterion; (2) Each item in a list has inherent worth; (3) A definite hierarchy of skills and knowledge exists in any skill or content area.

Criterion-referenced testing does not escape the need for a base of reference. The decision to place a task at a certain chronological or mental age level implies that a certain response is expected from the child. There is also a general lack of agreement as to what steps are necessary to insure reading success, which makes the establishment of a hierarchy of skills difficult.

Because criterion-referenced tests are specific, careful analysis of tasks to be learned is needed. Reading skill objectives are identified in children's reading texts, reading curriculum guides, and skills lists, such as *Basic Reading Skills List* (Barbe 1960). An example of a criterion-referenced reading test may be found in table 3–2.

Through criterion-referenced testing, efforts are being made to explore the segments of the reading task and to systematize the learning skills. One recent development is the use of management systems for the assessment of reading skills. Described in detail by Schmidt (1976), a management system analyzes a student's reading proficiency at different developmental points. It provides the teacher with prescribed instructional objectives to use in assessing students' strengths and weaknesses in reading skills and in planning supportive instructional activities. From a selection of appropriate skills, a list is ordered and posted on a reading skills progress chart. As children successfully pass competency tests for each skill, they paste markers under their names. In addition to encouraging the children to achieve mastery in many skills, the chart helps them manage their own learning activities. This system would help to integrate the handicapped reader into the regular classroom, since it provides for a wide range of abilities. It would also free the teacher to spend time with individual students, to provide immediate feedback, and to assist with problems.

One of the canons for developing program-related assessment presented by Venezky (1974) is that, "The content of assessment should be compatible with the content of instruction" (p. 9). Educators, not test designers, should decide on the content of reading instruction. Assessment procedures and assessment instruments can be designed or selected on the basis of the content. Criterion-referenced testing permits this compatibility to occur.

Determining Instructional Level

An *informal reading inventory* (IRI) is a teacher-implemented testing procedure used to determine how well individual pupils can read. Because it can be applied to any type of reading material (basal, content, magazine, newspaper), it is useful for teachers at every level.

The IRI is used to determine the appropriateness of any reading material for any child by letting him read and noting his specific word recognition and comprehension behaviors. Smith and Bentley (1975) present the following criteria for determining whether or not material is appropriate for instruction:

Independent Level	Word Recognition	Comprehension	Fluency
A level at which a student reads with obvious ease as illustrated by his reading accuracy	97% or more accuracy	80% or more accuracy	Smooth
Instruction Level			
A level where the student has some difficulties in one or more of the three areas. The difficulties supply the teacher with specific skills deficiencies.	92%–96%	60%–70%	Lacking
Frustration Level			
A level at which the student is unable to perform instructionally because of the lack of numerous skills	91% and lower	50% or lower	Poor

To build an IRI, the teacher chooses a well-graded series of readers which the child has not used. Two selections are chosen from the first part of each book, one to be used for oral reading and the other for silent reading. Selections from the preprimer through the second reader should contain from sixty to 120 words; for grades three to six, one hundred to two hundred words. The teacher then prepares three to five comprehension questions, avoiding those that can be answered yes or no. He also prepares a word list to check sight vocabulary by using every third or fourth word from the word list in the back of the reader and plans a way of checking similar to the methods used in standardized individual reading tests. Information gained from an IRI can be helpful in assigning instructional material for each child and enables the teacher to instruct the child at his own level of functioning (Gillespie and Johnson 1974).

Kohl (1973) presents an innovative and useful way of looking at reading. He has broken down the skill of reading into four different levels of competency: beginning, not bad, with ease, and complex. The skills at each level are presented as follows:

Levels		Skills
Beginning	1.	Knowing print
	2.	Known words
	3.	Words that connect and words that place
	4.	Alphabet
	5.	Sounds and combinations of sounds
	6.	Simple sentences
Not Bad	1.	Combinations of sounds
	2.	Complicated words
	3.	Complex sentences
	4.	Everyday reading
	5.	Paragraphs and stories
With Ease	1.	Unfamiliar words
	2.	Different forms of writing
	3.	Voice
	4.	Test taking
Complex	1.	Knowing about language
	2.	Special uses of words
	3.	Special languages
	4.	Critical analysis

(p. 133)

Several schools have defined these levels through printed material that seemed relevant to their students. The teachers at the schools brought in ten books, each ranging from simple to complex, and sorted the books into four piles according to some of the descriptions given in the chart. A diagnostic table was set up in the school with the four piles of books on it. The students were shown the chart and were asked to choose a book to read to a staff member of their choice. Over a period of a few weeks, each student had read several times and a level had been found. Some high school students who read on a beginning level commented that being a beginning reader felt different from being a 2.6 reader since 2.6 implied they had the intelligence of second-graders, while beginning implied nothing about their intelligence (Kohl 1973).

Assessment of the Handicapped Child

Because of requirements previously mentioned, many schools routinely administer group reading tests to all children. An annual test of this nature may provide the teacher with all the information he needs about some students. Venezky (1974) states that "the amount of assessment an individual receives within a program should be proportional to his needs within that program" (p. 13). The poorer readers, as defined relative to a given instructional program, should receive more extensive assessment than the better readers. A plan for testing reading subskills for children who vary widely in ability is suggested through a sequential assessment:

Step 1.   At the beginning of the year each student is assessed on oral reading, using a one-to-two-minute passage drawn from materials encountered after about the first month of school.

Step 2.   Children who had no difficulties in oral reading would be tested no further but would be observed informally, depending upon how much differential instruction they could be given. Students who did extremely poorly would be assessed with several finer procedures, beginning with basic word attack skills. The middle group would be assessed on oral reading again, but with easier materials.

Step 3.   If any uncertainty existed over the abilities of any of the lower group students, even finer assessment procedures would be used, starting with prereading skills assessment. By this procedure the best readers would have spent only a few minutes each in assessment, while the poorest readers may have received as much as an hour each (Venezky 1974).

Handicapped children will, in many cases, require intensive reading assessment. The resource teacher, who has a background in diagnostic testing, should work cooperatively with the classroom teacher in determining the needs of the child. Based on the needs and the instructional objectives established by the planning team, reading instruction can be implemented. In referring to the classroom, Farr and Brown (1971) declare, "It is in this setting that the potential resides for helping children become competent and interested readers, or for handicapping them in skill development and 'turning them off' from reading as a lifetime habit" p. 342).

Prerequisites to Reading

Lack of success in reading may be related to the requirements of the reading process. Edwards (1966) says:

Prerequisites common to success in beginning reading are an adequate background of experience, concepts, and general information; visual and auditory discrimination ability; oral language facility (in terms of both production and comprehension); physical and emotional intactness; reasoning ability; interests in learning to read; and, of course, a degree of native intelligence that will permit learning to take place (p. 358).

By definition, handicapped children lack many of the prerequisites considered essential to reading. Teaching them to read requires recognizing, assessing, and remediating problems related to the auditory, visual, emotional, intellectual, verbal, and physical factors.

Visual

Visual Acuity. Dechant (1970) states that "Reading is a visual process." Since the reader reacts visually to the graphic symbols, the child who is visually impaired is at a tremendous disadvantage. Provisions must be made for either an adequate alternative method for the input of information or an adequate method for the development of the child's seeing ability.

Blindness. In the case of the blind child, a very complicated skill must be acquired—learning to read by touch rather than by sight. Braille, a system of six embossed dots arranged in two vertical rows of three, is used for this purpose. These dots may be covered simultaneously by the pad of the finger tip. Grade-one braille is written with full spelling, while grade-two braille makes use of contractions and short forms.

The readability of the dots representing the letters of the alphabet is related more to the formation of the dots than the number of dots. Good readers use a uniform pressure in reading braille. While touch reading is much slower than normal reading, a good braille reader may read as many as 90 words per minute (L'Abate and Curtis 1975).

School readiness for the blind child involves the same factors as for the sighted child: chronological and mental age, emotional maturity, and background of experience. The manner in which these developmental factors are acquired may differ greatly. Lack of vision interferes with language development, opportunities for experiences, progress toward independence, and emotional stability within the family. It is important for the teacher of a blind child to realize that the countless tasks and experiences that seeing children learn and participate in through visual observation must be demonstrated or explained to blind children (Lowenfeld, Abel, and Hatlen 1969).

The formation of concepts requires the provision of numerous direct experiences. The language a child must know in order to read includes terms such as *alike* and *different* and *top* and *bottom*. Such abstract concepts must be learned by their connection with concrete experience.

Tactual discrimination is tremendously important for the blind child, since it is required for successful reading of braille. Opportunities for finer discrimination between sizes of objects, textures, and consistencies can be provided in any classroom, since every object has some unique tactual characteristic.

Lowenfeld, Abel, and Hatlen (1969) offer many suggestions providing readiness activities. They suggest the use of cards covered with various textured materials to be matched or separated; sorting games, using familiar objects such as buttons, spools, clothespins, coins, and eating utensils; and some of the Montessorial materials and commercially available toys, such as three-dimensional form-boards. Such materials assist the teacher in leading the child gradually from gross discriminations to fine tactual discriminations which require the use of small muscles and fingertips. The ultimate goal of this development is physiological readiness for reading braille.

The classroom teacher may feel that the responsibility of teaching a child to read braille is overwhelming. While braille is difficult to learn by touch, using it visually is quite simple. Sighted children are curious about it and view it as a code to be broken (see chapter 10). Teachers and children can decode braille very easily by referring to the chart.

In most cases, the classroom teacher will not be responsible for teaching braille. He is usually responsible for content in the total curriculum and is concerned with problems in the child's reading which may influence his performance in school. The resource or itinerant teacher will assume responsibility for specifics of braille reading and the location of suitable books and reference material. A special reading teacher may be paid for by the State Commission for the Blind or the Department of Social Services.

As the blind child advances in school, he will have to use other reading media. He will have to develop listening skills and learn to use sighted readers, audio texts, and reference works. He will have to consult with his teachers to plan his study through the use of braille, tape, or a sighted reader. Lowenfeld, Abel, and Hatlen (1969) suggest that the following pattern may be pursued when choices are available: select braille for the more technical work in language or science, tape for the longer assignments in social studies or literature, and use sighted readers for research references and other library research.

The two main sources of braille books are the American Printing House for the Blind, publishers of braille textbooks for children enrolled in the schools, and the Division for the Blind of the Library of Congress (see appendix A), the greatest source of books and periodicals for the blind in the United States. These books are distributed through the Regional Libraries for the Blind in various sections of the country. Other books may be purchased from braille printing houses and volunteer braille transcribers.

With an understanding teacher, the child can think of himself as a blind child who learns at his level most of the things that sighted children learn, though he must use different approaches and equipment. The teacher can understand his individual goals in much the same way as he does for each sighted child.

Low Vision. A majority of visually handicapped children, including those identified as "legally blind," are readers of print rather than braille materials. With appropriate teaching approaches, the visually handicapped student can utilize the same materials as his peers and achieve comparable levels of attainment.

For children who need materials in large type, a reference circular listing commercial and volunteer producers of large type materials is available from the Library of Congress, Division for the Blind and Physically Handicapped (*Reading Materials in Large Type* 1975). According to this reference circular, large type materials are produced by three methods: setting the material to be printed in type which is the desired size, the best method for achieving sharp, uniform letters; photographically reproducing and enlarging material already printed in ordinary type, a less expensive method, especially for a limited number of copies; typing on a large type typewriter, a method often used by volunteers to meet the individual needs of students and other partially sighted persons.

Sykes (1972) presents evidence that when visually handicapped children read under optimum reading conditions, and when corrective lenses for near vision have been prescribed for those students who need them, they perform as well in standard print as in large print on measures of reading speed and comprehension. It is suggested that teachers be more concerned with illumination and with the quality of print than with print size.

Some children with low vision require higher levels of illumination for reading, while some may require a reduction in lighting. A child who holds the printed page very close to his eye may be helped by a seat next to a window or by the use of a reading lamp. A portable reading lamp would give the visually handicapped child the power to control the lighting situation to suit his individual needs.

The quality of print is an important determinant of legibility. Teachers should do all that is possible to insure that print materials are clear, attractive, and meaningful. The use of ditto masters that will reproduce in red, green, or black is helpful, since the usual bluish-purple ink is difficult to read.

Posture in reading is important, since physical fatigue contributes to any visual fatigue the child may experience. Visual fatigue is brought about by the child expending maximum accommodation energy and reading in an uncomfortable position with the book close to his eyes.

Teachers should insure that students have received adequate correction for near vision and that those using optical aids and magnifying devices have been taught to use them properly. Frequent reevaluation is necessary as individual requirements may vary from grade level to grade level. The use of magnifiers, glare shields, or other equipment may be indicated. Another reference circular (1972) from the Library of Congress (*Aids for Handicapped Readers*) describes available reading aids.

Favorable opportunities for learning should be created through individualized instruction and the use of materials with a multisensory base so that all possible avenues of input may be explored. The primary mode of input for many low-vision children will be auditory in order to overcome the difference in reading rate between the sighted and the visually handicapped (Sykes 1972).

Visual Defects. The most common disorders that affect visual acuity are: *astigmatism,* which causes a generalized blurring of the vision and is often the result of irregular corneal curvature; *myopia,* or nearsightedness, which is a condition where sight is clear at near but blurred at far distances; and *hyperopia,* or farsightedness, where sight is clear at far but blurred at near distances. Referred to as *refractive* errors, these defects can usually be corrected by glasses, which help the eye to focus and lower eye strain but may fail to provide normal vision (Dechant 1970).

The classroom teacher should know his student's eye condition well enough to answer the following questions: Does the pupil need special reading materials? When should he wear glasses? Does he require special lighting? Can he read for prolonged periods of time (Dechant 1970)?

The teacher should be familiar with symptoms of visual difficulty (see chapter 1). Such symptoms as they relate to reading may be grouped as (1) avoidance symptoms, as in shunning reading tasks; (2) behavior symptoms, as squinting, fatigue, or excessive blinking; and (3) complaints, as dizziness, blurring, or double vision.

Teachers may learn to use various visual screening tests, such as:

Keystone Visual Survey Telebinocular. Keystone View Company, Meadville, PA 16335. Tests acuity, eye-muscle balance, and fusion in both distance vision and near vision, with additional tests of depth perception and color vision.

Reading Eye Camera. Educational Developmental Laboratories, Huntington, NY 11744. Measures the pupil's ability to use his eyes in reading.

T/O Vision Testers. Titmus Optical Company, Inc., Petersburg, VA 23803. Measures acuity (near and far), fusion, and color discrimination. Identifies persons with restricted visual fields and quickly identifies excessively farsighted children.

The Snellen Chart, formerly considered the acceptable screening test, identifies nearsightedness and measures visual acuity at a distance of twenty feet, but fails to detect astigmatism and farsightedness. Since nearsightedness frequently is associated with good rather than poor reading, the test is not too helpful in reading diagnosis (Dechant 1970).

The suggested vision tests are for screening purposes only. Any unexplained symptoms, referral indication, or doubtful results indicate that a competent professional vision examination is in order.

Visual Discrimination

Wallace and Kauffman (1973) state that "Many children who have normal visual acuity experience difficulties in differentiating, interpreting, or remembering different shapes, letters, or words" (p. 166). They suggest that children with visual skill deficiencies should learn to

1. Discriminate sizes and shapes
2. Discriminate specific letters
3. Discriminate the directionality of specific letters
4. Remember letter names and words
5. Remember particular words learned mainly by sight
6. Recognize structural parts of words (p. 166).

According to Spache (1964), visual discrimination or perception is derived from or based upon physical handling of objects. The child learns shapes and spatial relationships first with his hands and later with his eyes. During the preschool years, when vision is developing, the child learns to explore, recognize, and discriminate objects or forms by tactile and visual approaches, with gradually greater dependence upon visual clues.

Evidence of the lack of sufficient tactile and visual experience with objects, forms, and spatial relationships may be described by the teacher as (1) lacking visual discrimination or perception; (2) lacking hand-eye coordination; (3) lacking orientation to left and right; (4) inability to attend to near-point tasks; (5) lack of concentration or attention span and (6) pointing or using a marker while reading.

According to Cravioto and DeLicardie (1975), the ability to make gross discriminations among visually perceived figures, although a necessary component ability, does not constitute a sufficient refinement of perceptual skill for a task such as reading. In addition to making gross discriminations, a child must also respond to more differentiated forms if he is to learn to read.

The child's failure to respond to the spatial orientation of a visual

174

form can result in his confusing a number of letters identical in form but distinguishable by their spatial positioning. Letters such as *b, p, d,* and *g,* or *N, Z, W,* and *M,* represent equivalent shapes and depend upon the child's ability to respond to shape and to orientation in visual space.

Typical errors of visual perception made by children with learning disabilities indicate the confusion of similar letters and lack of discrimination between words in which the form is similar (*said* for *and, you* for *yes,* and *pretty* for *puddle*). The child's inability to organize letters accurately in their spatial sequence is responsible for many errors such as *stop* confused with *spot, three* with *there* and *of* with *for.* Reversals are common, such as *was* for *saw* and *no* for *on* (Strauss and Lehtinen 1947).

Reading demands such visual discriminations and perceptions as orientation to left and right, up and down, front and back; accurate binocular shifts from point to point; accurate focus and accommodation to distance; and a fine degree of parallel or coordinated action of both eyes. To read, the child must be able to note similarities and differences among words by the clues given by the shapes of their beginning and ending letters, by letters that ascend and descend above the line, and by the patterns or outlines formed by combinations of these elements of words (Spache 1964).

Formal tests such as the Bender-Gestalt Visual Motor Test and the Huelsman Word Discrimination Test will help the teacher to identify the problem of visual discrimination. Getman (1961) suggests that the observant teacher will be more clinically accurate than any test devised.

If she sees a child stumbling and reversing, losing his place or skipping lines, the chances are very great that this child does not have the ocular motilities he needs for reading comprehension. If she sees him reversing and confusing similar letters of words in his writing and spelling, the chances are very great he does not have the tactual perceptions of directionality that should underlie the visual perceptions of likes and differences that he needs for comprehension (p. 2).

Visual discrimination exercises may be found in many reading instruction books. Wallace and Kauffman (1973) offer a variety of suggestions. The following are examples of exercises which may be used in any classroom:

The child finds like objects (such as circles) that are a part of a total picture.

The child finds "hidden objects" in a picture.

The child estimates the distance between objects (spatial discrimination). Say, "Place these as far apart as those." A harder task requires the child to place two objects as far apart as the length of a desk or the width of a doorway.

The child matches silhouettes of an object to the actual picture of that object.

Use "what's-missing pictures" that require careful observation of details. For example, a picture of a child may show that he is ready to play in the snow, but has forgotten to put on one sock and shoe.

Many commercial products, such as Etch-a-Sketch and Dot Pictures, are effective developmental and remedial tools.

Auditory

Auditory Acuity

Deafness. Learning to read is one of the most important and most difficult tasks faced by pupil (and teacher) in the education of deaf children. Hart (1963) expresses the need and the problem:

The printed form represents the only medium of communication in which the deaf person meets intact language patterns in exactly the same form as anyone else. Therefore, reading would seem to be a lifeline of communication to the world of intellectual stimulation for the deaf. But the nature of the reading process is such, that despite the desire of the child to master this most attractive avenue of communication, his road is fraught with difficulty (p. 1).

Reading, or written language, is derived from spoken language. In order to understand the symbols reading represents, the child must have a background of language patterns which the symbols represent. Deaf children do not have this knowledge of auditory symbols. Dale (1967) states the situation in an interesting way.

When you read the word *korero* you probably have no idea of its meaning, i.e., the language is quite unfamiliar to you. If the word was placed in a sentence the context is not a great deal of help unless one knows most of it. For example, *Korero te wahine e te tamaiti* does not make the meaning of *korero* a great deal more clear. If one has more vocabulary, however, one might be able to read the above sentence as: The woman *korero* the boy." Now it is possible to guess that *korero* is a verb and may mean "spanked" or "kissed" or "washed" or something like that. In other words, the unknown word takes on *some* meaning. (*Korero* incidentally is the Maori to "talk" or, in this case, "talked to.") (pp. 174–175).

The deaf child is at a double disadvantage. He cannot easily convert written symbols into oral symbols, and his language grows so slowly that many of the words he is trying to identify in written form have no meaning to him in any form.

In general, a young deaf child requires experiences, and the language and concepts of such experiences, before he can learn to recognize printed symbols. The deaf child who, instead of being given language, speech, and reading drill, is encouraged to participate actively in the events and activities of school life, will in fact learn language, speech, and reading. Such skills will have more meaning to him if they grow out of his own direct experiences (Hart 1963).

Since the young deaf child has little or no place in his world for language, he experiences the world visually. Therefore in his formal reading program he may learn the concrete words which name the objects and visible things in his environment and fail to understand the intangible and abstract words. It is advisable, therefore, to delay the formal program until the child has acquired some meaning of sentence structure.

The language-experience approach to reading (described in chapter 5) is suggested by many educators for deaf and hard-of-hearing children. As the child advances in his language and reading ability, the vocabulary and the type of sentence presented to him may become more complex.

The camera has been suggested as a teaching aid to enable a deaf child with limited or no spoken language to recall experiences. Other suggestions are field trips to provide experiences, visual aids to help fill in gaps in the experiential background of the child, and the provision of a constant source of books and periodicals at all levels. A simple type of individual reading activity stressing sentence comprehension is matching sentences to pictures. Another language development activity is building stories around pictures. Most reading activities suitable for hearing children are adaptable for deaf children.

Hard of Hearing. Hard-of-hearing, as well as deaf, children should be provided with adequate alternative modes of reception (input) and expression (output) of information to compensate for their inability to hear adequately. To achieve as near a normal life as possible, the hard-of-hearing child must, to the best of his ability, be able to convey his ideas verbally. He may need auditory amplification and training to make use of his residual hearing.

Loss of hearing can aggravate reading deficiency. The auditory factor is especially important when there is a severe hearing loss, when the specific hearing loss involves high-tone deafness, or when instruction puts a premium on auditory factors. The exclusive use of the phonic method with a child who has suffered a hearing loss may prevent achievement in reading (Dechant 1970).

Early identification of children who have hearing impairment is crucial to educational growth. Any child who shows symptoms of hearing deficiencies should be screened with an audiometer.

The classroom teacher can do a great deal to develop the hearing-impaired pupil's auditory discrimination skills. He must train the child in the awareness of sound, in making gross discriminations, as between the sounds of a bell and a horn, in making discriminations among simple speech patterns, as differences between vowels, and in the finer discriminations necessary for speech.

Norwood (1976) reports that educational media are being recognized as a tremendous but relatively untapped resource for deaf and hard-of-hearing persons. The Captioned Films for the Deaf (appendix A) program is a free loan service of subtitled motion pictures similar in nature to the free loan service of Talking Books for the Blind. The Captioned Films and Telecommunications Branch of the Bureau of Education for the Handicapped is also involved in enhancing the instructional environment of deaf and hard-of-hearing people through the use of television.

The regular classroom teacher can stimulate development of reading skills of hearing-impaired children in his classroom. Vocabulary development can be facilitated by using a new word in a sentence and then asking related questions about it. Comprehension may cause difficulty for the child with limited hearing. Making comparisons and determining differences can be facilitated with questions such as "What does it look like? How are cats and dogs similar? How are they different?"

The academic stimulation of a regular classroom can create an ideal learning environment for the development of reading skills. With emphasis on comprehension and vocabulary development, the hearing-impaired child can learn to read with his hearing classmates (Bitter and Johnston 1974).

Auditory Discrimination

In referring to auditory skills in reading, Wallace and Kauffman (1973) state that "Children with auditory skill deficiencies may have normal hearing acuity. However, they experience difficulties in differentiating, synthesizing, and remembering the sounds of different letters and words" (p. 176). They claim the child must learn to discriminate among sounds, discriminate initial and final letter sounds, synthesize letter sounds into words, and remember the sounds of letters and words.

Wepman (1975) states that readiness to read can be safely assumed from the evidence to be as closely related to auditory perceptual factors as to visual. The three auditory perceptual processes—discrimination, memory span, and sequential recall—have been found to have a positive correlation to reading, writing, and spelling achievement.

Auditory discrimination is the ability to discriminate between the sounds or phonemes of a language, essential to success in reading. If a child cannot *hear* sounds correctly, he usually cannot *speak* them correctly. If he confuses sounds in speech, it may be impossible for him to associate the correct sound with the visual symbol.

According to Spache (1976) the goal of discriminating letter sounds and words is founded on many types of listening exercises. The child must first be able to discriminate pitch, loudness, duration, and rhythmic patterns or sequences of sounds, which are auditory cues to letters and words. Her suggestions for auditory memory and discrimination include the following exercises:

Children pretend they are in a cave where echoes bounce from wall to wall. The leader of the expedition makes various sounds, words, sentences. The followers repeat each one, trying to use the same inflections, pitch, and so forth, as an echo.

When children are waiting in line, the teacher says, "Raise your hand if . . ."

> your name begins like Billy.
> you're wearing something green (or other color).
> your birthday is in _____ (month).
> you got up before 7:00 this morning.

Children are given dittoed sheets marked with a large circle in which a path of squares has been drawn. Give each child a marker of some sort. The teacher claps two or three times, and children move their markers through the squares according to the number of claps they hear. Children who finish too soon or too slowly need further practice to improve these skills.

The children listen while you pronounce several unrelated words, such as *deer, candy, pencil, ring*. Students try to remember these words and supply the correct ones when you say "something sweet," "something to wear," "made of wood," "has four legs."

Tape voices and let members of the group listen to the tape and identify the voices they hear.

Record a collection of sounds on a tape recorder. After a small group listens to one sound, take time to discuss what it might be.

Several screening tests are available which enable the teacher to determine a child's ability to recognize fine differences between sounds in words. One is the Wepman Auditory Discrimination Test (1958); another is the Goldman-Fristoe-Woodcock Test for Auditory Discrimination (1970). If a weakness is indicated in this area, the teacher should use exercises to strengthen it and provide reading instruction not related to phonics until the auditory skills are developed.

Intellectual Functioning

Relationship to Reading

"Reading is essentially an intellectual activity, and a person's intelligence will play a major role in the level of reading development which he can attain" (Otto, McMenemy, and Smith 1973, p. 22).

While high scores on intelligence tests do not always indicate high reading achievement, there is a marked tendency for them to agree. The size of the relationship varies with grade level and tests used. On the Wechsler Intelligence Scale for Children (1949) there are few items requiring reading, but reading-related items such as picture completion and picture arrangement, are included. Picture completion measures the ability to visualize essential from nonessential detail and to identify familiar stimuli from school and home. Picture arrangement measures the ability to see a total situation based on visual comprehension and organization as well as environmental experiences.

On group intelligence tests, pictures are used in the primary forms; from the fourth grade up, most questions are in printed form. Thus, poor readers are at a distinct disadvantage and might indicate an intellectual level more in keeping with their reading level.

There is a substantial relationship between mental age and learning to read. However, present evidence does not justify the establishment of an absolute dividing line at any one mental age. The progress of the child depends upon the difficulty of the material used, the speed required, the specific methods used, and the amount of individualized help. However, most children who fail to learn to read in the first grade have mental ages below six years. More mature children not only learn more easily but also retain what they learn better than less mature children.

Program Development

The use of group readiness tests and group and individual IQ tests in the first grade makes it possible to locate the child whose rate of mental growth is below average. The reading program for such children can be adapted by prolonging the readiness program, extending the period of reading readiness activities, and gearing the pace of reading instruction to his rate of learning.

Skill Development

Experience and maturation alone do not guarantee success in reading. The child needs certain intellectual skills. Reading requires that he perceive likenesses and differences, that he remember the word forms and possess thinking skills. It requires him to tell stories in proper sequence, to interpret pictures, to make associations and inferences, and to think on an abstract level (Dechant 1970). A review of the educational characteristics of the mentally retarded child (chapter 1) suggests that the absence of many of these intellectual and sensory skills impedes reading progress.

Characteristics Related to Reading

Eisenberg (1966) says "Even moderately retarded children can learn to read enough to transact the ordinary business of life if teaching methods take into account the learning characteristics of the defective child" (p. 13). In considering the learning characteristics of mentally retarded children, one becomes aware that several deficits are particularly relevant to the reading process: memory, reasoning skills, language acquisition, perceptual development, and cultural factors.

Memory. Memory may be discussed as a factor in reading as it relates to auditory memory, visual memory, and sequential or serial memory (Gillespie and Johnson 1974). The acquisition of a sight vocabulary, the ability to remember details of stories, and the use of skills previously acquired depend upon a good memory. Games and activities may be used to increase visual and auditory memory skill.

Visual:
Present a picture with missing parts; ask the child either to draw in the missing part or tell which part is missing.

Printing words with a rubber stamp set calls attention to the sequence of letters.

Cut apart cartoon strips and paste them on oak-tag; ask the child to reassemble the cartoon in the correct order.

Auditory:
Tap or clap out rhythm patterns; have the child repeat the pattern.

Ask the child to repeat a sentence or phrase that you have said to him.

Present a series of movements to a small group of children and have them follow the sequence. For example, "Jump, hop, clap, and skip" (Wallace and Kauffman 1973, p. 181).

Reasoning Skills.   Reasoning skills have been linked with reading comprehension. Reading may be interpreted as a thinking process in which reading comprehension involves the use of problem solving, suspending judgments, and employing concepts (Gillespie and Johnson 1974). The retarded child's inability to deal with abstract relationships may hinder his ability to draw inferences and to make evaluations of the material that he reads. Newspapers are valuable in increasing these skills.

Select the key sentence in a newspaper article; underline it.
   Prepare a headline for an article.
   Answer the questions: who, where, when? in each of several articles.
   Remove the ending from an exciting story; have the student supply one.
   Ask: Why did they do that? What would you do if? What would happen if they did?

Language Acquisition.   Most educable mentally retarded children come from homes of low socioeconomic backgrounds and are at least one year behind normal children in development of language skills. The relationship of oral language to reading will be discussed later in this chapter, as will techniques that assist in the development of language for reading.

Many children who are developmentally retarded are also delayed in language development. It is essential that speech and language stimulation form the basis for the reading readiness program and that expectations for reading be related to the degree of language development in the child.

Perceptual Development.   Children with limited intellectual development are frequently lacking in good perceptual motor development, visual perception, and auditory perception. While perceptual-motor deficits are frequently found in students with reading disabilities, training in these skills does not appear to improve children's reading scores significantly (Gillespie and Johnson 1974). Activities designed to improve auditory and visual discrimination skills may be found in this chapter.

Cultural Factors.   Many mentally retarded children also have social, cultural, and economic disadvantages. Frequently they come from homes where there is a dirth of reading material and where academic achievement is not valued highly. A reading teacher working with a fourth-grade child was alarmed to find him reading two years below grade level. She made a home visit, telling his mother, "John is reading at a second-grade level." The mother was delighted. She then revealed that John was the only one in the family who could read at all. One of the problems confronted by children from disadvantaged homes is the nonrelevance of much of the reading material they encounter. Kohl (1973) suggests the use of the following materials:

1. A stamp set. Students can make their own signs and posters, play with designing a page of print, make poems, and so forth.

2. Stencils. Some students who don't have the patience to do elaborate work with stamps take to stencils.

3. A Dymo label maker. Label makers provide good practice for someone learning to read. Label the chairs in the room "The hot seat," "A funny chair," or "The seat of power."

4. Plastic or wooden letters. These come with little magnets and a metallic board and may be used to illustrate how words and sounds vary.

5. Scissors, index cards, rubber cement, old newspapers, and magazines. Pupils can make up interesting card games and "found" poetry from headlines, phrases, and sentences discovered in the printed material.

6. Cartoons. Cut cartoons from old magazines and newspapers, remove the captions, and paste the pictures on cardboard. Pupils make up their own captions, which can be printed and used as reading material.

7. Free and inexpensive reading material, such as billboard sections, telephone books, old ads and signs, posters and buttons of all sizes and shapes, street signs, comic books, and catalogues.

Kohl also has advice for the teacher:

If you do not believe young people or poor people or black people or yellow or brown people can learn with ease do not attempt to teach them. If you tend to look upon people who are different than you as damaged or inferior you can only do them harm by trying to teach them.

Finally, if you believe reading is a difficult and sacred skill most likely you will make it seem difficult and holy to your students and create learning problems for them. Reading and writing will be acquired naturally if you can be natural about it and believe it is worth doing (p. 173).

Emotional Adjustment

A child who cannot read or who cannot read as well as his age group is marked before all as a failure. He is reminded of being a failure many times a day and every day. Even a skilled classroom or corrective reading teacher often cannot restore his confidence in himself, since his classmates and worried parents often magnify his deficiency (Schiffman 1966, p. 244).

The incidence of maladjustment among poor readers is greater than among good readers. As indicated in chapter 1, it is difficult to establish a causal relationship; it is not known whether emotional maladjustment causes reading failure, or whether reading failure causes maladjustment. Not all emotionally disadvantaged pupils are poor readers, nor are all poor readers emotionally disadvantaged children.

Success in school is not possible without success in reading. Therefore, poor reading ability threatens social acceptance and leads to feelings of inadequacy. The poor reader, rejected by others and feeling unsuccessful with himself, may become shy, antagonistic, self-conscious, nervous, inattentive, defensive, discouraged, irritable, fearful, frustrated, defiant, indifferent, restless, and hypercritical. He may stutter, be truant, join gangs, and engage in destructive activity (Dechant 1970).

Emotional problems may precede reading failure and become the cause of inadequacy in that area. Because reading is the first academic subject to be systematically taught to children, it becomes the first major educational issue in which problems become apparent. Because successful reading requires application and sustained concentration, emotional problems that prevent a child from concentrating and paying attention also prevent him from learning to read (Harris 1961).

If there appears to be evidence of a marked emotional disturbance, the teacher should call the child to the attention of the school guidance counselor, psychologist, or principal. Efforts should be made to provide successful experiences for the child in school. Hewett (1969) states, "The teacher who sets realistic academic goals for the non-achiever and who helps him achieve success resulting in deserved praise and recognition will be shaping positive academic and social attitudes which may have far-reaching implications" (p. 261).

Berkowitz and Rothman (1969) describe techniques used with severely disturbed children who were receiving remedial reading instruction. The techniques could be used by the classroom teacher and might be interesting approaches to use with all readers who are encountering difficulty. With children who have developed a kind of fantasy world for themselves, it was felt that reading might be meaningful if they were permitted some distortion of reality and could base reading material upon their fantasies. The child was encouraged to articulate his fantasy in drawings, verbalize his accompanying idea to the teacher, who typed or printed the story right on the drawings, and then attempt to read this material. Reading became a satisfying activity, providing the child with the opportunity to express his own interests and to have those interests accepted by the teacher. When the program of fantasy reading is carried to its logical conclusion, the child develops a reading sight vocabulary which permits him to relinquish his fantasy material for available text-books.

Another attempt at using unusual material was made with songs. A special type of song, written for this purpose, was designed to encourage movement and action. When the children learned the songs and enjoyed participating in the musical experience, the words of the songs were rein-troduced in a new situation: reading. The words were duplicated on sep-arate sheets of paper and the child read from them while he sang (Berko-witz and Rothman 1969).

The use of "organic" words (described later in this chapter under Components of Reading) has been effective with emotionally disadvan-taged children. While Bruno Bettelheim was director of the Orthogenic School for severely emotionally disturbed children, he used words with a strong emotional load to help children learn to read. He found that when teachers began to help children learn to read words of their own choice, some of them who for years had not learned to read a single word learned to recognize, read, and spell a hundred words or more in a couple of weeks. He described one child who grew up in a variety of foster homes, was un-able to learn, and repeated first grade three times. He finally learned to read and print words such as *soldier, submarine, fireman,* and *fighting,* all in line with his feelings of hostility. He still could not learn to read simple words like *come here,* because no one had ever wanted him to come or had lovingly called out to him (Gray 1972).

Frequently children who fear academic activity because of past failure can be stimulated into learning with the presentation of different materials in an unusual manner. With methods that are presented in a structured learning situation and that guarantee success, progress can be made. The most productive approach, however, is one of prevention. In a classroom where differences in ability are accepted and where the value of each child is assured, emotional problems are less likely to occur.

Oral Language

Although oral communication skills for handicapped children were dis-cussed in the previous chapter, emphasis should be placed on their relationship to the reading process. Since reading is, as one child put it, "wrote down talking," the skills of reading are based upon the skills of speaking.

Evidences of delayed and immature speech can be seen in the deaf child, the blind child, the mentally retarded child, the learning disabled child, and the culturally disadvantaged child, as well as in the child who has been identified as having a speech problem as his primary difficulty. Therefore, any reading program designed for handicapped children must have a strong emphasis on language stimulation.

The interrelatedness of oral language and reading should be recognized by all teachers. Hall (1970) states the sequence of the relationship: "As children listen they are building their stock of words and knowledge. As children speak their powers of communication are sharpened. As they read they are drawing upon their previous knowledge of words and adding new thoughts and concepts" (p. 3). Thus, in asking why a child has difficulty in learning how to read, the teacher should first determine whether the child possesses the sensory experiences and the verbal background to which the written words refer (Ross 1976). The reading readiness program for the deaf child, for example, consists of the use of language association with his immediate activities. As his understanding and use of language develops, he will be able to get ideas from language when it is written as well as when it is oral (Hart 1963). The blind child who has had limited experiences will need structured opportunities for language development. Sequential types of experiences in which verbal communication is increased will have to be offered.

Learning to read is equated with language ability by many reading experts. This point is made clear by Joos (1966): "Talking must come first; reading ability cannot (at first) proceed beyond the language ability possessed" (p. 83). He adds that the reading ability (or disability) of a given person must be viewed in the light of the language ability he possesses.

The implications of the relationship between oral and written language for teaching reading may be stated as follows:

1. *The language of initial reading materials should represent the child's speech patterns.* In the beginning stages of instruction, reading will have more meaning for children when they learn to read the language patterns and vocabulary already employed in their speech.

2. *Reading instruction should build upon the relationship between spoken and written language.* As children decode printed symbols they relate those symbols to their existing knowledge of speech sounds and vocabulary.

3. *Reading experiences are taught as communication experiences even in the beginning stages.* Communication in reading does not overlook or minimize the importance of phonics and other word attack skills in decoding print. Children must be able to recognize printed words if they are to be successful in reading. However, as children are acquiring reading vocabulary, the meaning of the material read should be evident to them.

4. *Reading instruction must be related to the total language program.* As children receive instruction in oral language, this instruction enriches their total background for comprehending the printed language of reading materials. Attention in the total language program is given to vocabulary development, to language enrichment through literature experiences, and to the expression of thoughts in written language (Hall 1970, p. 4).

Physical Factors

Children who have errors of biochemical functioning (such as diabetes, glandular dysfunction, nutritional and circulatory problems), who fatigue easily, and who are ill for prolonged periods of time may have difficulty with any academic skills. There is no evidence that any specific reading disabilities occur because of such physical problems. If a child is absent from school for a long period of time, it may be necessary for the teacher to insure his acquisition of readiness and word attack skills he may have missed.

Maturation as a factor in reading has been widely discussed. There are many persons who believe that children can and should read as early as they talk (Melcher 1973). A review of the research (Dechant 1970) suggests the following conclusions:

1. Younger children make less progress than older ones of the same intelligence when they are exposed to the same program.

2. The best age for beginning reading is dependent upon the materials used, the size of the class, the pacing of the program, and teacher expectancies (p. 51).

One teacher, from a background of fifty years' experience, asked "Why is there such a hurry to have children read at five or six? At eight, children take to the three R's like ducks to water. As an informal experiment, I gave first-grade readers [books] to a class of eight-year-olds who had just started to learn to read. They read in a week what the six-year-olds had been struggling with for a month" (Cooper 1977, p. 46).

Motor and neurological development have been cited as determinants of reading ability and disability. While these factors are still controversial, there are some conclusions that may be helpful to the teacher.

Perceptual-Motor Training

Kephart (1960) and others have planned programs to develop motor and perceptual skills, with the assumption that such training will improve, among other things, reading skills. Kephart states this philosophy:

Classroom teaching . . . involves attention to both perception and motor ability, and especially to the very important feedback or matching between them, just as much as it involves attention to integration with its variables of experience and intelligence. Because of the cyclical nature of the process, physical education becomes a part of reading and the too frequent dichotomy between muscular or motor activities and intellectual activities becomes untenable (p. 65).

In discussing the issue, Bateman (1976) summarizes research which indicates there is no scientifically acceptable data demonstrating special effectiveness for any of the physical, motor, or perceptual programs used in the prevention or correction of reading or other learning disabilities.

Cratty (1971) further denies the relationship between reading and physical coordination. He states that reading is largely a cognitive act, which will more likely be improved with practice in reading than practice in walking balance beams.

Neurological Bases

Strauss and Lehtinen (1947), pioneers in working with children now identified as learning disabled, considered disturbances resulting from brain injury to be the predominant factors in causing the reading difficulties encountered. The reading problem was viewed as a manifestation of the general disturbances of perception and behavior. Thus the approach to the reading disability was an attack on the "organic disturbances" (p. 168). The techniques suggested to improve visual and auditory perception are excellent methods which the reading teacher will find valuable in improving visual and auditory skills in children.

The neurological basis for learning disabilities is still adhered to by many educators and psychologists. Gaddes (1975) feels that educators who possess some neuropsychological knowledge can better understand and teach children with learning disabilities.

188

In summarizing programs for children with reading and other learning disabilities, Ross (1976) finds that the hypothesis that learning disabilities are due to a malfunction in the brain has never been proved. He feels that there is some danger in recommending perceptual-motor training for learning disabled children regardless of the area of weakness. He concludes, "A child will learn reading only when one provides the opportunity to learn reading, by teaching him or her to read. No amount of perceptual-motor training can take the place of carefully individualized tutoring that takes the child's maturational level and prior learning into account" (p. 83).

Implications for the teacher are clear. If a child has poor physical development and coordination, he certainly needs remediation in that area. However, there is no support to the idea that such remediation will be reflected in his reading or in any academic area. Assessment of his reading will indicate areas of weakness, such as visual discrimination or comprehension. Training in the specific areas of weakness will improve those skills.

Components of Reading

Reading may be defined as a two-step process of translating the written medium to language and translating the language to thought. The translation of writing is *recognition* and the translation of language to thought is *comprehension*. Wallen (1972) identifies the categories as follows:

RECOGNITION

Recognizing Words by Sight
  Sight-Word Skills

Recognizing Words by Word Attack
  Readiness-Discrimination Skills
  Phonic Word-Attack Skills
  Structural Word-Attack Skills
  Syllable Word-Attack Skills

COMPREHENSION

Comprehending Word Meaning
  Word-Meaning Skills

Comprehending Paragraph Meaning
  Recall Skills
  Interpretation Skills
  Extrapolation Skills
  Evaluation Skills

Rate of Comprehension
  Rate Skills

(p.13)

It is assumed that the classroom teacher in the elementary school has a good background in teaching reading and is familiar with traditional textbooks and reading materials. The teacher with such a background can frequently group children for instruction based on the assessment of the reading problem, regardless of the handicapping condition represented.

In teaching the handicapped child to read, the teacher is, in many cases, dealing with a child who has not learned by the usual methods. A great deal of ingenuity and creativity is required; quick successes are not expected. However, good results are well worth the effort.

In September, Morris was referred to the resource teacher. The fourth-grade teacher and the parents were concerned that Morris was not reading. In the initial contact, Morris looked at the resource teacher, hung his head, and declared, "I can't read." Because she could work with him on a one-to-one basis each day, the resource teacher was able to help Morris build his reading skills and his confidence. Each success was shared with the classroom teacher, who praised Morris lavishly. One day in April the resource teacher told Morris it was time to return to his room after his regular half-hour session. Morris pleaded, "Can't I read one more book?"

Most children come to school knowing many words. A problem occurs when it is discovered they don't know the "right" words. Such children therefore do not know how to read for school; it is assumed that they have brought no prereading experiences with them.

Billy's mother had been told that he would never learn to read; that his intellectual functioning would not permit it. One day in the grocery store, Billy went to a carton he had seen on television many times, pointed and said, "Geritol." His surprised mother pointed out other items and heard the responses, "Colgate," "Dentyne," and "Bayer."

Kohl (1973) points out that people in our culture are constantly exposed to the written word through billboards, television, packages, product labels, street signs, and graffiti. The beginning level of reading should incorporate what the learner knows informally and add other skills.

Recognizing Words by Sight

The successful classroom environment is conducive to sight recognition of words. There are multipurpose, multiage materials available. There are things for house play and dramatic play; things to start a child on a line of exploration and interest and things brought in to feed an ongoing project or interest. Books of every kind and level are everywhere. These include telephone books, magazines, recipe books, and books made by the children

(Houghton 1974). There are many things in the room that require reading: a sign on the bathroom door indicating that it is vacant or in use; activity charts or lists that indicate choices or specify who has selected particular activities; experience charts recording shared activities; recipes that have been used for cooking; and records or graphs recording plant or animal growth or behavior changes.

Feinberg (1975) suggests that the mastery and application of a sight vocabulary requires proficiency in the perceptual and perceptual-motor areas and offers activities to build the skills with children who are mentally retarded. The following are exercises related to visual and auditory discrimination:

> Skill: Visual discrimination
> 1. Activity: Fasten six or so vocabulary words (printed on flash cards) to a cork board or bulletin board and have the student point out a particular word from the group.
> 2. Activity: Print letter combinations such as these on the board, STEP, SHOR, STQF, STOP, and STOR, and have the student find the word "stop."
>
> Skill: Auditory discrimination (with no visual cues)
> 1. Activity: Spell a word such as "g-i-r-l" and ask the student if the word spelled was "cat?", "boy?", "girl?" or "dog?" (p. 250).

The selection of words to present requires thought and should be adapted to the particular needs of the child. Words on standardized lists such as the Dolch Word List and the Kucera-Francis List are valuable both as diagnostic instruments and in content development. However, for handicapped children the lists are formidable and do not offer much hope for total success.

Kolstoe (1976) states that sight words should be taught in the context of meaningful activities. Words are selected and listed by categories:

Action words

stand	come	bend	whisper	laugh
draw	kneel	sit	go	hop
wave	touch	clap	run	jump
skip	fly	walk	nod	scratch
cry	write			

Objects

chair	wagon	plate	cow	pencil
telephone	table	truck	knife	horse
book	kettle	basket	block	fork
dog	crayon			

Prepositions

These were taught by pantomime.

up	out	behind	right	bottom
from	down	across	before	left
beside	beneath	in	around	on
top	under	between		

(p. 108)

Using cards on which the words were written, games were played with the children in which they were required to act out or pantomime the word.

Ashton-Warner (1963) states the philosophy quite simply: first words must mean something to a child. She finds that if words are chosen accurately, they prove to be one-look words. In selecting the appropriate words, she asked the Maori children she taught such questions as: Whom do you love most in the world? What is something that scares you? What did you dream about last night? The answers resulted in such words as *Daddy, Mummy, ghost, bomb, kiss, brothers, butcher knife, love, dance, wild piggy.* The words were written on large tough cards and given to the children to read.

At first, sight words may be keyed to pictures. Mitchell (1974) used the children's first names, the words *sad, mad, glad,* and *is* to make sentences. The sentences were: *Mark is sad. Jim is mad. Ricky is glad. Donna is sad.* Each sentence was followed by the picture of a face. Other words, with illustrations, were gradually introduced in teacher-made books. This technique (sight repetition and the use of context clues) was successful with mentally retarded children.

Old reading books may be used to advantage in building sight word vocabularies. Key words may be cut from the book and chosen by the child in the correct usage. This exercise also helps the child to learn to use context clues.

There are many high-frequency structure words that are difficult to remember because they cannot easily be represented by pictures. Houghton (1974) states that only thirty-two words make up one-third of the words used by a child (or adult). These are: *a, and, he, I, in, is, it, of, that, the, to, was, all, as, at, be, but, are, for, had, have, him, his, not, on, one, said, so, they, we, wish,* and *you.* These words should be used frequently in the language experience stories (discussed in chapter 5), in captioning stories, and in signs about the classroom. Specific drill on these words will help to assure success in beginning reading. A collection of games for this purpose may be found in the following section, Materials and Techniques.

The Language Master.   For children who have visual discrimination problems, the Language Master provides auditory input to help build a sight word vocabulary. It is also useful with hyperactive children, since it requires some manipulation. With young children, large blank cards may be used by the teacher to include picture clues or even manipulative objects. With older children, the standard cards, printed or teacher-made, permit a variety of clues to be used. The Language Master is a valuable instructional tool which may be placed in the regular classroom and used by handicapped students with or without earphones.

Kinesthetic Methods.   Some children may require tactile input to learn a sight vocabulary. A clay pan, referred to in chapter 5, is useful in learning such words through touch. Tracing activities of all sorts are helpful and may be utilized in any classroom. Laminated sheets can be prepared by the resource teacher or by the classroom teacher and kept in the handicapped child's folder for use at any time. The clues can be faded gradually until the child can write and read the words without help (see chapter 9).

Drawing Words.   The way that words look affects the reading of them. To provide opportunities to play with words, to become comfortable with them, and to enjoy knowing them, teachers may suggest that children "draw" words the way they feel about them or put words instead of people into the pictures they draw. Such drawings are attractive displays or mobiles in the room and provide additional stimulation for the entire class.

Phonetic Analysis.   A child is usually ready for phonics instructions when he has a fairly large sight vocabulary, when he is beginning to notice word "families" and when he sees words as made up of different letters and sounds that he sees in other words. He is ready to understand that knowing more about individual letters and combinations of letters will help him figure out new words (Houghton 1974).

Otto, McMenemy, and Smith (1973) combine the numbers of phonics systems into two approaches: word-family phonics and single-letter phonics. The word-family approach avoids the need for blending individual letter sounds by making use of "families," such as *an, at, in,* and so forth. Single-letter phonics consists of blending individual consonant and vowel sounds from the very beginning. Four general rules are suggested for teaching this important skill: Provide a great deal of practice in auditory perception; sounds should be smooth and continuous; proceed from the whole word to its parts; keep phonic and blending instruction brief.

Some children seem to learn sound-letter correspondence and even phonic rules and can sound out words letter by letter but are not able to blend the sounds. P-u-t remains p-u-t. To assist the child in learning to blend sounds, the teacher may briefly present words of two or three letters, pronouncing them. A brief span of time prevents the child from reading the word letter by letter. An extension of this method would be the use of a tachistoscope. The Language Master may be used for this purpose to introduce new words, so the child sees and hears them simultaneously (Frostig and Maslow 1973).

Kohl (1973) describes a way to master most of the phonic regularities without much effort. It is easier to think of syllables than of isolated sounds. One way of beginning is to start with a list of words generated by the students and begin to modify them:

	kill	love	nation
which can be	will	dove	station
transformed to	spill	but not	situation
	fill	stove which	
		brings up an	
		exception	

(p. 56)

Students can learn to make transpositions, to change letters, reverse letters, and keep one element constant and vary the others.

Word wheels may be used for drill in initial sounds, word families, final sounds, prefixes, and suffixes. Directions for making such wheels are in the following section, Materials and Techniques. Commercial word-building charts, flip cards, and word attack games are available at reasonable prices.

If a child has poor auditory discrimination abilities, a program should be chosen for him that permits him to use visual and kinesthetic word attack skills. At the same time, efforts should be made to improve his auditory discrimination skills in a separate instructional program. There are a number of commercial programs available which help in the development of auditory discrimination, auditory sequencing, and auditory memory.

Structural Analysis.   Structural analysis enables the child to recognize variations in words by identifying the pronunciation and meaning of the base or root word. This approach can and should be used in conjunction with phonic analysis. Otto, McMenemy, and Smith (1973) feel that many of the skills of structural analysis are learned inductively after a general foundation of awareness of words and word patterns is laid. The following elements are usually taught in the primary grades:

1. Compound words (always begin with known words): cowboy, afternoon, doorway
2. Plurals formed with -s, -es, and -ies: ball-balls, potato-potatoes, fly-flies
3. Doubling consonants before adding endings beginning with a vowel: can-canned, stop-stopped
4. Base words with variant endings: wanted = when -ed says ed, tricked = when -ed says t, loved = when -ed says d
5. Contractions: I am = I'm, I will = I'll, he is = he's
6. Possessive forms: boy's hat, boys' hat
7. Base words with prefixes: unkind, refill, export
8. Base words with suffixes: fearless, thankful, eagerly
9. Base words with both prefixes and suffixes: unkindly, unhappiness, unthankful (Otto, McMenemy, and Smith 1973, p. 171)

Comprehension.   During a reading workshop for a group of special education teachers, the instructor asked teachers at different levels to state their chief problem in teaching reading. The primary teachers indicated building a sight vocabulary, the intermediate teachers, word attack skills, and the advanced teachers, with one accord, comprehension. The instructor asked the teachers to consider that if comprehension were given major consideration at all levels, perhaps it wouldn't be a problem at the advanced level.

Reading programs may put so much emphasis on teaching word attack skills that comprehension is neglected. Certainly many children have reading problems because of difficulties in word attack sequences, which should be taught at every level. However, it must be remembered that the ultimate goal of reading is comprehension; word attack is a means to this end rather than an end in itself (Schiffman and Daniels 1971).

The assessment of comprehension skills is usually done on an informal and individualized basis, since there are few formal instruments designed to pinpoint specific comprehension difficulties. The assessment may begin with extremely simple sentences, asking key questions of who, what, where, when, why, and how. Otto, McMenemy, and Smith (1973) illustrate this technique:

1. Tom swims well.
   Q. Who swims?
      How does he swim?
2. Tom swam and played in the pool.
   Q. What did Tom do?
      Where did he do it? (p. 200).

With a series of success steps, the teacher proceeds to sentences of more complex construction. The child learns to see key words and develop sentence sense.

The paragraph is used to develop the concept of main idea, the use of pronouns, and words that show relationships. The pupil may develop paragraphs of his own or practice finding answers to the "what, who, when" questions in newspaper articles. Experience stories may be used to develop paragraph meaning by cutting apart the sentences and having children number them in order of their importance to the main idea.

The ultimate goal in comprehension—understanding the whole selection—requires the student to comprehend words, sentences, paragraphs, and the author's purpose. It requires him to draw conclusions and to generalize (Otto, McMenemy, and Smith 1973).

While some reading programs may not develop comprehension skills well, Chall (1967) feels that the basal reading programs emphasize reading for understanding and enjoyment from the start. She points out that teachers' manuals give a great deal of attention to preparing children for each story by establishing background and arousing interest. The follow-up activities also emphasize reading for meaning. An analysis of such activities reveals that most of them emphasize reading comprehension and word meaning.

Since comprehension is built on the understanding of concepts, on memory, on generalization and interpretation, it is particularly difficult for children who have deficits in these areas. Teachers working with handicapped children need to stress comprehension at every level.

It is important for children learning a sight vocabulary to know the meanings of the words they learn. Some of the suggestions made in the previous section emphasize this idea: using action words; pantomiming concepts such as "under"; using personal words (as in the Ashton-Warner method); and using pictorial clues.

Following directions is a valuable skill in itself; it also indicates comprehension of the sentence. With students who do not follow directions well, one direction at a time may be given: "Open your book to page 30." After the direction is followed, another can be given: "Read the title of the chapter." After students can follow one direction at a time, give them two to be followed consecutively: "Open your book to page 30 and read the title of the chapter." The directions must be clearly stated and in the students' realm of understanding (Burmeister 1974). This technique may be used by the classroom teacher to use the student's reading ability in content areas such as mathematics, social studies, and science. As his skills develop, lists of directions in these areas can be given to follow.

Exercises in reading for meaning can be provided through folders designed to provide sources of information. Tasks that require comprehensive reading may be suggested: What can you order with box tops from this cereal package?; How do you order it?; What are the ingredients listed on this label?; How would you use it?; What is the address on this match cover?; What sort of place did it come from?

Tovey (1976) believes that comprehension cannot be taught directly, but may be learned through situations that facilitate and encourage the processing of print into meaning. He feels questions should be asked regarding the appropriateness of instructional procedures and materials when evaluating a child's comprehension skills. He offers ten instructional guidelines for involving children in successful reading experiences to develop these skills:

1. Help children select books they can read.
2. Help beginning readers have successful reading experiences through the use of dictation.
3. Help children develop an understanding of the purpose and nature of reading.
4. Encourage children to read high interest material.
5. Encourage children to read books with content that is familiar to them.
6. Help children avoid meaningless oral reading.
7. Emphasize reading as communication.
8. Provide children who have comprehension problems with many short selections of high interest.
9. Extend children's interests and thinking related to books they have read.
10. Motivate children to read, read, read! (p. 291).

Understanding of the whole selection is difficult to assess. The usual technique is to ask the child to outline the main idea or to retell the story. Guthrie (1977) claims that children expect a story to have structure and remember it accordingly. Comprehension of a story, therefore, is not comprehension of haphazard facts or a main idea, but of the structure. It is composed of the setting, the theme, the plot, and the resolution. Teachers can help by checking the questions in the materials they are using and eliminating any haphazard questions. Teachers may use questions that will help reconstruct the story, recognizing the ability of children to search for and use abstract story structure as the basis for comprehension and memory. The following rules are offered to illuminate the structure of stories: (1) The story is defined as consisting of a setting, theme, plot, and resolution, usually in that sequence. (2) The setting consists of characters and usually the location and time of a story. (3) The theme of a story consists of the main goal of the main character (the goal may be to rescue the beautiful damsel from the dreadful dragon).

"The plot of a story consists of a series of episodes, which are designed to help the main character reach his goal. Each episode consists of a subgoal, an attempt to reach the goal, and a resolution of the attempt. For instance, our hero wants to get a horse to ride to the dragon's cave. His attempt may consist of asking the king for a horse, and the resolution occurs when the king grants him one. After several episodes, an outcome occurs which matches the goal of the main character, ushering in a final resolution. These rules apply to many stories, folk tales, and dramas and give us a common framework for understanding them" (Guthrie 1977, p. 575).

To help children understand the structure and sequence of stories, flannelboard figures may be used. There are a number of story figures available commercially, including structured stories and flexible sets, which can be used to create one's own story. After observing this technique, children can retell the story to demonstrate their understanding. Puppets and finger puppets can be used for the same purpose.

Children of all ages enjoy dramatizing stories. Imitation of characters, situations, and settings requires understanding of the story. Children who grasp the idea will be able to write and dramatize their own stories.

The following activities are designed to improve comprehension skills.

Find the Answer. From a chart or folder containing pockets marked "Questions" and "Answers," the student selects a card containing a question and matches it with the card containing the answer.

Form Sentences. An envelope is prepared which contains a series of word cards. The student arranges the words to form a sentence.

Newspaper Questions. The student selects a newspaper clipping. He reads to find the answers to the four questions that appear on the chart or folder: (*Who*) was concerned with the event? (*What*) happened? (*When*) did it happen? (*Where*) did it happen?

Old Reading Books. Old reading books may be used in two ways to help build comprehension skills: (1) Remove some of the pictures. Children will illustrate the stories on blank paper pasted where pictures were removed. (2) Remove the story; leave the picture. Children will write a story on blank paper to go with the picture.

Some handicapped children may not advance beyond literal comprehension; some will develop understanding of nonliteral language and will acquire critical reading and study skills. Regardless of the reading level, children should read for meaning, for enjoyment, and for learning.

Materials and Techniques

The Reading Teacher's Dilemma

I know I.T.A.,
I use SRA,
A knowledge of phonics is mine.
I've assigned my troops
To ability groups
I think basal readers are fine.

Linguistics are cool.
My class likes to fool
Around with experience charts.
My kids play Scrabble,
And I often dabble
In reading aloud, with two parts.

My tape recorder,
When not out of order,
Is ready to catch every word.
Earphones on one's head
While stories are read
Means words are seen as they're heard.

Individualize?
I've tried that for size.
I've set up a reading corner.
I let children use
Nasty words that *they* choose,
A la Sylvia Ashton-Warner.

Drill sheets are stellar
(Stored in my cellar

Are all of the Dittos I need).
One problem I find
Drives me out of my mind:
A lot of my students can't read!

Richard G. Larson (1974)

Handicapped children, like other children, do not always respond to teacher-designed procedures. While some children will be able to use the same reading materials as other class members, others will need special materials and techniques to reach their full potential.

Informal Materials

Through the use of informal materials, children may relate more readily to their environment and therefore to printed material. Kohl (1973) suggests such materials as the telephone book, *TV Guide,* bus and plane schedules, catalogs, menus, advertisements, instructions that are included with appliances, price lists in supermarkets, newspapers, campaign literature, posters, buttons, and "how to" manuals. As teachers begin to know their students' interests, they can put together packets of such material that will appeal to almost anyone.

The alert teacher will find many items of interest to the student in the environment. Reading may be motivated and strengthened by the use of baseball and football cards, greeting cards, joke books, bumper stickers, cereal and other food boxes.

Local Chambers of Commerce can provide teachers with many materials describing geographic areas, vacation points, and historical places, as well as maps of the city and state. Many magazines provide addresses to which the teacher or children may write for materials about quarter horses, the trucking industry, and almost any topic of interest. Materials files can be built to provide a number of reading levels and topics.

Special Reading Programs

In addition to the basal readers, programmed instruction, trade books, and other series, some unique programs have been designed for students with special problems. If other systems have not been successful, the teacher will want to investigate the following programs and others which are available.

The Ball-Stick-Bird Method. Developed for use with severely retarded children in an institutional setting, Ball-Stick-Bird is now used with all children, including normal three-year-olds and learning disability students. Using three basic forms—a line, a circle, and an angle—the child learns words after he knows only two letters and reads action adventures from the beginning. The author describes tests which indicate that the students comprehend what they read and that they understand the difficult Ball-Stick-Bird vocabulary. Information concerning this program is available from: Ball-Stick-Bird, P. O. Box 592, Stony Brook, NY 11790.

Edmark Reading Program. The Edmark Reading Program teaches a one hundred fifty–word vocabulary and provides activities to use reading skills and to develop comprehension and language. Activities include word recognition lessons, direction books, picture-phrase matching, and a storybook. Pretests and review tests are provided throughout the program to confirm the student's progress. This program is designed for students with extremely limited skills. For information, write to: Edmark Associates, 655 S. Orcas St., Seattle, WA 98108.

The New Streamlined English Series. Developed by Dr. Frank C. Laubach to teach adults with no reading skills, this program is being used increasingly with students for whom other methods have proved ineffective. The method is based on the use of pictures with letters superimposed on them. The lesson format guarantees success by eliciting the correct response from the student and reinforcing it. Each lesson includes phonics, reading sight words, comprehension checks, structural analysis, and vocabulary development. Information may be obtained from: New Readers Press, Division of Laubach Literacy, Inc., Box 131, Syracuse, NY 13210.

High Interest Books. Pickering (1977) suggests the following series of books for children who are reading below their grade level expectations. The interest level is geared to the chronological age of the reader rather than to his reading ability.

Series	Publisher	Reading Grade Level	Interest Grade Level
American Adventure Series	Harper & Row 10 E. 53rd St. New York, NY 10022	2–6	4–9
Checkered Flag Series	Field Education Publications 609 Mission St. San Francisco, CA 94105	2	6–10

(continued next page)

Series	Publisher	Reading Grade Level	Interest Grade Level
Cowboy Sam Books	Benefic Press 10300 W. Roosevelt Road Westchester, IL 60153	1–3	1–4
The Deep Sea Adventure Series	Field Educational Publications	2–4	3–9
Discovery Books	Garrard Publishing Co. Champaign, IL 61820	2–4	3–6
The Interesting Reading Series	Follett Educational Corp. 1010 W. Washington Blvd. Chicago, IL 60607	2–3	4–9
Morgan Bay Series	Field Educational Publications	2–4	4–9
Sprint Library 1	Scholastic Book Services 904 Sylvan Avenue Englewood Cliffs, NJ 07632	2	3–8
Sprint Library 2	Scholastic Book Services	2	3–8
Sprint Library 3	Scholastic Book Services	3	3–8
Sprint Library 4	Scholastic Book Services	3	3–8
The True Books	Children's Book Centre 140 Kensington Church St. London W8, England	2–3	2–8

(pp. 109–110)

Instructional Techniques

Cohen (1971), in evaluating reading instruction, finds the question frequently asked is: What reading program gets better results? He feels the question should be: What is it that more successful teachers do that less successful teachers do not do? He cites studies indicating that more successful teachers individualize reading and spend more time in reading instruction.

The integration of the handicapped child into the reading program of the regular classroom certainly requires individualization and a great deal of time. When the reading program is totally different for one or several children, specific techniques are helpful.

Peer Teaching. Reading instruction permits the good reader to help the poor reader and the poor reader to help the younger reader. The programs described in the previous section may be taught by students who have been instructed in the simple steps. Good readers can read to small groups of children, helping them understand and react to the stories.

Cross-grade matching enables the poor reader to help younger children learn to read or learn to listen. Several children from a fourth grade were asked to read to a small group of kindergarten children. They had never been asked to read before; they wanted to be perfect. Practice sessions, tape recording, and prolonged preparation preceded the experience. Reading skills were improved; self-concepts were lifted!

Tape Recording.   A great deal of material from the regular curriculum can be recorded. Passages from science, social studies, language arts, math, or any other material the student is expected to read can be taped and listened to at a learning station or with earphones. Books and articles of interest to the student may be taped and placed with the written material; the student may follow the print while he reads. This amount of recording is time-consuming, but the teacher can usually find help with it. Smitherman (1974) suggests obtaining the help of a friend (perhaps one who is convalescing) who would be willing to record. College and high school students, through service clubs or individually, can help with this process.

The tape recorder may also be used to give directions to students who do not read well. At the start of a reading lesson key words may be presented and directions given for follow-up exercises. This can be accomplished at a listening station and can accommodate a number of students at different levels. As described by Yates (1969) this technique has several advantages: (1) Most disadvantaged students have a positive attitude toward audiovisual equipment; (2) The lesson can be carefully structured to provide success and reinforcement; (3) The students are not just listening; they are "doing" as well; (4) They can turn the teacher off—literally— until they catch up or understand.

Learning Packets and Centers.   The techniques described in chapter 4 are extremely useful in teaching reading at multiple levels. Fairleigh (1977) describes an excellent learning center in which the newspaper is the focus. Activities are suggested to use advertisements, the index, advice columns, and other sections to build reading comprehension, classification, and analysis. With directions and materials in a file folder format, students at many levels can work at the same center.

Contracting.   Through the use of contracts, independent classroom work on specific reading skills may be designed by the resource teacher and supervised by the classroom teacher (Wilhoyte 1977). The use of contracts may facilitate communication between the classroom teacher and the resource teacher who share responsibility for the student's total reading program. The resource teacher is able to extend the time the child works on personally prescribed activities and the classroom teacher doesn't have to spend time preparing an individual lesson.

Games. The drill required in the acquisition of word attack skills can be very dull unless presented in creative ways. The use of games permits an unlimited variety. In addition to skill-building properties, games provide excellent opportunities for peer teaching and interaction.

Numerous reading games are commercially available. One source, Little Brown Bear Learning Associates, Inc. (P. O. Box 561167, Miami, FL 33156) lists a key to selecting the appropriate game as determined by the reading skill goal and prerequisite skills. Kits for making games provide dice, plastic markers, and flexible boards to be used in many situations and changing demands.

With minimal preparation and expense, the following games can be used successfully.

Games to Teach Basic Sight Vocabulary

Post cheers on charts:

We want a touchdown!

Go, team, *go!*

Get that ball!

Block *that* kick!

Two, four, six, eight,
Who do we appreciate?

Two bits, *four* bits, *six* bits, a dollar;
Everybody *from* Fairview, stand *up and* holler!

We've got *the* pep, we've got *the* steam
But most of all, we've got *the* team!

Look at the clock, *look at the* score;
Come on, team, *we want more!*

Fish

Prepare a deck of cards with three cards for each word:

Small group plays fish, asking in turn for matches for the words in each hand; three of a kind makes a book. The first one out of cards is the winner.

Bingo

Bingo cards are made with high-frequency words in the squares. Small cards with matching words are called and asked for if a match occurs. The game is beneficial for the caller as well as for the players and may be entirely pupil directed.

Dominoes

Dominoes can be played with word cards intead of the usual dots. The student must match words instead of dots. This will provide practice in reading and matching words, as well as in discriminating between words that may be substituted for each other.

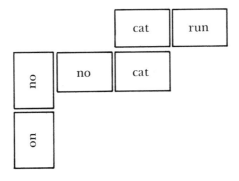

Making small words out of larger ones

Have the student make as many words as he can out of the letters in large words, such as government: go, me, govern, men, never, ever, even, ten, move, etc.

Decoding

Write simple sentences or stories for the student, omitting the vowels. Have the student complete the sentences: Wh-n w-nt-r c-m-s, c-n spr-ng b-f-r b-h-nd?

Word Wheels

Word wheels may be used for drill in initial sounds, common word elements, final sounds, prefixes, and suffixes. Cut two cardboard circles, one slightly smaller than the other. On the larger wheel, print the required letters. Then cut a slot in the smaller wheel, making sure that it is positioned to expose all of the words in turn as it is rotated. Place the smaller wheel on top and clip them together using a paper fastener.

Thus, for drill in the initial *br*, the upper wheel would read *br* next to the window opening. The lower wheel would shown *own, at, eak, ush, ing, ink, ake, ain, ute.*

205

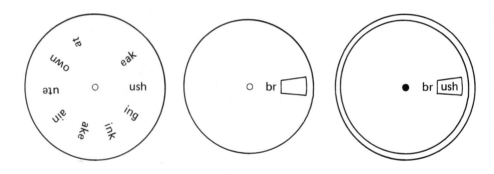

Additional games may be found in the following sources:

Fretz, Peggy. *Reading Games that Teach: Words—Phrases and Sentences.* Monterey Park, CA: Creative Teaching Press, 1969.

Hall, Nancy A. *Rescue.* Stevensville, MI: Educational Service, 1969.

Keith, Joy L. *Word Attack Joy.* Naperville, IL: Reading Joy, 1974.

Mallett, Jerry J. *Classroom Reading Games Activities Kit.* New York: Center for Applied Research in Education, 1975.

Pierros, Betty. *How to Create Reading Centers.* Carson, CA: Educational Insights, 1974.

Platts, Mary E. *Spice.* Stevensville, MI: Educational Service, 1973.

Optimism. A book salesman related an experience in calling on the reading consultant in a small school system. The consultant's office was strewn with books, magazines, and papers. The consultant was comfortably seated with his feet on the desk. The book salesman approached him, asking how many nonreaders there were in the school system. The consultant thoughtfully responded, "We don't have any nonreaders. We do have some children who haven't learned to read yet."

References and Suggested Readings

Aids for handicapped readers. 1972. Reference circular. Washington, D.C.: Library of Congress, Division for the Blind and Physically Handicapped.

Ashton-Warner, S. 1963. *Teacher*. New York: Simon and Schuster.

Barbe, W. B. 1960. Basic reading skills list. Reprinted from *Educator's guide to personalized reading instruction*. Englewood Cliffs, N.J.: Prentice-Hall.

Bateman, B. 1976. Teaching Reading to Learning Disabled Children. Paper presented at Reading Conference, University of Pittsburgh.

Berkowitz, P., and Rothman, E. 1975. Remedial reading for the disturbed child. In H. Dupont, ed., *Educating emotionally disturbed children*. New York: Holt, Rinehart and Winston.

Bitter, G. B., and Johnston, K. A. 1974. *Facilitating the integration of hearing impaired children into regular school classrooms*. University of Utah. Filmstrip.

Burmeister, L. E. 1974. *Reading strategies for secondary school teachers*. Reading, Mass.: Addison-Wesley.

Cegelka, P. A., and Cegelka, W. J. 1970. A review of research: Reading and the educable mentally handicapped. *Exceptional Children* 37:187–200.

Chall, J. S. 1967. *Learning to read: The great debate*. New York: McGraw-Hill.

Cohen, S. A. 1971. Dyspedagogia as a cause of reading retardation: Definition and treatment. In B. Bateman, ed., *Learning disorders,* vol. 4. Seattle: Special Child Publications.

Cohn, S. M., and Cohn, J. 1967. *Teaching the retarded reader*. New York: Odyssey Press.

Cooper, T. T. 1977. Following a child's lead. *Teacher* (April):46–47.

Cratty, B. J. 1971. *Active learning*. Englewood Cliffs, N.J.: Prentice-Hall.

Cravioto, J., and DeLicardie, E. R. 1975. Environmental and nutritional deprivation in children with learning disabilities. In W. W. Cruickshank and D. P. Hallahan, ed., *Perceptual and learning disabilities in children,* vol. 2. Syracuse, N.Y.: Syracuse University Press.

Dale, D. M. C. 1967. *Deaf children at home and at school*. Springfield, Ill.: Thomas.

Dechant, E. V. 1970. *Improving the teaching of reading,* 2nd ed. Englewood Cliffs, N.J.: Prentice-Hall.

Durkin, D. 1970. *Teaching them to read*. Boston: Allyn and Bacon.

Durost, W. N. 1971. Accountability: The task, the tools, and the pitfalls. *The Reading Teacher* 24:291–304.

Edwards, T. J. 1966. Teaching reading: A critique. In J. Money, ed., *The disabled reader*. Baltimore: Johns Hopkins Press.

Eisenberg, L. 1966. The epidemiology of reading retardation and a program for preventive intervention. In J. Money, ed., *The disabled reader*. Baltimore: Johns Hopkins Press.

Fairleigh, R. A. 1977. Extra! extra! the newspaper center. *Teacher* (February): 50–58.

Farr, R. and Brown, V. 1971. Evaluation and decision making. *The Reading Teacher* 24:341–346.

Feinberg, P. 1975. Sight vocabulary for the TMR child and adult: Rationale, development and application. *Education and Training of the Mentally Retarded* 10:246–251.

Frostig, M., and Maslow, P. 1973. *Learning problems in the classroom.* New York: Grune and Stratton.

Fuller, R. 1974. Severely retarded people can learn to read. *Psychology Today* (October):97–102.

Gaddes, W. H. 1975. Neurological implications for learning. In W. M. Cruickshank and D. P. Hallahan, eds., *Perceptual and learning disabilities in children,* vol. 1. Syracuse, N.Y.: Syracuse University Press.

Getman, G. N. 1961. Visual success is reading success. *Journal of the California Optometric Association* XXIX (Reprint).

Giangreco, C. J., and Giangreco, M. R. 1970. *The education of the hearing impaired.* Springfield, Ill.: Thomas.

Gillespie, P. H., and Johnson, L. E. 1974. *Teaching reading to the mildly retarded child.* Columbus, Ohio: Merrill.

Goldman, R., Fristoe, M., and Woodcock, R. 1970. *Test of auditory discrimination.* Circle Rines, Minn.: American Guidance Service.

Gray, F. 1972. Mommy, ghost, blood and learning to read. *Learning* (November):70–72.

Guthrie, J. T. 1977. Research views. *The Reading Teacher* (February): 574–577.

Hall, M. A. 1970. *Teaching reading as a language experience.* Columbus, Ohio: Merrill.

Hall, M. A. 1972. *The language experience approach for the culturally disadvantaged.* Newark, Del.: International Reading Association.

Hardin, B. and Ray, C. 1976. On the reading horizon. *Teacher* (January): 53–56.

Harris, A. J. 1961. *How to increase reading ability.* New York: David McKay.

Hart, B. O. 1963. *Teaching reading to deaf children.* Washington, D.C.: Alexander Graham Bell Association for the Deaf.

Hewett, F. M. 1969. A hierarchy of educational tasks for children with learning disorders. In H. Dupont, ed., *Educating emotionally disturbed children.* New York: Holt, Rinehart and Winston.

Houghton, C. 1974. Reading for the beginner: Open but deliberate. *Learning* August/September):90–94.

Johnson, M. S., and Kress, R. A. 1971. Task analysis for criterion-referenced tests. *The Reading Teacher* 24:355–359.

Joos, L. W. 1966. Linguistics for the dyslexic. In J. Money, ed., *The disabled reader.* Baltimore: Johns Hopkins Press.

Kephart, N. C. 1960. *The slow learner in the classroom.* Columbus, Ohio: Merrill.

Kirk, S. A. 1940. *Teaching reading to slow-learning children.* Cambridge, Mass.: Houghton Mifflin.

Kirk, S. A., Kliebhan, J. M., and Lerner, J. W. 1978. *Teaching Reading to Slow and Disabled Learners.* Boston: Houghton Mifflin.

Kohl, H. 1973. *Reading, how to.* New York: E. P. Dutton.

Kolstoe, O. P. 1976. *Teaching educable mentally retarded children,* 2nd ed. New York: Holt, Rinehart and Winston.

L'Abate, L., and Curtis, L. T. 1975. *Teaching the exceptional child.* Philadelphia: Saunders.

Larson, Richard G. 1974. The reading teacher's dilemma. *The Reading Teacher* (November):588. Reprinted with permission of R. G. Larson and the International Reading Association.

Laubach, F. C. 1945. *The silent billion speak.* New York: Friendship Press.

Livingstone, I. 1977. Sight words. *Elementary Teacher's Ideas and Materials Workshop* (April):5.

Lowenfeld, B., Abel, G. L., and Hatlen, P. H. 1969. *Blind children learn to read.* Springfield, Ill.: Thomas.

Melcher, D. 1973. Johnny still can't read. *School Library Journal* (October): 3109–3117.

Mitchell, J. R. 1974. Getting poor readers ready to read. *Teaching Exceptional Children* 6:103–110.

Myers, M. 1975. Uncle Sam's a reading puppeteer. *Learning* (November):20–26.

Norwood, M. J. 1976. Captioned films for the deaf. *Exceptional Children,* 3:164–166.

Otto, W., McMenemy, R. A., and Smith, R. J. 1973. *Corrective and remedial teaching.* Boston: Houghton Mifflin.

Pickering, C. T. 1977. *Helping children learn to read.* New York: Chesford.

Popham, W. J., ed. 1971. *Criterion-referenced measurement.* Englewood Cliffs, N.J.: Educational Technology Publications.

Prescott, G. A. 1971. Criterion-referenced test interpretation in reading. *The Reading Teacher* 24:347–354.

Reading materials in large type. 1975. Reference information. Washington, D.C.: Library of Congress, Division for the Blind and Physically Handicapped.

Reinert, H. 1976. *Children in conflict.* St. Louis: Mosby.

Ross, A. O. 1976. *Psychological aspects of learning disabilities and reading disorders.* New York: McGraw-Hill.

Ruddell, R. B. 1974. Preface. In R. L. Venezky, *Testing in reading.* Urbana, Ill.: ERIC Clearinghouse on Reading and Communication Skills and National Council of Teachers of English.

209

Schiffman, G. B. 1966. Program administration within a school system. In J. Money, ed., *The disabled reader.* Baltimore: Johns Hopkins Press.

Schiffman, G. B., and Daniels, P. 1971. Comprehension: A constellation of many factors. In B. Bateman, ed., *Learning disorders,* vol. 4. Seattle: Special Child Publications.

Schmidt, T. 1976. Make your own reading management system. *Teacher* (January):60–62.

Smith, P. B., and Bentley, G. I. 1975. *Curriculum.* Austin, Tex.: Education Service Center, Region 13.

Smitherman, D. W. 1974. A hand-up for slow readers. *Learning* (November): 87.

Spache, E. B. 1976. *Reading activities for child involvement,* 2nd ed. Boston: Allyn and Bacon.

Spache, G. D. 1964. *Reading in the elementary school.* Boston: Allyn and Bacon.

Strauss, A. A., and Lehtinen, L. B. 1947. *Psychopathology and education of the brain-injured child.* New York: Grune and Stratton.

Sykes, K. C. 1972. Print reading for visually handicapped children. *Education of the Visually Handicapped* 8:4.

Tovey, D. R. 1976. Improving children's comprehension abilities. *The Reading Teacher.* 30 (3):288–292.

Urell, B. 1976. They call that reading! *Teacher* (January):64–68.

Vandever, T. R., Maggart, W. T., and Nasser, S. 1976. Three approaches to beginning reading. *Mental Retardation* 14:29–32.

Venezky, R. L. 1974. *Testing in reading.* Urbana, Ill.: ERIC Clearinghouse on Reading and Communication Skills and National Council of Teachers of English.

Wallace, G., and Kauffman, J. M. 1973. *Teaching children with learning problems.* Columbus, Ohio: Merrill.

Wallen, C. J. 1972. *Competency in teaching reading.* Chicago: Science Research Associates.

Wechsler, D. 1949. *Wechsler intelligence scale for children.* New York: Psychological Corp.

Wepman, J. M. 1958. *Auditory discrimination test.* Chicago: Language Research Associates.

Wepman, J. M. 1975. Auditory perception and imperception. In W. M. Cruickshank and D. P. Hallahan, eds., *Perceptual and learning disabilities in children,* vol. 2. Syracuse, N.Y.: Syracuse University Press.

Wilhoyte, C. H. 1977. Contracting: A bridge between the classroom and resource room! *The Reading Teacher* 30:376–378.

Yates, J. R., Jr. 1969. Use of a listening station for introducing a reading lesson to disadvantaged EMR junior high school students. *Education and Training of the Mentally Retarded* 4:29–31.

Chapter Seven

Teaching Arithmetic

Photograph by John Rosenthal

Many handicapped students mainstreamed in regular classes are at a significant disadvantage in regard to success in arithmetic. Some types of handicapping conditions have a higher probability of interfering with arithmetic achievement than others. Students handicapped with cognitive impairment, learning disabilities, and sensory disadvantages (visual and hearing) will most likely need adaptation in the arithmetic curriculum to achieve maximum gains. However, physically handicapped students— for example, with impairment only in their lower limbs—may need no special adaptation. It is important to remember, however, that all students, handicapped and nonhandicapped, need some individualization to accommodate their particular strengths and weaknesses. Systematic instruction based on the diagnostic-prescriptive approach discussed in chapter 4 is the framework in which an arithmetic program focused on individual needs can be developed.

Assessment

In order to plan an arithmetic program, it is necessary for the teacher to find the answers to two questions (Lowenbraun and Affleck 1976): What is the student's level of functioning in the sequence of arithmetic skills? What skills should the student learn next? Selection of assessment tools is the first step in answering these questions. Assessment tools appropriate to use fall into the categories of standardized tests, criterion-referenced tests, and structured observation (see chapter 3 for a description of each category). Regardless of the particular type of tool, there are some general guidelines that apply across the board in arithmetic assessment, including the following:

Assessment should occur before arithmetic instruction is initiated—at the beginning of the school year for the majority of students. As new students transfer into the school during midyear, the teacher should establish the habit of immediately pinpointing the student's repertoire of arithmetic skills.

Arithmetic assessment tools that are correlated as much as possible with the type of curriculum approach used in the classroom should be chosen. For example, if the student will be expected to engage in frequent pencil and paper tasks in the classroom, an assessment device which only requires the student to point to the correct answer should not be used exclusively.

Assessment should be on-going. Sometimes students may be nervous or lack self-confidence when testing is initiated at the beginning of the year. Errors related to these factors could be misinterpreted by the teacher as lack of skill development. The possibility of unreliable information is curtailed as teachers continue to check on the student's progress.

In-depth analysis of all assessment data should be made. Paying attention only to the number of correct and incorrect responses is a very superficial way to interpret student performance. Teachers need to observe closely the types of errors that the student makes and the reasons that seem to be contributing to the errors. This type of information leads directly to remediation. Error analysis will be discussed in greater detail later in the chapter.

Assessment can be a shared responsibility with other educators in the school. It should not automatically be the sole responsibility of the classroom teacher. If a special education resource teacher or a school psychologist participates in the process of arithmetic assessment, it is important for the assessment results to be clearly communicated to the classroom teacher.

Standardized Tests

Standardized assessment tools used in arithmetic are usually of two types: achievement and diagnostic tests. Achievement tests generally provide an overview of arithmetic achievement by sampling a variety of skills with a limited number of items per skill. The results of achievement tests are typically reported in the form of grade equivalent scores. For example, the Peabody Individual Achievement Test profile might indicate that a student in the fifth grade is on a 3.4 grade level in arithmetic. This means that the student performs on arithmetic tasks similarly to the average student in the fourth month of the third grade. At first glance this type of score might seem to provide information to answer the two crucial assessment questions: What is the student's current level of functioning in the sequence of arithmetic skills? What skills should the student learn next?

When we stop and analyze the meaning of a 3.4 grade level, the precise sequence of mastered skills and skills that need to be introduced on "Monday morning" are still not pinpointed. Teachers need to realize that quantitative scores do not always provide the assessment information necessary to develop a systematic instructional program.

The second type of standardized assessment is diagnostic tests. Although diagnostic tests in arithmetic vary widely, they tend to be more specific and precise than achievement tests. Usually they provide more in-depth analysis of several subcomponents of arithmetic such as computation, reasoning, fractions, and measurement. This type of profile is more likely to result in the identification of individual strengths and weaknesses. One arithmetic diagnostic test that is systematically and comprehensively constructed is the KeyMath published by American Guidance Service, Inc. (Circle Pines, MN 55014). Items on the KeyMath are organized according to the following format:

I. Content
   A. Numeration
   B. Fractions
   C. Geometry and Symbols

II. Operations
    A. Addition
    B. Subtraction
    C. Multiplication
    D. Divison
    E. Mental Computation
    F. Numerical Reasoning
III. Applications
    A. Word Problems
    B. Missing Elements
    C. Money
    D. Measurement
    E. Time

The KeyMath is individually administered and requires only minimal writing responses. Included in the manual is an instructional objective for each test item which promotes the generalization of test results into identification of the specific skills for programming. The test is designed so that teachers or teacher aides can administer it. Other achievement and diagnostic tests frequently used to assess arithmetic skills are identified and briefly described in table 7–1.

Table 7–1
Standardized Tests—Arithmetic

Title: Peabody Individual Achievement Test
Publisher: American Guidance Service, Inc.
Circle Pines, Minnesota 55014
Description: This test measures achievement in several areas, including mathematics. It yields grade equivalents, age equivalents, standard scores, and percentile ranks.

Title: SRA Achievement Series
Publisher: Science Research Associates, Inc.
259 East Erie Street
Chicago, Illinois 60611
Description: This achievement test is useful for testing children in grades two through six. It measures skills in the areas of concepts, reasoning, and computation.

Title: Stanford Diagnostic Arithmetic Test
Publisher: Harcourt Brace Jovanovich, Inc.
Test Department
757 Third Avenue
New York, New York 10017

214

Table 7–1 Continued

Description:	This test is provided in two forms that overlap and cover the second through the eighth grades. The test gives information in the form of stanines, percentiles, and grade level equivalents. Also this test can be scored by a computer with a programmed readout for interpretation and recommendations.
Title:	Metropolitan Achievement Tests
Publisher:	Harcourt Brace Jovanovich, Inc.
	Test Department
	757 Third Avenue
	New York, New York 10017
Description:	This test is given to children in the third through the ninth grades and offers two scores: computation and problem-solving concepts.
Title:	California Achievement Tests
Publisher:	California Test Bureau
	McGraw-Hill Division
	Del Monte Research Park
	Monterey, California 93940
Description:	The subtest for arithmetic gives three scores: reasoning, fundamentals, and total tests. It may be used in grades one through nine.
Title:	Wide Range Achievement Test
Publisher:	Western Psychological Services
	12031 Wilshire Boulevard
	Los Angeles, California 90025
Description:	The WRAT is provided in two forms; the range is from kindergarten to college level. The arithmetic sections on both forms are designed virtually to eliminate reading. The test is individually administered and can be completed within 10 minutes.
Title:	Los Angeles Diagnostic Tests
Publisher:	California Test Bureau
	McGraw-Hill Division
	Del Monte Research Park
	Monterey, California 93940
Description:	These tests are used with children in grades two through nine and measure skill in the four basic computational areas and in reasoning.
Title:	Diagnostic Arithmetic Tests
Publisher:	California Test Bureau
	McGraw-Hill Division
	Del Monte Research Park
	Monterey, California 93940

215

Table 7–1 Continued

Description: This test measures skill development in the four computational areas: weights, percentages, measures, and fractions.

Title: Pattern Recognition Skills Inventory

Publisher: Hubbard Press
2855 Shermer Road
Northbrook, Illinois 60062

Description: This instrument is for use with children between the ages of five and ten years. It analyzes the development of pattern recognition ability and the relationship of this ability to the development of other cognitive concepts. The inventory enables teachers to understand why students display knowledge of certain concepts and not others.

From Bill R. Gearheart, *Teaching the learning disabled.* St. Louis, 1976, The C. V. Mosby Co. Reprinted by permission of the publisher.

Criterion-Referenced Tests

The distinguishing characteristics of criterion-referenced tests are a sequential arrangement of tasks and the specification of the criteria the student is expected to reach in order to attain proficiency. Teachers can develop criterion-referenced tests in arithmetic that insure a direct link between assessment and instruction. Teachers should adhere to the following procedure in developing criterion-referenced tests:

1. Specify the arithmetic skills which are important for the student to know;
2. State the desired criteria to indicate proficiency;
3. Develop a test question(s) to assess the skill; and
4. Record student's performance.

An example of a teacher-constructed, criterion-referenced test in the area of multiplication processes is presented in table 7–2. There are several ways to develop criterion-referenced tests which can be used repeatedly. One approach would be to mimeograph skill sequences in checklist form and to develop a laminated index card file of test items keyed by skill number to the checklist. Different students might follow the same sequence and the mimeographed copies of skill checklists would provide an individual record for each student. Skills could be dated as they were mastered. The laminated index cards would enable the test items to be used repeatedly without any extra preparation, beyond the initial effort of

Table 7-2
Criterion-Referenced Test in Multiplication Processes

Skills (Partial Listing)	Criteria	Sample Test Questions	
1. Multiplies a 2-digit multiplicand with a 1-digit multiplier, involving no carrying in equations and word problems.	90%	1. (a) $\begin{array}{r} 23 \\ \times\ 2 \end{array}$	(b) If there are 11 groups of people with 6 people in each group, how many people are in all the groups?
2. Multiplies a 3-digit multiplicand with a 1-digit multiplier, involving no carrying in equations and word problems.	90%	2. (a) $\begin{array}{r} 123 \\ \times\ 3 \end{array}$	(b) A school has 123 classrooms with each having 3 erasers. How many erasers are in the whole school?
3. Multiplies a 4-digit multiplicand with a 1-digit multiplier, involving no carrying in equations and word problems.	90%	3. (a) $\begin{array}{r} 2314 \\ \times\ 2 \end{array}$	(b) There are 4 schools in the district. Each school has 1021 children. How many children are in the school district?
4. Multiplies a 2-digit multiplicand with a 1-digit multiplier, involving carrying in equations and word problems.	90%	4. (a) $\begin{array}{r} 35 \\ \times\ 3 \end{array}$	(b) If a car goes around a 25-mile track 5 times, how far has it traveled?
5. Multiplies a 3-digit multiplicand with a 1-digit multiplier, involving carrying to the 10's place in equations and word problems.	90%	5. (a) $\begin{array}{r} 128 \\ \times\ 2 \end{array}$	(b) There are 4 piles with 217 rocks in each pile. How many rocks are in all the piles?
6. Multiplies a 3-digit multiplicand with a 1-digit multiplier, involving carrying to the hundred's place in equations and word problems.	90%	6. (a) $\begin{array}{r} 384 \\ \times\ 2 \end{array}$	(b) If 5 trucks each have 141 boxes, how many boxes are in all the trucks?

217

organization, by the teacher. When the skills involved in the construction of criterion-referenced tests are being learned initially by the teacher, test construction can be time-consuming. The substantial payoff is that the assessment sequence is the same as the instructional sequence. Behavioral objectives are the natural by-product of criterion-referenced tests. As teachers master the task of specifying skill sequences in arithmetic, it is likely that this systematic approach to arithmetic programming will facilitate the progress of all students.

Criterion-referenced assessment also provides the opportunity for in-depth error analysis. Again, it is important for teachers to pinpoint the types of errors that the student is making and the cause of those errors. Reisman (1972) has developed an error analysis chart, depicted in table 7–3, which provides examples of frequently made computation errors with

Table 7–3
Error Analysis Chart

Analysis	Example
1. Lacks mastery of basic addition combinations.	$3\lceil 2$ $+4\lceil 3$ $7\lceil 4$
2. Lacks mastery of basic subtraction combinations.	$3\lceil 8$ $-2\lceil 5$ $1\lceil 2$
3. Lacks mastery of basic multiplication combinations.	$3\lceil 2$ $\times\;\;3$ 86
4. Lacks mastery of basic division combinations.	$35 \div 5 = 6$ 6 $9\overline{)56}$ -56 0
5. Subtracts incorrectly within the division algorithm.	$3)\;73\;\text{R}1$ 70 $3\overline{)230}$ -21 $10 \longleftarrow$ -9 1

218

Table 7–3 Continued

6. Error in addition of partial product.

$$
\begin{array}{r}
432 \\
\times\ 57 \\
\hline
3\ \boxed{0}\ 24 \\
21\ \boxed{6}\ \ 0 \\
\hline
24\ \boxed{0}\ 24
\end{array}
$$

7. Does not complete addition:
   a. Does not write regrouped number.

$$
\begin{array}{r}
85 \\
+43 \\
\hline
28
\end{array}
$$

   b. Leaves out numbers in column addition.

$$
\begin{array}{r}
4 \\
8 \\
2 \longleftarrow \\
+\ 3 \\
\hline
15
\end{array}
$$

8. Rewrites a numeral without computing.

$$
\begin{array}{r}
\searrow 72 \\
+15 \\
\hline
\longrightarrow\quad 77
\end{array}
$$

$$
\begin{array}{r}
\longrightarrow\quad 32 \\
\times\ 3 \\
\hline
\longrightarrow\quad 36
\end{array}
$$

9. Does not complete subtraction.

$$
\begin{array}{r}
582 \\
-35 \\
\hline
47
\end{array}
$$

10. Does not complete division because of incompleted subtraction.

$$
\begin{array}{r}
1)\ 41 \\
40) \\
7\overline{)397} \\
-280 \\
\hline
7 \\
7 \\
\hline
\end{array}
$$

11. Fails to complete division: stops at first partial quotient.

$$
\begin{array}{r}
50 \\
7\overline{)370} \\
350
\end{array}
$$

12. Fails to complete division; leaves remainder greater than divisor.

$$
\begin{array}{r}
80\ R9 \\
9\overline{)729} \\
720 \\
\hline
9
\end{array}
$$

219

Table 7–3 Continued

13. Does not complete multiplication within division algorithm.

$$\begin{array}{r} 201 \text{ R}3 \\ 200 \\ 3\overline{)603} \\ 600 \\ \hline 3 \end{array}$$

14. Does not add by bridging endings—should think $5 + 9 = 14$, so $35 + 9 = 44$.

$$\begin{array}{r} 35 \\ +9 \\ \hline 33 \end{array}$$

15. Lacks additive concept in addition.

$$\begin{array}{r} 35 \\ +20 \\ \hline 50 \end{array}$$

16. Confuses multiplicative identity within addition operation.

$$\begin{array}{r} 71 \\ +13 \\ \hline 73 \end{array}$$

17. Lacks additive identity concept in subtraction.

$$\begin{array}{r} 43 \\ -20 \\ \hline 20 \end{array}$$

18. Confuses role of zero in subtraction with role of zero in multiplication.

$$\begin{array}{r} 37 \\ -20 \\ \hline 10 \end{array}$$

19. Subtracts top digit from bottom digit whenever regrouping is involved with zero in minuend.

$$\begin{array}{r} 30 \\ -18 \\ \hline 28 \end{array}$$

20. Confuses role of zero in multiplication with multiplicative identity.

$$7 \times 0 = 7$$

21. Confuses place value of quotient by adding extra zero.

$$\begin{array}{r} 20 \\ 30\overline{)60} \end{array}$$

22. Omits zero in quotient.

$$\begin{array}{r} 30 \text{ R}3 \\ 4\overline{)1203} \\ 1200 \\ \hline 3 \end{array}$$

23. Lacks facility with addition algorithm:
    a. Adds ones to ones *and* tens;

$$\begin{array}{r} 37 \\ +2 \\ \hline 59 \end{array}$$

Table 7–3 Continued

b. Adds tens to tens *and* hundreds;

$$\begin{array}{r} 342 \\ +36 \\ \hline 678 \end{array}$$

c. Adds ones to tens *and* hundreds;

$$\begin{array}{r} 132 \\ +6 \\ \hline 798 \end{array}$$

d. Is unable to add horizontally:

$$345 + 7 + 13 = 185$$

Thinks: $3 + 7 + 1 = 11$; writes 1
$4 + 3 \quad = 7 \quad (+ 1 \text{ carried})$
$5 \quad = 5$

$$\begin{array}{r} 8 \\ 5 \\ \hline 185 \end{array}$$

24. Does not regroup ones to tens.

$$\begin{array}{r} 37 \\ +25 \\ \hline 52 \end{array}$$

25. Does not regroup tens to hundreds (or hundreds to thousands).

$$\begin{array}{r} 973 \\ +862 \\ \hline 735 \end{array}$$

26. Regroups when unnecessary.

$$\begin{array}{r} 43 \\ +24 \\ \hline 77 \end{array}$$

27. Writes regrouped tens digit in ones place; carries ones digit (writes the 1 and carries 2 from "12").

$$\begin{array}{r} ② \\ 35 \\ +7 \\ \hline 51 \end{array}$$

28. When there are fewer digits in subtrahend:
a. Subtracts ones from ones *and* from tens (*and* hundreds);

$$\begin{array}{r} 783 \\ -2 \\ \hline 561 \end{array}$$

b. Subtracts tens from tens *and* hundreds.

$$\begin{array}{r} 783 \\ -23 \\ \hline 560 \end{array}$$

29. Does not rename tens digit after regrouping.

$$\begin{array}{r} 54 \\ -9 \\ \hline 55 \end{array}$$

Table 7–3 Continued

30. Does not rename hundreds digit after regrouping.

$$\begin{array}{r} 532 \\ -181 \\ \hline 451 \end{array}$$

31. Does not rename hundreds or tens when renaming ones.

$$\begin{array}{r} 906 \\ -238 \\ \hline 778 \end{array}$$

32. Does not rename tens when zero is in tens place, although hundreds are renamed.

$$\begin{array}{r} 803 \\ -478 \\ \hline 335 \end{array}$$

33. When there are two zeros in the minuend, renames hundreds twice but does not rename tens.

$$\begin{array}{r} 5 \\ \cancel{6}_{11} \\ \cancel{7}00 \\ 326 \\ \hline 248 \end{array}$$

34. Decreases hundreds digit by one when unnecessary.

$$\begin{array}{r} 3\,7\;1 \\ -\;1\,3\;4 \\ \hline 1\,3\;7 \end{array}$$

35. Uses ones place factor as addend.

$$\begin{array}{r} 32 \\ \times\;4 \\ \hline 126 \end{array}$$

36. Adds regrouped number to tens but does not multiply. $(7 \times 5 = 35;\ 30 + 30 = 60)$*

$$\begin{array}{r} 35 \\ \times\;7 \\ \hline 65* \end{array}$$

37. Multiplies digits within one factor. $(4 \times 1 = 4;\ 1 \times 30 = 30)$*

$$\begin{array}{r} 31 \\ \times 4 \\ \hline 34* \end{array}$$

38. Multiplies by only one number.

$$\begin{array}{r} 457 \\ \times\;12 \\ \hline 914 \end{array}$$

39. "Carries" wrong number.

$$\begin{array}{r} 8 \\ 67 \\ \times\;40 \\ \hline 3220 \end{array}$$

Table 7–3 Continued

40. Does not multiply one times tens.

$$\begin{array}{r} 32 \\ \times\ 24 \\ \hline 648 \end{array}$$

41. Reverses divisor with dividend.

(Thinks $6 \div 3$ instead of $30 \div 6$)*

$$\begin{array}{r} 2* \\ 6\overline{)30} \end{array}$$

42. Does not regroup; treats each column as separate addition example.

$$\begin{array}{r} 23 \\ +8 \\ \hline 211 \end{array}$$

43. Subtracts smaller digit from larger at all times to avoid renaming.

$$\begin{array}{r} 273 \\ -639 \\ \hline 446 \end{array}$$

44. Does not add regrouped number.

$$\begin{array}{r} 37 \\ \times\ 7 \\ \hline 219 \end{array}$$

45. Confuses place value in division:
    a. Considers thousands divided by ones as hundreds divided by ones;

$$\begin{array}{r} 1) \\ 200)\ 201 \\ 3\overline{)6003} \\ 6000 \\ \hline 3 \\ 3 \end{array}$$

    b. Records partial quotient as tens instead of ones:

$$\begin{array}{r} 50) \\ 100)\ 150 \\ 7\overline{)735} \\ -700 \\ \hline 35 \\ 35 \\ \hline \end{array}$$

    c. Omits zero needed to show no ones in quotient.

$$\begin{array}{r} 2\ \text{R1} \\ 3\overline{)61} \\ 6 \\ \hline 1 \end{array}$$

46. Ignores remainder because:
    a. Does not complete subtraction;
    b. Does not see need for further computation;

$$\begin{array}{r} 80 \\ 7\overline{)562} \\ 560 \\ \hline \end{array}$$

    c. Does not know what to do with "2" if subtraction occurs, so does not complete further.

From F. K. Reisman, *A guide to the diagnostic teaching of arithmetic.* Columbus, Ohio: Charles E. Merrill Publishing Co., 1972. Reprinted by permission of the publisher.

a brief statement indicating the possible cause of each error. It is also possible to carry out error analysis in the area of arithmetic reasoning. As for solving word problems, errors may be related to any of the following factors: lack of attention; poor reading comprehension; inability to recognize words; overlooking important cues such as "how many all together" which indicate which computational process to use; inability to disregard irrelevant numbers included in problem; writing down the problem correctly on paper; knowledge of the correct computation process; and general carelessness.

Each type of error is different and, therefore, requires a different approach to correction. Error analysis is important for all students, but it is particularly relevant for assessing students having handicaps associated with cognitive impairment or learning disabilities. Students who experience substantial difficulty in arithmetic make the most systematic progress when errors are consistently identified and then eliminated.

Observation

In every arithmetic lesson, teachers have the opportunity to conduct further error analysis and to identify arithmetic strategies and activities which the handicapped student appears to enjoy and around which he achieves success. Taking advantage of opportunities involving seatwork, workbooks, games, large group activities, and small group activities, in addition to teacher constructed tests, can provide valuable assessment information on a continuous basis during the student's natural classroom routine. Although the means of conducting this type of observational assessment is far more informal than in the case of standardized or criterion referenced tests, the insights available to teachers can be invaluable.

Developing Goals and Objectives

Once arithmetic assessment has been completed and the teacher has identified the skills the student has already mastered, he needs to develop long-term goals and short-term objectives or intermediate steps to reach those goals. It is difficult to know how much progress to expect handicapped, as well as nonhandicapped students, to make throughout the school year. Long-term goals rather than being rigid dictates are guides to instruction. Teachers should write down their general expectations, realizing that it is always possible to increase or decrease the complexity of the goals later.

A major decision related to setting goals is deciding what to teach or identifying the specific body of arithmetic concepts and skills important for a handicapped student to know. Assessment might have revealed that a student with significant learning problems in the fourth grade has the following skills: can count to 100 by ones, twos, fives, and tens but cannot go past 100; has mastered basic addition facts and column addition with no carrying; is ready to learn two-digit addition with carrying; is able to tell time only by the hour; can count change to 25 cents; can measure in feet and inches, but is unfamiliar with event the vocabulary of the metric system; and can identify various geometric figures, but is unable to use a compass to construct a circle or angle.

Where does the teacher start? One of the first considerations is that handicapped students who achieve significantly below grade level in arithmetic will, in the majority of cases, never completely catch up with grade level expectations. These students may have handicaps attributable to impaired cognitive ability or a learning disability in arithmetic. The end result of the concepts and skills these students will master in arithmetic will probably be less than the majority of other students; therefore, teachers need to identify the most *relevant* arithmetic curriculum to serve as the core for setting long-term goals. This means leaving out the "trimmings" that are not essential for daily living situations. In order to begin to pinpoint relevant skills, stop and ask yourself what arithmetic skills you have used in the last twenty-four hours. You might consider making notes of the arithmetic skills you use over the next several days. Also identify jobs that handicapped students might be likely to have as adults and list the arithmetic skills associated with success on that particular job. The fundamental nature of daily arithmetic requirements is often surprising. It is also important to remember that the student's parents should have the opportunity of defining goals and objectives as part of their participation in the development of their child's individual education plan. There might be arithmetic deficiencies around which the parents would particularly like remediation to occur. Further, handicapped students, depending upon their age and maturity, might also help to define the arithmetic curriculum in terms of what they would most like to learn. Thus, the responsibility and accountability of goal-setting may be shared among various persons. When one realizes the importance of individual differences and that no one guideline applies to all students, a general framework within which to plan arithmetic instruction for students with significant learning problems might be: (1) number concepts, (2) facts and processes, (3) money, (4) time, and (5) measurement

These subcomponents of arithmetic have the most direct tie to

225

everyday living skills. Working within this framework, a teacher could construct a long-term goal for each subcomponent and then break the long-term goal into short-term objectives. For the fourth-grade student whose profile was presented earlier in this section, examples of an annual goal and objectives (Turnbull 1976) in each subcomponent area are as follows:

1. Number Concepts
    A. Present level of performance: Can count to 100 by ones, twos, fives, and tens, but cannot go past 100.
    B. Long-term goal: By the end of the academic year, the student will be able to read, write, and manipulate numbers from 101 to 500.
    C. Short-term objectives:
        (1) Rote counts beginning with any three-digit number from 100 to 200 up to a designated number, 200 or below.
        (2) Reads any number from 100 to 200.
        (3) Writes from memory any number from 100 to 200.
        (4) Tells the missing number in an incomplete oral sequence using the numbers 100 through 200.
        (5) Writes the missing numbers in an incomplete written sequence using the numbers 100 through 200.
        (6) States, both verbally and using the appropriate mathematical symbols ($>$ and $<$), whether a given number is less than or greater than another number, for numbers between 100 and 200.
        (7) Rote counts beginning with any three-digit number from 200 to 500 up to a designated number, 500 or below.
        (8) Reads any number from 200 to 500.
        (9) Writes from memory any number from 200 to 500.
        (10) Tells the missing number in an incomplete oral sequence using the numbers 200 through 500.
        (11) Writes the missing number in an incomplete written sequence using the numbers 200 through 500.
        (12) States, both verbally and using the appropriate mathematical symbols ($>$ and $<$), whether a given number is less than or greater than another number, for numbers from 200 to 500.
2. Facts and Processes
    A. Present level of performance: Has mastered basic addition facts and column addition with no carrying; is ready to learn two-digit addition with carrying.
    B. Long-term goal: By the end of the academic year, the student will have mastered carrying in two- or three-digit numbers and will begin learning basic subtraction facts.

C. Short-term objectives:
    (1) Adds a two-digit and a one-digit number with carrying.
    (2) Adds a two-digit and a two-digit number with carrying.
    (3) Solves column addition with three two-digit addends with carrying.
    (4) Adds a three-digit and a one-digit number carrying to the ten's place.
    (5) Adds a three-digit and a two-digit number carrying to the ten's place.
    (6) Adds a three-digit and a three-digit number carrying to the ten's place.
    (7) Solves column addition with three two- or three-digit numbers carrying to the ten's place.
    (8) Adds a three-digit and a two-digit number carrying to either the ten's or hundred's place.
    (9) Adds two three-digit numbers carrying to either the ten's or hundred's place.
    (10) Solves column addition with three two- or three-digit numbers with carrying to either the ten's or hundred's place.
    (11) Solves subtraction problems using real objects with basic facts 0 through 9.
    (12) Solves subtraction problems using pictures with basic facts 0 through 9.
    (13) Subtracts any two one-digit numbers.
3. Time
    A. Present level of performance: Is able to tell time only by the hour.
    B. Long-term goal: By the end of the academic year, the student will be able to tell time to the minute.
    C. Short-term objectives:
        (1) Points to and understands the function of the hour and minute hands.
        (2) States that 60 minutes equals one hour.
        (3) Tells time by the hour with 100 percent accuracy.
        (4) Understands that 30 minutes equals one-half hour.
        (5) States that when the minute hand is pointing to six, it is the half-hour.
        (6) Tells time by the half-hour.
        (7) Uses the terms *past* and *after* to tell time in five-minute intervals between 12 and 6 o'clock.
        (8) Uses the terms *before, to,* and *till* to tell time in five-minute intervals before the new o'clock hour.
        (9) Reads and writes time equivalents.
        (10) Tells time by the minute.

4. Money
   A. Present level of performance: Can count change to 25 cents.
   B. Long-term goal: By the end of the academic year, the student will be able to count coins to one dollar and bills to 20 dollars.
   C. Short-term objectives:
      (1) Recognizes the cent value of all coins.
      (2) Recognizes the monetary relationships of all coins to each other up to 50 cents (e.g., 5 nickles = 1 quarter, 2 quarters = one-half dollar).
      (3) Counts coins to 50 cents.
      (4) Solves addition and subtraction problems with sums to 50 cents.
      (5) Writes monetary values using the cents sign or dollar mark.
      (6) Recognizes and counts bills representing one, five, ten, and twenty dollars.
      (7) Recognizes the monetary relationships of all coins to each other up to one dollar.
      (8) Counts coins to one dollar.
      (9) Solves addition and subtraction problems with sums to one dollar.
      (10) Counts to one dollar using a variety of coin combinations.
      (11) Makes correct change from purchases up to one dollar.
      (12) Counts change and bills for amounts up to 21 dollars.
5. Measurement
   A. Present level of performance: Can measure in feet and inches but is unfamiliar with even the vocabulary of the metric system.
   B. Long-term goal: By the end of the academic year, the student will be able to use a metric ruler to make a measurement in centimeters.
   C. Short-term objectives:
      (1) States the history of the metric system.
      (2) Uses the metric vocabulary related to linear measure.
      (3) Uses a metric ruler to measure classroom objects in approximate terms.
      (4) Recognizes and uses the measure of a centimeter.
      (5) Can identify objects whose length can be measured in centimeters.
      (6) Can identify the relationship of meters and centimeters to feet and inches and can convert from one measure to another.
      (7) Uses a meter stick to measure in whole and fractional parts.
      (8) Can estimate the approximate length of objects in meters and centimeters.
6. Geometry: Assessment revealed that the student can identify various geometric figures, but is unable to use a compass to construct a circle

or an angle. This area seems to have the least relevance to everyday arithmetic skills, and the teacher might decide not to include goals and objectives in geometry as part of the student's arithmetic curriculum. Rather than teaching concepts related to geometry as a formal part of the arithmetic curriculum, the teacher could integrate these concepts into art activities. For example, the student might identify and draw geometric forms in use such as a bicycle, roof, and house. It is difficult to know where to trim the curriculum; however, curtailment is necessary for students whose achievement is significantly below grade level and whose learning rate will likely be slower than the majority of students in the class. While classroom peers are working on geometry during arithmetic periods, handicapped students with significant lags in achievement can pursue the mastery of the specified objectives in the other subcomponents of their program. (It should be remembered that all handicapped students do not achieve below grade level. Students with physical, sensory, and emotional/behavioral disadvantages may not need adaptation in curriculum content. These students, however, may require adaptation in the method of instruction, which will be discussed in the next section.)

After the goals and objectives have been identified, teachers must make the decision of ordering the content to be taught in the various arithmetic subcomponents. The question here relates to *when* to teach the specified skills and concepts. Students who are handicapped in their learning potential and/or achievement have more systematic success when they are provided with the opportunity to practice new concepts and skills to the point of proficiency before moving on to something new. This means that when the concept of carrying is introduced, for example, the student should focus entirely on this area with practice distributed over enough days to solidly master each objective before moving to the next objective representing an increased level of difficulty. Success at each step insures the development of a strong foundation in arithmetic. Some students find it frustrating to work routinely on one or more subcomponents (e.g., money, time) during the first part of the week and another subcomponent (e.g., measurement) during the latter part of the week. When learning is more difficult anyway, constantly expecting the student to "change gears" can be an ineffective instructional strategy. Teachers might consider units of instruction with each unit focusing on separate subcomponents. Of course, one must always review periodically objectives that have been mastered previously.

After teachers decide when to teach the specified goals and objectives comprising the arithmetic curriculum for a handicapped student, they may proceed to introduce the objectives systematically. As was pointed out in chapters 3 and 4, many objectives must be broken down further into a series of smaller steps. This process, known as task analysis, is most applicable to the subject of arithmetic. Teachers should carefully analyze the prerequisite skills involved in the mastery of each objective and teach these skills in a step by step fashion. The value of this type of ordered and meticulous approach to teaching cannot be overstated relative to the successful achievement of handicapped students. Many students with handicaps are further penalized in schools when teachers assume they know skills that they do not, expect them to make huge leaps in skill development, or expect that they will learn arithmetic or other skills incidentally. Classroom success will be enhanced when teachers accurately assess students to pinpoint what they have learned and what they need to learn next, provide step-by-step instruction in a sequenced format, and actively teach the skills and concepts to handicapped students.

Instructional Adaptations

The instructional adaptations discussed in this section are directly related to some of the educational characteristics of handicapped students identified in chapter 1. These characteristics are associated with various types of handicapping conditions and are likely to interfere with the arithmetic achievement of students unless curriculum accommodations are made. The learning characteristics to be included relate to attention, concept development, memory, generalization, learning rate, delayed language, and fine motor problems.

Attention

Many handicapped students—for example, those with emotional/behavioral and cognitive disadvantages—have difficulty directing their attention to the appropriate objective during instruction. Various factors may contribute to this difficulty. Some students who have difficulty maintaining attention may sit in the back of the room and think about other things during arithmetic instruction. Teachers should consider changing the seating arrangement so that the students who seem to experience problems attending to arithmetic are seated in close proximity to the teacher. Cues —for example, touching the student, signaling with the hand with a predetermined and established gesture, or giving verbal prompts such as "think" or "listen"—may be used. The handicapped student might also be seated in close proximity to attentive peers who could serve as appropriate behavioral models.

Some handicapped students may fail to pay attention during arithmetic because they do not understand the content of the lesson or the directions for a particular assignment. If assessment and goal setting have been done properly, the student should be working on tasks commensurate with his achievement. When the complexity of materials appears to be too difficult, the teacher should back up in the sequence of skills. Readjustment of objectives is often necessary before the exact achievement level is pinpointed. Making sure that the student understands the directions of the task is a very important teacher responsibility. Suggestions which might be beneficial include:

1. Using consistent language easily understood by the student.

   1. *Example:* When the vocabulary of the metric system is introduced, be sure the student understands one term before another is introduced.

2. Using routine formats of seatwork assignments.

   2. *Example:* If arithmetic contracts are used, they should be set up in a routine way with standard organization for identifying activities, materials, and requirements.

3. Using a peer tutor to explain directions to a handicapped student.

   3. *Example:* If the student is expected to work ten problems on page 38 of his arithmetic workbook, have a peer check to see if he understands and finds the right page. If not, the peer can explain directions.

4. Using the tape recorder to provide a more detailed explanation to the handicapped student.

   4. *Example:* If the student is assigned a task on number concepts and the teacher believes that review or a thorough explanation is necessary, a recorded message could be put on the tape recorder. The student could then refer to the message several times if necessary.

Another problem associated with focusing attention appropriately is that many textbooks and workbooks, particularly in arithmetic, are distracting in terms of the particular content composition on each page. On a given page of a workbook, there might be ten addition, subtraction, and multiplication problems placed around various examples, charts, written directions, and pictures. The print on the page may be in several different scripts and make use of three or four different colors. For some students, this diverse composition might be intriguing; however, for many handicapped students it can be a significant obstacle to focusing attention properly. With so many different stimuli, some students can become frustrated and distracted. Teachers should be aware that the performance of some students will improve if their arithmetic textbooks and workbooks have problems representing a single or limited number of concepts on each page, a controlled number of "distractors," and the response required is consistent rather than frequently changing (e.g., supplying a missing addend; computing the sum of a problem).

A final attention problem relates to attention span or the length of time a student is capable of maintaining attention on a given task. Many arithmetic periods in regular classes range from thirty minutes to one hour; many handicapped students have attention spans far briefer than this period. For a student with an attention span of ten minutes, the teacher might plan three ten-minute arithmetic tasks. After each task is completed, the student might be able to have two to five minutes of free time. Another option is to arrange periods of structured arithmetic assignments interspersed with games like *Monopoly, Concentration,* or *Dominoes.* Games are often not as taxing on attention requirements, yet are valuable approaches to learning arithmetic skills. Interesting lessons can boost the length of a student's attention span. Sometimes the topic of a lesson is the differential factor. If a student is highly motivated to learn to count money but is having a difficult time attending to lessons on place value, teachers should take advantage of the student's interest. Place value concepts can easily be couched in the context of monetary values and taught in that framework. On the other hand, students might be more attentive to arithmetic lessons involving a manipulative rather than written response. The student might have an increased attention span when using the abacus, rather than paper and pencil, to solve subtraction problems. As teachers identify arithmetic topics and strategies which motivate the student, these should be capitalized upon and expanded in order to minimize the disadvantage of some handicapped students' attention problem.

Concept Development

A significant component of arithmetic instruction for handicapped students should be directed toward developing concepts and problem-solving skills. Because of many handicapped students' learning disadvantages, teachers sometimes believe that these students are incapable of higher level conceptualization leading to problem solving. This is an unfounded assumption. Handicapped students can understand higher-order concepts and solve problems if they are systematically taught these skills. Often the arithmetic problems of handicapped students relate to the fact that emphasis on computation and problem solving occurred in school prior to the student's developmental foundation for understanding numbers (Hammill and Bartel 1975) or that instruction was based on rote learning. Piaget (1952) has described concepts central to the development of understanding numbers. These concepts are briefly described below with an example of an instructional activity for each concept.

Concepts	*Activity*
1. Classification Grouping objects according to distinguishing characteristics.	1. Students could group objects of different shapes, verbally identifying the shape of each.
2. One-to-One Correspondence Recognizing the relationship that one object in a given set is the same number as one object in a different set regardless of dissimilar characteristics.	2. Matching each ball in a set of three balls with a bat in a set of three bats.
3. Seriation Ordering objects according to a distinguishing characteristic such as size, weight, or color.	3. Ordering Cuisenaire rods (to be discussed later in the chapter) according to height.
4. Conservation The number of objects in a set remains constant regardless of the arrangement of the objects.	4. Make two balls of play dough of identical size. Have the student roll one out into a "rope" and state whether the objects contain the same amount of play dough.

5. Reversibility
   Objects in a set, regardless of their rearrangement, can be returned to their original position without changing their relationship.
	5. Pictorially depict the following equations with plastic chips:
	   $4 + 2 = 6$
	   $6 - 4 = 2$
	   $4 + 2 = 6$

6. Developing Number Concepts Associated with Numerals Recognition of the number of objects corresponding to a particular numeral.	6. Have the students place the number of clothespins, corresponding to the numerals, on tagboard cards.

It is essential that handicapped children master these basic concepts which are precursors to higher-order arithmetic functioning. Many arithmetic problems will be encountered later if this developmental foundation is weak. In teaching these basic concepts, teachers should start with activities employing real objects and opportunities for manipulation, proceed to the use of pictures, and finally work toward the more abstract level of paper and pencil and verbal responses. Initial introduction should also include a minimum of objects or distinguishing elements and gradually move to more complexity as the student's concept development increases.

Cawley and Vitello (1972) have developed a comprehensive model specifying components of the arithmetic instructional system for handicapped students. The four major units included in the model are learning set, interactive, verbal information processing, and conceptual processing. The interactive unit component includes an excellent framework for teachers to use in developing arithmetic instruction for handicapped students (Smith 1974). First, the unit is divided into two sections: Input (the teacher) and output (the student). These sections can be categorized into three cells: Do, see, and say. Table 7–4 illustrates arithmetic programming according to all the combinations of presenting and responding to curriculum content. The "do" level basically involves manipulation of objects and pictures in tasks employing constructing, ordering, arranging, and other similar skills. The "see" level involves responding to pictures or a visual model by pointing or marking; the "say" level emphasizes spoken or written language. As depicted in table 7–4, there are nine combinations of these cells. This model can be a helpful guide for teachers in teaching concepts to handicapped students. Generally, the sequence of difficulty is from the "do-do" combination, at the easiest level, to "see-see" and then "say-say." The following activities related to teaching place value and multiplication concepts, which are often areas of particular difficulty for handicapped students, illustrate the "do," "see," and "say" levels of instruction for student output:

Place Value

"Do"

1. Use the abacus to represent numbers by moving the correct number of beads illustrating values of the one's and ten's place.
2. Have students make a place-value box or chart with compartments representing the one's, ten's, and hundred's places. Sort the appropriate number of plastic chips, straws, sticks, or other small objects into the compartments to represent numerical values.

"See"

1. The teacher or peer tutor presents the student with two bundles of ten sticks in each bundle (on the left) and three individual sticks (on the right). The student is asked to point to the numeral on a work-

sheet which has the same number of tens and ones as represented by the sticks: 29   23   32.
2. The teacher or peer tutor calls out a number between 11 and 19. The student points to the number of dimes and pennies which represents the numerical value.

"Say"
1. A game is played in which one student describes a number by stating how many hundreds, tens, and ones. Other students must call out the number which corresponds to the description.
2. Cards are flashed with numbers ranging from two to three digits. The teacher or peer tutor ask various questions such as, which number is in the one's place? Students must respond verbally.

Multiplication

"Do"
1. Arrange poker chips to find the answer and understand the concept of 4 fives.
2. If the student already understands basic monetary relationships, arrange the combination with coins (two nickels equal one dime) to illustrate that 2 fives equal 10.

"See"
1. The teacher presents the student with various cards representing domino patterns. The student points to the cards representing the concept of 3 twos.
2. The teacher presents strips with sets depicted, such as ... ...   The student points to the correct number of sets, indicating the value of 3 threes.

"Say"
1. A card game similar to *Go Fishing* is played. The student asks for a card by indicating the multiplication combination, such as 4 ones. The student being asked must respond by stating the correct answer, as well as indicating whether or not he has the card.
2. Flashcards can be used with peer tutors or among small groups of students to reinforce combinations after understanding of multiplication concepts has been mastered.

Some students are unable to receive or respond to information in certain ways. Blind students will be unable to perform at the "see" level; therefore, teachers should capitalize on "do" and "say." Some physically handicapped students, unable to use their hands and arms, may be blocked in the output responses of the "do" channel, but are fully capable of benefiting from instruction with the "see" and "say" combinations. On the

Table 7-4
The Interactive Unit of Cawley's Arithmetic Program

	Do	See	Say
Input			
Output			

Examples of each of the nine possible combinations:

Mode combination		Teacher behavior illustrated	Student behavior illustrated
Input	Output		
Do	Do	The teacher has three toy cars and three balls. She says, "Watch me." She groups the three toy cars into a set and the three balls into another set. She says, "Now you do what I did."	The child has the same kind and number of toy cars and balls. He is expected to group the objects into two sets similar to his teacher's groups.
Do	See	The teacher lays seven pieces of string on a table. All of the pieces are of the same color and texture, three are five inches shorter than the other four, all of which are the same size. She separates the three short ones from the four longer ones—making two sets.	The child is shown four pictures, only one of which contains two sets. The remaining three pictures contain more than two sets. The child is asked to point to the picture that is like the display which the teacher constructed.
Do	Say	The teacher combines three sets of blocks, each of which contains two blocks.	The child is asked to write the algorithm that describes what was done and to solve the problem.
See	Do	The teacher presents the following stimulus to the child: $8 - \square = 6$	With a group of blocks, the child is asked to solve the problem by stacking the number of blocks that belong in the box.

		The teacher presents the following problem: $3 + 2 - 1 =$	The child is asked to point to the correct response among the following alternatives: 5 1 2 4 6 0
See	See		

		The child is presented with the following stimulus and asked to tell what time it is: (clock face showing 3 o'clock)	The child is expected to say, "Three o'clock."
See	Say		

		The teacher says to the class, "With your Cuisenaire Rods, prove that $6 + 2$ is the same as $4 + 4$ and that both are different from $5 + 4$.	The children manipulate the rods so that they have a combination of rods for each of the three algorithms. They place the three groups side-by-side to prove the relationships which the teacher requested.
Say	Do		

		The teacher presents the following problem in written form: "Bill has four dogs, Bertha has two cats, and Mark has a hamster. How many more animals does Bill have than Bertha and Mark together?	The child points to one of the following alternatives: 7 1 3 5 2
Say	See		

		The teacher says, "How many ways can you think of to make six?"	The child responds verbally with as many ways as he can generate.
Say	Say		

From Robert M. Smith. *Clinical teaching: Methods of instruction for the retarded.* New York: McGraw-Hill Book Co., 1974.

other hand, deaf students might favor "do" and "see" approaches rather than "say." Teachers should also consider that students able to receive or respond to information at all levels may have preferred methods of learning. Some students may respond to one approach more successfully than another or benefit from a combination of approaches. This model lends itself to capitalizing on the strengths and minimizing the weaknesses of the handicapped student in programming arithmetic and can help teachers greatly in analyzing classroom tasks.

A final area of conceptualization to be discussed in this section is related to verbal problem solving or "word problems." Handicapped students should be taught verbal problem solving in conjunction with computational and process skills. Additionally, verbal problem solving should accompany skill development in the areas of money, time, and measurement. When problem solving is sequenced according to the skill hierarchy, it becomes an integral of the arithmetic curriculum. One way to organize this instruction is for the teacher to compile an index file of word problems keyed according to the sequential order of skills. Problems could be written in different colors to depict the various skill levels. For example, a sequence in arithmetic might be:

	Skill	*Color*		*Problem*
1.	Basic facts—sums 0 to 5	Red	1.	Mary has two books. Bill has three books. How many books do Mary and Bill have all together?
2.	Basic facts—sums 6 to 10	Yellow	2.	There are six girls and three boys in the class. How many children are there in all?
3.	Column addition—three addends	Green	3.	Jane has three apples. Joe has four apples and Sam has four apples. How many apples do Jane, Joe, and Sam have together?
4.	Two-digit and one-digit addition without carrying	Blue	4.	There are 22 pennies in Sally's bank. She puts 5 more pennies in the bank. What is the total number of pennies in Sally's bank?
5.	Column addition with three two digit numbers without carrying	Orange	5.	Jay earned 12 stars, Amy earned 11 stars, and Kate earned 16 stars. Find the sum of the stars the children earned all together.

238

6. Three-digit and one-digit addition without carrying	Brown	6. There are 112 seats in the auditorium. Six more chairs can be placed in front of the stage. What is the total number of people who can be seated in the auditorium?

The teacher or a volunteer might prepare five to ten cards with one problem per card at each level of difficulty. Answers could be put on a separate card to provide for self-correcting. This type of system encourages individualization and independence, since the student can proceed without the teacher always having to find word problems at the appropriate level. For handicapped students unable to read, the problems could be put on a cassette tape or a peer tutor could read the problems to the student. Additionally, the peer tutor or a volunteer could prepare the tapes. Another strategy for teaching problem solving would be to develop learning activity packets (LAPs) described in chapter 4. The LAPs could be programmed so that real objects or pictures were available for the student to manipulate as he solved the problems. The reference dictionary (to be described in the next section) can be used to help the handicapped student focus on cues important in indicating the appropriate process to use in solving a word problem (e.g., find the sum; how much all together?). Goodstein (1973) warns against teachers promoting mechanical rather than conceptual understanding by teaching the student to scan the word problem for cue words. Teaching the student cues should be couched in the total process of teaching comprehension of verbal problems in problem solving. Proficiency in comprehension of problems should include an instructional sequence of using problems with extraneous information, categorizing information as a step in problem solving, using problems with more than one operation involved, and leaving out essential information and having the student identify the necessary missing elements. Again, successful problem-solving instruction must proceed from simple to complex in a step-by-step fashion.

Memory

Attention and concept development are necessary ingredients of memory. In order to remember, a student must first actively attend; therefore, the strategies included in the previous sections to aid attention also are applicable to the improvement of memory. Memory is greatly enhanced by meaningfulness of the material to be learned. Arithmetic concepts become meaningful as they are understood through systematic instruction programmed at the "do," "see," and "say" levels. Many memory problems associated with arithmetic are, therefore, eliminated when students selectively pay attention to the relevant cues and have a solid understanding of concepts.

Memorization plays a vital role in arithmetic proficiency. Number recognition, rote counting, basic facts, time equivalents, measurements tables, and monetary relationships are but a few of the arithmetic area that require memorization of one kind or another to attain mastery. Many handicapped students have the distinct disadvantage of having a hard time remembering information. As pointed out in chapter 1, strategies to improve the memory skills of handicapped students systematically may be used.

One of the most fundamental aspects of the arithmetic curriculum involving memorization is learning the basic facts in addition, subtraction, multiplication, and division. It is generally preferable for handicapped students to memorize the combinations of the basic facts after prerequisite concepts have been mastered. Ineffective instruction and lack of motivation on the part of handicapped students has often resulted in their being excused from learning the basic facts. In far more cases than not, these students are capable of mastering this memorization requirement. However, memorization should only occur *after* the student has demonstrated an understanding of the basic number concepts described by Piaget as necessary for arithmetic proficiency and concepts integrally associated with the computation of facts and processes (e.g., associative and communicative operations). Emphasis should be placed first on adequate concept development and then on memorization. The beginning point of instruction in memorizing the basic facts is assessment. If the student is working on addition, he should be pretested on all combinations of the basic facts. The pretest can be either written or oral. The student should be instructed to answer only the problems he knows immediately. Each student's level of performance should be recorded, since the particular combination of problems mastered and not mastered will vary from student to student. After the teacher has identified which facts the student knows and which facts he must learn next, the student's preferred methods of learning the facts should be established. The teacher might consider a variety of methods at the "do," "see," and "say" levels including counting objects, using the abacus, using the number line, counting on fingers, using card games, drilling with fact cards, or drilling with records. Again, some students may respond to one particular approach while others benefit from a combination. To identify preferred learning styles, the teacher should experiment assigning the student a specified number of facts to learn and a particular method of practice. Based on the student's performance and his expressed preferences, the teacher can document effective strategies. There are several important considerations in teaching various counting systems. A major factor is that some handicapped students may not ever master rote memorization; therefore, it is important to use a system which will not stigmatize them in upper grades or adult life if they need to continue using it. Seeing a handicapped adult counting on his fingers to compute in his checkbook while standing in line at the bank is evidence of the importance of this consideration related to social acceptability. A method which has demonstrated effectiveness with handicapped students (Kramer and Krug 1973; Kokaska 1973) is counting fixed reference points on numerals.

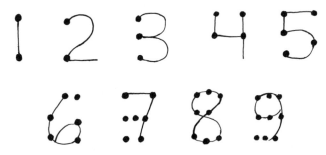

Kramer and Krug (1973) state the advantages of using this system as providing consistency in perception of the numbers and the immediate association between the number and its value. This method lends itself to a sequenced transition from using cues to memorization.

Step 1	Permanent dots first placed and then counted.
Step 2	Dots counted as placed and becoming less prominent.
Step 3	Dots begin to fade and maybe pencil touches or eye fixations. The top number may not have dots.

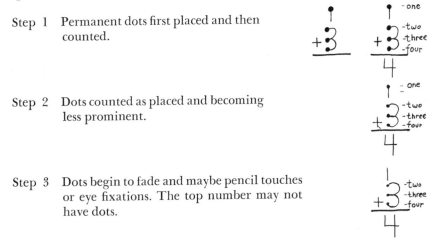

Step 4   Complete transition to rote mastery.

After the method the student will use in learning the facts has been identified, the teacher should next pinpoint the student's learning rate for facts. Some handicapped students may be able to learn five or six new facts per day, while others may have a rate of one or two facts per week. To establish learning rate, the teacher could use the following procedure:

1.   Make an educated guess in assigning the student a certain number of facts to learn during a daily arithmetic lesson.

2.   Use methods already identified as successful for the student for practice. Remember that some students will need more drill than others.

3.   Evaluate the student on the assigned facts at the end of the day and at the end of the week. The number of basic facts learned per day which the student successfully completes on the evaluation at the end of the week becomes the student's daily learning rate.

When learning rate has been established, the student should be assigned that specified number of facts per day for practice and drill. Facts may have to be adjusted up or down based on the student's performance. The goal is for the handicapped student to master as many facts as possible working at a success level. If the student is consistently missing a number of problems on the mastery test every week, it is an indication that either the learning rate is too high, the method of instruction is inadequate, or the student is not approaching the task as conscientiously as he should. Students might keep records of their progress, graphing the number of problems they learn each week and keeping charts of the particular combinations they learn. In this way, the reinforcement procedure (graphing and charting) for memorizing the basic facts provides the opportunity for learning different arithmetic skills. The probability that handicapped students will learn the basic facts is greatly increased when the instruction is geared to the student's level of achievement, preferred learning styles, and rate of learning. The student's awareness of his continuous and consistent progress often provides a renewed impetus to master arithmetic skills. These same principles of programming memorization of basic facts apply to other aspects of the arithmetic curriculum requiring memory skills such as measurement tables and monetary relationships.

A strategy used with handicapped students with great success is the development of a reference dictionary (Scott 1968), which is basically a compilation of sheets including examples or referents representing the instructional objectives on which the student is working. The reference dictionary is continually updated as the student progresses from one objective to the next and covers approximately twenty days of work at any given point. The sheets may be bound in a notebook or folder. The purpose of the dictionary is to provide a model the student can refer to in order to maximize his success on a task covering his total academic program. In the area of arithmetic, the reference dictionary can be a tremendous source of ameliorating memory deficits of handicapped students. Examples of arithmetic skills and corresponding sheets the teacher or a volunteer could develop for the reference dictionary are as follows:

Skills	*Reference Dictionary Sheets*
1. Basic facts	1. A sheet with the facts and answers that a student is in the process of mastering.
2. Monetary relationships	2. One nickel = five pennies One dime = ten pennies (Could be written or in pictorial form. Real coins could also be taped to sheet to depict relationships.)
3. Time concepts	3. *2 o'clock*
4. Computational processes	4. $\begin{array}{r} \square \\ 2\ 6 \\ +\ 1\ 5 \\ \hline \end{array}$ Visual prompt for setting up and solving an addition problem.
5. Symbols of metric units	5. mg—milligram g—gram Kg—Kilogram
6. Word problem clues	6. Clues to knowing when to add: a. What is sum? b. How many all together?

When handicapped students can refer to an easily accessible guide when they do not remember necessary information to complete a problem or assignment, their independent work habits and overall task success are promoted. The reference dictionary is also an excellent source of review when the student finishes an assignment early or has free time. Essentially this strategy insures that the student has information he needs so that he does not have to rely totally on his memory. Some teachers may believe they are being too easy on the student by providing a ready source of reference material and correct answers for the student as he needs it, but this viewpoint is pedagogically unsupportable. Programming for success is a characteristic of excellent instruction, not leniency. In addition to reducing the detrimental educational implications of memory problems, the reference dictionary can also be a source of reinforcement for the student. As the handicapped learner masters the various concepts included in the dictionary representative of his instructional objectives, he can underline the concept with a colored magic marker. Generally, students not only enjoy indicating their successes, but they also have "visual proof" of the progress they are making. In the area of basic facts, for example, a good feeling on the part of the student and his parents is practically assured when the goal of underlining *every* addition or subtraction fact in the dictionary has been accomplished. Thus, the dictionary can be the basis of on-going record keeping and reinforcement.

A final benefit of the dictionary is that it can be a vehicle for coordinating the instructional programs between the resource and regular classroom programs. The resource teacher might initially set up the dictionary based on the arithmetic assessment and give the child assignments related to using the information from the dictionary while he is in the regular classroom. Again, the dictionary facilitates independent work, since the student has the information needed to complete problems successfully. While his nonhandicapped peers are working on other arithmetic objectives, the handicapped student may proceed on his own assignment. Individualization, in turn, becomes more of a reality in the regular classroom.

Other strategies are effective in increasing the memory of handicapped students. Memory is enhanced when skills and concepts are meaningful to the student. It can be very difficult to memorize information that is not understood or seems to be irrelevant to the student. For example, if the objective is for the student to memorize common metric kitchen measures, a handicapped student will probably be more successful with this task when he is provided with the opportunity to use metric kitchen measures in following recipes and can associate favorite foods that can be prepared or measured with the metric units. This type of experiential instruction promotes a clear understanding of concepts, as well as long-term retention. Handicapped students often have difficulty remembering because they do not employ active strategies when they are confronted with a task in which memory is required (Ellis 1970). This point may be illustrated by examining typical ways in which adults remember new information. Stop when you get to the end of this paragraph and look for a time period of approximately eight seconds at the number which is written.

After the eight seconds is completed, cover the number in the book and write it from memory on a piece of paper. Ready?

8   1   3   5   9   2   7   0   6

The important point to consider is not so much whether you were 100 percent correct, but rather what you did to try to help you remember. Think about the strategy you used. Some people tend to group a series of numbers into clusters and remember the clusters as one unit, such as: 813, 592, 706. Another strategy may have been to associate the individual numbers or clusters with something that is meaningful. For example, the first two digits, 81, might be associated with the fact that a person used to wear that number on his football jersey. Other strategies could involve saying the numbers over and over to oneself (rehearsing) or picturing them in the mind's eye (imagery). Whatever the particular strategy, the majority of adults actively try to remember when faced with a memory task. A problem of many students who have learning handicaps is that they do not automatically employ strategies when required to use their memory; however, these students can be taught to be more "active" learners. During arithmetic instruction, teachers can help handicapped students by teaching them memory strategies such as clustering, associating, rehearsing, and imagery. An example of each strategy as it relates to arithmetic follows:

Strategy	*Example*
1. Clustering	1. Learns social security number by grouping digits into three separate units.
2. Associating	2. Learns the number of days in each month by association with the verse "Thirty Days Has September."
3. Rehearsing	3. Learns to repeat the sequence of solving a problem, such as:

Work from right to left

16   Multiply in one's column first

x 3   Cross-multiply in ten's column

Double-check

4. Imagery	4. If a student cannot remember how to form the number 8, he could refer to his reference dictionary and then close his eyes and visualize the 8 and the kinesthetic motions required to form an 8.

In teaching the aspects of the arithmetic curriculum that involve memory, the teacher should work toward overlearning with handicapped students (Gearheart 1976). This means that often a substantial amount of practice and drill is required for students to gain solid proficiency. Once overlearning has occurred, handicapped students are capable of long-term retention. Some teachers have the erroneous impression that teaching handicapped students is a hopeless task, because these students are incapable of remembering information over a long period of time. The teacher may believe, for example, that the student will forget the basic facts he learns one day after a couple of weeks has elapsed. When this type of forgetting occurs, it means that the students had not attained total proficiency in the first place. If the handicapped student is provided with sufficient practice and drill during the memorization process, he will generally be capable of long-term retention.

One final consideration is that every handicapped student will not be able to attain proficiency in memorizing arithmetic skills and concepts. Some students will be at a greater disadvantage relative to memory than others. When students have particular difficulty, it is important to help them compensate or work around this problem. The notation system—using fixed reference points on numbers—is one strategy applicable to continued use. Another strategy to consider is using a low-cost pocket calculator (Bitter 1977). These calculators are extremely accessible and handy and may be used to compute the basic facts, as well as more complicated arithmetic processes. Other uses in the classroom can be for drill and self-checking. An important consideration in terms of use in the adult life of handicapped students who do not memorize basic arithmetic facts is that using a calculator is far more socially acceptable than many other counting systems.

Generalization

The generalization of arithmetic skills to experiences of everyday living is a particularly crucial area for handicapped students, yet it is one that is often overlooked. Since handicapped students need a significant amount of drill to master basic facts and processes, sometimes teachers may provide one worksheet after another of isolated computation and fail to help the students make the generalization between the computation and the arithmetic demands likely to be encountered in everyday living. Since some handicapped students are often at a disadvantage in making generalizations on their own, the result is that arithmetic skills and concepts may not carry over into needed situations.

Teachers can help these students with the generalization of arithmetic skills by providing meaningful arithmetic instruction related to the experiences which the student has already encountered or is likely to encounter. Teaching the arithmetic content in the areas of money, time, and measurement in a relevant context is easy to accomplish. An excellent strategy for teaching the generalization of money skills is through setting up a classroom store (Schulz 1973). The students learn skills related to the cost of food and other products, making change, sales tax, special sales, budgeting, record keeping, reading newspaper advertisements, writing checks, and occupational awareness. Thus students immediately have the opportunity to use arithmetic and related skills in a relevant context representative of everyday living demands.

Another consideration in teaching for generalization is that the skills learned in one situation must be transferable to another. An unfortunate example that highlights the importance of this consideration happened to Billy, a cognitively impaired student of elementary school age. A major objective in his arithmetic curriculum was learning to tell time. Billy, his teacher, and his parents all worked very hard providing a great deal of practice for him to learn this important skill. Realizing how hard he was working, his grandparents promised him a new watch when he had accomplished his goal of telling time. Finally, when mastery had been accomplished, Billy received the watch in the mail with great anticipation. He tried to tell his parents the time from his new watch, but he was at a complete loss. The watch had Roman rather than Arabic numerals, and the skills he had worked so hard to accomplish were not immediately transferable. This problem illustrates what often happens to handicapped students, yet it can be significantly minimized as teachers realize the importance of applying newly acquired skills in a variety of ways. Billy's teacher and parents might go back and help him generalize his time-telling skills to clocks with Roman numerals, digital clocks, clocks with no numerals, and clocks representing a variety of shapes, sizes, and types. In this way, generalization can be assured.

When handicapped children are learning basic facts and computational processes, it is important for them to use these skills immediately in the context of daily problems at the "do," "see," and "say" levels in order to promote generalization. For example, when students are learning the basic addition facts with sums 0–5, these facts should be introduced through the use of experiences and real objects—for example, counting children in the classroom, books, desks, or pencils. The problem, such as $2 + 3 = 5$, takes on meaning as it is introduced in a relevant context; furthermore, the experiential context helps the student generalize the skill to daily situations. As each level of increasing difficulty of facts and processes skills is introduced, generalization to everyday situations should be made. Many teachers tend to wait to introduce experiential problems until after a large portion of the facts and processes skills have been learned. This results in the mechanical use of these skills for a long period of time, which can lead to difficulty in their suddenly having to apply the skills in the form of "word problems." Emphasis on generalization should not be withheld until culminating skill development on a particular topic, but rather generalization to daily experiences should be an integral part of the introduction of arithmetic skills, as well as a consistent part of practice leading to mastery.

Learning Rate

Since learning rate has been discussed throughout the total chapter, the purpose of this section is merely to summarize those points.

1. Learning rate is a major consideration in the successful instruction of handicapped students. It takes more time for many handicapped students to master arithmetic concepts than it does for nonhandicapped students. It is important to allow sufficient time for practice of skills at each level so that mastery will be reached.

2. No two handicapped students are exactly alike as to their rate of learning. Factors that may influence learning rate are achievement level, instructional methods and materials, whether prerequisite skills are mastered, meaningfulness of the material, selective attention, type of reinforcement, and general interest in the subject. Techniques can be used by classroom teachers to assess a student's learning rate in various areas of the arithmetic curriculum. A procedure for conducting a learning rate test was previously outlined in this chapter. Since learning rate in influenced by various factors, it often increases or decreases. Teachers need to observe carefully the performance of handicapped students and make adjustments, if necessary, in learning rate expectations. Many students with sensory, physical, or emotional/behavioral disadvantages develop accelerated learning rates when appropriate instructional strategies are used.

3. The result of a lowered learning rate is that the handicapped student often falls farther and farther behind his nonhandicapped classmates. The need for individualization increases in proportion to the discrepancy between the achievement of the student and the general achievement level of his peers. It is important to remember, however, that all students in the class will differ on learning rate in the various subject areas. Adaptations are necessary for all students, not just handicapped ones.

Delayed Language

Students having delayed language development can be at a disadvantage in arithmetic, as well as in language arts areas. Regardless of whether the language delay is attributable to cognitive impairment, a learning disability, or a hearing impairment, teachers can help students minimize this problem. One strategy is for the teacher to use a simple arithmetic vocabulary with linguistic consistency. Rather than using all the terms, *regrouping, renaming,* and *carrying,* to refer to the same concept, the handicapped student's confusion can be reduced by using only one label (Lowenbraun and Affleck, 1976). In the area of telling time, a source of confusion can result from referring to 8:45 as "quarter 'til," "quarter to," "15 minutes before," or "8:45." Consistency in terminology is important. Teachers should encourage handicapped students to let them know when they do not understand the language used in a classroom discussion or in directions for an assignment. Students are more likely to let teachers know when they need clarification if teachers respond positively to their requests rather than with exasperation because the student does not understand. When students do not understand particular vocabulary words or language structures, teachers might systematically teach these language concepts. An important consideration is that just because a handicapped student is deficient in an area is no indication he cannot significantly improve his skills with sound instruction. Therefore teachers should not necessarily drop the use of language the handicapped student does not understand; rather, they might include language skills related to arithmetic as part of the curriculum.

The reference dictionary can be used to minimize language disadvantages. Vocabulary lists related to various arithmetic objectives could be kept in the dictionary with possibly a picture or a written definition, depending upon the student's achievement level, to explain the meaning of the word or concept. In the area of time, the vocabulary list might include clock, hour hand, minute hand, o'clock, 30 minutes after, before, second, sixty, A.M., P.M., and many others. When the handicapped student hears the word in class or runs across it in an assignment and is unsure of the meaning, he may look it up in the dictionary. As vocabulary lists are mastered, more difficult ones may be introduced.

Some handicapped students with language delays benefit more from visual prompts or demonstrations than from lengthy verbal explanations. In teaching the student how to set up a division problem, the teacher might work several examples to provide the student with a model format, such as,

$$
\begin{array}{r}
8 \\
8\,)\overline{6\ 6} \\
6\ 4 \\
\hline
2\ \text{R}
\end{array}
\qquad
\begin{array}{r}
\square \\
6\,)\overline{3\ \ 7} \\
\square\ \square \\
\hline
\square\ \text{R}
\end{array}
$$

and/or provide a simply stated procedural outline for solving the problem. The emphasis of arithmetic programming might be on the "do" and "see" levels of instruction rather than the "say" for students with language delays.

Fine Motor Problems

Handicapped students with fine motor problems may encounter difficulty in arithmetic in making written responses and manipulating objects during instruction. Students who have significant writing deficiencies are probably going to have difficulty learning to form numerals and engaging in the written requirements involved during arithmetic instruction in most regular classes. When numerals are initially introduced, it may be helpful for the student to start making large numerals on the chalkboard and on pieces of newsprint and gradually reducing the size of the numerals on notebook paper. Students might trace stencils of numerals and use visual prompts which could gradually be faded:

Some students benefit from physical guidance—actual help in moving their pencil in the desired direction. If writing interferes with the student's ability to demonstrate an understanding of arithmetic skills, the teacher could allow opportunities for oral tests, with the student responding either directly to the teacher, peer tutor, or using a tape recorder. Although it probably would be difficult for students to type most arithmetic assignments, typing would be one alternative. Students with fine motor problems may be very slow in completing their work, and writing will probably be more fatiguing for them than for other classroom peers. One easy to implement adaptation is simply cutting down the length of an arithmetic assignment.

The other major arithmetic consideration for students with fine motor problems is that they may not be able to use some instructional materials involving manipulation, such as Cuisenaire rods, adequately. If students do not have the necessary coordination to pick up small objects, teachers should use alternate methods of instruction.

Instructional Materials

Only a limited number of arithmetic instructional materials have been developed specifically for handicapped students; however, many instructional materials developed primarily for nonhandicapped populations are also useful with handicapped students. In selecting materials, teachers must match the instructional objective and the student's learning characteristics with the particular instructional materials. Since students respond differently to various instructional materials, a major component of individualization is matching the student with his material preferences. No two students, handicapped or nonhandicapped, are exactly alike in their instructional needs. A brief overview of some of the arithmetic materials that may be considered for handicapped students follows.

Stern Structural Arithmetic. *Structural Arithmetic* was designed particularly for handicapped students covering kindergarten through third-grade levels. It is a sequenced program using concrete materials to teach number relationships and arithmetic processes. A teacher's guide and mastery tests are included in the program. For information, write to: Houghton-Mifflin Co., 53 West 43rd St., New York, NY 10036.

Sullivan Programmed Math. This programmed series of workbooks emphasizes the development of computational skills. It requires minimal reading, and has progress tests and a teacher's manual. For information write to: Webster Division, McGraw-Hill Book Co., 30th Floor, 1221 Avenue of the Americas, New York, NY 10020.

Distar Arithmetic. Distar is a highly structured and sequential program covering kindergarten to third grade. It covers basic arithmetic facts, processes, and fractions. The program strongly emphasizes a verbal approach. For information, write to: Science Research Associates, Inc., 259 East Erie St., Chicago, IL 60611.

The Learning Skills Series. This series of four workbooks was specifically designed for handicapped students at the junior high level. Prevocational skills are emphasized with content on facts and processes, as well as skills related to reading road maps, newspaper ads, recipes, and thermometers. The four workbooks are correlated so that they are appropriate for four different achievement levels. For information, write to: Webster Division, McGraw-Hill Book Co., 30th Floor, 1221 Avenue of the Americas, New York, NY 10020.

Individualized Arithmetic Instruction. This workbook contains drill and practice sheets on the basic facts. The sheets are open-ended so that they may be used with various processes and multi-ability groups. For information, write to: Love Publishing Co., Denver, CO 80222.

251

Sequential Mathematics. Developed specifically for handicapped students, this individualized program covers skill development in basic facts and processes (addition, subtraction, multiplication, and division). The major components of the program include a diagnostic test, activity segments, mixed practice, and word problems. It is highly sequential, focuses on one skill at a time, and eliminates distracting elements from workbooks. A teacher's guide is available. For information, write to: Harcourt Brace Jovanovich, Inc., 757 Third Ave., New York, NY 10017.

Cuisenaire Rods. Cuisenaire rods are made of wood and vary in length from one to ten centimeters. They are useful in teaching manipulative and conceptual skills at kindergarten through sixth-grade levels. They emphasize a visual and tactile approach to learning. For information, write to: Cuisenaire Company of America, Inc., 12 Church St., New Rochelle, NY 10805.

Developmental Learning Materials. A wide variety of arithmetic aids and games is available, such as clock puzzles, fraction puzzles, money dominoes, sorting box and game, and a multiplication game. The materials are highly motivating, durably constructed, and cover a grade span of kindergarten through upper elementary school. For information, write to: Developmental Learning Materials, 7440 Natchez Ave., Niles, IL 60648.

Pacemaker Arithmetic Program. This program, designed for students with learning problems, includes student worksheets on carbon masters covering readiness skills (shape recognition, quantitative concepts, and basic vocabulary) and number concepts through ten. A teacher's manual is included. For information, write to: Fearon Publishers, 6 Davis Dr., Belmont, CA 94002.

Arithmetic: Step-by-Step. This program contains ten units on topics such as counting, sets, addition, and the calendar. Three hundred carbon masters are included, with the same topic programmed at three levels of difficulty. For information, write to: Continental Press, Inc., Elizabethtown, PA 17022.

"The Six Wonderful Records of Facts." These records present addition, subtraction, multiplication, and division facts at presentation rates of both six and four and one-half seconds. The facts are divided into easier and harder sections. For more information, write to: John D. Caddy, Box 251, Canoga Park, CA 91305.

I'm OK, You're OK: Let's Go Metric. This workbook includes metric activities covering linear, area, volume, temperature, liquid, and weight skills.

Activities are programmed at four reading levels ranging from no skills required to high levels. For information, write to: Midwest Publications Co., Inc., P.O. Box 129, Troy, MI 48084.

Clockface with Raised Print and Braille Numbers. This plastic frame clock has both raised numerals and braille numerals on its face as an aid in teaching blind children to tell time. The hands are attached to gears inside the frame so that the hour hand follows the minute hand in proper sequence. For information, write to: American Printing House for the Blind, 1839 Frankfort Ave., P.O. Box 6085, Louisville, KY 40206.

Metric-English One-Foot Braille Rulers with Caliper Slides. With the purpose of teaching the relationship between metric and English systems of measurement, raised lines and braille numbers indicate one inch, one-fourth inch, one centimeter, and one-half centimeter intervals. For information, write to: American Printing House for the Blind, 1839 Frankfort Ave., P.O. Box 6085, Louisville, KY 40206.

Abacuses. The Cramner abacus is a pocket-sized device which can be used to teach arithmetic facts and processes. It has one bead above the bar and four beads below. An enlarged abacus is also available which is easier to manipulate for students who have fine motor problems. Additionally, two instructional books in both braille and large print may be ordered. For information, write to: American Printing House for the Blind, 1839 Frankfort Ave., P.O. Box 6085, Louisville, KY 40206.

Guidebooks for Teachers

Plus. This book contains dozens of activities, games, and independent work ideas in areas of counting, time, facts, numbers, money, fractions, and others. For information, write to: Educational Service, Inc., P.O. Box 219, Stevensville, MI 49127.

Kids' Stuff Math. This guidebook of ideas covers areas of numeration, sets, fractions, problem solving, and others. For information, write to: Incentive Publications, Box 12522, Nashville, TN 37212.

Activities Handbook for Teaching the Metric System. Classroom activities in the areas of linear measurement, volume and capacity, area and perimeter, temperature, and mass are included, as well as a basic introduction to the metric system. For information, write to: Allyn and Bacon, Inc., 470 Atlantic Ave., Boston, MA 02210.

253

Guidebook for Parents

Telepac. These programmed workbooks were developed specifically to aid parents in teaching basic arithmetic skills to their handicapped child. Two areas included are number symbols and counting. For information, write to: Exceptional Child Center UMC–68, Utah State University, Logan, UT 84322.

References and Suggested Readings

Bitter, G. 1977. The calculator and the curriculum. *Teacher* 64–67.

Cawley, J. F., and Vitello, S. J. 1972. Model for arithmetic programming for handicapped children. *Exceptional Children* 39:101–110.

Ellis, N. R. 1970. Memory processes in retardates and normals. In N. R. Ellis, ed., *International review of research in mental retardation,* vol. 4. New York: Academic Press.

Gearheart, B. R. 1976. *Teaching the learning disabled.* St. Louis: Mosby.

Goodstein, H. A. 1973. The performance of educable mentally retarded children on subtraction word problems. *Education and Training of the Mentally Retarded* 8:197–202.

Hammill, D. D., and Bartel, N. R. 1975. *Teaching children with learning and behavior problems.* Boston: Allyn and Bacon.

Kokaska, S. M. 1973. A notation system in arithmetic. *Education and Training of the Mentally Retarded* 8:211–216.

Kramer, T., and Krug, D. A. 1973. A rationale and procedure for teaching addition. *Education and Training of the Mentally Retarded* 8:140–144.

Lowenbraun, S., and Affleck, J. Q. 1976. *Teaching mildly handicapped children in regular classes.* Columbus, Ohio: Merrill.

Piaget, J. 1952. *The child's conception of numbers.* London: Routledge & Kegan Paul, Ltd.

Reisman, F. 1972. *A guide to diagnostic teaching of arithmetic.* Columbus, Ohio: Merrill.

Schulz, J. B. 1973. Simulation for special education. *Education and Training of the Mentally Retarded* 8:137–140.

Scott, F. 1968. Personal communication.

Smith, R. M. 1974. *Clinical teaching: Methods of instruction for the retarded.* New York: McGraw-Hill.

Turnbull, A. P., ed. 1976. *Carolina arithmetic inventory.* Chapel Hill: University of North Carolina.

Chapter Eight

*Teaching Science, Social Studies,
Physical Education, Music, and Art*

This chapter covers five major curriculum areas, including science, social studies, physical education, music, and art. These subjects are particularly important in mainstreaming, since they often represent the portions of the curriculum in which many handicapped students spend the greatest amount of time in regular classes. Although most resource teachers probably spend the majority of their time working with handicapped students on skills and concepts primarily associated with language arts and arithmetic, it is important for resource teachers to help facilitate the instructional and social integration of handicapped students in the five curriculum areas to be discussed in this chapter. As with all aspects of mainstreaming, shared responsibility among educators is a necessity.

Science and Social Studies

The areas of science and social studies are considered together, since the nature of curriculum adaptation for handicapped students tends to be similar in these two subjects. Kirman and Nay (1975) discuss the similarities between science and social studies as both subjects incorporate an inquiry approach and share a major concern for values development. Handicapped students often are placed at a disadvantage in achieving success in science and social studies classes, yet many of these disadvantages can be significantly minimized through appropriate instructional strategies. Students who are mentally retarded or learning disabled frequently experience difficulty in keeping up with the academic requirements of science and social studies classes, such as reading the textbook, comprehending technical vocabulary, writing reports, following the many directions of an experiment, and other such requirements. Sensory handicaps (vision and hearing) can also interfere with science and social studies achievement.

Carolyn, a blind student in the eighth grade, reported that her biology teacher constantly used visual models to clarify his lectures. Rather than explaining in detail the nature of chromosomes, he used pictures as illustrations. During his lectures, he frequently said, "You can see on the chart that . . ." He was right about most students, but he was wrong about Carolyn. She could not see.

Just as visual impairment has implications for curriculum planning, hearing handicaps should also be considered. A significant portion of science and social studies classes involve lecture, discussion, and verbal interaction in small groups. Students with hearing impairments can often be successfully integrated into these classes if instructional strategies can be adapted to accentuate their strengths and minimize their handicaps. This chapter will focus on such curriculum adaptation by suggesting specific methods and materials.

Assessment

The first step to educational planning for handicapped students who require "specially designed instruction" in order to progress successfully in their classes is the development of the individual education plan (see chapter 3). The teacher responsible for science and social studies instruction should develop the individual education plan for each handicapped student in cooperation with the special education resource teacher, the student's parents, and any other members of the committee responsible for devising the program. The development of the individual education plan brings together all considerations which contribute to meaningful concept development.

The beginning point of the individual education plan is assessment, which must be completed to identify the student's level of performance in the content area. Since few commercial tests are available which adequately cover the variety of topics comprising the science and social studies curriculum, teachers often have to construct their own assessment tools. One method of doing this is to specify the major concepts and skills to be covered throughout the year. In science, at one of the intermediate grade levels, these topics might include living things (humans, animals, plants) and space exploration. Teachers might break down each major topic into subtopics, specifying the important skills and concepts to be taught. For example, the study of animals might include classifications, care of animals, needs of animals, defense mechanisms, adaptations to the environment, training animals, and others. Many state and/or system-adopted curriculum guides provide a comprehensive analysis of the component skills and concepts in the various topical areas the teacher plans to cover. Teachers might consider collecting curriculum guides in science and social studies from various sources to help with the task of skill and concept specification. Textbooks may also be helpful.

After the teacher has identified the general curriculum, which will serve as a core of the science and social studies program, a test sampling readiness for the content may be given to handicapped students. These tests may be administered orally by a volunteer or teacher aide. The purpose is not to ask every possible question on every topic, but rather to probe the student's level of knowledge in order to get an indication of whether or not the student is ready to progress according to "grade level" expectations. For example, in the topical area of geography in social studies, a major objective might be map-reading skills. The teacher might plan to use a map of the United States. Upon testing, the teacher may find that a student with learning problems not only has no skills in reading a map of the United States, he may also be unable to read a state map, community map, neighborhood map, or a map depicting the route from his house to the school. In a situation such as this, a teacher clearly learns that instruction must start on a much lower level than what might have been anticipated. Requiring that students "keep up with the class" when they do not have necessary prerequisite skills almost assuredly leads to failure. Planning sound instruction means identifying whether or not a student has the necessary prerequisite skills. Students who have disadvantages associated with mental retardation and learning disabilities will probably lack some important prerequisites. These can, in turn, be incorporated into the student's education plan as teachers engage in the process of task analysis (see chapter 3).

An important type of assessment is documentation of the student's reading level in content area texts. Johnson and Vardian (1973) analyzed sixty-eight social studies texts from grades one through six to pinpoint readability levels. A startling finding was that intermediate texts had a readability range from two to twelve years. Generally, their findings suggested that many elementary social studies texts have readability levels above grade level expectations. It is suspected that similar findings would also apply to science texts. The assessment implications are that the reading level specified in the child's cumulative folder might be inapplicable to making immediate assumptions about the student's capability of reading the social studies or science texts. For example, a student's reading level might be recorded to be at the low fourth-grade level; however, the fourth-grade social studies or science text might have a readability level of sixth grade. Based on the student's reading level, the teacher might understandably expect the student to be able to read the text, unless the teacher is knowledgeable about the readability level of the book. As for assessing the student, the teacher may administer an individual reading inventory, as explained in chapter 6, using content from the social studies or science text (Turner 1976). The procedure for constructing the inventory is identical to that described in chapter 6. The documentation of the student's reading level correlated to the available texts clearly guides the teacher in planning appropriate instruction.

A final type of assessment is identification of the student's preferred learning styles. There are several ways to do this. Sample questionnaires, which may be used to gain information on students on preferred learning style, are described in chapter 3. Questionnaires of this nature are one option for the science and social studies teacher to consider. Another strategy is to talk with the student's former teachers, the student's parents, and the student to find the types of learning situations most conducive to successful achievement. This particular strategy is of particular importance when planning instruction for sensory impaired students. Questions might include: What seating arrangement seems to be the most beneficial? Does the student need large print books, magnification, taped texts, or braille?

Is the hearing impaired student able to read lips? How can the student best be prepared to understand the technical vocabulary of the content area? What is the student's attention span? Does the student have adequate listening comprehension? Does the student have any problems with handwriting? Will language problems interfere with the student's confidence and capability to participate in class discussions and to make oral reports?

Another method of answering these questions is through observation. Teachers might use a combination of all three strategies—questionnaires, interviews, and observation—to accurately identify learning styles in order to plan appropriate social studies and science instruction for the handicapped student.

Concept Development

After assessment information has been collected, the teacher can begin to adapt the curriculum in order to insure adequate concept development. Three major decisions to be made with respect to concept development include the body of content to be taught, the amount of instructional time devoted to each concept, and the instructional methods most likely to result in success.

Content. The body of content is a particularly crucial issue in the science and social studies curriculum when planning for students whose achievement is significantly below grade and age level expectations. As discussed in the previous section on assessment, these students typically lack many of the prerequisites necessary to proceed in higher order concept development; however, they are capable of advancing in the hierarchy of concept development when necessary prerequisites are in place. Sequencing the content to be taught is a major consideration in the development of the individual education plan for science and social studies. At that time, the sequence of short-term objectives, which will serve as the stepping stones to mastery of the annual goals, must be specified. The central concern when making the decision as to when various concepts will be introduced is that students have the necessary prerequisites to be successful in the new learning task. Again, this is particularly important in the cases of students with learning problems. It is virtually impossible to meet the unique needs of every student in the class during every class period, but teachers have to work on foundation skills with students who are achieving substantially below grade level. In the subsequent section on instructional methods, specific strategies for adapting the content of the science and social stud-

259

ies curriculum to the individual levels of handicapped students will be discussed.

Another content consideration is that some students with learning problems will never catch up entirely with their peers. This means that they may never learn some skills and concepts in the general social studies and science curriculum. Therefore decisions must be made about what is most relevant and most necessary for adult adjustment and community living skills. Sometimes the issue of relevant curriculum decisions about adult adjustment and community living is postponed until the senior high years. By that time, some handicapped students have wasted inordinate amounts of time on topics that have no personal value to them. Science and social studies instruction even at the early elementary levels is preparing the student for lifelong adjustment. Students who are handicapped by mental retardation, for example, need the most careful use of instructional time. In almost every case, they are going to learn less than their chronological age peers, and they will probably have lower problem-solving abilities as adults. As a result, there is a high premium on the value of every instructional hour that they spend in school. Relevance to concept development is a central curriculum concern. For every topic the teacher considers including in the science and social studies curriculum, questions should be asked: Will it help the student be more independent in the community, employment setting, and/or at home? What is the jeopardy of the student not knowing this information? Will the student be receiving this information from other sources?

As the responses to these questions are analyzed, teachers can identify the long-range goals and short-term objectives necessary for the effective development and implementation of the individual education plan. One strategy for systematically identifying the most relevant content is for committees of sciences or social studies teachers in the school system jointly to make the decision on the most essential skills and concepts which should comprise the basic core curriculum. This relevant core could be drawn from the state or system-adopted curriculum guide. When the scope and sequence of relevant skills are specified by a systemwide committee, the probability of sequential concept development from grade to grade is increased.

Timing. Handicapped students often require more instructional and practice time before a new skill or concept is mastered. Students who are mentally retarded typically have a slower learning rate. Other students handicapped by deafness may require more time to learn the technical vocabulary associated with science and social studies content. The problems associated with learning disabilities warrant careful consideration.

260

Joe has been diagnosed as having a learning disability. Science seems to be his most difficult class. It's the last period of the afternoon, when Joe usually is feeling tired and "hassled." It seems to take him most of the period to settle down and get to work. He wanders around the room, sharpens his pencil over and over, and tries to involve his peers in conversation. That is the reason Joe rarely completes his assignments by the end of class. He is falling farther and farther behind his peers.

The implication of arranging the curriculum so that handicapped students are afforded appropriate amounts of time to master concepts is that often the rest of the class is ready to move ahead while the handicapped student needs additional practice on previously introduced concepts. Again, more individualization is required to manage this situation in the classroom. As stated in the previous section, some portions of the general curriculum will be deleted for students who are achieving substantially below grade level. Leaving out some concepts frees up time to concentrate more intensively on more relevant concepts.

Instructional Methods.   Four basic categories of instructional methods in typical science and social studies classes include discussion, media, reading, and "doing." Each of these categories will be considered separately with respect to the concept development of handicapped students.

   Discussion. Herman (1969) examined teacher-pupil interaction patterns in a sample of fifth-grade social studies classes. His results indicated that 77 percent of the children's time was devoted to listening to the teacher, other students, or teacher-student exchanges. It is clear that discussing facts and concepts is a frequently used instructional strategy. Handicapped students with disadvantages characterized by a short attention span, memory problems, language delays, and inappropriate behavior may require curriculum adaptation to extended periods of lecture and class discussion.

   Students with a short attention span may be unable to stay in their seat and/or maintain listening behavior for more than a brief period of time. If lectures and discussion are overused, these students may simply tune out. Teachers might consider varying instructional approaches, interspersing periods of lecture and discussion with more active learning experiences. Many students with short attention spans are helped by class periods that include two to three change-of-pace activities. These could include conducting an experiment, completing activities at a learning center, using audiovisual aids, playing a game, working with a peer tutor or volunteer, completing a learning activity package, writing/illustrating a story about the concept being studied, or other such activities. When

261

lecture and discussion are being used, students with attention span problems might be helped by being seated close to the teacher, having a structured outline on the board to follow, and having questions directed at them in an effort to elicit their responses. Experiencing success on the questions often encourages them to be more attentive. The behavior management strategies to be discussed in chapter 9 may also be helpful in increasing attention.

Students with disadvantages associated with memory often do not learn very effectively through a lecture and discussion approach. Typically, inadequate repetition is provided for these students to overcome their memory deficits. The result is that they forget important information. The problems of these students can be minimized through providing a summary of the key points to remember and following up the discussion with exercises and activities. These exercises and activities should provide a context to apply the content in a fashion personally meaningful to the student, and they should aid the students in linking the new information with concepts they have already mastered.

Language delays, which can interfere with lecture and discussion approaches to instruction, may be directly related to delayed vocabulary development and language problems associated with hearing impairment. The technical language of science and social studies may be difficult for students with delayed vocabularies to understand. Not only do some students not understand the technical word itself, but they may also have inadequate comprehension of the words that the teacher uses to explain the technical term. It can be difficult, for example, to explain the terms photosynthesis or electromagnet to students with significant delays in vocabulary development. It is often helpful to introduce these students to new vocabulary prior to the time the vocabulary will be used in the context of a lesson. If the students have dictionary skills, they might look up the new words and write definitions on an index card. Also on the card they might write the word in a sentence and either draw a picture or find a picture in a magazine as a form of illustration. All cards could be kept in a file box. Reviewing the word cards could become an activity the students could do as an assignment or in their free time. Students who have not yet mastered dictionary skills will need guidance in initially defining the new vocabulary. This can be done by the teacher, teacher aide, special education resource teacher, volunteer, or peer tutor.

Learning new vocabulary can also be included in activities associated with the instructional methods of using media, reading, and "doing" to be discussed in the following sections. In class discussions, the teacher should be aware of the need to use familiar words in a context that is comprehensible to the student. Certainly new words should be introduced consistently; however, their meaning should be systematically taught to handicapped students before the teacher simply interjects the word into a lecture or discussion. Children with learning problems are generally poor incidental learners. Teachers cannot automatically assume that these students will easily infer the meanings of new words.

The "glue" of class discussions frequently is the teacher's ability to guide the students' thinking through the use of questions. Although learning the use and levels of questioning is generally not given a great deal of emphasis in teacher-training programs, skillful questioning by the teacher can significantly contribute to the degree of individualized instruction. This is a particularly important curriculum concern as it relates to students handicapped by language delays. Teachers may tend to leave these students out of discussions, direct only low-level questions to them (simple recall), and/or not give them as much time to respond as is typically given to other students. The teacher's reason for doing this may be based on the desire not to embarrass the students or create a failure experience for them. Although this may be justified in limited instances, students with language delays need systematic instruction in higher levels of thinking, just as any other student does. Consistently excusing them from language tasks is one way to insure the permanence of their delays. Handicapped students can learn to respond to questions according to Bloom's (1956) categories of thinking. These categories include:

1. Memory: the student recalls or recognizes information.
2. Translation: The student changes information into a different symbolic form or language.
3. Interpretation: The student discovers relationships among facts, generalizations, definitions, values, and skills.
4. Application: The student solves a lifelike problem that requires the identification of the issue and the selection and use of appropriate generalizations and skills.
5. Analysis: The student solves a problem in the light of conscious knowledge of the parts and forms of thinking.
6. Synthesis: The student solves a problem that requires original, creative thinking.
7. Evaluation: The student makes a judgment of good or bad, right or wrong, according to standards he designates (Sanders 1966, p. 3).

These categories can serve as a guide in the assessment process in pinpointing the student's level of performance. If the science or social studies teacher finds that the student is able to perform successfully at the levels of memory and translation, the teacher can begin to structure questions and activities for the student at the interpretation level and continue to move upward.

Language delays can be obstacles to progressing through the taxonomy of questions, but these students can benefit from systematic and sequential instruction. Individualizing questions according to the level of the students, always striving toward sequential development, can have substantial payoffs in the science and social studies curriculum for handicapped students.

As for language problems associated with hearing impairment, science and social studies teachers should be cognizant of the suggestions included in the hearing impairment section of chapter 1 (Adaptations in Classroom Procedures). Most of these suggestions directly relate to minimizing language difficulties during classroom discussions. The information on teaching vocabulary and individualizing the use of questions have direct applicability to hearing-impaired students who have language delays, as well as to students whose language delays are attributable to mental retardation and learning disabilities.

Media (visual and audiovisual) such as pictures, charts, films, filmstrips, maps, and graphs can be effective instructional materials for many handicapped persons. Students with disadvantages associated with mental retardation and learning disabilities can benefit from experiences and activities that do not penalize them for a lower level of reading achievement. Additionally, these students often associate visual and audiovisual materials with higher motivational appeal.

Teachers must remember that blind students are unable to take advantage of the typical visual media used in social studies and science classes. For example, the maps and globes used in social studies will be meaningless to the blind student with no residual vision; however, alternative materials are available from the American Printing House for the Blind (see appendix A for address), many state libraries for the blind, and possibly regional instructional materials centers. The latter two sources frequently lend materials free of charge. These materials include relief maps of a molded plastic texture, dissected maps of continents, relief globes and mileage scales, large type outline maps, and landform models. In science, the American Printing House for the Blind has biological models representative of invertebrate animals and plant phyla which are constructed to emphasize tactually the most important biological features. These materials may be ordered from the American Printing House and used as alternatives for blind students for concept development. These materials enable the blind student to participate in class activities related to visual methods of instruction. When the class is examining and discussing a map of the United States, the blind student can work with the relief map. Thus, an "audio-tactile," rather than audiovisual method of instruction is being employed.

Many hearing-impaired students are unable to hear the audio portion of films, filmstrips, or video-tapes. In some cases, seating close to the machine will help. For students with extremely limited residual hearing, teachers should consider ordering captioned films. These films and filmstrips provide a written statement on each frame or in each sequence correlated with the verbal content. Through the use of these films hearing-impaired students can read what other students are hearing. For information on ordering captioned films, teachers should write to the Special Office for Materials Distribution at Indiana University (see appendix A for address). Many films are loaned free of charge.

Reading. Karlin (1969) has estimated that 25 percent of the high school population do not possess the reading skills necessary to read the materials and textbooks they are expected to comprehend. The reading problem at the elementary and junior high level is also very severe. Reading deficiencies can significantly interfere with successful performance in social studies and science unless instructional adaptations are made.

As discussed in the section on assessment, the situation is complicated by many content area textbooks having a readability level above the equivalent grade level expectation. Lunstrum (1976) points out that two important factors to consider in regard to readability are vocabulary loading and concept loading. Vocabulary loading refers to the problem of the textbook including many unfamiliar words that have not been systematically introduced and defined. Concept loading occurs when textbooks fail to provide for sequential development of concepts, pacing is inappropriate, or the complexity or number of concepts exceed the student's cognitive ability to process the information. When choosing textbooks, teachers should consider these factors carefully.

Handicapped students, particularly those with learning problems, often have disadvantages associated with reading achievement. Reading problems occur in the areas of word recognition, comprehension, and study skills (reading tables, using the index, scanning, paraphrasing). Some suggestions for minimizing reading problems, and at the same time working to improve reading performance, follow:

Have a peer tutor and a student with a reading problem complete the reading assignment together. Both students might read orally, with the tutor helping his partner identify words that have not yet been learned. When this strategy is used with blind students, the peer tutor, of course, would need to do all the reading.

Have students who excel in reading make summaries of chapters for less able readers. The less able reader might participate in the overall development by illustrating the summary with pictures from old textbooks or magazines or binding several summaries to make booklets. Summaries can be laminated or covered with clear contact paper so that they may be used over and over (Turner 1976).

The teacher, volunteers, or a peer tutor can underline or highlight the key concepts on each page of the text. If the child is a slow reader and overwhelmed by the length of the chapter, singling out the most important concepts can increase the likelihood of the handicapped student reading them.

Volunteers or peer tutors can tape-record the textbook for students who read significantly below grade level. Introductory "organizers" can be included on the tape. For example, a student might be told in advance which points to listen for or the main idea of the selection. Study questions can also be included after paragraphs to check the student's comprehension. This strategy can also be helpful for blind students. For blind students who comprehend information easily, the introductory "organizers" and study questions may be superfluous.

The language experience approach to reading instruction (see chapter 5) may be used as a way of promoting concept development in science and social studies. After information has been presented (through discussion, media, textbook, inquiry experiences), have students summarize the major points in their own words. If they are unable to write or spell adequately, a peer tutor or the teacher could write their summary for them. They could find pictures in magazines or draw pictures to "visually paraphrase" (Turner 1976) the concepts they are learning. A similar approach could be used to write stories about the concepts rather than more objective summaries. Through this method, students can increase their reading skills simultaneously with mastering science and social studies concepts.

Learning centers with textbooks, reference books, and activities can be developed. Turner (1976) describes such a center in which students plan learning activities and experiences for their peers from a section of a chapter. It could be in the form of questions, inquiry activities, an oral report, a group project, or various alternatives. Both the students planning and completing the activities have the opportunity to expand their skills.

Some partially sighted children need large print textbooks. Teachers can possibly borrow these from the State Library for the Blind and Physically Handicapped. If books are not available on loan, magnification equipment might be used or portions of the basic text could be retyped with a primary typewriter. Before pursuing this, teachers should make sure that primary type print is large enough for the particular student needing the modification. If so, perhaps a volunteer could be located to do the typing (the high school typing teacher might know of willing students) or the Lion's Club might be contacted about providing financial help.

Another reading alternative which might be considered is using a textbook on a lower grade level for students with severe reading delays. This situation can sometimes create a dilemma for the student and teacher. Basically, students have different preferences on using textbooks at lower grade levels.

Don is in the fifth grade and reads on a third-grade level. He has had a series of unfortunate experiences in school when teachers have expected him to read texts which were impossible for him to read. Reading assignments have often resulted in a high level of frustration for Don. He does not want his peers to know about his reading problem and sometimes "pretends" he is reading a book when he is really unable to recognize the majority of words. Don's teacher found a primary science book that was brightly colored and filled with interesting illustrations. It covered some of the same concepts as the fifth-grade text used in the class but in a more simplified fashion. The teacher asked Don if he would like to use the book. When he looked through the first chapter, he squealed with delight, "I can read it. I can read it. Where did you get this book that I can read?" Don was elated and read the book from cover to cover dozens of times.

Ray is also in the fifth grade. He has a learning disability in the area of reading. His teacher felt strongly that Ray could master skills and concepts in content areas if the reading obstacle could be eliminated. The teacher searched the school's storage room for books and found a couple of social studies and health books on a lower grade level. He introduced them to Ray and explained that these books would help him learn important information and would enable him to complete assignments with success. Ray said very little to the teacher as he sheepishly put the books in his desk. He recognized one of them as a book his younger sister was using, and he immediately told himself that he would never take it home. These books represented one more reminder of his academic failures.

These two examples illustrate students' different reactions to having textbooks on a lower grade level. Teachers should strongly consider the preferences of the student and avoid humiliating the student by insisting that he use the book when he clearly is rejecting it. If the teacher chooses to use books on a lower level, some problems can be avoided by locating books with motivational appeal, rather than the ragged and tattered books often shelved in the storage room, and by choosing books that are not presently nor have in the past been used in the lower grade of the school in which the student is enrolled. Commercial book jackets might also be used.

> I hear and I forget;
> I see and I remember;
> I *do* and I understand.
> —Indian proverb

Doing. Active learning or doing has many advantages for handicapped students. Some are high motivational appeal, change of pace involvement—which can minimize attention span problems, multisensory approaches capitalizing on learning style preferences, the opportunity to individualize according to the achievement level and interests of the students, and the potential for promoting positive peer relationships through participation in group activities.

Instruction that emphasizes doing can take a variety of organizational patterns. Some are learning centers, learning activity packets, inquiry activities, conducting experiments, and involvement in out-of-school settings such as community-based experiences. Whatever the particular organizational pattern, there are guidelines to this type of curriculum development which should be considered. Blackburn and Powell (1976, pp. 44–46) have discussed guidelines in planning individualized instruction that are applicable to the development of active learning experiences in science and social studies for handicapped students.

1. Are the alternatives designed for individuals with varying interests, learning styles, and levels of ability? (Blackburn and Powell 1976, p. 44).

In order to meet this guideline teachers might consider such factors as: the complexity of directions; level of independent activity required; reading level; writing requirements; length of assignments; whether architectural barriers could prevent a student from participating in an experience; consideration given to mobility implications for blind students, and activity alternatives for students achieving below grade level, as well as students achieving in the average and above-average range.

For students achieving below grade level science teachers at the junior high level should consider the instructional program entitled *Me Now* and *Me and My Environment.* (Hubbard, 2855 Shermer Road,

Northbrook, IL 60062). The program was specifically designed for mildly retarded students and incorporates an activity orientation to learning. A thorough description of this science curriculum is provided by Menhusen and Gromme (1976).

An excellent activity-oriented program in social studies specifically designed for elementary and junior students with cognitive disadvantages is the Social Learning Curriculum (Charles E. Merrill Publishers, 1300 Alum Creek Rd., Columbus, OH 43216). This program combines instruction in thinking (e.g., analysis and synthesis) and subject area skills (e.g., mathematics, language arts, science, physical education) with social learning concepts in the broad areas of self-identification, self-perception, and interaction. It is based on an inductive learning process and includes workbooks, stimulus pictures, spirit duplicating masters, and a teacher's guide.

A further consideration is providing learning alternatives for students with sensory handicaps. For blind students, a variety of adapted equipment for science experiments and social studies projects is available from the American Printing House for the Blind. Further, a curriculum entitled Adapting Science Materials for the Blind has been developed as an outgrowth of the Science Curriculum Improvement Study (Schatz et al. 1976; Linn 1972). This curriculum focuses on adaptations of instructional strategies and materials found in typical science programs rather than the development of an instructional program with minimal correlation to that occurring in most classrooms. Further information on this science program for blind students may be obtained by writing to Field Coordinator, Adapting Science Materials for the Blind, Lawrence Hall of Science, University of California, Berkeley, CA 94720.

Learning alternatives for deaf students in science and social studies should provide concrete and meaningful experiences through which these students may master language concepts. Collea (1976) reports on a successful science program with deaf students in which new concepts are presented in a minimum of six or seven different ways. Active learning based on a "doing" approach to instruction can promote concept mastery if appropriate learning alternatives are provided to students.

> 2. Are the learning alternatives likely to help students accomplish the objectives for which they were designed? (Blackburn and Powell 1976, p. 44).

It is important not only that activities be related to the objectives, but that handicapped students understand the relationships. When the purposes of learning activities are clear and relevant to the needs of the students, higher motivation is likely to result.

3. Are the alternatives explained fully and concretely enough so that they can be used by students and teachers? (Blackburn and Powell 1976, p. 44).

Careful consideration should be given to wording directions to insure that students with learning problems comprehend them. This means attending to such factors as vocabulary, reading level, complexity of sentence structure, and number of directives. For students reading on a low level, pictures might accompany the written directions to provide context clues.

Arrangements should be made to tape directions for blind students or for a teacher or a peer tutor to explain them verbally. Students might be given alternatives to follow if they do not understand directions, such as asking a friend, signaling for the teacher's attention, or proceeding to a different activity.

4. Are there alternatives available for small group activity as well as individual activity? (Blackburn and Powell 1976, p. 45).

Instruction based on doing has the advantage of capitalizing on small group interaction. Since handicapped students often experience difficulty with forming peer relationships, alternatives for small group activity in social studies and science classes are particularly important. Teachers should consider ways for handicapped students to contribute to and receive from the group. Excellent science lessons could involve the amplification system of hearing aids, magnification equipment used by partially sighted children, or the technology of equipment developed for the blind. The concept of individual differences is central in a social studies curriculum. Small group activities in science and social studies can provide a natural opportunity to help classroom peers become more knowledgeable about and sensitive to handicapping conditions, as well as laying the groundwork for peer interactions.

5. Do the alternatives provide for the continuation and reinforcement of desired basic skills? (Blackburn and Powell 1976, p. 45).

Many handicapped students with special interests and talents in the areas of science and social studies can effectively learn basic skills (reading, writing, spelling, arithmetic) as part of their curriculum. As teachers plan activities and experiences, they should take advantage of opportunities to correlate subject matter.

6. Does the alternative include all essential information for the student, including:
   a. What he is to do (read, construct, write, draw, dramatize, listen, view),

b. Where to find information, and what media to use (read books in the classroom library, construct a model of a stage, write your feelings about ecology, draw a scale model of the United Nations, dramatize scenes from your favorite story or play, listen to the lecture on atoms on the cassette tape player in the learning center, view the film on how to play basketball),

c. Whàt to do with any products or results from the alternative (place your chart on the classroom bulletin board, prepare and present a puppet show to the class depicting your findings, display your model in the school library) (Blackburn and Powell 1976, pp. 45–46).

A major objective of a doing approach to instruction is to teach the students to discover answers for themselves; however, self-discovery does not mean that the student is left to flounder and offered no guidelines. Structure is very important, particularly for some handicapped students who do not generate their own structure and organization. Generally, before students can "do" science and social studies activities, teachers must provide a basic core of information.

The subjects of science and social studies are adaptable to meet the particular needs, interests, and capabilities of handicapped students. Science and social studies teachers have the opportunity to meet the challenge of mainstreaming.

Physical Education

Concept Development

Many people typically associate concept development in physical education strictly with the psychomotor domain; however, physical education incorporates a much broader array of concepts and skills. Sherrill (1976) suggests a model (see table 8–1) to illustrate the interrelationships of cognitive-perceptual-psychomotor-affective development considered to be an integral part of the physical education program. Many of these behaviors are learned through normal development/maturation and in informal physical activities in the neighborhood by many nonhandicapped children. Handicapped children, on the other hand, frequently have special needs which require alternative instructional strategies to enhance the probability of their success in learning the underlying concepts and behaviors comprising well-balanced physical development.

A framework proposed by Puthoff (1976) directs attention to individual differences which should be considered in physical education instruction. The application of this individualized guide could have a sig-

271

Motor Development	Perceptual-Motor Integration and Language Development	Perceptual-Motor-Cognitive Integration	Application-Analysis-Synthesis-Evaluation
1. Gross movement patterns requisite to body control and safe locomotion	5. Body image, concept, cathexis	11. Wide variety of play interests	15. Sufficient weekly exercise for optimal health and fitness.
2. Fine motor coordinations requisite to self-help skills and daily living activities	6. Fine motor coordinations requisite to academic and/or vocational success	12. Sufficient physical recreational skills, knowledges, and understandings for group acceptance and self actualization	16. Knowledge and understandings requisite to enjoyment of sports, dance, and aquatics as a spectator, a consumer of television, radio, and other media, and as a participant in discussions
3. Gross motor patterns requisite to play activities	7. Personal attractiveness requisite to social acceptance	13. Relaxation and release of neuromuscular tensions	17. Knowledges and understandings requisite to optimal use of community recreation resources and to intelligent decision-making as a voter, citizen, consumer, and parent
4. Perceptual-motor skills related to motor learning and motor performance	8. Physical fitness	14. Motor skills, knowledges, and understanding requisite to success in one or more physical activities with carry-over values	
	9. Positive attitudes toward body, self, others, movement, play, and competition		
	10. Creativity in exploring use of time, space, and energy		

The Infant

The Preschool Child

The Elementary School Child

The Middle School Student

The Secondary School Pupil

From Claudine Sherill, *Adapted physical education and recreation*, Dubuque, Iowa: Wm. C. Brown Co., 1976. Reprinted by permission of the publisher.

Table 8–1
Spectrum of Behaviors for Which the Physical Educator Is Responsible

nificant positive influence on the concept/behavioral development of handicapped students. This framework includes (1) modification of content; (2) modification of learning rate; (3) teaching/learning style options; and (4) internal class environmental settings.

Modification of Content

Physical education content can be adapted for handicapped students through the use of differentiated objectives. The decision as to which objectives would constitute an appropriate curriculum for a particular student should be based on evaluation of the student's skill level in physical development and motor performance. There are some formal tests, such as the American Alliance for Health, Physical Education, and Recreation (AAHPER) Youth Physical Fitness Test (Hunsicker and Reiff 1976), which may be used to assess skill levels. The AAHPER Youth Fitness Test includes six test items that provide an overall indication of the fitness of students in grades five through twelve. National norms are available. Adaptations have been made in several of the test items in tailoring this physical fitness test to the special needs of mentally retarded students, in addition to establishing norms for mildly retarded students within the age range of eight to eighteen (AAHPER 1976). The majority of physical education assessment, however, is likely to be informal evaluation using observation as a basis of pinpointing strengths and weaknesses. Examples of such informal instruments are illustrated in tables 8–2 and 8–3.

Table 8–2
Informal Inventory in Physical Education Based on Observations

---

What do you consider to be his or her major health problem or handicapping condition?

1. _____
2. _____

What is the average number of school absences in a semester?

| 0–3 | 4–7 | 8–15 | over 15 |

Which seems to be his physical education preference and/or strength?

| Dance | Developmental Exercise | Individual Sports |
| Aquatics | Gymnastics, Stunts | Team Sports |

Table 8–2 Continued

In which developmental stage of play should he be classified?

Solitary or parallel	Games and dance with "I" emphasis
Cooperative or shared	Activities emphasizing team or group goals
Small group (6 or less)	Regulation sports, dance, aquatics

In which developmental stage of competition should he be classified?

Competes with self against his own best performance
Tries to attain specific individual goals
Cooperates with others in achievement of a team goal
Competes against one other
Cooperates with partner in competition against 2 opponents
Cooperates with team members in competition against a team

At which level of game complexity should he be classified?

1. Everyone does same thing in same direction as in Follow the Leader, Musical Chairs, Hot Potato, Red Light-Green Light, Catch My Tail, or Teacher Ball.
2. Everyone runs from one base to another on the same cue to escape an "it"; this "it" remains the same throughout the game as in Midnight and Old Mother Witch.
3. Same as 2, but with a different "it" for each exchange of bases.
4. Some children remain stationary whereas others run, chase, or flee in response to a cue number or word. All movement is in the same direction as Fire Engine, Mickey Mouse, Circle Call Ball, and Steal the Bacon. The more children who remain stationary, the easier the game.
5. The same as 4 except that the direction varies as in Squirrels in the Trees and Two Deep.
6. Some children play an offense role while others play defense as Dodgeball, Brownies and Fairies, and Trades.
7. Role changes frequently, direction of movement varies, and penalties are enforced when fouls or violations are made like Keep Away.
8. Same as 7, except score keeper must keep track of number of points earned by each team as in Kick Ball.

Can participate in games based upon the following locomotor activities and/or motor skills;

walk	dodge	bounce
run	squat	dribble
leap	throw	catch
jump	kick	volley
hop	strike	pivot
tag	bat	

Table 8–2 Continued

Can participate in rhythmic or dance activities based upon the following loco-motor movements and/or basic skills:

walk	gallop	waltz
run	slide	two-step
leap	skip	polka
jump	step-hop	bleking
hop	schottische	draw

Which is his level of rhythmic performance and/or temporal perception?

No evidence of understanding concept nor ability to move in time to stimulus.	Can move in time to metronome or drum beat.	Can move in time to verbal stimulus Up-2-3, Down-2-3	Can move to music with well defined beats and accents.	Can move to any kind of music without problems.

Which of the following visual problems does the pupil exhibit?

accommodation	double vision	ocular muscle imbalance
nearsightedness	suppression of one eye	convergence insufficiency
farsightedness	squint (cross-eye)	horizontal tracking
astigmatism	binocular coordination	vertical tracking

What correction or training is the pupil receiving for his visual problems?

none	prescribed eye exercises
corrective glasses	prescribed gross motor activities
patch over one eye	prescribed tracking activities

Which problems of visual perception does the pupil exhibit?

form discrimination	object constancy
color discrimination	phi phenomenon
figure-background	retinal inhibition
depth perception	form constancy
directional constancy	

Which problems of auditory perception does the pupil exhibit?

pitch discrimination	figure-background
intensity discrimination	directionality of sound
tonal quality discrimination	temporal perception

275

Table 8–2 Continued

Which problems of proprioception does the pupil exhibit?

duplication of specific joint positions	static balance
imitation of movements	dynamic balance
directional accuracy in moving objects	spatial balance
distance accuracy in moving objects	size estimation
weight discrimination	force production

Which two sense modalities appear to be the strongest?

visual	tactile	kinesthetic
auditory	vestibular	olfactory
gustatory		

Which stimulus is most effective as an attention getting device and a starting and stopping signal?

voice	bell	raised arm
whistle	flicker of lights	flag raised or thrown in air
drum	hand clapping	other _____

Observe the pupil in his attempts to learn a gross motor skill. At which level does his learning appear to break down?

Perception	Formulation of the Motor Plan Central Processing	Motor Output
sensory input	visual memory and sequencing	readiness (set)
mental awareness	auditory memory and sequencing	perceptual-motor matching
discrimination	haptic memory and sequencing	imitation of movements
organization (parts into wholes)	mental practice (motor planning)	duplication of joint positions
cue selection (figure-background)	mental creativity	perceptual-motor sequencing
		motor feedback
		total assembly
		automatic response (relaxation)
		fixation (consistency under stable conditions)
		diversification (consistency under changing conditions)

Table 8–2 Continued

In comparison with the average of other children in his group, which behaviors does this child exhibit to a greater degree than the others?

motor awkwardness	distractibility
poor spatial orientation	perseveration
immature body image	social imperception
negative self-concept	low frustration tolerance
hyperactivity	crying
loneliness	aggression toward others
self-destructive acts	

Which of the following conditions which may affect balance are evidenced?

hydrocephalus	visual deficits
amputation	chronic ear infections
taller than average height	history of meningitis
extremely long legs	semicircular canal impairment
excessively large busts	cerebellar ataxia
small or defective feet	gait abnormalities
absence of big toe	spasticity
poor postural alignment	athetosis
lack of body part symmetry	imbalance of muscular strength
inconsistent opposition of limbs	poor kinesthesis
unequal length of legs	fear of heights
takes medications which may affect balance	

Put an x in the proper box to denote special strengths and weaknesses. Every box should not have an x.

Component	Strengths to Be Built upon	Weaknesses to Be Remediated or Compensated for
Static (extent) flexibility		
Dynamic flexibility		
Speed in changing direction		
Running: explosive strength		
Explosive arm strength (throwing)		
Explosive leg strength (jumping)		
Static strength		
Dynamic arm strength		
Dynamic leg strength		

Table 8–2 Continued

Component	Strengths to Be Built upon	Weaknesses to Be Remediated or Compensated for
Hanging strenth		
Abdominal strength		
Upper back strength		
Lower back strength		
Circulo-respiratory endurance		

From Claudine Sherrill, *Adapted physical education and recreation*, Dubuque, Iowa: Wm. C. Brown Co., 1976.

After initial evaluation has been made, an individual education program (see chapter 3) should be prepared for all handicapped students who require any specially designed physical education instruction. Differentiated objectives may be specified at this time. For example, the objective in basketball for a seventh-grade student with poor motor coordination might be to dribble a basketball continuously on an open court for one minute whereas an objective for the top athlete in the class might be to dribble the ball successfully for a period of ten minutes while being closely guarded.

Table 8–3
Informal Inventory of Ball Handling

1. Circle answers which best describe ball handling behaviors.

Task	Throwing			Kicking		
	Yes		No	Yes		No
Uses same limb consistently	Right	Left		Right	Left	
Uses other limbs in opposition	Always	Usually	Seldom	Always	Usually	Seldom
Transfers weight	Always	Usually	Seldom	Always	Usually	Seldom
Aims accurately	Always	Usually	Seldom	Always	Usually	Seldom
When aim is inaccurate, it usually goes too far in which directions?	Right High	Left Low	Inconsistent	Right High	Left Low	Inconsistent

Table 8–3 Continued

2. In comparison with the average of other pupils of his same age and sex, this child's ball handling skills can be described best by which adjectives?

Motor Skill	Superior	Average	Inferior
Throwing			
Catching			
Batting			
Pitching			
Bunting			
Place kicking			
Shooting baskets			
Volleying			
Other			

In comparison with the average of other children in his group this pupil can be described best in the physical education setting by which phrases? Circle only one under each heading.

Attention
attentive
average
nonattentive
distracted
confused
not there
scatterbrained

Memory
remembers well and
 retains
remembers fairly well
forgets easily
never remembers

Imitation
imitates easily and well
imitates fairly well
average
imitates little and with
 difficulty
can do things only his
 own way

Initiative
a self-starter
has considerable
 initiative
average
responds to prodding
relies entirely on others

*Understanding of
Instructions or
Explanations*
grasps instructions
understands after asking
 questions
average
confused, but knows he
 doesn't understand
thinks he understands,
 but really doesn't
confused and helpless

Mental Flexibility
receptive to new ideas
average
prefers the old and
 familiar
resents change
perseverates

279

Table 8–3 Continued

In which area is the pupil stronger?

receptive language
expressive language

Which phrases best describe the pupil's language functioning?

no problem	expressive language deficit
inner language deficit	gesture and/or sign language
receptive language deficit	no usable language

Which extrinsic award and/or social incentive works best as a motivator?

verbal praise	coins or tokens
hug	stars on wall chart
food (specify kind)	point system
hand clapping	other _____

From Claudine Sherrill, *Adapted physical education and recreation,* Dubuque, Iowa: Wm. C. Brown Co., 1976.

Activities and materials based on the objectives specified for the student must be selected—another way to modify physical education content. In the next section on mobility, adapted activities and materials for handicapped students will be described.

Modification of Learning Rate

All students differ in the rate in which they learn physical education skills and concepts. Some handicapping conditions impede learning rate more than others, and even the same handicapping condition will impede some persons more than others. The important point is that learning rate must be considered carefully. Many physically handicapped students have the disadvantage of muscle weakness which results in their becoming fatigued in a physical education class fairly quickly; it may also be more difficult for them to develop coordination. Because they can engage only in short periods of exertion, their learning rate may be slower than other students'. On the other hand, it might take students with learning problems longer to master the scoring system of tennis or rules of football. Consideration of learning rate in the development of physical skills and concepts is essential if successful mainstreaming is to occur.

Teaching/Learning Style Options

A range of teaching/learning style options should be considered for handicapped students in physical education. Arnhein and Sinclair (1975) have suggested the following:

Visual guidance. A visual cue is provided (teacher demonstration, filmstrips, charts, pictures, observing other students, watching an organized sporting event), and students are expected to model the performance they have witnessed. This visual approach is not an option for visually impaired students.

Manual guidance. This technique involves manipulating the child's body parts to take him through the sequence of correct movements. It is based on the premise that kinesthetic feedback or the awareness of how the action feels is a facilitator of motor learning. Kinesthetic feedback may be increased by having the student wear weights on the body part being moved and through the application of manual resistance by the instructor or a peer tutor (Arnheim and Sinclair 1975). Manual guidance can be an effective learning style for blind students. Arnheim, Auxter, and Crowe (1977) suggest that an instructor who wants to use visual guidance for the majority of the class in teaching a new skill might provide manual guidance to a blind student while other class members observe.

Verbal guidance is generally considered less effective than visual and manual guidance; however, it may be an effective style for some students. When using verbal guidance, the physical education teacher should use simple and consistent language. Key words such as *up, run,* and *jump* may be substituted for sentences. Students concentrating on motor performance could be confused and distracted by an overload of lengthy directions. Verbal guidance is ineffective for some hearing-impaired students. The noise level of physical education classes during activity sessions is often high and can drown out the beneficial effects of amplification received through hearing aids. Also in gymnasiums and on large playing fields, the distance between the teacher and students can prevent the opportunity for the student to lip-read. When specific content is being taught, physical education teachers should try to minimize the factors that create interference to verbal guidance for hearing-impaired students.

Multisensory instruction. Visual, manual, and verbal guidance may be combined effectively in a wide variety of activities through a multisensory approach. In learning basic swimming skills such as the side stroke, a student could observe the arm and leg patterns of the teacher swimming the side stroke; receive kinesthetic feedback by having a peer tutor guide her arms or legs through the proper movements, and receive verbal guidance such as *pull* and *kick* while practicing the side stroke. The combina-

281

tion of sensory input is generally believed to be an advantage to successful learning and performance.

Movement exploration approach. Sherrill (1976) advocates the movement exploration approach to physical education instruction, particularly for students with physical/orthopedic handicaps, low fitness, and poor coordination. This approach capitalizes on a process of discovery and inquiry in encouraging students to assume responsibility for identifying problems and developing a plan to solve them. A visually impaired student may discover the most advantageous method of learning to bowl accurately by establishing his own objectives and instructional strategies. In testing out the instructional strategies, the student could learn his own strengths and weaknesses and perhaps discover an appropriate adaptation that never occurred to the teacher. This type of instruction can help teach the student a problem-solving process that can be used continuously throughout adult life as physical/motor adaptations must be made.

Internal Class Environmental Settings

Teachers should structure the learning environment within a physical education class according to the particular needs of the handicapped student. Consideration may be given to one-to-one instruction with a peer tutor or volunteer, small group instruction, large group instruction, learning center, and independent work.

Consideration must also be given to such other environmental factors as the elimination of architectural barriers for students in wheelchairs and on crutches and the location of any special equipment these students might require; the identification of alternatives to outdoor play on chilly or damp days for students with chronic health conditions associated with respiratory problems; the creation of an environment tailored to the needs of students with chronic health conditions associated with asthma and allergies, considering such factors as the extent of pollen and dust in the air and the availability of equipment made of nonallergenic materials; and the identification of safety precautions for blind students such as roping off the entrance to a swimming pool, removing any glass from playing fields, and providing an orientation to the environmental arrangement of the instructional area (Sherrill 1976).

Mobility

Much of a physical education program requires varying types and degrees of mobility. Mobility adaptations vary according to different handicapping conditions and the strengths and weaknesses of each handicapped

282

student participating in the program. The most substantial adaptations in games and sports will most likely have to be made for physically handicapped and blind students. Table 8–4 outlines specific suggestions for possible adaptations for these two groups of students in the following games

Table 8–4
Suggested Adaptations in Selected Physical Education Activities for Physically Handicapped and Blind Students

A. Archery
  1. Physically Handicapped
     a. Students in wheelchairs should position chairs at a right angle to the target and reach over the side of their chair to draw bow.
     b. Students on crutches can prop themselves on the crutches in order to free their arms for shooting.
     c. Students in wheelchairs or on crutches may need a "buddy" to help retrieving arrows.
     d. For students with only one arm, the bow could be attached in the correct position to a sturdy pole secured in the ground. The student could draw the string and arrow back, aim, and release (Fait 1972).
  2. Blind
     a. A tow line can be installed by attaching a rope from the middle of the top of a target to a foot board marking the correct shooting position. This rope can enable the blind student to walk to the target and can also serve as a guide in aligning the bow in a horizontal position to the target (Adams et al. 1972).
     b. In teaching blind students how to pull the bow correctly, two poles can be placed in the ground and positioned in line with the target. One pole can serve as a guide for the correct hand position of the extended arm and the other pole for the correct wrist position of the hand pulling the string (Fait 1972).
     c. The opportunity for self-scoring can be afforded by covering each color on the target with a different texture (e.g., terry cloth, satin, vinyl) and having the students feel the texture and associate it with a specified number of points (Adams et al. 1972).

B. Bowling
  1. Physically Handicapped
     a. Students in wheelchairs or those who have difficulty with ambulation may use an extra arm swing before the ball is released. They might swing the ball back, forward, back again, and then forward in the release. The extra swing can help increase momentum (Fait 1972).

Table 8–4 Continued

    b. Students with muscle weakness in their hands can use a lap rack made of metal upon which the ball could roll down to be released to the alley. They could also use lightweight balls made of polyethylene (Fait 1972).

  2. Blind.

    a. A guide rail can be placed along the approach lane to aid in directing the student in releasing the ball (Arnheim et al. 1972).

    b. A blind student will need a buddy to report the number of pins knocked down.

    c. Blind students can learn to distinguish the sound of the bowling ball traveling down the lane from the sound of the ball in the alley.

C. Tennis

  1. Physically Handicapped

    a. A student who has had both arms amputated can play tennis by taping or strapping a racquet to the remaining stump. Padding should be placed between the stump and racquet. These students can learn to serve by balancing the ball on the face of the racquet and tossing the ball in the air by making a quick upward movement of the racquet. Loose balls can be picked up by edging them on the face of the racquet and bouncing them up to be returned (Fait 1972).

    b. Students in wheelchairs or on crutches might play on only the front half of the court and may be given the allowance that the ball can bounce two times and still be kept in play.

  2. Blind

    a. Tennis is one of the more difficult games to adapt for blind students. One strategy would be to use balls with bells or electronic balls with beepers. Information about these balls can be obtained from the American Foundation for the Blind. Orange or yellow tennis balls should be used for partially sighted students (Sherrill 1976).

D. Basketball

  1. Physically Handicapped

    a. Wheelchair basketball is a popular sport in many states. Rules for playing may be obtained from the National Wheelchair Athletic Association, 40–42 62nd St., Woodside, N.Y. 11377.

    b. For students with restricted arm movement, baskets may be lowered, the ball may be trapped between the arm and the body, and passes may be made with one hand.

Table 8–4 Continued

2. Blind
   a. A basketball with an audible bell or beep can be used. The goal can also be rigged with a bell so that the student will know when a basket has been made.
   b. When passing to a blind student, the sighted peer should use a bounce pass and should call the blind student's name immediately prior to passing the ball. When the blind student is passing, the sighted peers can hold their hands up and snap their fingers as a guide to the blind student in judging height, direction, and distance (Arnheim et al. 1977).
   c. When teaching the blind student to shoot, the teacher should use manual and verbal guidance. A sighted peer may stand under the basket talking to the blind student to aid in judging distance and direction (Arnheim et al. 1977).

E. Swimming
   1. Physically Handicapped
      a. The side stroke is generally the most effective stroke for persons who have lost one limb. For individuals unable to use either leg, the crawl is the most satisfactory stroke (Fait 1972).
      b. Persons who have lost both arms can learn any kick which can be done on the back (Sherrill 1976).
      c. Ramps should be available for entrance into the swimming pool for students in wheelchairs and on crutches.
   2. Blind
      a. A rope should be used to separate the shallow pool and deep ends of the pool.
      b. Through manual and physical guidance, blind students can learn a variety of strokes and safety measures.
      c. Devices such as a metronome or radio should be located at the side of the pool to serve as an orientation guide to the blind student (Arnheim et al. 1977).

and sports: archery, bowling, tennis, basketball, and swimming. The appropriateness or inappropriateness of these adaptations can be judged only in light of the individual needs of each physically handicapped or blind student. Teachers should pick and choose the adaptations which might be helpful, realizing that some of them may be inapplicable to particular persons and situations.

In designing a physical education program for physically handicapped students, the teacher must first assess the particular implications

285

of the mobility handicap. As pointed out in chapter 1, mobility must be evaluated in light of the locus of involvement (e.g., legs, arms), the nature of involvement (e.g., paralysis, lack of coordination, loss of limbs), and the rate and stability of motion (e.g., agility, endurance). After evaluating the student's skill level and specifying appropriate objectives, the teacher, with the help of special education resource teachers and a physical therapist (if one is available), should proceed to adapt or develop physical education activities for the student. A rule of thumb is that games and sports should be changed to the minimum extent necessary in order to insure the handicapped student's success and safety. Wheelchair Athletics, a nationally organized competition program, offers an example of the athletic prowess of thousands of handicapped people. The Paralympics, Olympics for paraplegics (persons who are disabled in their lower extremities) is held annually. Some of the events included are basketball; fencing; field events including discus, shotput, and javelin; track events including 40-yard dash, 100-yard dash, 440-yard dash, and one mile; swimming; archery; table tennis; and weight lifting (Sherrill 1976). This program alone points to the possibilities in physical education programs when handicapping conditions are minimized through curriculum adaptations. Although those programs include only handicapped persons, similar types of adaptations can be used in regular physical education classes to accommodate a handicapped student.

A common misconception is that epileptic students should not engage in physical education. On the contrary, physical activity is recommended for many persons with epilepsy. The American Medical Association endorsed the participation of epileptic students in physical education programs, with the exceptions of long periods of underwater swimming, body contact sports that may produce head injuries, and gymnastic and diving activities where heights could be dangerous in the event of a fall (AMA 1968). Students with cardiac conditions, asthma, and allergies can also benefit from inclusion in the physical education program. Working with their physician and parents, the teacher can plan a program alternating short activity periods and rest. A major objective of the program for some of these students might be relaxation exercises.

Mobility considerations for visually impaired students involve mobility training as well as adapting games and sports as suggested in table 8–4. Mobility training during the physical education program could involve the following activities, which could be done in the regular class with the assistance of a peer tutor.

1. Practice walking a straight line. All sightless persons tend to veer about 1.25 inches per step or walk a spiral-shaped pathway when at-

tempting to traverse a straight line. The ten-year-old, however, should not veer more than ten feet when attempting to walk forward for fifty feet nor more than thirty feet when moving forward 150 feet.

2. Practice facing sounds or following instructions to make quarter, half, three-quarter, and full turns. Blind adults tend to turn too much (100–105 degrees). Full turns are the most difficult with the average person moving only 320–325 degrees.

3. Practice reproducing the exact distance and pathway just taken with a partner.

4. Take a short walk with a partner and practice finding the way back to the starting point alone.

5. Outside, where the rays of the sun can be felt, practice facing north, south, east, west. Relate these to goal cages and the direction of play in various games.

6. Practice determining whether the walking surface is uphill or downhill or tilted to the left or right; relate this to the principles of stability and efficient movement.

7. Practice walking different floor patterns. Originate novel patterns and then try to reproduce the same movement (Sherrill 1976, pp. 342–343).

Mobility considerations must also be examined in light of the special needs of hearing-impaired students. Because the semicircular canals of the ear are damaged, some deaf students have problems associated with balance and coordination. Teachers should assess these students carefully to document the existence of a problem. If one exists, balance and coordination exercises such as dancing and gymnastics might be prescribed to develop greater skill in this area. Precautions should be taken in climbing activities to insure against placing a student with balance deficiencies in a dangerous situation.

As discussed in chapter 1, students with learning disabilities often have difficulty with gross and fine motor development. In physical education classes, these students are sometimes described as clumsy and awkward. Many students with such problems benefit from basic movement experiences involving activities with the balance beam, trampoline, dance, and rhythm. High activity levels can sometimes interfere with success in physical education programs. To aid students in controlling their level of activity, teachers might provide a quiet period after periods of intensive stimulation, restricted boundary areas limiting the space dimensions in which activity takes place, and reduction of a wide range of choice in activities and schedules. A structured lesson can contribute to a successful experience for these students. Many students with learning disabilities are extremely sensitive to their low motor performance. Teachers can help to reduce these feelings by teaching games and sports which tend to be less competitive than others—for example, swimming, jogging, and bike riding.

The physical development and motor performance of mildly mentally retarded students is generally equal to chronological age expectations. Many of these students compete very successfully in interscholastic athletics. Although there are no unique mobility considerations for this population, it is worth noting that many retarded persons rely on motor skills more heavily than intellectual skills in vocational endeavors as adults. For this reason the physical education program can be an integral part of their vocational training. Teachers should recognize this responsibility and develop motor proficiency to the highest possible level. Cratty (1969) has suggested many games and activities which have been successfully used with mentally retarded students.

The overview of mobility implications in this section has been far briefer than the topic warrants. Teachers interested in more detailed suggestions are referred to the work of Sherrill (1976), Fait (1972), Adams, Daniel, and Rullman (1972), Daniels and Davies (1975), Arnheim and Sinclair (1975), Arnheim, Auxter, and Crowe, (1977), and Moran and Kalakian (1974).

Academic Difficulty

Many handicapped students experiencing difficulty with academic achievement can improve academic, as well as motor, skills in a well-balanced physical education program. Arithmetic skills related to counting, number facts, and processes can be taught by having students learn to keep score in various games and sports. Setting up a volleyball or tennis court is an excellent opportunity to teach and reinforce measurement skills. Numerous opportunities exist for working on time concepts—for example, keeping up with the regulation time of a basketball or football game and clocking the time for track events. Some students who do not respond to more traditional arithmetic approaches might benefit from learning arithmetic skills in the meaningful context of physical activities.

Language arts is another curriculum area that can be closely related to physical education. Students might learn to read the rules of games and sports they find particularly appealing and improve writing skills as they have the opportunity to order special material and equipment. Library books, newspapers, and magazines related to sports might enhance the relevance of the student's reading program and his desire to learn to read. Every academic subject has possible ties to physical education. When students find their greatest motivation and interest in experiences provided in physical education, teachers should seize the opportunity to increase the students' academic performance as well. This does not require the physical education instructor to teach all subjects; rather, the classroom teacher might plan units of instruction and lesson plans around physical education themes. Coordination of objectives and strategies is essential to maximum student gain.

Peer Relationships

Physical education activities can provide a foundation for facilitating positive peer relationships of handicapped students. The nature of physical activities often involves groups, as in basketball and volleyball teams; interaction can be a natural by-product. Teachers should try to structure opportunities in which handicapped students can contribute successfully to group goals. Joe, a learning disabled seventh-grader, reported that he was called "Blockhead" and "Bungle Bum" by his peers in physical education. He was naturally embarrassed by this type of ridicule. Negative interaction can have disastrous effects on self-concept. Teachers can help minimize it by making sure that all students have the opportunity to be recognized for their strengths. Joe almost consistently struck out in the softball games, but he could do more sit-ups during calisthenics than almost anyone in the class. It is important for Joe to be recognized for those things he does well and not merely for his deficiencies.

With respect to sensitivity to students' feelings and trying to promote positive peer interactions, teachers should carefully consider the implications of letting the "captains" choose teams for sports and games. What happens in most classes? One student consistently gets picked last. The student may be clumsy, awkward, physically handicapped, mentally retarded, or have some other disadvantage judged to be a team liability by classmates. Whatever the cause, being picked last is a continual reminder to everyone, including the student, that he is a "loser." Handicapped students often need help in being perceived in high-status rather than low-status positions. There are many alternatives to the "pecking-order" approach in dividing into teams.

Involvement in physical activities is an excellent vehicle for mainstreaming handicapped persons into community programs—for example, the YMCA, YWCA, city recreation department, league teams (football, soccer, and others), swimming clubs, physical fitness organizations, and other such groups. It is shocking how frequently handicapped persons are almost automatically excluded from consideration for this type of community participation. Once they have developed skills in their physical education program at school, they are better able to demonstrate their capability for active and meaningful participation in community programs. If one of the purposes of education is to prepare a person for adult independence, maximizing the handicapped person's potential for community integration is a high-priority goal. It is from this type of participation that meaningful peer relationships can evolve. Many nonhandicapped persons might take community recreation for granted; however, the opportunities do not come naturally to many handicapped persons. The school-based physical education program can be the beginning point of moving out into community-sponsored physical education programs.

Music

Concept Development

As with other subjects, it is important to assess the student's music skills and concepts and to analyze the errors he makes, to provide the basis for planning instruction. Error analysis provides valuable information in identifying the source of a problem so that appropriate remediation can be planned. If a student is having difficulty learning to play the autoharp, the source of the problem may be reading music, remembering how particular chords are formed, positioning the autoharp in his lap, lack of sufficient coordination, short attention span, or possibly other factors. The sequential development of musical concepts to be taught through the use of the autoharp will be dependent upon pinpointing the types of problems the student is having and tailoring instruction to overcome those problems.

There are curriculum considerations in the area of music that can help students progress in concept development. The teacher should use music that is meaningful to and valued by the student. When concepts are introduced, the music selected should clearly illustrate the concept to be learned. The lesson plan should move gradually toward using many different music examples, requiring finer degrees of discrimination and understanding, so that mastery is possible. Some students learn more efficiently through one sensory channel than another or from responding to music through one form or another. Generally it is a sound educational approach to provide practice on music concepts in various ways, using diverse materials. Welsbacher (1972) advocates the multisensory approach when teaching upward movement of melody by having students *move* their hands up as the music portrays upward movement; *sing* sequences that move upward; *play* instruments, such as the xylophone, to depict upward movement; and *look* at pictures illustrating upward movement. By approaching concept development through different experiences and providing sufficient practice for mastery, teachers can help handicapped students' progress in the quality and rate of their concept formation.

Hearing-impaired students require adapted instructional approaches in music to develop musical concepts. As was discussed in chapter 1, hearing impairment must be considered according to each student's individual hearing pattern related to frequency (pitch) and intensity (loudness). Hearing-impaired students vary in the pitch range of their handicap. Thus, some of these students might be less handicapped in learning musical concepts when examples are used at a high rather than low pitch level or vice versa. Also, some students benefit from amplification more than others in minimizing intensity disadvantages. The music teacher should work with the audiologist and speech therapist in planning the most appropriate way to teach musical concepts for each hearing-impaired student.

Even students with severe hearing impairments can be successful in musical concept development. Deaf students can experience music through touch and vision and, thus, learn concepts through those sensory channels. By touch, these students can associate the sounds of instruments through feeling the vibrations. Fahey and Birkenshaw (1972) suggest that large drums or the timpani, bass xylophones, and base metallophones have been found to be most helpful in training deaf students to distinguish vibrations of musical instruments from other environmental sounds. Students can also feel the vibrations of the piano and rhythm band instruments. Activities such as having students feel the instrument and indicate when the music starts and stops can be used to reinforce their tactile perception of sound. Visual clues can be provided to deaf students in the area of rhythm through the use of a metronome, so they may "see" fast and slow tempos. They can observe another student dance to a musical selection and then go through the steps of the dance themselves. Fahey and Birkenshaw (1972) outline a multitude of specific instructional strategies in teaching musical concepts to deaf students for readers who would like more information. Often teachers have assumed that the ear is the most essential factor in successful musical experiences. It must be remembered that all handicaps can be minimized with adapted instructional approaches. Epley (1972) describes her personal experience of playing the bass drum and cymbals in the university band following an accident which resulted

291

in her becoming deaf. She stated that "alert eyes, strict counting, and self-confidence" enabled her to play successfully and find enjoyment with the rest of the band.

Why did I ask to join the band and risk the work of the other band members and the director? Why did I decide to make participation in music an aspect of my whole life? Aaron Copland once said that to stop the flow of music would be like the stopping of time itself, incredible and inconceivable. In my opinion he is absolutely correct. Music can provide a feeling of achievement, give a personal pleasure as well as pleasure to other people, and in general, furnish an individual with a way to express himself. For these reasons, I want to continue taking part in soundless musical activities. This can only be possible, however, if musicians will open up their world to me and the thousands of other handicapped persons and let us join in their music-making (p. 39).

Teaching musical concepts to visually impaired students involves making adaptations to insure that instruction is not visually oriented. Students might learn concepts through verbal instruction and physical guidance. For example, a blind student learning to play a guitar might be given a verbal explanation of finger positioning for a particular chord and could be guided into the particular position by the teacher actually placing his fingers into the position. Since blind students typically have developed keen auditory abilities, the students might learn to play instruments or sing musical selections by "ear." To capitalize on this approach, the teacher might tape selections for them so they can listen to the example or model over and over. The American Printing House for the Blind and the Division of the Blind and Physically Handicapped of the Library of Congress (see appendix A for addresses) have a wealth of resources which can be made available to music teachers. Some of these include slow taping of instrumental music, large print and braille music, books explaining the braille music code, and records and tapes of music periodicals (Mooney 1972). Teachers are encouraged to take advantage of these valuable services.

Mobility

Portions of the music curriculum, such as singing, dancing, rhythm development, and playing instruments, require movement of one type or another. Each curriculum subcomponent of music incorporates different types of mobility requirements focused on various body parts including the oral cavity, lower trunk, arms, hands, and fingers. Some music experiences, such as playing a flute, require fine motor control whereas clapping to keep time with rhythm is a gross motor activity. Mobility rate and stability are also important factors to consider as related to music. The rhythm of group music activities typically sets the rate at which students should perform or participate in the activity. Students who have slow rates of mobility may have a difficult time keeping up with a fast tempo whether singing, playing instruments, or engaging in any other type of music experience. Finally, stability of motion becomes an important consideration in music when activities requiring physical endurance because of extended lengths of movement are considered. These activities include participation in the marching band, frequent and extended practice and performance sessions of the school orchestra, and dancing classes. Mobility adaptations can be made in the music curriculum to minimize the disadvantages of blindness, deafness, and physical handicaps.

On the whole, visual impairment is less of a handicap in music than in some other areas of learning. One subcomponent of the music curriculum that warrants special consideration, particularly when a visually impaired child is young and is just learning skills related to orientation and mobility, is rhythmic movement. Some visually impaired students may not be as secure or coordinated in rhythmic movement as their peers, owing to possible previous limited opportunities to fully explore the endless variations of movement. Rhythmic activities are channels for aiding the development of mobility skills. Visually impaired students may begin with large free movement, with gradual emphasis toward the refinement of the movements. In helping to structure rhythmic activities for the visually impaired student, the teacher can use verbal directions and physical guidance which involves helping to move the student's limbs or body in the desired manner. Rhythmic movements can be valuable in teaching the visually impaired student concepts related to motion, such as a wheel rolling, trees swaying in the wind, and an elephant's walk. Special emphasis might also be given to teaching the visually impaired student popular dance steps to enhance their social acceptance, participation, and self-confidence at school social functions.

Deaf children may use movement to learn rhythms they are unable to hear. They may observe a particular rhythmic sequence done in different meters and then reproduce the pattern through clapping or playing rhythm instruments. This kinesthetic approach to teaching rhythm can be a valuable teaching strategy (Fahey and Birkenshaw 1972). Movement exercises combined with music can improve all students' agility, posture, and physical fitness.

Adaptations in the music program should be considered for physically distabled students. Students unable to walk might crawl, roll over, clap their hands, or engage in some other response when rhythmic experiences are being shared by the class. Students with physical handicaps might learn rhythm through observation of activities such as dance or gymnastics or by combining rhythmic activities with their physical therapy sessions. Playing instruments is another music experience which can be adapted for students with mobility disadvantages. Teachers should analyze the various degrees of coordination and types of movement required by different instruments. For example, students able to make only gross motor responses might play the drums or tambourine. Sand blocks or rhythm sticks may be played by striking them on another surface for students able to use only one hand, or sleigh bells may be fastened to various parts of the body, depending upon the locus of a physical disability. Eddy (1972) tells of an experience teaching instrumental lessons and band to a young student, Barbara, who tried out to play clarinet in the band. Although Barbara had no fingers on either hand, she did have rather small stubs of various sizes. After considering various alternatives, in spite of the marked handicap, Eddy decided she could try to play a mellophone as a precursor to a horn. Barbara made phenomenal progress, to the point of playing a horn in the elementary band. As she progressed to junior and senior high, Barbara continued as a member of the marching band. There were other obstacles for her to overcome, since she was born with a twisted leg and malformed foot. Working against these disadvantages, she marched in parades up to three miles long and participated in the complex band maneuvers on the football field. Eddy states: "She has grown up to be a well-adjusted, happy person, and I like to think that learning to play the horn and conquering the obstacles of becoming a good band member have contributed to her happiness and the confidence that she has in herself" (p. 46).

Communication

Music activities provide excellent opportunities for helping students with communication handicaps. Many students who have problems associated with stuttering typically have more fluency when singing than when talking. Singing provides a structured rhythm that can be an excellent therapeutic tool. Instructional strategies need to be carefully coordinated among the music teacher, classroom teacher, and speech therapist to maximize the overall benefit of music experiences for the child with communication handicaps. The procedures of the speech therapist can be incorporated into the music curriculum. The speech therapist can suggest ways to help a child who stutters to minimize this handicap through music, which might generalize to other communication experiences. Additionally, if music poses no problems for the student who stutters, situations might be devised for him to sing in the school chorus or to have other such experiences to gain recognition for his strength in this area.

Problems associated with articulation lend themselves to possible remediation activities in the area of music. Teachers and students can make up songs with words composed of the particular sounds which the student is working on in speech therapy. An example might be with the *M* sound.

> Miles away there is a man
> Who makes the children happy.
> Miles away this merry man
> Sings songs to make them happy.
> (Flowers 1963, p. 104)

While the student is being provided practice in speech, instruction on music concepts, such as melody, harmony, and rhythm, may also be built into the experiences with song writing. Another opportunity for improving articulation is to provide vocal warm-up drills to exercise the lips, tongue, and larynx. Students can also be helped to learn particular positioning of the parts of their oral cavity. This can help students learn to produce sounds correctly and carry over to lipreading training for hearing-impaired students.

Music is an excellent vehicle for helping students disadvantaged by voice problems related to pitch, intensity, quality, and flexibility (chapter 1 includes an explanation of these communication handicaps). For example, students can be taught rhythm, which is necessary for appropriate flexibility in speaking, by clapping the accents of words or phrases, walking the rhythmic sequence, or illustrating it by playing percussion instruments (Fahey and Birkenshaw 1972). Practice should be structured to insure generalization to speech patterns. Activities can also be provided to help students identify various pitch levels of instruments and to experiment with matching their speech with the range in levels. Students with speech problems associated with pitch will be helped best if music teachers coordinate their program with that of the speech therapist. In order to provide appropriate practice for students with voice problems and to promote generalization of communication skills learned through music to other speech and language experiences, teachers should pick songs and experiences that emphasize natural rhythmic accents, tonal inflections, and pitch.

Academic Difficulty

Music is an excellent channel for teaching many academic skills, as well as musical concepts. "Sesame Street" productions certainly exemplify the merit of this approach. Some students who are placed at a significant disadvantage by having a very low reading level as compared to their peers might learn concepts through music that they fail to master from reading their textbooks. Skills in language arts, arithmetic, social studies, physical education, socialization, and all other curriculum areas may be reinforced through music experiences. Reichard and Blackburn (1973) include many suggestions for correlating academic and music instruction. In order to maximize beneficial outcomes for students, all teachers must coordinate their instruction. Depending upon the available personnel in a school working with handicapped students, coordination might occur among the classroom, resource, speech, and music teachers.

Peer Relationships

Music activities may be planned to provide opportunities for handicapped students to share experiences with their nonhandicapped peers, develop hobbies that would increase the likelihood that peer relationships would continue outside of school, and receive positive recognition accentuating their strengths, which could result in heightened classroom status. The group nature of many music activities provides an excellent setting for interaction between handicapped and nonhandicapped students. Teachers should try to insure that handicapped students have the skills to make a positive contribution to the group. For example, if several students are working together to write a song and the handicapped student in the group has severe language delays and is poor in penmanship, this student probably will not be able to participate effectively in this assignment. Positive peer relationships involve both giving and receiving. Teachers should structure situations so that the handicapped student may contribute to and draw from the resources of other group members. The student with language and writing problems may be very successful in a group activity aimed at devising a folk dance. Handicapped students should be considered for the school chorus, orchestra, and other music activities on the same basis as other students. They should not be ruled out automatically simply because they are handicapped.

Hobbies related to music can be enjoyable leisure time activities over one's entire life. Hobbies also can be socializing catalysts in neighborhoods and the community. Students who have special difficulty forming friendships with others might be aided by developing hobbies that could provide a natural tie with another person. In the area of music, these hobbies might include playing in a rock or folk band, participating in choral groups, collecting records, attending concerts, singing in the church choir, joining a dancing group, or other such activities. For handicapped students so inclined, teachers should encourage the development of such hobbies and try to structure the opportunity for the hobby to be shared during class with others. Sharing hobbies within class can help build the bridge to sharing outside of the school day.

Some handicapped students with talent in music might achieve more in this curriculum area than in any other. Being at a significant disadvantage in some subjects makes it particularly important to "shine" in others. If music is the student's strength, teachers should capitalize on this success experience to help the handicapped student receive respect from his peers. The student might be asked to conduct the class's singing, write a class song, demonstrate how to play an instrument, have the lead in a musical performed by the class, participate in school-sponsored and community-based special events in music, or act as a peer tutor to other students in the school on music activities. This should not be viewed as showing special favoritism to the handicapped student and certainly similar opportunities should be extended to nonhandicapped students talented in music.

Art

Concept Development

Art education is often provided in elementary and junior high schools in a random rather than systematic fashion. Much instruction in art can be characterized as a series of unconnected activities rather than as a developmental process. This random approach to art instruction can penalize handicapped as well as nonhandicapped students in developing artistic interests, abilities, and talents. In order for handicapped students to progress maximally in artistic concept development, systematic instruction is a basic requirement.

As pointed out in all other subject areas, assessment is the first step to planning appropriate instruction. A meaningful assessment requires that the teacher be knowledgeable of the developmental sequence of skills and concepts which should be mastered. In this case, it is important for teachers to be aware of the stages children go through in art development. Lowenfeld and Brittain (1964) have provided a developmental sequence of artistic abilities which is included in table 8–5. This model outlines a hierarchy of skills and concepts which can be used as a guide in pinpointing a child's level of art performance. Most assessments in the area of art are done informally by teachers through observation of children's art work.

Summary: Preschematic Stage—Four to Seven Years

Characteristics	Human Figure	Space	Color	Design	Motivation Topics	Materials
Discovery of *relationship* between drawing, thinking, and environment. Change of form symbols because of constant search for definite concept.	Circular motion for head, longitudinal for legs and arms. Head-feet representations develop to more complex form concept. Symbols depending on active knowledge during the act of drawing.	Self as center, with no orderly arrangement of objects in space: "There is a table, there is a door, there is a chair." Also emotional relationships: "This is *my* doll."	No relationship to nature Color according to emotional appeal.	No conscious approach.	Activating of passive knowledge related mainly to self (body parts).	Crayons, clay, tempera paints (thick), large bristle brushes, large sheets of paper (absorbent).

Table 8–5
Summary of Developmental Stages

Summary: Schematic Stage—Seven to Nine Years

Characteristics	Human Figure	Space	Color	Design	Motivation Topics	Materials
Formulation of a definite concept of man and environment. Self-assurance through repetition: repetition of form symbols, schemata. In pure schema no intentional experience is expressed, only the thing itself: "the man," "the tree," etc. Experiences are expressed by deviations from schema. Use of geometric lines.	Definite concept of figure depending on active knowledge and personality, through repetition: schema. Deviations expressing experiences can be seen in— (1) Exaggeration of important parts. (2) Neglect or omission of unimportant parts. (3) Change of symbols.	First definite space concept: base line. Discovery of being a part of environment: important for cooperation and reading. Base line expresses— (1) Base (2) Terrain Deviations from base line express experiences. Subjective space: (1) Folding over (egocentric). (2) Mixed forms of plan and elevation (3) X-ray pictures. (4) Space-time representations.	Discovery of relationship between color and object: through repetition: color schema. Same color for same object. Deviation of color schema shows emotional experience	No conscious design approach.	Best motivation concentrates on action, characterized by *we, action, where.* Topics referring to— (1) Time sequences (journeys, traveling stories). (2) X-ray pictures (inside and outside are emphasized), factory, school, home, etc.	Colored crayons. Colored chalks. Tempera, poster paint. Large paper. Bristle and hair brushes. Clay: (1) Synthetic (2) Analytic

Table 8–5 Continued

Summary: Stage of Dawning Realism—Nine to Eleven Years

Characteristics	Human Figure	Space	Color	Design	Motivation Topics	Materials
Gang age.	Attention to clothes (dresses. uniforms), emphasizing difference between girls and boys.	Removal from baseline expression.	Removal from objective stage of color.	First conscious approach toward decoration.	Self-awareness stimulated by characterization of different dresses and suits (professions).	Paper cutting.
Removal from geometric lines (schema).		Overlapping. Sky comes down to base line.	Emphasis on emotional approach to color.	Acquaintance with materials and their function.		Crayons.
Lack of cooperation with adults.		Discovery of plane.				Poster paint.
	Greater stiffness as result of egocentric attitude, and the emphasis on details (clothes, hair, and so forth). Tendency toward realistic lines.	Filling in space between base lines.	Subjective stage of color. Color is used according to subjective experience.		Cooperation and overlapping through group work.	Flat, colored chalk.
Greater awareness of the self and of sex differences.		Difficulties in spatial correlations as result of egocentric attitude and lack of cooperation.			Clay.	
	Removal from schema.				Subjective cooperation through type of topic: "We are building a house." Objective cooperation through team work.	Papier-mâché.
						Wood.
						Collage materials.
						Metal.
						Prints.

Table 8–5 Continued

300

Table 8–5 Continued

Summary: Pseudonaturalistic Stage—Eleven to Thirteen Years

Characteristics	Human Figure	Space	Color	Design	Motivation Topics	Materials
Developed intelligence, yet unawareness.	Joints. Visual observation of body actions.	Urge for three-dimentional expression.	Changes of color in nature for distance and mood (visually minded).	First conscious approach to stylizing.	Dramatic actions in environment.	Water color.
Naturalistic approach (unconscious).	Proportions. Emphasis on expression by nonvisually minded.	Diminishing sizes of distant objects.	Emotional reaction to color (nonvisually minded).	Symbols for professions. Function of different materials with related designs.	Actions from imagination and posing (with meaning, like scrubbing).	Gouache (water color and tempera).
Tendency toward visual—or nonvisual mindedness.		Ho·· line (visually minded).			Proportions through emphasis on content.	Poster paint.
Love for dramatization and action.		Environment only when significant (nonvisually minded).			Color moods.	Bristle brush.
						Hair brush.
						Clay.
						Linoleum.
						Papier-mâché.
						Textiles.
						Wood.

From Viktor Lowenfeld and W. Lambert Brittain. *Creative and Mental Growth*, 4th ed. New York: The Macmillan Company, 1964, pp. 396–400.

Lowenfeld and Brittain's model can aid teachers in the refinement of their observational skills, since it identifies the skills and concepts for which the teacher should be looking. This model, however, is based on the normal developmental process and generally assumes that the child's senses, intelligence, and motor skills are intact. When one considers the disadvantages associated with handicapping conditions, adaptations in the sequence must be made.

Joe is nine years old. He has been blind since birth. Although Joe loves to use crayons, chalk, and paint, he has no concept of color. Unless a peer helps him pick particular colors, he might be coloring a sky with a green crayon.

Mary is a seventh-grader. She has gifted intelligence and is one of the best readers in the class. Polio struck Mary at a young age, leaving one arm and hand totally nonfunctional and the other arm and hand with minimal usage (movement in two fingers). Mary enjoys art activities involving fine motor movements. She is able to use a felt pen, magic markers, chalk, paint brush, and crayons; however, her drawings have characteristics associated with those of younger children. The art activities which pose the greatest difficulty for Mary are ones requiring large motor movements, such as modeling clay and making papier mâché objects. Mary also has difficulty with activities which need two hands, such as macramé. One of the reasons Mary enjoys art is because her teachers have always encouraged her, in spite of her lowered performance in some areas.

After initial assessment has been accomplished and teachers have an idea of a particular student's strengths and weaknesses, adaptations in the art curriculum may be needed to accommodate the student's unique needs. Curriculum adaptations may have to be made in what is to be taught (content), how the content is to be taught (methods/materials), and when the content is to be taught (timing/sequence). This decision has to be made individually, based on each student's needs. Many characteristics associated with handicapping conditions may necessitate content modification of the art curriculum. Learning disabled or mentally retarded students may have short attention spans or difficulty in remembering directions. These characteristics often require adaptation of the curriculum in timing and sequence. Additionally, lowered functioning in some academic subjects may create problems in art. For example, if the students are expected to read a poem and illustrate it with a painting, students with learning problems may be unable to read the poem initially. Use of a peer tutor or a tape presentation could eliminate this particular problem. Some students with learning problems have difficulty with spatial orientation, which is an important prerequisite to higher level artistic functioning. These students may be unable to draw a human figure without gross body distortions. The problems of some students may be remediated through sound instruction and practice; other students may always have significant spatial problems. Teachers should help students compensate or work around their deficiencies by developing students' interests and talents in other artistic endeavors which they can perform successfully. Many students with learning problems have strong talents in art. When this is the case, teachers should seize the opportunity to capitalize on the artistic channel for teaching other academic skills, as well as for improving self-concept.

Blind and partially sighted students, as well as physically handicapped students with hand and arm involvement, often require all three types of adaptation in the art curriculum—content, methods/materials, and timing/sequence. Because of limitations imposed by the handicap, students may be below the developmental level in art predicted on the basis of chronological age (table 8–5). Teachers have to zero in on these students' level of performance and provide instruction at that level in order to establish a strong foundation of artistic skills and concepts. The teaching/learning style options described in the previous section on physical education are also applicable to art education. These include visual guidance, verbal guidance, multisensory instruction, and the movement exploration approach (see section on physical education for description).

As for multisensory instruction, blind students typically learn best through a combination of auditory, tactile, and kinesthetic experiences. When teaching blind students macramé, the teacher might provide verbal instruction in how to make a particular knot, have the student feel the texture of the knot (loose, tight, smooth, pointed) and guide the student's hands and fingers through the sequence of steps involved in making the knot. Other art activities that have been mastered and enjoyed by blind students include experiences with clay, sculpture, printmaking, collages, finger painting, papier mâché, and ceramics. A variety of textures should be used and explored by blind students as a way of familiarizing them with their environment and refining tactile skills necessary for learning braille. Art media to choose from include paper (regular, sandpaper, tracing paper, wax paper), wood, textiles, wet sand, string, yarn, pipe cleaners, wires, rubber, plastic, glass, and a host of others.

Often the adaptation that must be made in order for concept development to proceed is in the sequence in which the art activity is accomplished.

Figure 8–1

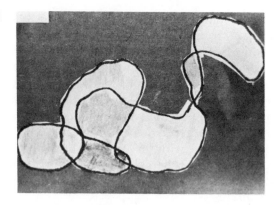

Collage by David Gates, Photograph by Richard Clontz

The sixth grade class was making crayon collages by coloring a sheet of paper with all different colors. After the coloring was completed, they outlined each different color section by glueing string around its border. Larry, a blind student, participated in the activity by reversing the procedure: first he glued string in various patterns on the sheet and then he colored the inside of each section. His collage, depicted in figure 8–1, was one of the nicest in the class.

Modification of methods and materials for art education requires divergent thinking on the part of the teacher. It often boils down to taking an activity which teachers have been "programmed" to do in one way and turning it around so that the activity can be done in another way. Lowenfeld and Brittain (1964) state five important factors of the creative process which seem to embody the concepts and objectives inherent in the philosophy of art education. They include sensitivity, fluency, flexibility, originality, and capacity to refine or reorganize. It is conjectured that these factors lead to a teacher's capability to adapt the art curriculum to the particular strengths and weaknesses of handicapped students. The likelihood of students learning the creative process can be facilitated by the teacher's demonstration of the creative process in teaching.

Mobility

Art experiences and activities almost always require movement of one type or another. Some movements are of a gross nature, such as finger painting, and others require very fine control, such as sketching or carving very small figures. Physically handicapped students, particularly those who have limited mobility in their arms, hands, and fingers, may require

304

adaptations in the art curriculum. Some students may not be able to hold a pencil, crayons, or a paint brush in the typical fashion. Sometimes a ball of clay or a foam rubber sponge may be put on the brush to provide a better grip. Another problem that students may have is that jerky or uncoordinated movements may result in their paper frequently slipping off their desk, paint being spilled, or crayons being knocked to the floor.

To position the paper, teachers may use masking tape to affix the paper to the student's desk or table. Students who have uncontrolled movements or who are particularly clumsy may be provided a special work table away from any of the major material storage areas in the classroom. Limits might be placed on how many materials they may have on their table at one time and a special area of the table may be set aside for materials and supplies. By reserving one area of the table for materials, students may establish the habit of being particularly careful with haphazard movements in that direction. A sturdy rack with holes cut to hold paint jars snugly may also prevent spillage. Some students with physical limitations may also have extreme difficulty manipulating small objects. Rather than making a collage or junk sculpture with small pieces of material, they may have to use larger ones that are easier to handle. Other students have more severe limitations and require more substantial adaptations.

Peg's hands are twisted and turn in toward her body. She has no movement in them. In art class, she enjoys blow painting through a straw and printmaking. When printmaking, Peg uses a plastic stick with a small platform at the end. She holds one end of the stick in her mouth and the print (potato, textiles, leaves) is attached to the platform. She then uses head movements to make a picture. Peg's favorite art activity, which she does more at home than at school, is foot and toe painting. She puts paper on the floor, dips her toes or whole foot in tempera paint to design both abstract and realistic compositions. When one of Peg's classmates saw her "foot art," the peer exclaimed, "Peg's hands may not work, but she has got the best feet of anyone I know."

Art activities involve a tremendous range of mobility requirements. Because of the variety of activities from which to choose, teachers are afforded tremendous flexibility in making needed adaptations for handicapped students.

Communication

He seems to be striving to find his Self. Silently, yet eloquently through his drawings, he reveals his thought and his feelings. Usually happy—for that is the mood of childhood even in adversity—but sometimes lost and bewildered in a voiceless appeal for help, he may be trying to tell us where it hurts (DiLeo 1970, p. 379).

Art is a method of expression. A student can express what he sees and feels. He can become more sensitive to his own ideals and feelings and communicate these with peers and adults through art. Art is an important form of communication for all students, but it may have especially important implications for students who have handicaps associated with language, and who thus have impairment in some channels of communication.

Deaf students, or students with severe stuttering problems, may be able to express visually through art work many of the thoughts and feelings they are unable to explain verbally. Often art is used as a form of therapy for emotionally/behaviorally disturbed students who are having difficulty with personal development and interpersonal relations. Kramer (1971) has provided an excellent description of the use of art as therapy. As teachers encourage students to communicate with themselves and others through art experiences, teachers have to be sensitive to the student's expression, yet avoid the pitfall of constantly analyzing the student or overly attaching psychological meaning to the student's compositions.

Sam's teacher became very concerned as he reviewed Sam's art work. The concern stemmed from the fact that all of a sudden Sam was using the color black more than any other color. He painted black clouds, houses, books, food, and clothes. Every picture Sam painted or colored had a foreboding overtone according to the interpretation of his teacher. This alarmed the teacher who proceeded to set up a parent conference to find out if Sam's parents believed their child to be depressed, anxious, and having morbid thoughts. When the teacher showed the pictures to Sam's mother, she immediately realized what was happening. Sam had recently gotten a black Labrador Retriever. He named the dog Blackie and quickly became very devoted to her. One of his favorite home activities was to brush Blackie's coat every night to see how much it would shine. The more it shone, the more Sam talked about what a pretty color black is. When Sam's mother related these incidents to the teacher, a completely different message was interpreted from Sam's art work.

Teachers must beware of diagnosing emotional/behavioral problems through art work. If the student seems to have disturbances that warrant attention, the teacher might discuss his concerns with the school counselor, school psychologist, or special education resource teacher responsible for teaching emotionally/behaviorally disturbed children. Further observations and evaluation should be done to document the teacher's initial concerns. There is a difference between art education and art therapy. Art therapy requires specialized training and should not be practiced by persons without the appropriate qualifications. Some school systems employ art therapists on a full-time or part-time basis. Qualified therapists can play a valuable role in facilitating communication through art experiences for handicapped students.

Academic Difficulty

Art has countless applications to the improvement of academic achievements. Students with learning problems, particularly those who have special interests and talents in art, can benefit tremendously from a correlated approach to instruction. The language experience method of teaching reading (see chapter 5) has traditionally been a vehicle for incorporating art. Students describe their experiences; the teacher or a peer writes down the words of the student, the student illustrates the words through art projects and learns to recognize and comprehend the words in written form. Art can be a very important component of the language experience approach to reading instruction.

In the social studies curriculum, art can play a major role. Many students unable to read the textbook can learn concepts about foreign customs, for example, by analyzing pictures and other visual media; and they can demonstrate their knowledge of these customs by constructing collages, shoebox stories, murals, and props for a play. This instructional strategy should not be used in an entirely singular fashion, but rather combined with other strategies into a multisensory approach.

Teaching measurement in the arithmetic curriculum has tremendous potential for correlation with art. Learning the metric system can be incorporated into a variety of art projects. Furthermore, art can be the channel of teaching skills and concepts in the area of time, such as days of the week, months, seasons, and holidays. The combination of arithmetic and art can be meaningful, enjoyable, and substantive.

The relation of art to other subject areas is discussed by Jefferson (1969). Let it suffice here to state that some handicapped students, disadvantaged in academic achievement, may make significant gains when academics are taught within the context of art which is often a less threatening and more motivating subject for these students. Furthermore, many of these students may find pleasure in art which they do not find in other subjects. Every opportunity should be taken to capitalize on the joy of learning.

Peer Relationships

Art education can provide many opportunities for students to work together to share their expertise. When handicapped students have special talents in art, an opportunity should be provided for them to receive peer recognition and classroom status.

Molly is deaf. She struggles to keep up academically and tends to be isolated from most informal peer groups in her seventh-grade class. Molly has a distinctive talent in cutting out silhouettes. The teacher asked her to cut out a silhouette of each of her classmates to hang around the room in preparation for the PTA-sponsored "Parent's Night." The students were excited over watching Molly cut the silhouettes. When parents visited the classroom they were encouraged to identify their child's silhouette and to take it home with them. It was fun for the parents, students, and teacher. It was more than fun for Molly—it was her "ticket" to social acceptance.

Art instruction can be planned to encourage small group interaction. For example, group murals can be a vehicle for learning artistic skills and concepts, academic skills and concepts, and increasing positive peer interaction. Teachers must try to insure that handicapped students make a positive contribution to the group and be considered assets rather than liabilities.

Hobbies related to art which stem from school experiences can carry over into neighborhood and community experiences. These hobbies can initiate lifelong, leisure-time interests. As community experiences and leisure-time interests develop, handicapped persons increase their opportunities for interacting with peers. Art can serve as the bridge among people of similar interests.

References and Suggested Readings

AAHPER. 1976. *Special fitness test manual for mildly retarded persons.* Washington, D.C.: AAHPER Publications.

Adams, R. C., Daniel, A. N., and Rullman, L. 1972. *Games, sports, and exercises for the physically handicapped.* Philadelphia: Lea and Febigel.

AMA. 1968. The epileptic child and competitive school athletics. *Pediatrics* 42:700.

Arnheim, D. D., and Sinclair, W. A. 1975. *The clumsy child.* St. Louis: Mosby.

Arnheim, D. D., Auxter, D., and Crowe, W. C. 1977. *Principles and methods of adapted physical education.* St. Louis: Mosby.

Blackburn, J. E., and Powell, W. C. 1976. *One at a time all at once: The creative teacher's guide to individualized instruction without anarchy.* Pacific Palisades, Calif.: Goodyear.

Bloom, B. S., Engelhart, M. D., Furst, E., Hill, W., and Krathwahl, D. R. 1956. *Taxonomy of educational objectives, handbook I: Cognitive domain.* New York: David McKay.

Cratty, B. J. 1969. *Motor activity and the education of retardates.* Philadelphia: Len and Febigev.

Daniels, A. S., and Davies, E. 1975. *Adapted physical education.* New York: Harper and Row.

DiLeo, J. H. 1970. *Young children and their drawings.* New York: Brunner-Mazel.

Eddy, Clark. 1972. No fingers to play a horn. In Malcolm E. Bessom, ed., *Music in special education.* Washington, D.C.: Music Educators National Conference, 1972. Copyright © 1972. Reprinted with permission.

Epley, Carol. 1972. In a soundless world of musical enjoyment. In Malcolm E. Bessom, ed., *Music in special education.* Washington, D.C.: Music Educators National Conference, 1972. Copyright © 1972. Reprinted with permission.

Fahey, J. D., and Birkenshaw, L. 1972. Bypassing the ear: The perception of music by feeling and touch. In Malcolm E. Bessom, ed., *Music in special education.* Washington, D.C.: Music Educators National Conference.

Fait, H. F. 1972. *Special physical education.* Philadelphia: Saunders.

Flowers, A. M. 1963. *The big book of sounds.* Danville, Ill.: Interstate.

Herman, W. L. 1969. Reading and other language arts in the social studies instruction: Persistent problems. In R. C. Preston, ed., *A new look at reading in the social studies.* Newark, N.J.: International Reading Association.

Hunsicker, P., and Reiff, G. G. 1976. *Youth fitness test manual.* Washington, D.C.: AAHPER Publications.

Jefferson, B. 1969. *Teaching art to children.* Boston: Allyn and Bacon.

Johnson, R., and Vardian, E. R. 1973. Reading, readability, and the social studies. *The Reading Teacher* 26:483–488.

Karlin R,. 1969. What does educational research reveal about reading and the high school student? *The English Journal* 58:386–395.

Kirman, J. M., and Nay, M. A. 1975. Joint planning for integrating social studies and science. *Social Education* 39:77–80.

Kramer, E. 1971. *Art as therapy with children*. New York: Schocken.

Linn, M. C. 1972. An experimental science curriculum for the visually impaired. *Exceptional Children* 39:37–43.

Lowenfeld, V., and Brittain, W. L. 1964. *Creative and mental growth,* 4th ed. New York: Macmillan.

Lunstrum, J. P. 1976. Reading in the social studies: A preliminary analysis of recent research. *Social Education* 40:10–17.

Menhusen, B. R., and Gromme, R. O. 1976. Science for handicapped children—Why? *Science and Children* 13:35–37.

Mooney, M. K. 1972. Blind children need training, not sympathy. In M. E. Bessom, ed., *Music in special education*. Washington, D.C.: Music Educators National Conference.

Moran, J. M., and Kalakian, L. H. 1974. *Movement experiences for the mentally retarded or emotionally disturbed child*. Minneapolis: Burgess.

Puthoff, M. 1976. Instructional strategies for mainstreaming. *Mainstreaming physical education*. The National Association for Physical Education of College Women and the National College Physical Education Association for Men.

Reichard, C. L., and Blackburn, D. B. 1973. *Music based instruction for the exceptional child*. Denver, Colo.: Love.

Schatz, D., Franks, F., Thier, H. D., and Linn, M. C. 1976. Hands-on science for the blind. *Science and Children* 13:21–22.

Sanders, N. M. 1966. *Classroom questions*. New York: Harper and Row.

Sherrill, C. 1976. *Adapted physical education and recreation*. Dubuque, Iowa: Brown.

Turner, T. N. 1976. Making the social studies textbook a more effective tool for less able readers. *Social Education* 41:38–41.

Welsbacher, B. T. 1972. More than a package of bizarre behavior. In M. E. Bessom, ed., *Music in special education*. Washington, D.C.: Music Educators National Conference.

■ Chapter Nine

Changing Behavior

Photograph by Richard Clontz

Traditionally, children have been referred to special classes, remedial situations, and segregated units because their behavior is inappropriate for the regular classroom. Therefore, behavior change is one of the primary focus points in planning for the handicapped child's integration into a normal setting. Two facets of behavior have to be considered. First is the curtailment of inappropriate behavior:

David never enters a room; he falls into it. He stalks about the room, breaking things, creating confusion, and being the class clown. The other children laugh at him, and he destroys all my well-laid plans.

311

Second is the increase of appropriate behavior:

I have twenty-five fourth-graders and Tony. Tony reads at the preprimer level. How can I help him with basic reading skills and still meet the needs of the other children?

The handicapped child may have acquired immature or antisocial behavior for many reasons. He may have been overprotected in the home, where temper tantrums, interruptions, or overbearing attitudes were permitted. He may have been enrolled in a special school or special class, where standards for behavior were not as high as in other situations. He may be functioning at a level where most persons do not expect normal behavior from him. Regardless of the reason, inappropriate behavior can be eliminated and acceptable behavior substituted. This change alone can make a tremendous difference in the degree to which a child is accepted by his teachers and by his peers.

After talking with David about his behavior, we listed things that needed to be changed. We made a chart, with space for check marks each time he entered the room quietly, put his books away promptly, etc. With each five checks, David can spend thirty minutes working on his string art, which he loves to do. We also set up a check system for the other children, giving them checks for not laughing at David, and removing checks when they did laugh. I feel that David is gradually assuming responsibility for his own behavior.

The increase of appropriate behavior refers to what is commonly called learning. Since behavior includes any performance or activity, it describes reading, speaking, computation, and any other area of knowledge or skill acquisition. The handicapped child has been isolated because he hasn't learned as much as his normal peers; this learning (or behavior) needs to be increased if he is to remain an active part of the regular classroom.

After working out specific objectives for Tony's reading program, I asked another pupil to help him with his phonics drills. The other pupil then got compensatory time at a chosen activity. Soon other children wanted to help, and now they are all interested in Tony's progress.

Numerous techniques for changing behavior in the classroom have been developed in recent years. Based primarily on studies of behavior by B. F. Skinner and his associates (Skinner 1953), such techniques are often referred to as *behavior modification*. Wallace and Kauffman (1973) describe behavior modification as "any systematic arrangement of environmental events which produces a specific change in observable behavior" (p. 17).

The effectiveness of behavior modification with atypical children has been documented (Macmillan and Forness 1970), with references to retarded, learning disabled, autistic, emotionally disturbed, and brain damaged children. Descriptions of behavior modification strategies employed to reduce disruptive behavior, to increase kindergarten students' ability to follow instruction, and to develop and maintain a variety of academic behaviors (Thompson and Grabowski 1972) present a convincing rationale for its use in changing behavior. There has been some criticism of behavior modification as a tool for manipulating people. With the understanding that this technique is primarily a positive approach, embodying strategies long used by parents and teachers, such criticism may dissolve.

Many teachers, when presented with the principles of behavior, exclaim "Why, I've been doing that for years!" They have been rewarding good behavior and ignoring or punishing bad behavior. Certainly, behavior modification is not new. The new aspect is the systematic approach to using the principles of behavior. In using the definition presented above, focus is on *systematic, specific,* and *observable.* In other words, the techniques formerly used haphazardly are being employed in an organized, scientific way. Because behavior is predictable, the systematic use of behavior modification is effective.

In addition to its effectiveness, there are other advantages to the use of behavior modification techniques in the classroom. Although based on clinical observations, frequently of one person as opposed to a group, it has been found that the same principles work on a group basis. Thus within the group, individual differences in behavior can be accommodated while the group as a whole can make and abide by class rules.

Once understood, the principles of behavior can be explained to peers, paraprofessionals and volunteer helpers in the classroom. Because the objectives are specific, communication between the teacher and other assistants is facilitated. Thus directions for procedures can be given and followed with the full intent of the teacher carried out by anyone he designates.

Principles of Behavior

A young mother took her three-year-old daughter to an egg hunt. Because there were older children participating and the competition was keen, Mary found no eggs. Her mother was surprised, therefore, to see that she had one of the prizes. Asked how she got the prize, Mary replied, "I cried for it."

Children learn at a very early age that their behavior produces consequences. In contemplating behavior change, therefore, the teacher seeks to arrange the consequences to promote the desired behavior.

Behavior is a term that can be ambiguous. Although frequently associated with social actions, in the scientific framework underlying behavior modification, behavior is seen as any activity that can be observed, measured, and evaluated. This definition includes motor, intellectual, verbal, social actions—any performance that can meet the above criteria.

Two kinds of behavior are delineated: *respondent* and *operant*. Respondent (reflex) behavior refers to those responses that are elicited by special stimulus changes in the environment (Keller 1969). It is usually associated with involuntary muscular movements such as the contraction or dilation of the pupils of the eyes; response to touching a hot stove; watering of the mouth at the taste of some particular food.

Operant (voluntary) behavior, on the other hand, is conscious responses to one's environment, maintained through reinforcement. Thus operant behaviors are of major concern to teachers who wish to change children's behaviors. Whether or not operant behaviors are changed depends on what happens following each operant behavior (Reinert 1976). The general rule in behavior modification is that desirable behavior should be rewarded (reinforced) and that undesirable behavior should not be rewarded. Behavior which is reinforced tends to be repeated; behavior which is not reinforced tends not to be repeated (Thompson and Grabowski 1972).

Increasing Behavior

One way to increase the likelihood of a behavior recurring is to follow that behavior with a positive or favorable event. This is called *positive reinforcement.*

In the school cafeteria, Henry picked up Miss Lassiter's lunch tray and carried it to the table for her. Miss Lassiter smiled and said, "Thank you, Henry. That was very thoughtful."

It must be remembered that one can increase the likelihood of undesirable behavior as well as desirable behavior by positive reinforcement.

Jamie pulled at Mr. Owen's jacket, "Mr. Owen, let me have the ball." Mr. Owen ignored Jamie; Jamie continued to pull at his jacket. Mr. Owen said, "Oh all right, Jamie, you can have the ball, but stop pulling my jacket!"

It also must be noted that sometimes teachers inadvertantly *punish* desirable behavior rather than rewarding it.

"Teacher, I've finished all my math problems." "Fine. Here are ten more for you to do."

There are two conditions required to make positive reinforcement work:

1. Make the positive event come *after* the desired behavior.
2. Be sure the consequence is favorable (Mager 1972).

Another way to increase the likelihood of a behavior recurring is to follow the behavior by taking away an unpleasant event. This is called *negative reinforcement.*

Tom was very annoyed by Cindy, who chattered constantly. When he did not do his work, Cindy was instructed to sit next to Tom. When Tom was working well, Cindy was moved to the other side of the room.

In many cases a desired behavior must be broken into small steps. This is done for two reasons: first, the child may not perform the entire behavior and therefore cannot be reinforced for it; second, teaching a task through a series of small steps minimizes the number of errors made by the student. In behavior modification, there are several techniques by which tasks may be broken into small steps.

Shaping. Shaping is the process of reinforcing a child for closer approximations to the desired response. The first step is to state the desired (or target) response. The first response (approximation) that occurs, which roughly resembles the target behavior, should be reinforced. When the child has been reinforced for this response repeatedly, he is required to make a closer approximation before he is reinforced.

"Susan, sit in the chair." The first approximation is for Susan to look in the direction of the chair. She is reinforced. When Susan has been reinforced for this response several times and is looking at the chair often, more is required. The next approximation is for her to take a step toward

the chair in order to be reinforced. The sequencing of events continues until sitting in the chair is all that is reinforced.

It is important to raise the standards for reinforcement so the child will go on to the next step. However, standards should not be raised so rapidly that the child cannot receive reinforcement.

Chaining. For most learning tasks, one response does not complete the criteria for learning the entire behavior. Chaining techniques are used to teach behaviors that occur in a sequence. The complex behavior is broken into simple components to be learned one at a time and chained together to obtain the complete behavior. The distinguishing characteristic of chaining is that reinforcement is delivered after the last step. Frequently referred to as *backward chaining*, this technique requires completion of the task before reinforcement and is a powerful teaching device.

A picture puzzle is assembled except for the last piece, which is placed adjacent to its proper place. Only a small effort is required for the child to complete the task and see the final product. Reinforcement is delivered for finishing the task. Later, two pieces are omitted from the puzzle and reinforcement is delivered for completion. Finally, the child completes the entire task and is reinforced.

There are several conditions to chaining. First, the child must know how to perform each unit; second, the child must perform each unit in the proper sequence; third, the units must be performed in rapid succession to be sure they are linked together; fourth, the chain must be repeated until the learning has taken place; fifth, reinforcement must be present in the learning of chains and the reinforcement must be immediate.

To set up a chain of events, the teacher must acquire the skills of task analysis, pertinent to any target behavior. Task analysis was defined and described in chapter 3.

Fading. In using fading, the stimuli are varied until a response made in one situation is made in another. Changes are made in the condition under which the behavior occurs rather than in the nature of the task itself. An example cited by Thompson and Grabowski (1972) is teaching children to color inside a heavy raised outline (cardboard template or yarn); later the height of the outline is reduced and still later replaced by a heavy drawn outline. Ultimately the outline is the usual printed one. A similar technique is illustrated in Figure 9–1.

Figure 9–1
Example of Fading

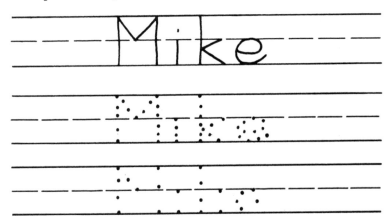

Decreasing Behavior

Behavior is weakened or suppressed by *punishment* or *extinction*. When a behavior is followed by punishment, the likelihood of the behavior recurring decreases. The use of an aversive event (such as spanking) is the form generally used. A second type of punishment (response cost) is used when positive reinforcement is withdrawn. A third type of punishment (time-out) involves isolating the subject from reinforcement for a stated time.

To be effective, punishment must be intense and last long enough to be viewed as aversive and must be administered every time and immediately following the undesirable behavior (Blackham and Silberman 1975).

The effects of punishment are less predictable than those of reinforcement. Some of the undesirable side effects may include avoidance of the punisher; model for aggression provided by the teacher; and increase of fear, withdrawal, and tenseness.

Blackham and Silberman (1975) present guidelines to avoid such side effects from punishment:

Use punishment infrequently and never as the only method for controlling or eliminating undesirable behavior.

Specify clearly the acceptable and unacceptable behavior and the consequences for each. When a child is punished, he or she should know the reasons for the punishment.

Punish the undesirable behavior as soon as it appears; do not wait until the behavior has run its course.

Provide desirable behavioral alternatives for the child.

While punishing the undesirable behavior, reinforce the behavior you wish to promote.

Be consistent in punishing behavior you wish to eliminate. Inconsistent punishment may make the undesirable behavior more durable (p. 71).

A second way to reduce the likelihood of a behavior occurring is *extinction*. Since behavior is maintained by positive or negative reinforcement, withdrawal of the reinforcement weakens the behavior.

Jamie pulled on Mr. Owen's jacket, "Mr. Owen, let me have the ball." Mr. Owen ignored the pulling. Jamie continued to pull his jacket, but when she didn't get the ball, she stopped.

Ignored behavior usually increases at first; this is part of the extinction process. Many teachers do not continue to ignore the behavior long enough; it is difficult to do. However, it does help eliminate nonproductive and disruptive responses since these behaviors are often attention-getters.

There are certain behaviors that are potentially dangerous and cannot be ignored. Physical attacks, horseplay with scissors, and self-injurious behavior cannot always be handled by removal of reinforcement. In such cases, various forms of punishment should be considered. The choice of aversives may progress from those for children functioning at very low levels to those which apply to mature persons: electric shock; spankings; withdrawal of love, affection, or approval; denial of privileges or removal from a rewarding setting; scolding or social disapproval; and self-disappointment. The punishment should be selected in terms of the functional maturity of the child and should be perceived by the child as aversive. When punishment is used, it is important that it be used consciously and systematically (Macmillan, Forness, and Trumbull 1973).

Basic Procedures

Observing and Recording

Once the principles of behavior are understood, there are basic procedures to be followed to insure maximum success from the method. The first procedure is to *define and describe operationally the behavior to be changed.* The behavior must be defined in observable, countable, and repeatable terms. Educators frequently use ambiguous terms in describing children's behavior. For example, the phrase "short attention span" could refer to inability to sit still for five minutes, inability to listen for half an hour, inclination to roam about the room, or any number of behaviors.

The test for *observable* behavior is: Can other persons (who agree on the definition of the behavior) see the same behavior at the same time? Do they all agree as to when the behavior did or did not occur? Do they agree on how many times it occurred and the force or intensity with which it occurred? If such agreement can be reached, the behavior is observable.

When the behavior has been pinpointed, a target must be set, in observable terms. Thus the goal "to decrease John's aggressiveness" would be inappropriate. The target "to decrease John's kicking" would be observable, countable, and therefore subject to change. In addition to the question stated above, a very simple test of observable behavior is: Can you count it?

Neisworth and Smith (1973) suggest that the teacher avoid the use of expressions such as "ability to," "potential for," "capacity for," and so forth. The teacher is not interested in Sue's ability to add two-digit numbers; he is interested in her *doing* it.

When the target behavior has been identified and stated in operational terms, the teacher should *observe and record* that behavior. Sometimes viewed as a chore and a time-consuming effort, this process is a time-saver and an essential element in successful behavior management strategies. Many trial-and-error methods which have been used traditionally in the classroom are not discarded because there is no proof that they do or do not work. If good records are maintained, the teacher can easily keep or reject a particular intervention, dependent upon the recorded results. Another important advantage is that such records are reinforcing to the teacher, to the parent, and to the child. Jens and Shores (1969) report the use of behavioral charts as strong reinforcers in motivating the work performance of mentally retarded adolescents.

In observing and charting behavior, frequently the teacher realizes that the behavior does not occur at the frequency he supposed it did. Upon consideration, the behavior may be seen to be annoying to the teacher only and not of sufficient frequency or duration to need altering.

There are two types of observation of concern in the classroom. The *frequency count* is a measurement of the number of times a behavior occurs. A frequency count could be taken of the number of times Ann cries

319

Figure 9–2
Record of Baseline Data

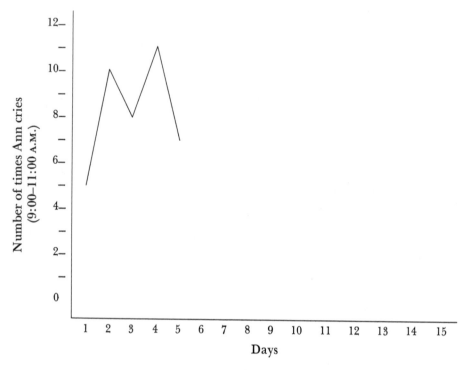

during a stated observation period. The *time interval* observation is a measurement of the length of time a behavior is exhibited. The length of time Ann cries may be more pertinent than the number of times she cries.

An accurate measurement of behavior before intervention is referred to as the *baseline*. Since the purpose is to record an average of the behavior, the recording may be done for a short length of time each day over a five-day period. It is desirable that the behavior be recorded in the setting where change is desired. Data obtained during the baseline period are usually plotted on a graph. (See figure 9–2). The line and bar graphs are most frequently used. The horizontal axis in both types of graph usually identifies the time period while the vertical axis denotes the criteria used to evaluate intervention effects.

Frequency can be counted by recording a mark on a sheet of paper each time the behavior occurs (See figure 9–3) or by the use of a mechanical counter or a stop watch. Kubany and Sloggett (1974) describe an ef-

Figure 9–3
Form of Recording Frequency

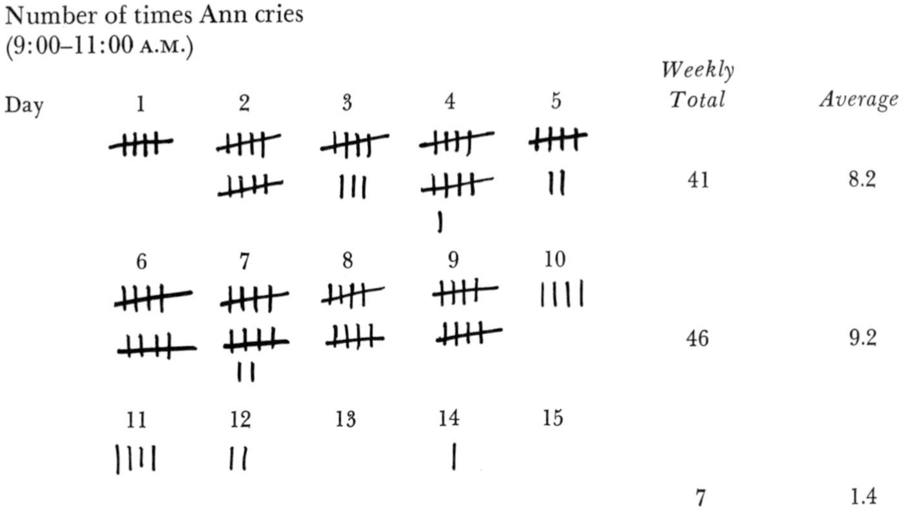

Number of times Ann cries
(9:00–11:00 A.M.)

Day	1	2	3	4	5	Weekly Total	Average
	̶H̶H̶ ̶H̶H̶	̶H̶H̶ III	̶H̶H̶ ̶H̶H̶	̶H̶H̶ II I	̶H̶H̶ II	41	8.2
	6	7	8	9	10		
	̶H̶H̶ ̶H̶H̶	̶H̶H̶ ̶H̶H̶ II	̶H̶H̶ ̶H̶H̶	̶H̶H̶ ̶H̶H̶	IIII	46	9.2
	11	12	13	14	15		
	IIII	II		I		7	1.4

fective method for teachers to use. The teacher sets a timer to correspond with the intervals indicated on the chart to be kept; when the timer bell rings, the teacher glances at the student and identifies what he is doing at that instant. After recording the behavior the teacher immediately resets the timer and proceeds with instruction.

Teachers who feel they cannot manage recording while teaching may employ other methods. If paraprofessionals, volunteer aides, or parents are available, they can be classroom recorders. The children themselves can record certain behaviors. Moving the recording task from the teacher to the children in sequenced steps increases the students' potential for self-direction. For example, if the teacher is recording class behaviors, such as in seat on time, on a daily chart, students can assume this responsibility. Individual behaviors can be recorded on a piece of masking tape on a child's desk. After observing the teacher's method, the child can record his own behavior (Sarason, Glaser, and Fargo 1972).

Recording is continued after the intervention is introduced (see figure 9–4) to determine the effectiveness of the plan. Although day-to-day fluctuations will occur, a well-planned program will usually produce the desired effects. If the teacher is uncertain about what produced the de-

Figure 9–4

Record of Intervention Effect

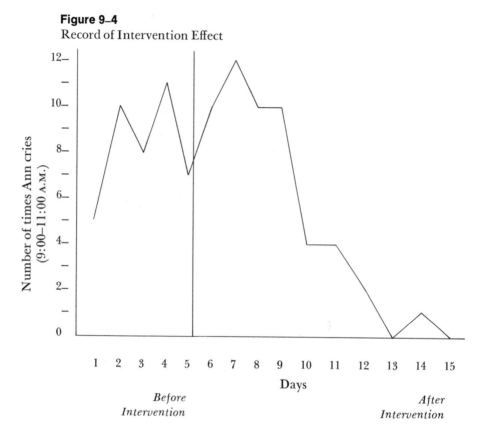

sired effect, or suspects that other variables have contributed, the intervention may be stopped and the recording continued. The results will indicate whether or not the intervention is effective. However, most teachers are reluctant to withdraw a plan that is working!

Recording behavior change is useful even if the particular intervention does not appear to be effective. For example, Bill is sent from the room every time he kicks a classmate. The kicking behavior is recorded and does not decrease with the intervention. Rather than being discouraged, the teacher may discard this intervention and seek another one. At least, one technique has been tried and proved ineffective. This is certainly more productive than continuing a poor strategy.

Once the baseline data have been charted, the teacher can decide whether or not to proceed with an intervention. The successful arrangement of consequences requires specific attention to behaviors and how they are affected by reinforcement. Arranging consequences requires the teacher to decide which reinforcers to use, how much reinforcement is necessary, and the schedule of reinforcement to employ.

Reinforcers

Since reinforcement is contingent on the emission of a response, it can be used to increase appropriate behavior or to decrease inappropriate behavior. The *selection of the reinforcer* demands sensitivity from the teacher. Care must be exercised that the event chosen by the teacher is rewarding to the child.

Tommy made an outstanding score on his achievement tests. As a reward, the teacher suggested that he go home an hour early. Tommy walked home, miserable and lonely, and waited for his friends to join him.

Since a reinforcer is defined by its effect on behavior, it is a highly individual event; it is the teacher's task to find reinforcing events for specific children. This can be done by observing what the child does with free time, asking the child what he would work for, or systematically arranging a consequence and observing its effect on his behavior (Wallace and Kauffman 1973). Lists of potential reinforcers may be found in appendix F.

Neisworth and Smith (1973) present a hierarchy of reinforcer categories:

1. Self-generated reinforcers (satisfaction with a job well done, etc.)
2. Self-management of tangible reinforcers (allowing yourself to watch television only after you've completed an unpleasant chore)
3. Social approval, attention
4. Management of tangible reinforcers (tokens, trinkets, food, water) by others (p. 87).

It is suggested that one should use reinforcers as high in the hierarchy as possible and revert to basic reinforcers only if the higher ones are unsuccessful.

Marc Gold, who has demonstrated some remarkable accomplishments in training individuals who are severely handicapped, states the following rules of reinforcement:

1. The best reinforcers are the natural and permanent ones: the tasks themselves.

2. The fewer contrived factors that are added to the reinforcer, the less there are to be removed.

3. When the learner knows the trainer (or teacher) is attending, no other reinforcement is needed (Gold, 1975).

Schedules of Reinforcement. Success of reinforcement depends on the timing of its presentation as well as the selection of the reinforcer. The more promptly reinforcement follows an act, the more effective it will be. Papers and examinations graded and returned immediately are more effective than those returned a week later. Teachers who walk about the classroom observing and commenting on their pupils' accomplishments are more effective than those who wait until the work is completed. While learning is more likely to occur when every response is reinforced, continuous reinforcement is not as effective as variable reinforcement for maintaining it. The four major patterns of reinforcement are summarized in table 9–1.

On a *fixed ratio schedule* reinforcement follows a fixed number of behaviors. It may be on a one-to-one basis or continuous reinforcement. For example, every time Jenny writes her name, she receives an M & M. However, it need not be continuous. Another fixed ratio schedule would be giving Jenny an M & M for every three times she writes her name. This ratio would be 3:1 rather than 1:1.

A variable ratio schedule means that the number of responses required for reinforcement is not fixed. Behavior is reinforced randomly. In the ordinary classroom, most reinforcement occurs on a variable ratio schedule. For example, a child raises his hand to volunteer an answer to a question. He may be called on to answer after raising his hand once or after raising it five times. Behavior that has been on a variable ratio schedule is much more durable than behavior that has been reinforced on a fixed schedule. Sarason, Glaser, and Fargo (1972) point out that if the child never knows whether the reinforcement is coming, he won't be disappointed on the one hand or bored on the other.

Building a behavior succeeds best on a continuous 1:1 reinforcement schedule. Once it is established, however, it will last longer if the reinforcement is gradually changed to a variable ratio schedule (Neisworth and Smith 1973). Thus if a child is building a sight word vocabulary, the teacher might give him a token for each word recognized. As his word recognition is rising and becoming stable, the teacher could reinforce intermittently. The teacher could reinforce on the *average* of every three words (every three words would be a fixed ratio), then move to an average of every five words.

Ratio schedules provide for reinforcement of number of responses.

Table 9–1
Schedules of Reinforcement

Schedule	Behavior	Reinforcer
Fixed Ratio (FR)	Child correctly solves 3 arithmetic problems	1 token
	Every time child uses toilet correctly	Adult praise
Variable Ratio (VR)	Child makes his bed each day	Receives 50¢ once or twice a week
	Child erases chalkboard every afternoon	Given extra dessert by teacher on the average of once a week
Fixed Interval (FI)	Child listens to story for 10 minutes	1 cookie
	Child does not interrupt teacher all morning	work on model airplane
Variable Interval (VI)	Child stays outside during entire recess	Teacher comes out to play ball on the average of every 3 days
	Child works in carrel for half an hour without asking for help	Takes messages to office on an average of twice a week

With interval schedules, reinforcement occurs after a set period of time. The best example is a weekly or monthly paycheck. On a *fixed interval schedule* reinforcement occurs following the first correct response after the specified interval has elapsed. When a group is attending to a story read by the teacher, after every five minutes of attending, each member of the group is given a Life Saver. On a *variable interval schedule* the reinforcement comes at irregular intervals. Life Savers would be dispensed intermittently as the group attended to the story.

As with the variable ratio schedule, the variable interval schedule produces stable performance patterns. Once the reinforcement system is operating satisfactorily, it is important to spread the same amount of reinforcement over a longer period of time or a larger number of responses.

Fixed ratio schedules are usually more satisfactory than fixed interval schedules because the reinforcement depends on the child's performance rather than a time lapse. However, there are events, such as remaining in one's seat, which must be reinforced on a time basis.

The teacher needs to choose a schedule of reinforcement which best fits the learning objectives and the child's needs. However, if a behavior modification procedure is not working, a change in the schedule of reinforcement may produce the desired results.

Interventions

The final step in the behavior management process is the *choosing and implementation of a particular strategy*. The choice will depend on the behavioral level of the children, the resources available, and the preference of the teachers. There are advantages and disadvantages to each of the systems presented. The teacher is encouraged to experiment with each and to discover techniques appropriate for his particular situation and students. Reinforcement systems that are used in schools may be classified as primary, social, token, and contingency management.

Primary Reinforcement. Primary (tangible) reinforcers are particularly effective with children who exhibit immature or bizarre behavior. When paired with praise and approval, they can be starting points toward nontangible reinforcers. Most children respond to edibles, such as cookies, ice cream, or candy.

There are several precautions to be taken in using primary reinforcers. The reinforcers need to be changed frequently so the child doesn't become satiated and therefore not reinforced. The strength of edible reinforcers may be increased if used prior to meal time. If the child is obese or has diet problems, special consideration must be given to the choice of edibles. Diet colas, crackers, raisins, or cereal may be used instead of the usual cookies and candy.

The cost of primary reinforcers must be taken into consideration by the teacher who plans to use them. Some schools allow instructional material funds to be used for purchasing reinforcers; some reinforcers may be obtained from the school cafeteria. A team of fourth-grade teachers devised an ingenious method. Rather than asking several parents to furnish refreshments for a school party, they asked every child to bring something. The leftover cookies, potato chips, and candy were put into canisters to be used for primary reinforcers. Many teachers purchase reinforcers out of personal funds. Since this can be expensive, teachers are advised to utilize the resources available to them.

Because reinforcement systems are chosen to suit the students, there may be just a few children who receive edible reinforcers. It is important for the class members to understand that rewards may differ. This difference will not present a problem if each child knows that his appropriate behavior is being rewarded in some way.

Social Reinforcement. Social interaction or attention is another powerful reinforcer. The strength of social reinforcement is demonstrated in a study reported by Dmitriev and Hawkins (1973). A child had refused to speak for two years and had been placed in a remedial class. After many trial and error patterns of treatment, a behavior modification specialist suggested that teacher attention be withdrawn. The child was prompted to speak selected words and when she did not speak, all teacher attention was withdrawn. Within twenty-two days of this treatment, the child was speaking over four hundred words a day and was reinstated in a regular classroom. She had been receiving teacher attention (social reinforcement) for *not* speaking.

Approval from the teacher and from peers promotes desirable behavior in most children. Smiles, pats, and verbal approval have worked well for teachers for many years. Easy to administer, inexpensive, and adaptable to any age group, social reinforcers are ideal. However, depending on the teacher's interaction with the child, the child's previous experience with teachers, and the severity of the child's behavior problem, social reinforcement may not be effective with some children. In this event, it may be paired with a primary or token reinforcer. As appropriate behavior increases, the tangible reinforcer may be faded out. One teacher, who wished to establish good behavior in his classroom, gave a Fruit Loop (cereal) for attention, academic performance, and so on. Inappropriate behavior was ignored. With the Fruit Loop, he always said something like "I like a good worker." He later discontinued the cereal, relying on the praise as a social reinforcement.

A classic study of the effects of teachers' behavior on children's behavior (Thomas, Becker, and Armstrong 1968) indicates that teachers who use approval for good behavior will find that frequency and duration of appropriate behavior will increase. It further suggests that teachers who ·try pleasantly to get children to stop inappropriate behavior, and who talk to them in an attempt to get them to understand what they're doing wrong, will find an increase in inappropriate behavior. The authors conclude that "unless an effort is made to support desirable classroom behaviors with appropriate consequences, the children's behavior will be controlled by others in ways likely to interfere with the teacher's objectives" (p. 45).

The rule which seems to work is to give praise and attention to behaviors that facilitate learning. Tell the child what he is being praised for. Try to reinforce behaviors incompatible with those you wish to decrease. Inappropriate behavior may be strengthened by paying attention to it even though you think you are punishing (Madsen, Becker, and Thomas 1968).

Token Economy. The token system of reinforcement is usually implemented in classrooms when social reinforcers such as teacher approval have been ineffective in controlling children's behavior. Skinner (1953) defines the token as a generalized reinforcer distinguished by its physical specifications. He cites money as the most common example, since it can be exchanged for primary reinforcers of great variety. This system involves the presentation of a token (checkmark, poker chip, star, school money, points) following specified behaviors. When the child has accumulated a sufficient number of tokens, he is able to exchange them for "back-up" reinforcers, such as candy, toys, school supplies, or desirable activities (see appendix E).

The tokens initially function as neutral stimuli, acquiring reinforcing properties by being exchangeable for the back-up reinforcers. Teacher praise and approval may be paired with the tokens, increasing the effectiveness of praise and approval as reinforcers. A general goal of token systems is to transfer control of responding from the token systems to other conditioned reinforcers such as teacher praise and grades (Kuypers, Becker, and O'Leary 1968).

Token systems have been used effectively with exceptional children in many situations. Their success has been demonstrated with retarded children (Birnbrauer et al. 1965), with emotionally disturbed children (Hewett 1967), socially maladjusted children (Kuypers, Becker, and O'-Leary 1968), children with cerebral palsy Stone 1970), children with learning disabilities (McKenzie et al. 1968), and with normal children (O'Leary and Drabman 1971). The system offers many advantages to the regular classroom teacher who has exceptional children in his classroom, since it may be highly individualized. It also overcomes many of the objections to using a primary reinforcement system, such as one child asking "How come Johnny gets candy for sitting still and I don't?" Tokens are available to all class members and may be earned by achieving the individual goals set for them.

Several organizational patterns to token economies have been suggested. Hewett (1967) refers to his highly structured situation as an engineered classroom, in which the emphasis is on alerting the student to the work efficiency orientation of the classroom. As each student enters the class in the morning, he picks up a work record card ruled into squares. As he moves through the day, the teacher and aide recognize his accomplishments by checking off squares on the card the student carries with him. The student saves his completed work cards and exchanges them on a weekly basis for candy, small toys, or trinkets. An exchange board in the room displays tangible rewards available for one, two, or three cards filled with checkmarks. The philosophy of the program says to the student, "We want you to succeed at all costs. If you will meet us half way and function reasonably well as a student, we will give you tasks you can do, need to do, and will enjoy doing, and we will reward you generously for your efforts" (p. 466).

Another token system utilizes a point system (O'Leary and Becker 1967). On the first day of the token period, instructions are written on the chalkboard: In Seat, Face Front, Raise Hand, Working, Pay Attention, Desk Clear. The procedure is explained to the students; the tokens are ratings placed in booklets on each desk. Ratings from one to ten are given, reflecting the extent to which the students follow instruction. The points may be exchanged for back-up reinforcers. The number of ratings given is gradually decreased from five to three and the number of points required to obtain a prize is gradually increased. Group points are also given for total class behavior, to be exchanged for popsicles at the end of the week. Since teacher time may be a factor, it is interesting to note that in this particular program, the ratings took only three minutes.

In a program for physically handicapped children who exhibited deviant behavior, the class day was divided into five learning periods. A behavior chart was supplied for each period. At the end of each period, the children were given one penny if they had carried out all the behaviors and lessons on the chart. At the end of class, the children who had earned five pennies could buy a toy from the teacher (Stone 1970).

The choice of tokens can be as varied as the choice of reinforcers. One teacher used S & H green stamps as tokens, with a field trip to the redemption store scheduled twice a year (Lankford 1974).

One of the greatest advantages of the token system is that tokens can be dispensed immediately following the desired behavior, providing an ideal situation for building new behaviors. They may be dispensed by the teacher or the aide, and should be accompanied by a comment such as "Good work, Sue!"

To help the child learn to delay reinforcement and thus deal with society's reward systems, the time for exchange of tokens is gradually extended. In the beginning tokens may be exchanged at the end of each day; later at the end of each week. The exchange period is reinforcing in itself and may follow a less desired activity. Tokens should be easy to dispense, easily transportable from the place of dispensing to the area of exchange, and their value should be understood by all the children. They may be given for approximations of the desired behavior and for progress in any specified activity.

An efficient token system should gradually withdraw material reinforcers (e.g., candy, toys) and rely on reinforcing activities. If this is the goal, the teacher might consider advancing to a contingency management program.

Contingency Management.   The term *contingent* implies that there is a relationship between what one does and what happens afterward. Salaries are contingent upon job performance; teaching positions are contingent upon certification. The contingencies of our environment control our behavior. Therefore, a teacher can control (change) a child's behavior by arranging contingencies (Haring and Phillips 1972). A contractual agreement between the teacher and the child, contingency management helps the child to assume responsibility for motivating his own behavior, and facilitates the shift from external control to self-management (Homme et al. 1970).

In a preschool class for mentally retarded youngsters, a little girl was observed to go to her teacher for a task (a lacing board), go to her desk and complete the task, return the board to her teacher, and go to the sand table to play.

Contingency management is based upon the Premack Principle (Premack 1959) which states that a low-probability behavior (such as working math problems) can be increased in frequency when its performance is followed by the opportunity to engage in a high-probability behavior (such as listening to a favorite record). This system, like the token system, is particularly suitable for use with handicapped children in a regular classroom, since it may be individualized and has been used successfully with atypical as well as with normal children.

In a Crisis Class a belligerent, low achieving fifth grader was presented with the various contingencies open to him if he entered into contracts with the teacher. He was delighted to receive free time or the teacher's undivided time. He found that when he did not get his work done, he was not involved in the play period or free time. After eight weeks, he returned to the regular class, where he found he could set up contracts with his regular teachers on his own initiative (Dee 1972).

Langstaff and Volkmor (1975) outline the procedures in planning a contingency management program:

Setting up a reinforcement (RE) menu. A list of reward activities high-probability behaviors) from which students may choose. RE activities are available to the student only upon completion of a specified task (low-probability behavior) (see figure 9–5).

Figure 9–5
RE Menu

RE MENU

Games
Checkers o oo
Parcheesi
Candy Land
Dominoes
Puzzles
Pick Up Sticks

Art
Paint
Clay
Crayons
Collage

Listening, Looking
Records
Music
Stories
Language-Master
Filmstrip Viewer

Relaxing
Reading
Talking with
a friend
Writing
Rocking
Watching fish

331

Figure 9–6
Classroom Arrangement

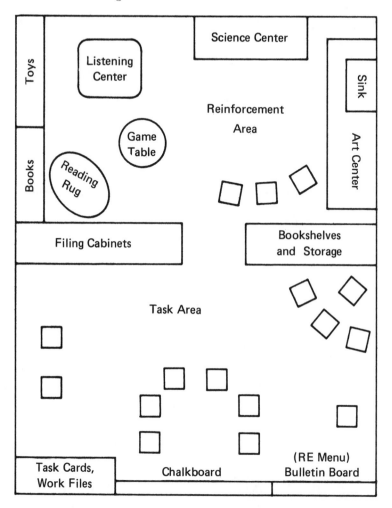

Arranging the classroom. In the beginning, it is helpful to divide the room into two areas—a task area where students can work quietly and an RE area where they may spend their free time (see figure 9–6). Arrangements may be flexible to accommodate a self-contained classroom, a resource room, or an open situation.

Scheduling task and RE time. At first, the schedule should be designed so that all students start tasks at the same time, finishing within two to three minutes of each other. When the child finishes, he signals for the teacher to come and check his work and he is immediately excused to the RE area. The RE time should be kept to five- to eight-minute periods.

A desk signal is used by the student to indicate task completion. A teacher signal is used to call the students back to the task area from the RE area.

Preparing tasks for students. Initial tasks should be slightly below competency level to insure success when the program begins. Directions should be clear; task cards or individual folders should be presented. Students should be observed as they work and helped if they are confused. Group work may be conducted while individual students are working on assignments.

Explaining the system to the students. A chart may be posted explaining the system:

Do some work . . .
Have some free time . . .
Do some more work . . .
Have some more free time . . .

Work is whatever is assigned,
Free time is whatever you want to do

IF

1. Your work is finished correctly.
2. You respect the right of others.
3. You remember safety rules.
4. You remember school rules.

(Langstaff and Volkmor
1975, p. 63)

One teacher evaluated her program in a learning disabilities resource room:

My recent experience with contingency management has produced a much more effective and successful learning atmosphere. The implementation of the program involved a great deal of organization and preparation. I explained the program to the children and made it possible for them to offer suggestions in regard to their potential reinforcers.

The reward area consisted of an art center, listening center, game area, and relaxation area. It is crucial to remove activities which have little or no reinforcement value from the reward area.

The task area was structured to provide easy access for teacher-student interaction and emphasized individualized instruction. A horseshoe-type seating arrangement permitted me to sit in the center, easily accessible for each child.

The students became involved by having the opportunity to make a nonverbal sign that was used for signifying they were working, needed help, or had finished their assignment. A timer was used to indicate a return to the task area from the reward area, or to return to their regular classes.

An individual folder was prepared for each student to contain his work for that day. Folders were given to the students each day and assignments explained.

I was pleased with the results I saw; the children enjoyed the program and expressed a desire to continue with it.

Besides promoting desirable behavior, contingency management has other advantages. Because the RE items are not consumable, there is little expense involved. There is little opposition from parents or school critics because the reward is an activity. Most important, this system involves the child in the decision-making process and leads toward his self-direction.

Toward Self-Management. It is hoped that the value of tokens, of tangible items, of reinforcing events will give way to the satisfaction of succeeding in school and receiving recognition as a student from one's peers, teachers, and parents. The teacher is interested, therefore, in building study behavior. In order to do so, he must first teach the child how to learn and how to behave appropriately in the classroom.

If he is to learn to manage his own behavior, the child should be involved in changing it.

Tommy, who was considered incorrigible, was asked by his teacher to list things about himself that he would like to change. Without hesitation, he stated that he would like to "quit talking so much and learn to ignore trouble-makers."

Many children who respond to reinforcement systems with enthusiasm decide at a later time that they don't need them. This is the ultimate goal of behavior modification: to help children realize that their actions produce consequences and that they, themselves, can change their actions and thus achieve goals that they set.

References and Selected Readings

Axelrod, S. 1971. Token reinforcement programs in special classes. *Exceptional Children* 37:371–379.

Becker, W. C. 1971. *Parents are teachers.* Champaign, Ill.: Research Press.

Bijou, S. W., Peterson, R. F., Harris, F. R., Allen, K. E., and Johnston, M. S.

1974. Methodology for experimental studies of young children in natural settings. In E. J. Thomas, ed., *Behavior modification procedure: A sourcebook.* Chicago: Aldine.

Birnbrauer, J. S., Wolf, M. M., Kidder, J. D., and Tague, C. 1965. Classroom behavior of retarded pupils with token reinforcement. *Journal of Experimental Child Psychology* 2:219–235.

Blackham, G. J., and Silberman, A. 1975. *Modification of child and adolescent behavior.* Belmont, Calif.: Wadsworth.

Carter, R. 1972. *Help! these kids are driving me crazy.* Champaign, Ill.: Research Press.

Dee, V. D. 1972. Contingency management in a crisis class. *Exceptional Children* 38:631–634.

Dmitriev, V. and Hawkins, J. 1974. Susie never used to say a word. *Teaching Exceptional Children* 6:68–76.

Freschi, D. F. 1974. Where we are, where we are going, how we're getting there. *Teaching Exceptional Children* 6:89–97.

Fullmer, W. H. 1972. Changing the behavior of the retarded in the special education classroom. In T. Thompson and J. Grabowski, eds., *Behavior modification of the mentally retarded.* New York: Oxford University Press.

Gearheart, B. R., and Weishahn, M. W. 1976. *The handicapped child in the regular classroom.* St. Louis: Mosby.

Gold, Marc. 1975. Training the Mentally Retarded. Address at Cherokee, N.C.

Haring, N. G., and Phillips, E. L. 1972. *Analysis and modification of classroom behavior.* Englewood Cliffs, N.J.: Prentice-Hall.

Hewett, F. M. 1967. Educational engineering with emotionally disturbed children. *Exceptional Children* 33:459–467.

Hewett F. M. 1968. *The emotionally disturbed child in the classroom.* Boston: Allyn and Bacon.

Homme, L., Csanyi, A. P., Gonzales, M. A., Rechs, J. R. 1970. *How to use contingency contracting in the classroom.* Champaign, Ill.: Research Press.

Jens, K. G., and Shores, R. E. 1969. Behavioral graphs as reinforcers for work behavior of mentally retarded adolescents. *Education and Training of the Mentally Retarded* 4:21–27.

Johnston, M. S., Kelley, C. S., Harris, F. R., and Wolf, M. M. 1966. An application of reinforcement principles to development of motor skills of a young child. *Child Development* 37:379–387.

Keller, F. S. 1969. *Learning: Reinforcement theory.* New York: Random House.

Keller, F. S., and Ribes-Inesta, E. 1974. *Behavior modification applications to education.* New York: Academic Press.

Kubany, E. S., and Sloggett, B. B. 1974. Coding procedures for teachers. In

E. J. Thomas, ed., *Behavior modification procedure: A sourcebook.* Chicago: Aldine.

Kuypers, D. S., Becker, W. C., and O'Leary, D. K. 1968. How to make a token system fail. *Exceptional Children* 35:101–109.

Langstaff, A. L., and Volkmor, C. B. 1975. *Contingency management.* Columbus, Ohio: Charles E. Merrill.

Lovitt, T. C., and Smith, D. D. 1974. Using withdrawal of positive reinforcement to alter subtraction performance. *Exceptional Children* 40:357–358.

McKenzie, H. S., Clark, M., Wolf, M. M., Kothera, R. and Benson, C. 1968. Behavior modification of children with learning disabilities using grades as tokens and allowances as back up reinforcers. *Exceptional Children* 34:745–752.

Macmillan, D. L., and Forness, S. R. 1970. Behavior modification: Limitations and liabilities. *Exceptional Children* 37:291–297.

Macmillan, D. L., Forness, S. R., and Trumbull, B. M. 1973. The role of punishment in the classroom. *Exceptional Children* 40:85–96.

Madsen, C. H., Jr., Becker, W. C., and Thomas, D. R. 1968. Rules, praise, and ignoring: Elements of elementary classroom control. *Journal of Applied Behavior Analysis* 1:139–150.

Mager, R. F. 1972. Who did what to whom? Champaign, Ill.: Research Press.

Neisworth, J. T., and Smith, R. M. 1973. *Modifying retarded behavior.* Boston: Houghton Mifflin.

O'Leary, D. K., and Becker, W. C. 1967. Behavior modification of an adjustment class: A token reinforcement program. *Exceptional Children* 33:637–642.

O'Leary, D. K., and Drabman, R. 1971. Token reinforcement programs in the classroom: A review. *Psychological Bulletin* 75:379–398.

Premack, D. 1959. Toward empirical behavior laws: I. Positive reinforcement. *Psychological Review* 66: 219–233.

Reinert, H. R. 1976. *Children in conflict.* St. Louis: Mosby.

Sarason, I. G., Glaser, E. M., and Fargo, G. A. 1972. *Reinforcing productive classroom behavior.* New York: Behavioral Publications.

Skinner, F. B. 1953. *Science and human behavior.* New York: Macmillan.

Stone, M. C. 1970. Behavior shaping in a classroom for children with cerebral palsy. *Exceptional Children* 36:674–677.

Thomas, D. R., Becker, W. C., and Armstrong, M. 1968. Production and elimination of disruptive classroom behavior by systematically varying teacher's behavior. *Journal of Applied Behavior Analysis* 1:35–45.

Thompson, T. and Grabowski, J., eds. 1972. *Behavior modification of the mentally retarded.* New York: Oxford University Press.

Volkmor, C. B., Langstaff, A. L., and Higgins, M. 1974. *Structuring the classroom for success.* Columbus, Ohio: Merrill.

Wallace, G. and Kauffman, J. M. 1973. *Teaching children with learning problems.* Columbus, Ohio: Merrill.

Films

Behavior Modification in the Classroom. Berkeley: University of California, Extension Media Center.

Who Did What to Whom? Champaign, Ill.: Research Press.

Filmstrip and Tape

Contingency Management. Columbus, Ohio: Merrill.

Chapter Ten

Enhancing Social Integration

A key element to successful mainstreaming is the creation of a positive
school environment in which the human differences of all students are
accepted and respected. Merely placing handicapped students in regular
classrooms without attending to their needs for self-development and peer
interaction is not truly implementing the concept of mainstreaming. In
chapter 2, it was emphasized that mainstreaming is the *social,* as well as
the *instructional,* integration of handicapped students in educational settings with their nonhandicapped peers. The purpose of this chapter is to
examine issues related to social integration and to suggest strategies for
bridging the gap that sometimes exists between handicapped students and
significant other persons in educational settings. Social integration issues

and strategies will be discussed in relation to the interdependent relationships among the teacher, handicapped students, and nonhandicapped students.

Teacher/Handicapped Students/ Nonhandicapped Students

It has been documented over and over again that the teacher's view of the student is a strong force in determining the nature of the interaction between the teacher and student and, in turn, the student's achievement (Rosenthal and Jacobson 1968; Good 1970; Brophy and Good, 1974; Purkey 1970). The teacher constantly communicates important messages to students about his attitudes toward individual differences. It becomes obvious to all students whether the teacher favors the high-achieving students; feels respect, pity, or disgust for students who have special problems; believes that every person has inherent value; or is prejudiced against people who are different. Teachers generally are far more transparent than they might like to believe. Both in verbal and nonverbal ways, a teacher's behavior can substantially affect the manner in which a handicapped student views himself and the manner in which the nonhandicapped peers view the handicapped student. This section, therefore, deals with the interactions among the teacher/handicapped students/nonhandicapped students. Since these relationships are interdependent, they should be viewed as a total process rather than as discrete units.

Kate, a third-grader, has been classified as educable mentally retarded on the basis of formal diagnostic tests. Kate goes to the resource room for one and one-half hours every day. Her classroom teacher tends to exclude her from almost all activities on the basis that "no child with her limited development can effectively participate in the regular classroom." When other students in the class fail to achieve according to the teacher's expectations, the voiced threat by the teacher is, "If you cannot do your assignments, you will have to go with Kate to work with the other EMRs in the resource room." Both Kate and her peers get the message.

Although this is an extreme example, it is a true story. The teacher's views and behavior can be extremely influential in defining respect for differences within the classroom.

Purkey (1970) distinguishes two aspects of the teacher's role in affective development—the attitudes conveyed and the atmosphere developed. These two areas will be discussed in relation to the teacher and the students.

Attitudes

When considering teacher attitudes toward handicapped students, the most basic question teachers might ask themselves is: Does less able mean less worthy? Each teacher might analyze the response to this question by documenting whether he genuinely believes that handicapped students should be entitled to consideration for placement in a regular class and whether they deserve the same rights, privileges, and responsibilities as their nonhandicapped peers. If teachers can honestly affirm that "less able does not mean less worthy," a commitment needs to be made to translating that belief into behavioral patterns such as spending equitable portions of time with the student, working to include him in extracurricular activities, exposing him to a variety of career options, and assisting him in accentuating his strengths. Teachers should check themselves constantly, because sometimes people tend to avoid handicapped persons without realizing it. If it takes the child who stutters longer to say something, it might be easier to overlook the fact that he would like to communicate rather than to take the time to allow him to stammer throughout his response. Similar situations occur with students representing the range of handicapping conditions. It often requires more time and effort for the teacher to make curriculum adaptations and to arrange situations to promote social integration for handicapped students who need help in this area than for students who are "automatically" accepted by their peers. If the teacher believes that these students are just as worthy as other students, the extra investment of time and effort does not create negative barriers between the teacher and handicapped students.

Many teachers may believe that "less able does mean less worthy." This does not necessarily mean that these teachers are cold and insensitive people and have no place in the teaching profession. It often reflects situations in which these teachers have had extremely limited contact with handicapped persons. Because separate classes, schools, and residential centers for the handicapped have been the rule in the past rather than educational settings which bring together handicapped and nonhandicapped persons, many practicing and prospective teachers may never have known a handicapped person. When this lack of exposure and awareness exists, many people tend to imagine far more "difference" than really exists. Sometimes negative stereotypes based on imagination or myths can cloud a person's perception of other human beings. This is an understandable phenomenon, but it does not have to be prolonged into lifelong attitudes. People's attitudes toward the handicapped can be changed by obtaining accurate information and experiencing positive encounters.

Theresa had just graduated from college and was considering the possibility of entering graduate school in the field of education. Her roommate, who was a member of the local Association for Retarded Citizens (ARC), convinced Theresa to come along on an ARC recreational function which involved taking approximately forty-five handicapped children (mentally retarded, severely emotionally disturbed and multiple handicapped) on a hayride and picnic. Theresa was hesitant about going along for several reasons. Although she had never been around handicapped persons to any significant degree, she had the idea that it might be dangerous to be with them. She wondered if they would bite her, make inappropriate sexual advances, or start a fire in the hay. On the one hand, Theresa told herself that she was being ridiculous, but on the other hand, she had strong reservations. Theresa's roommate insisted that she come along, and Theresa hesitantly decided to go. As the trucks were loaded with children. Theresa began to relax a little as she began to join in with the children's singing. She looked closely at the children. Some were attractive, and some were unattractive. Some seemed to have only minor handicaps, and others seemed to be significantly impaired. Some were talkative, and some were shy. There seemed to be a great variety of shapes, colors, sizes, and personalities. When they arrived in the country at the setting for the picnic, the children started walking through the meadows, playing games, eating hotdogs, laughing, fighting, joking, and generally doing the things that children do. Toward the end of the picnic, Theresa wandered over to her roommate and whispered, "Where are the handicapped children?" Not understanding Theresa's question, the roommate gave her a puzzled look. Theresa repeated, "Where are the handicapped *children? These are* just children."

Teachers can experience the same insight. Just because teachers have had limited opportunities to develop positive attitudes toward handicapped persons does not mean that they cannot begin to develop them.

Two types of strategies have been beneficial to many teachers in developing positive attitudes. One is to receive systematic and relevant training either at the preservice or inservice level, which results in the teacher feeling competent to teach handicapped children. It is conjectured that some teachers react unfavorably to handicapped students when they feel threatened in their capability to teach them successfully. Knowledge leading to self-confidence can be the forerunner to positive attitudes. A second strategy is to get to know handicapped people as *people*. The fear of the unknown can be removed by finding out handicapped persons' likes and dislikes, strengths and weaknesses, hobbies, interests, and future plans. Some-

342

times teachers only get to know handicapped children as students. They might know the student's level of performance, particular disability, curriculum needs, and learning styles; that is not enough. It is also important that teachers get to know handicapped children as children and, furthermore, to find joy and naturalness in their relationships.

When teachers and nonhandicapped students encounter handicapped children for the first time, and perhaps before they are entirely comfortable with their new relationships, they might follow some helpful guidelines.

People should try to be themselves in the presence of handicapped persons. Being tense, oversolicitous, or sympathetic toward handicapped persons can be offensive. Conversation can be the same as with other persons; attitudes of pity or charity are unproductive. Ideally, attitudes of equality and respect should form the foundation of attitudes toward the handicapped.

The disadvantages associated with a person's handicap may be an inconvenience for him, but his handicap may not prevent him from full participation in regular class activities. Handicaps are often in the eye of the beholder. Teachers and peers need to be careful not to impose a greater handicap on the person than might really exist by their negative attitudes and perceptions.

Overprotectiveness represents an unfavorable attitude toward handicapped persons. Encouraging independent behavior of handicapped students is often more difficult than with the nonhandicapped. Sometimes there is a natural tendency to want to protect or to prevent failure; however, it is important for teachers to strike the proper balance between needed support and encouragement of independence. This balance may have a slightly different definition in each individual situation.

Handicapped persons should be viewed as people, rather than as deviant, abnormal, or defective. They are persons with many of the same interests, talents, needs, and career goals as anyone else.

A poem written jointly by an English teacher and a group of blind students expresses the reactions of blind students to interactions with their teachers and peers. It can help prospective and practicing teachers put themselves in another person's shoes.

On Being Blind

They act like you can't hear.
They ask your best friend,
    with you standing right there,
        "Does *she* want a coke?"
        "Can *she* dress herself?"
        "Can *she* feed herself?"

They gather around—in two's and three's
     to watch you eat.
I'd like to say,
     "Twenty cents admission, please."
In class, when you find your seat,
     "You're a miracle!" they say.
Can't they see
     that it's just your normal way?
They fear the word "blindness."
They try to ignore . . .
     and make it seem more.
They call us "sightless,"
     and "visually handicapped."
They're nervous . . . uptight.
In conversation when they say, "You *see*?"
They quickly apologize to you,
     "Oh! I'm sorry!"
Can't they relax and try to be themselves
     like we do.
Can't they see how we feel,
     and treat us for real?
When we're doing braille,
     they ask, "What are you reading?"
       "I'm studying math."
Dumb questions come out
     like: "What's it *about?*"
They feel my braille.
I touch their hand;
     they jerk away.
I only wanted them to know
     I understand . . .
       and it's good.
But they're embarrassed and say,
     "Oh! I'm sorry!"
Can't they relax?
Oh, I wish they would!
The new student teacher asked,
     "Would you like to feel my face?"
I laughed and shook my head.
     "No thank you," I said.
I was sorry to hurt his feelings.
He was so excited,
     trying to be kind.
He'd heard somewhere, I guess,
     that you're *supposed* to let the blind
       feel your face.

> But I don't want anyone feeling *my* face;
>> and I didn't want to feel *his*.
> They use taking you to the bus
>> as an excuse
>>> to get out of class.
> If that makes them happy,
>> Well—it's O.K.
> They hold their fingers up and say,
>> "How many fingers?"
> They ask,
>> "What color am I?"
>> "What color are *you?*"
> Why can't they relax
>> and be themselves?
> Why can't they laugh—
>> like *we* do?
>>>> Ellen T. Johnson (1976)

This poem represents the views of one particular group of handicapped students. Certainly it is not reflective of everyone. Many handicapped students have just as much or greater difficulty relaxing and being themselves as anyone else. It is important to remember that individual needs exist in the area of social integration just as in all other aspects of the school program.

Mainstreaming is a reality. Teachers have both the opportunity and the responsibility to develop the attitudinal conviction that "less able does not mean less worthy" and to react accordingly as they serve as a model for nonhandicapped students to form positive attitudes.

Atmosphere

The classroom atmosphere the teacher creates can significantly influence the interactions among the teacher and the handicapped students. Additionally, this interaction often determines the quality of interaction between the handicapped student and his nonhandicapped peers. Three factors related to classroom atmosphere that can substantially facilitate mainstreaming include open and honest communication, success, and respect.

Open and Honest Communication.

Joe is hearing impaired. His second-grade classmates wonder why he wears "the funny wires that go in his ears." At the beginning of the year, they frequently asked Joe and Mr. Parks, their teacher. Mr. Parks quickly told them to "mind their own business" and to "not be so cruel." They finally

345

stopped asking, but they still wondered. The main thing they figured out from Mr. Parks' response was that it must be something dirty or shameful. Joe was also confused by Mr. Parks's reaction. He decided that Mr. Parks must not like hearing aids. That meant, in his way of thinking, that Mr. Parks must not like him either.

If handicapped students are to be socially integrated in regular classes, open and honest communication must characterize the classroom atmosphere. The teacher's degree of comfort in acknowledging strengths and weaknesses provides the foundation for this type of atmosphere to develop. As the teacher can acknowledge his own strengths and weaknesses students can be encouraged to do likewise about themselves. The best reader in the class may be the most uncoordinated person on the playground. It is important to remember that handicapped students have strengths and nonhandicapped students have weaknesses. As the classroom atmosphere, largely influenced by the teacher, communicates to students that it is psychologically safe to be honest about oneself, the context for being open and honest about differences significant enough to be characterized as handicaps is developed.

Teachers should consider the preference of handicapped students and their families when making the decision as to the degree of open communication among the teacher, handicapped student, and nonhandicapped students about the specific handicap. Dealing with blindness, deafness, and physically handicapping conditions can sometimes be less ticklish than the situation of discussing handicaps with students disadvantaged by mental retardation, learning disabilities, and emotional problems. Teachers, however, need to be comfortable with explaining why some students learn more slowly than others or why some students engage in puzzling or inappropriate behavior.

Nellie, a student in Ms. Wilson's third-grade class, goes to the resource room for instruction thirty minutes each day. The resource room is referred to as the EMR class around the school. Some of Nellie's peers teased her about going to the resource program and started calling her EMR and retardo. Nellie came to Ms. Wilson and asked, "What does it mean to be an EMR?" Ms. Wilson's heart dropped. How should she respond? She did not want to hurt Nellie's feelings; yet she valued honest communication with her students. She responded to Nellie by indicating that EMR stands for educable mentally retarded. She went on to explain that the term educable mentally retarded is sometimes used to refer to students who have more difficulty learning school subjects than some of their classmates. She asked Nellie if sometimes her reading and arithmetic lessons were hard for her to understand. Nellie affirmed that they were. Ms. Wilson reassured Nellie that educable mentally retarded does not mean that Nellie cannot learn at all nor that she has difficulty learning everything. Nellie's performance in art projects was pointed out as an area where she had less difficulty than many of her classmates. Ms. Wilson reminded Nellie that all people have difficulty learning some things. The point that individual people have different strengths, weaknesses, interests, and learning rates was strongly stressed. Although this is important to remember, Ms. Wilson told Nellie that she could understand how she did not like being called EMR. Ms. Wilson encouraged Nellie to remember the progress she was making from going to the resource program and to ignore students who have not yet learned that name-calling is unkind.

After this initial conference, Ms. Wilson and Nellie jointly chose some representative work assignments that Nellie had done in the resource room. These were shared with the class during a "show and tell" period, along with a description of the types of work done in the resource room. Ms. Wilson also worked with the class during language arts in writing scripts and producing puppet shows on sensitivity to feelings. Some of the students who had been doing the name-calling had puppets cast in roles of needing special help in order to understand their school work. Through the simulated experience with the puppets, these students began to get the message of what it is like when the shoe is on the other foot. Ms. Wilson realized that name-calling would not be eliminated immediately, but that systematic steps could be taken to teach respect for differences. She knew that merely punishing the students who were teasing Nellie might only teach them to call others names when they knew the teacher would not find out. Replacing the negative attitudes and behavior with positive attitudes and behavior was Ms. Wilson's goal.

In all situations, teachers can get an idea of the interest of handicapped students in discussing the handicap by carefully listening to what they say both to adults in the school and their peers. Many families teach their handicapped children to be open about the particular condition; many others do not. By consulting with the parents, the teacher can learn what type of communication makes the child comfortable at home and in the neighborhood. If handicapped students are accustomed to explaining their particular condition at home, they are likely to do the same at school.

Sherry has a physical disability referred to as cerebral palsy. She uses a walker to get around her third-grade class. When her peers ask her about why she uses the walker, she immediately tells them that the walker's name is Hi-O Silver and that Hi-O can help her get anywhere she wants to go.

347

She goes on to tell them that she has a disease known as cerebral palsy which means that her muscles have not developed in the same way as most other people's. She invariably affirms that someday she will be able to walk and run. Sherry's parents helped her learn to respond to questions in this fashion. Her teacher established the type of classroom atmosphere in which questions and responses could be discussed in an honest and open fashion.

Teachers are encouraged to deal with issues and concerns directly related to the handicap, rather than avoiding it. When classroom peers ask specific questions about the handicap, these questions should be viewed as natural and worthy of an honest answer. The teacher might talk with the handicapped students, his parents, and the school counselor in planning a method of providing information to the nonhandicapped classmates at the beginning of the school year. Many handicapped children can explain the nature of their handicaps succinctly to their peers. This ability to provide a self-explanation is very important, since handicapped students frequently get quizzed about "what's wrong" when the teacher is not around.

Another form of preparation is structured lessons related to the nature and implications of handicapping conditions. An example is a learning center on communication. The objective of the center is for students, through the acquisition of a new form of communication, to be aware that people communicate in many ways. Materials available in the center include:

Patches of the twenty-six flags making up the international Mariner's Alphabet (Navy Opportunity Information Center, P.O. Box 2000, Pelham Manor, NY 10803);

The one-hand manual alphabet used by deaf-blind people (American Foundation for the Blind, 15 West 16th St., New York, NY 10011);

Braille alphabet and numbers used by the blind (American Printing House for the Blind, 1839 Frankfort Ave., Louisville, KY 40206);

Special braille edition, *My Weekly Reader* (American Printing House for the Blind).

Display of Morse Code (Boy Scouts of America Handbook), Procedure: Two students decide upon a system of communication to learn. As a pair, they learn to communicate in a new way and demonstrate their new skill to the class. Other students follow.

Finally, open and honest communication about handicapping conditions can be promoted through the use of commercial materials. Developmental Learning Materials (7440 Natchez Ave., Niles, IL 60648) has published a curriculum entitled "Accepting Individual Differences." The four target areas are visual, hearing, motor impairment, and mental retardation/learning disabilities. Curriculum guides in each area suggest instructor and student activities, and large spiral-bound books provide photographs of handicapped children. A host of other commercial materials is available. A book entitled *Special People Behind the Eight-Ball* (Mullins and Wolfe 1975) provides a comprehensive listing and description of books, magazines, and films related to handicapping conditions. Most of the listings emphasize humanistic aspects of handicapping conditions, rather than technical definitions or descriptions of different disabilities. This book is an excellent resource guide for teachers in locating commercial materials that can help in the process of enhancing social integration. Additionally, an inherent value of using materials centered around handicapped characters is that handicapped students in the class can feel some identity with them. How many basal textbooks provide stories and pictures of blind or physically handicapped children? Handicapped students need role models with perceived similarities to themselves; however, they rarely have this opportunity in most classrooms.

Success.   Success is important for all students, but it can be of special significance to handicapped students. Some handicapped students, unfortunately, experience overwhelming amounts of failure in their school careers. Sometimes the failure is more teacher-based than student-based, as when teachers routinely set expectations for handicapped students on a much higher academic level than their achievement level would indicate. Inaccurate or insufficient assessment can lead directly to failure. Teachers can reduce a large portion of failure experiences by planning appropriate instruction. The individual education plan can be the focal point of successful instruction.

Purkey (1970) suggests questions that teachers might consider in developing a classroom atmosphere characterized by success. These questions include:

> Do I permit my students some opportunity to make mistakes without penalty?
> Do I make generally positive comments on written work?
> Do I give extra support and encouragement to slower students?
> Do I recognize the successes of students in terms of what they did earlier?
> Do I take special opportunities to praise students for their successes?
> Do I manufacture honest experiences of success for my students?
> Do I set tasks which are, and which appear to the student to be, within his abilities? (p. 56).

As handicapped students experience success, they can become more confident about their strengths and more positive in their view of themselves. Likewise, their nonhandicapped peers have the opportunity to view them as "winners." All of these factors can contribute to the enhanced social integration of handicapped and nonhandicapped students.

Respect.   A classroom atmosphere characterized by open and honest communication and successful experiences is the context in which respect for individual differences can grow. Respect means far more than merely tolerating differences; it involves valuing the individuality of each human being.

The manner in which the teacher interacts with handicapped students will reflect whether or not the teacher respects the student. Furthermore, the teacher's interaction largely determines whether or not nonhandicapped students develop respect for their handicapped classmates. Three strategies have been used successfully in promoting respect: placing the handicapped student in positions of status; the "similarity-attraction model" (Byrne, 1961); and buddy systems.

The first strategy calls for the teacher to make sure that the student is provided opportunities associated with status in the classroom. Often the handicapped student receives, but does not have the opportunity to provide, peer tutoring. In many situations, handicapped students are not chosen to be captains of the ball teams, stars in the class play, or editors of the classroom newspaper. These situations, however, typically are associated with status positions in most elementary and junior high classes. Teachers cannot always arrange peer relationships and determine which student is chosen by his classmates for a special honor, but the teacher's influence and guidance can serve as a strong model. It is important for teachers to be sensitive to opportunities within the classroom and school that might capitalize on the strengths and interests of the handicapped student. These opportunities should also be generally associated with status and prestige.

Charles is in his last year of elementary school. He is mentally retarded and has low academic achievement in all areas. He also has some emotional problems. At the beginning of the year, his teacher was acutely aware of his inferior class position. When basketball season started, Charles was very disappointed because he knew he was not skilled enough to go out for the team. He loved basketball and spent every afternoon practicing. His teacher had a great idea—Would the coach allow Charles to be the basketball manager? The teacher carefully described the situation to the coach

Figure 10–1

Photograph by John Rosenthal

and stated reasons why he thought Charles would do a very good job as team manager. The coach agreed to give Charles a chance to prove himself. When the teacher told Charles of this opportunity, he was overwhelmed with excitement. He could hardly wait until the first day of practice. Faithfully and diligently Charles worked at his job and performed in an outstanding manner. The coach and team grew to respect him as their manager and friend. Charles had the opportunity of traveling with the team to all out-of-town games and being recognized at the sports banquet. Figure 10–1 is a picture of Charles and his teacher sharing congratulations over Charles's plaque awarded at the sports banquet. The opportunity to be basketball manager was the beginning of new peer perceptions toward Charles. No longer was he the "kid with problems" or the "EMR student." Charles was the basketball manager. That position carried status.

In addition to being manager, some handicapped students are able to participate in interscholastic athletics.

351

Figure 10–2

Photograph by John Rosenthal

Kathy and Frances also are upper elementary students with significant learning problems. They were first-string players on the school's volleyball team. Their classmates came to games to cheer them on. The school letter each received, depicted in figure 10–2, is their most prized possession.

Handicapped students may be in the school chorus, members of an honor club, active in drama productions, members of the safety patrol, members of the school newspaper staff, or peer tutors of other students. Whatever the nature of involvement, the important point is that handicapped students have opportunities to excel in areas valued by others. The end result is usually increased self- and peer respect.

The second strategy for promoting respect is the "similarly-attraction model" (Byrne 1961). This model stipulates that perceived similarity is the basis of increased attraction between and among persons. This model suggests that in the classroom the teacher guide handicapped and non-handicapped students in discovering common characteristics and interests. Thus, students would learn to see themselves as more alike than different, with perceived similarities in many areas—arithmetic, music, physical education, food preferences, hobbies and/or favorite television programs.

Davis (1961) has suggested three stages of development in social relationships between physically handicapped and nonhandicapped persons. It is conjectured that the same three stages are likely to apply to other handicapping conditions, as well as to physical disabilities. These stages include:

The first is "fictional acceptance," in which the norm of our society operates so that when we first meet people we function on the basis of equality and normalcy, irrespective of how different the other person may be from us. This norm provides the handicapped person with the initial opportunity to establish a social relationship although, as the Kleck et al. (1966) experiment shows, the nonhandicapped person's behavior is, in fact, often influenced by the presence of the handicap even though he may be unaware of his modifications in behavior. The second stage that Davis postulates is "breaking through," when the nonhandicapped person ceases to be aware of the handicap and reacts to the other's personal characteristics. The third stage, "amending and qualifying the normal relationship," is one in which the nonhandicapped person is aware of the functional impairment and takes it into account but does not allow it to interfere with the social relationship (Richardson 1969, p. 1058).

Aiding students in identifying similarities could be particularly important in stage 2, breaking through, of Davis's (1961) acceptance process, the point at which the nonhandicapped child's attention is transferring from the handicap to the handicapped child's other attributes (Westervelt 1977). Teachers can facilitate this process by arranging small group situations that highlight similarities among handicapped and nonhandicapped students, using books and films with handicapped characters (as discussed in the last section), generally finding incidental opportunities in the classroom to share commonalities and similarities, and bringing handicapped adults into the classroom as consultants. Keller (1976), a scientist who was stricken with polio at the age of seventeen, wondered how many children had ever seen a handicapped doctor or scientist on television—the handicapped adult is rarely highlighted on television. Teachers do not have to rely on television for this type of experience; handicapped adults can be brought into classrooms to point out similar interests, talents, and career potentials in handicapped and nonhandicapped persons. A blind poet might read his poems; an adult paralyzed from the waist down might demonstrate methods of increasing upper body strength; a pottery lesson might be given by a deaf person. These types of situations provide opportunities to accentuate similarities rather than differences.

A third strategy for increasing classroom respect is setting up buddy systems between students. In these situations, a peer may be formally or informally assigned to a handicapped student who needs special help.

353

Ellen serves as the buddy for Joanna, who uses crutches to get around her classroom. When Joanna has a load of books to carry, Ellen helps her. Through the opportunity to know each other, Ellen and Joanna have become good friends. Joanna always catches on quickly to arithmetic. Sometimes she helps Ellen with her arithmetic homework. They visit at each other's houses after school and are planning to go to summer camp together.

"Helping relationships" often turn into friendships. The nonhandicapped student may be amazed at the adaptations and compensations that his handicapped buddy is able to make on his own. Through the opportunity to become aware of each other's strengths and weaknesses, respect for individual differences can be the natural by-product. It is important for teachers to remember that handicapped students should have opportunities to offer, as well as receive, assistance. If respect is to ensue, buddy relationships must be "two-way streets." The "two-way" interaction is illustrated in the example of Ellen and Joanna: Ellen helps Joanna carry her books; Joanna helps Ellen with arithmetic homework.

Achieving Social Integration

When careful attention is given to the development of positive attitudes toward handicapped students and to the establishment of a classroom environment characterized by open and honest communication, success, and respect, social integration will be maximized.

Mark has a long history of school failure. He has been ostracized frequently by his peers. When Mark reached the fourth grade, his teacher made a commitment to try to create an environment more conducive to learning for him. She first referred him for special education services. Mark was tested, and it was found that he qualified for services from the learning disabilities resource program. A committee comprised of Mark's classroom teacher, resource teacher, coordinator of special education services, and parents was established to develop an individual education plan for him. The committee worked very hard to pinpoint Mark's level of achievement and to plan the next steps.

When the plan was completed, Mark's teacher, Ms. Turner, felt that she had a good idea of where to start. With the help of the resource teacher, she gathered some instructional materials on Mark's level. As the year progressed, Mark systematically moved toward higher levels of mastery.

He was proud of what he learned and appeared to be a happier and more outgoing child overall.

Ms. Turner arranged for Mark to lead storytime in a first-grade class one day a week. Because of the work he had done and knowledge he had obtained at home in his parent's garden, he became "Chief Advisor" for the classroom window garden. He took excellent care of the plants and always seemed to know what to do when one began to droop. Mark's peers admired him for his gardening skills.

Ms. Turner observed that classroom peers gradually began to include Mark in more and more activities as "one of the guys." This pleased her very much, and one day she expressed her pleasure to a nonhandicapped peer who invariably included Mark in informal classroom groups. The peer was puzzled that Ms. Turner would make such a statement. The peer's reply was, "What's the big deal about including Mark? He is neat."

Perhaps the ultimate goal of social integration for handicapped and non-handicapped students is for it to be so natural that it is not a "big deal."

A day in the life of Ms. Winters' class exemplifies the natural social integration of handicapped and nonhandicapped students.

Ms. Winters' Class

This morning the kids had found in the science corner a huge tank full of muddy water and thirteen crayfish with rubber bands holding their pinchers shut. A big boy and a little boy stood beside each other at the long table and watched three crayfish pile on top of each other.

"See how they're fighting again? That's what the book said . . . crayfish fight each other to see who's going to rule. They've got a definite social order."

"Yeah, but Bob, look at these over here . . . the rubber bands are off their claws and they're not fighting . . . and they're both males," he added, checking.

The older boy scratched his head. "You know, I wonder . . ."

Doug's eyes gleamed. "Could we train them . . ."

"Yeah! Not to fight! Doug, is that an instinct or . . . wait a minute." He turned and bent over the ten-year-old retarded boy who was tugging at Bob's pants leg.

"Can I take dese off?" he asked, pointing to the blue rubber bands on his crayfish's pinchers.

"Okay, Sammy," grinned Bob, looking around for Billy. "Okay, but Sammy," he said slowly, touching the boy's shoulder so that he looked up, "be careful. Those pinchers can bite you, hurt you. Don't put your fingers in the pinchers . . . Hey Bill, 'scuse me. Will you show Sammy how to pick up the crayfish so it won't bite him?"

"Sure, Bob." Billy put down his book and stood up.

"And then help him take off the rubber bands, okay?"

Bob and Doug moved to the other side of the table and planned excitedly. Billy sat down on the floor beside Sammy. "See Sammy, hold him like this," he said as he picked up the crayfish, put it down again, and slowly guided Sammy's hands to the shell behind its head.

Ten-year-old Cindy sat by herself at the end of the table with a crayfish and some lesson cards. She read a card that said

> Watch how the crayfish moves across the table.
> How many ways can he move?
> In how many directions can he move?
> Can you guess how your crayfish swims?
> Put him in water and see if you guessed right.

Cindy put her head down on the crayfish's level and watched him come toward her. She mumbled to herself, "Can't he go backwards?"

Nine-year-old Tommy sat on the floor beside the shelf that held books, plants, and the aquarium and opened a book full of 8 x 12 glossies of crayfish. His lesson cards said

> Where do crayfish live?
> What do crayfish eat?
> What good things do crayfish do?
> Why do crayfish have shells?

But he couldn't read all that. He held the first card, looked at the jumbles of letters and remembered what Cindy had told him the first one said. "Where do crayfish live?" he heard her asking him. "Where do they live?" He leaned against the shelf and looked at the pictures. "They live . . ."

Lisa sat on the other side of the shelf in the green sunlight that flickered through the aquarium. She was humming to herself and cutting up a *Ladies' Home Journal* in search of pictures of words that start with *s* and *st*. Every now and then she looked up and watched Robert doing wild, furious pull-ups on the exercise bar wedged between a cabinet and the wall that made the doorway. When he was red in the face and completely out of breath, he staggered over and threw herself down beside Lisa. "... (gasp) Whatcha makin'?"

"Sounds. *Stool* starts with *st* an' *sssoap* an' *ssssalt* an' *cereal* start with *s*."

Robert fell backwards and lay spread-eagle, breathing. "*Cereal* don't start wif *s*."

Lisa stopped cutting and looked up. "It does so, *ssssereal!*"

"It's a *c*."

"*Sssssssssssssereal,* Robert!!"

"*C*."

Robert propped himself up on his elbows and looked at Lisa. "Sometimes *c*'s sound like *s*'s. . . . Thas right Lisa. It's real hard sometimes."

Lisa frowned and thought for a minute, and then she crumpled up the cereal picture. She looked at the page she was cutting and asked, "Robert, does *celery* start with an *s*?"

"Yeah Lisa, *celery!* Thas a good one. I gotta go do my math." He jumped up and walked over to Melinda's corner.

Melinda was surrounded by books, papers, her braille typewriter, and records of *Macbeth*. She was smiling as she listened through the headphones to Sir Ralph Richardson. Robert stood behind her and put his hands over her eyes. Melinda laughed. "Hi, Robert. Go do your math!"

Marilyn and Suzie were cuddled up in the Secret House . . . a big square cardboard box turned upside down with blankets and a light inside. Suzie, nine years old and having some emotional problems, was reading to Marilyn. Marilyn's left hand had a bandage on it—a reminder of yesterday's lesson. Suzie loved Marilyn very much and today she was sorry she had scratched her, but she was afraid yesterday, so afraid.

Ms. Winters smiled as she handed Shelley the story she had written for her writing program for the day. "I really enjoyed reading your story. It made me laugh!" Shelley grinned and went off to her corner to read Ms. Winters' comments and begin her work. Ms. Winters sat down at a low table beside Keith and asked him, "Well, sir, what word would you like today?"

"*Rattlesnake!*"

"*Rattlesnake?*"

"Yeah. I saw it on TV last night, a big rattlesnake. An' it sounded like shshooshooshokashookashooka."

Ms. Winters laughed. "That's a big word Keith. This says *rattlesnake*," she told him, printing big letters on a card.

"Un-*huh!* Thas a big word all right!"

"Sure is. Can you write it? Good, Keith. That's just fine. Now what's the word again?"

"*Rattlesnake!*"

"Keith, this part says *rattle* and this part says *snake*. What is this word?" she asked, covering *rattle* and running her first finger under *snake*.

"It says *snake!*"

"Good. Now can you tell me all the letters in *rattlesnake?*"

"*Rrrr* – *r* – *a* – *t* – *t* – *l* – *e* – *s* – *n* – *a* – ("I forget that one"; "It's a *k*," whispered Ms. Winters) *k* – *e*."

"Good! Tell me the word again."

"*Rattlesnake* . . . I won't forget this one!"

Ms. Winters smiled. "I'll bet you won't, Keith. Now go study your word cards—go find someplace quiet. And then go tell your words to Lisa— I don't think she knows *rattlesnake* yet. And, Keith, wait a minute! I've got a book for you.

"About rattlesnakes?"

"No, but we'll get one of those too, okay? See you later."

Ms. Winters got up and moved down the table to a chair beside Eddy. He was eleven and had some learning problems, and he'd been practicing writing yesterday's word, *wind*.

"What word would you like today, Eddy?" she asked, touching his arm.

"*Hot dog.*"

"Okay ... *hot dog* ..."

Ms. Winters sat at her table and read the note Maria and Lyn had left her when they blew in from outside, cold and pink-cheeked and excited, a few minutes before.

> We got all colors of leafs for our books. It's 33 degrees outside. That is the coldest this week. If we put the thermamiter in the sun will it *really* be hotter outside? (Bob said it would.) We saw 3 squirrills. If we catch a squirrill can we keep him? We took the camera out.
> Love,
Maria and Lyn

Ms. Winters smiled as she lay the note down and thought, "Squirrels, huh? ... Let's see, it's 11:00 now. Ms. Winton's coming for speech at 11:20. Robert's first today; he'll get restless about then. Mr. Lawrence has Randy now. Ms. Lowery for Melissa at 1:30. And Paul and his friend are going to do art with the kids at 2:00."

Little Renie was sitting in the corner under, almost in, the big fern, rocking and patting her cheeks. She was eight and very tiny.

"Hi, Honey," said Ms. Winters.

"Hi, Honey," repeated Renie.

Ms. Winters gathered her up and carried her to the rocking chair by Lisa. "Nice pictures, Lisa. Come show me?"

"Yeah!"

Ms. Winters sat down in the rocking chair with Renie and Lisa wriggled up onto the edge of the table and held up her pictures for Ms. Winters to see. "This is a *s* word! *Sssssand!* At the beach." Ms. Winters nodded and smiled. "An' this is *sssoup*. An' *ssssalt*. An' *ssselery*. An' ..."

"Now Lisa, about *celery* ..." (Thompson 1972).

References and Suggested Readings

Brophy, J., and Good, T. 1974. *Teacher-student relationships—Causes and consequences.* New York: Holt, Rinehart and Winston.

Byrne, D. 1961. Interpersonal attraction and attitude similarity. *Journal of Abnormal and Social Psychology* 62:713–715.

Davis, F. 1961. Deviance disavowal and normalization. *Social Problems* 9:120–132.

Good, T. 1970. Which pupils do teachers call on? *Elementary School Journal* 70:190–198.

Johnson, E. 1976. Unpublished poem.

Keller, E. C. 1976. A challenge to teachers from handicapped scientists. *Science and Children* 13:16.

Kleck, R., Ono, H., and Hastorf, A. H. 1966. The effects of physical deviance upon face-to-face interactions. *Human Relations* 19:425–436.

Mullins, J., and Wolfe, S. 1975. *Special people behind the eight-ball.* Johnstown, Pa.: Mafex Associates.

Purkey, W. W. 1970. *Self concept and school achievement.* Englewood Cliffs, N.J.: Prentice-Hall.

Richardson, S. A. 1969. The effect of physical disability on the socialization of a child. In D. A. Goslin, ed., *Handbook of socialization theory and research.* © 1969 by Rand McNally College Publishing Company, Chicago, p. 1058.

Rosenthal, R., and Jacobson, L., 1968. *Pygmalion in the classroom: Teacher expectation and pupils' intellectual development.* New York: Holt, Rinehart and Winston.

Thompson, C. *Ms. Winters' Class.* Unpublished manuscript.

Westervelt, V. D. 1977. Influence of a filmed intervention on the preference of non-handicapped children for physically handicapped children. Unpublished manuscript, University of North Carolina.

Professional and Conreums
Organizations

For more information on exceptional children, you may want to communicate with the following organizations:

Alexander Graham Bell Association
    for the Deaf, Inc.
3417 Volta Pl.
Washington, DC   20007
(202) 337–5220

American Association on Mental Deficiency
5201 Connecticut Ave., N.W.
Washington, DC   20015
Dr. John J. Noone, Director
(202) 244–8143

American Foundation for the Blind
15 West 16th St.
New York, NY   10011

American Printing House for the Blind
1839 Frankfort Ave.
P.O. Box 6085
Louisville, KY   40206

American Psychological Association
1200 Seventeenth St., N.W.
Washington, DC   20036

American Speech and Hearing Association
9030 Old Georgetown Rd.
Washington, DC   20014
(202) 657–2000 or (202) 530–3400

Association for Children with Learning
    Disabilities
5225 Grace St.
Pittsburgh, PA   15236
(412) 811–1191

Association for the Education of the
    Visually Handicapped
919 Walnut, Fourth Floor
Philadelphia, PA   19107
(215) WA3–7555

Captioned Films for the Deaf
Special Office for Materials Distribution
Indiana University
Audio-Visual Center
Bloomington, IN   47401

Clearinghouse on Programs and Research
    in Child Abuse and Neglect
Herner and Company
2100 M St., N.W.
Suite 316
Washington, DC   20037
(202) 293–2600

Closer Look
National Information Center for the
    Handicapped
1201 Sixteenth St., N.W.
Washington, DC   20036

Council for Exceptional Children
1920 Association Dr.
Reston, VA   22091

Division for the Blind and Physically
    Handicapped
The Library of Congress
Washington, DC   20542

Epilepsy Foundation of America
1828 L Street, N.W.
Washington, DC   20036

International League of Societies for
    the Mentally Handicapped
12 Rue Forestière
Brussels—5
Belgium

National Association for Creative Children
and Adults
8080 Springvalley Dr.
Cincinnati, OH   45236
Ms. Ann F. Isaacs, Executive Director
(513) 631–1777

National Association for Retarded Citizens
2709 Avenue E East
Arlington, TX   76010
(817) 261-4961

National Association of State Directors
of Special Education, Inc.
1201 Sixteenth Street, N.W.
Washington, DC   20036

National Association for the Visually
Handicapped
3201 Balboa St.
San Francisco, CA   94121
(415) 221–3201

National Association of the Deaf
814 Thayer Ave.
Silver Spring, MD   20910

National Center on Educational Media
and Materials for the Handicapped
Ohio State University
220 West Twelfth Ave.
Columbus, OH   43210

National Easter Seal Society for
Crippled Children and Adults
2023 West Ogden Ave.
Chicago, IL   60612
(312) 243–8400

National Foundation
March of Dimes
1275 Mamaroneck Ave.
White Plains, New York   10605
Mr. A. J. Caruso
Division of Health Information and
School Relations
(914) 428–7100

National Society for Autistic Children,
  Information and Referral Service
306 Thirty-first St.
Huntington, WV   25702
Ms. Ruth C. Sullivan, Director
Home: (304) 523–8269
Office: (304) 697–2638

United Cerebral Palsy Association
Program Department
66 East 34th St.
New York, NY   10016
(212) 889–6655

We Are People First
P.O. Box 5208
Salem, OR   97304
Ms. Valerie Schoof, President

Individual Education Program:
Total Service Plan

Child's Name _____

School _____

Date of Program Entry _____

Prioritized Long-term Goals:

_____

_____

_____

Summary of
Present Levels of Performance:

_____

_____

_____

_____

_____

_____

Short-Term Objectives	Specific Educational and/or Support Services	Person(s) Responsible	Percent of Time	Beginning and Ending Date	Review Date

Percent of Time in Regular Classroom

_____

Placement Recommendation

Committee Members Present

_____

_____

_____

_____

Dates of Meeting _____

_____

Committee Recommendations for
Specific Procedures/Techniques, Materials, Etc. (include information about learning style)

Objective Evaluation Criteria for each Annual Goal Statement

Individual Education Program:
Individual Implementation Plan

Complete one of these for each goal statement specified on Total Service Plan

Child's Name _____   Goal Statement: _____

School _____   _____

Date of Program Entry _____   Short Term Instructional Objectives:

Projected Ending Date _____   _____

Person(s) Completing Form   _____

Behavioral Objectives	Task Analysis of Objectives	Strategies and/or Techniques	Materials and/or Resources	Date Started	Date Ended	Comments

■ Appendix C

Learning Style Questionnaire

Name _____ Teacher _____

Class _____ Date _____

Directions: (To the student)—Answer *True* or *False* to
each of the following questions.

I. Environmental Stimuli

A. Sound

	True	False
1. I study best when it is quiet.	—	—
2. I can work with a little noise.	—	—
3. I can block out noise when I work.	—	—
4. Noise usually keeps me from concentrating.	—	—
5. Most of the time I like to work with soft music.	—	—
6. I can work with any kind of music.	—	—
7. I often like to work with rock music playing.	—	—
8. Music makes it difficult for me to work.	—	—
9. I can work if people talk quietly.	—	—
10. I can study when people talk.	—	—
11. I can block out most sound when I study.	—	—
12. It's difficult to block out TV when I work.	—	—
13. Noise bothers me when I am studying.	—	—

Totals: (To be completed by the teacher)

From R. Dunn and K. Dunn, *Educator's self-teaching guide to individualizing instructional programs,* p. 95. Copyright © 1975 by Parker Publishing Company, Inc. Published by Parker Publishing Company, Inc., West Nyack, New York.

■ Appendix D

Developmental Scale for Language Levels

Developmental Scale

Receptive Language	Expressive Language
6 Months	
Turns to sound of bell without seeing it.	Crows, laughs, makes sounds for pleasure. Imitates sounds—babbling.
7 Months	
	Puts two sounds together, like "ma-ma," "bye-bye."
8 Months	
Responds to "bye-bye" by waving "bye-bye."	
10 Months	
	Makes sounds during play.
11 Months	
Adjusts to commands: knows what "come here," "no," "don't touch" mean.	Says one word to name or describe something—like "mama," "bye."
12 Months	
Responds to "no," "don't touch."	Two-word speaking vocabulary.
15 Months	
	Uses "jargon" and gestures (jargon is his own make-up language; likes talking to toys).
18 Months	
Points to nose, eyes, hair.	One-word responses include naming, exclamations, and greetings. Half of vocabulary is names in speech. Uses initial vowels, consonants (says first sounds of words).
2 Years	
Can point to four parts of body when given the name; can point to a few	One-third of words are nouns.

Receptive Language	Expressive Language

2 Years

objects by name. Obey simple commands "Give me," "Put spoon in cup."	Sentence length two to three words; asks to go to toilet by verbal or gesture indication. Uses "I, you, me" fairly well.
Can repeat from memory, four words. Can fill in words or phrases of poems or songs.	Refers to self by name. Can tell what just happened.

2½ Years

Can tell what you cook on, what you sit on, what is good to eat.	Naming objects.
Child is able to "put one block on paper."	Three-word simple sentences. Vocabulary consists of 25% nouns, 25% verbs and pronouns.
Repeats two numbers. Can point to more objects by name. Can name something in picture. Can tell you what burns, what barks, what blows. Can give the objects of six actions as what flies, sleeps, bites, scratches, swims.	Use of "I" in reference to self.

3 Years

Repeats three numbers.	Uses three-to-four word sentences. Can tell what happened in more
Responds to prepositions: "Put the ball on the chair" "Put the box under the table." Can give the use of common objects, e.g., "What do we do with the spoon?" —Answer: "Eat."	detail. Adjectives, adverbs, pronouns, conjunctions, increasing in use. When looking at picture book, the child will answer when asked, "What is he doing?" Articulation: Consonants mastered: y, b, p, m. He knows songs and rhymes.

3½ Years

Obeys simple commands: "Put the book on the table."	Sentence length four-to-five words. Better use of pronouns.

Receptive Language	Expressive Language
3½ Years	
Names more things—pictures. Can name more things; When asked, "What do you use to . . ." (like lock the door). Can give good answer.	Articulation: Consonants mastered: *w, h.*
4 Years	
Can tell what is happening in picture.	Sentence length four to five words.
Memory for sentences: "We are going to buy some candy for mother."	Pronouns, prepositions, conjunctions, are in good use.
Responds appropriately with gesture and words to "What do you do when you are thirsty, sleepy, hungry?"	Articulation: Consonants mastered: *d, t, g, k.*
	Compound and complex sentences begin to appear.
The child carries out requests with four prepositions (in, out, beside, behind, under, in front of).	Future and past tense in common use.
4½ Years	
Repeats four numbers.	Parts of speech: 19% nouns, 25% verbs, 15% adjectives, 21% pronouns, 7% ad-Par.
Can follow three commands in order; carries out complex orders in three parts.	Consonant: production 90% or more correct.
Knows some things that are opposite; like "brother is a boy, sister is a girl."	Sentence length four to five words.
5 Years	
Can give a good answer: "What is a ball?"	Picks out and names red, yellow, blue, green.
Memory for sentences; can repeat a sentence of about seven words.	Sentence length four to five words.
	Can tell story correctly. Can tell about things and action in picture. Can name following coins: penny, nickel, dime.
	Articulation: masters consonants *f* and *v.*

Receptive Language	Expressive Language
6 Years	
Vocabulary: can tell what several words mean.	Tells more about picture; responds to picture.
Child knows the difference between A.M. and P.M. and answers questions "When does afternoon begin?"	Average sentence length six to seven words.
	Says numbers up to thirties.
6½ Years	
	Articulation: voiced *l, th*.
7 Years	
Repeats five numbers.	Girls' speech is quite grown up.
Similarities: "In what way are . . . and . . . alike?	
Can tell what is silly about something.	
7½ Years	
	Mastered consonant sounds, *s, z, r, sh, ch,* and consonant blends such as *bl, dr, tr*.
8 Years	
Can tell why some things are alike and some things are different. Remembers points of a story; can tell why some things happen, such as "What makes a sailboat move?"	Boys' speech is quite grown up.

■ Appendix E

Spelling Games

Detective

Write a word on the board from the current spelling lesson leaving out one or more of the letters, depending on the level of the group. Give a definition of the word and call on students to fill in the missing letters. This may be done orally or written.

As the class matures, leave out more strategic letters. By giving one point for each correct word and allowing the children to keep their own scores, everyone has more incentive to study the words before the game is played.

I Spy

The children make a vertical fold on their paper. Have them list all the concrete nouns from the current spelling lesson in the left column. They are to place the remainder of the words in the right column. The children may be told to list the words that show taste, smell, time, color, questions, size, and so forth.

Give one point for each correct answer.

Find It

Each child has a word list, a pencil, and a piece of paper on his desk. The teacher gives definitions of words from his lists. The children find the word, and write it on their paper. The teacher then picks a student to write the word on the board while the others check his answer against their own.

As the group progresses, they may give definitions to each other.

Grab Bag

The teacher writes each word on the board three times. Two of the spellings are incorrect, The children have to choose the correct spelling, either writing their choice on paper or responding orally.

An occasional insertion of a ridiculous letter results in added stimulation.

It is wise to make many choices quite apparent at the start of this game so that even poor spellers will achieve a degree of success.

Association

Each word in any given spelling lesson has something in common with another word in that list. That association may be found in common beginning letters, letter combinations, prefixes, suffixes, or merely the identical number of letters.

The children have to find as many pairs of words as possible within a period of time and list them. Give special recognition to the children finding the greatest number of "associations."

Funny Friends

Some children may be able to write limericks about imaginary friends using the new and review words in the current lesson. Encourage fun rather than extreme criticism.

Jumbled Words

Transpose the letters in all the words in the spelling list for the week. When the class becomes accustomed to this activity, it is fun to add one or two extra letters that tend to make the game more difficult. This activity is most successful when it is reproduced on a ditto. Mistakes are more common when material is copied from the board.

Word Pictures

To begin the game, the teacher describes a word phonetically from the current spelling lesson. The word *like*, for example, would be described as "a one-syllable word beginning with a consonant and ending with a vowel."

The teacher calls on a child to find the word. He in turn will describe a word and call on a classmate to answer his question. The game continues until the list is completed.

Baseball Game

This is an old game which has been used constantly with school children. They invariably enjoy it and apparently profit from it.

The teacher draws a baseball diamond on the board, and the room is divided into two equal teams.

The two top spelling students may be chosen as pitchers to give the words to the opposing team.

Each team is given three words—one each to the first three batters. If the first person spells the word correctly, he is given a "single" and he moves to base, standing in front of first base on the board. If he misses the spelling, he is out.

If, before he is given the word, the batter specifies "home run," his correct spelling will clear the bases and that number of runs will be given to his team. In the event he misses the word, it is automatically three outs and the side is retired. Three outs must be registered before the opposing team takes the field.

Football Game

Two teams play this game.

The ball is placed on the 50-yard-line of the scale football field drawn on the board.

One team is given six plays, or six straight words, to advance the ball. With each correct word, the ball advances ten yards towards the opponent's goal line. For each word missed, the offensive team loses ten yards.

A score of six points is given a team each time it crosses the opponent's goal line.

Crossword Puzzle

Make up a crossword puzzle (or have the children make one) using new and review words in the current lesson.

It is difficult at times to use all the words in a fifteen by fifteen square puzzle. To fill in, use everyday words and those found in the social studies unit. The children are greatly interested, and they learn not only to spell the words, but their meaning as well. The puzzle may be drawn on the board and filled in on paper by the children at their desks.

Potential Reinforcers

Tangibles

candy
cereal
chewing gum
pop corn
Cracker Jacks
miniature marshmallows
cookies
crackers
soft-drinks
fruit drinks
coffee, tea, milk
peanuts
potato chips

pencils
crayons
books
note pads
jewelry
make-up
play money
badges
patches
toys (marbles, cars, dolls)
stamps
colored paper
clay
balloons

Activities

Being . . . .

read to
hugged
kissed
patted
swung around
pulled in a wagon
pushed on a swing
played ball with
teacher helper
first in line

Allowed to . . . .

talk to a friend
help in the cafeteria
write on the chalkboard
play with blocks, games
listen to records
use typewriter
use tape recorder
draw and paint
model with clay
turn on flashlight
pop corn
perform before group
perform science experiments
go to learning centers
sit in rocking chair
teach someone

Activities

Allowed to . . . .

staple papers together
give a test
operate audiovisual equipment
read
write
do arithmetic
clean chalkboard
sharpen pencils
do nothing

Index